SOCIAL SECURITY

John Attarian

SOCIAL SECURITY

False Consciousness and Crisis

Transaction Publishers
New Brunswick (U.S.A.) and London (U.K.)

368.43
A88N

Coy

Library of Congress Catalog Number: 2002072126
ISBN: 0-7658-0127-2
Printed in the United States of America

Library of Congress Cataloging-in-Publication Data

Attarian, John.
   Social security : false consciousness and crisis / John Attarian.
        p. cm.
   Includes bibliographical references and index.
   ISBN 0-7658-0127-2 (alk. paper)
      1. Social security—United States. I. Title.

HD7125 A85 2002
368.4'3'00973—dc21   2002072126

Dedicated to the Valiant
Soldiers of Truth about Social Security

Carl T. Curtis

Judd Benson

Dillard Stokes

Ray Peterson

A. Haeworth Robertson

Peter G. Peterson

"And ye shall know the truth,
and the truth shall make you free."
—John 8:32

Contents

Part 3: What Now?

List of Tables

Chapter 1

Chapter 2

Acknowledgements

My deep gratitude goes first of all to the Earhart Foundation, for the grant which made possible the research for this book and the completion of the first draft, and to the referees for my grant. Dr. Antony T. Sullivan, Earhart's secretary and director of program, merits special thanks for his faith in this project and his sage counsel.

A heartfelt salute to A. Haeworth Robertson, chief actuary of Social Security in 1975-1978, president and founder of the Retirement Policy Institute, and one of the unsung heroes in the battle to educate the country about Social Security. The tribute on the dedication page is the least he deserves. Warmly supportive of my own efforts in that cause, Mr. Robertson not only served as a referee for my grant but read and closely criticized the first three chapters of the first draft. Professor Charles E. Rounds, Jr., of the Suffolk University Law School and an authority on trusts, read and criticized my treatment of the Social Security "trust fund" in chapter 6. My work is better for their criticisms. Any remaining errors are mine alone.

I got by with more than a little help from my friends. One of my goals was to produce a book accessible to a broad audience, in hopes of having a constructive impact on the Social Security debate, and Damon Demady, a dear friend and my apartment-mate during the research and drafting period, generously took time out from work on his doctorate in clinical pharmacology to read and criticize the entire first draft for clarity, accessibility, and intelligibility of argument to educated general readers, noneconomists, and nonspecialists in Social Security. Dr. John Wilhelm, a competent economist and good friend, served as a patient and discerning sounding board for several of my criticisms of Social Security privatization. Jeffrey Tucker of the Ludwig von Mises Institute in Auburn, Alabama, gave wise editorial and marketing advice.

Last, but emphatically far from least, a special, warm thanks to Dr. Irving Louis Horowitz, chairman and editorial director of Transaction. His frank and rigorous criticism of the first draft was invaluable in prompting a more fruitful framing of the analysis. Together with an anonymous referee, he made valuable criticisms and suggestions for revisions to the final draft which made for a much stronger book, in particular for a further explication and honing of the concept "false consciousness" as used here. His enthusiastic support is much appreciated—as is his prompt, crisp, and businesslike response to correspondence, a very rare thing among publishers.

Preface

One of today's most important national concerns is the projected bankruptcy of Social Security some time in the next few decades and its consequent inability to pay full benefits on time.

Yet despite almost two decades of warnings about this, nothing is being done. The saying that Social Security is the third rail of American politics—touch it and you die—holds true. Ever since ferocious opposition routed President Ronald Reagan's 1981 proposal to cut some benefits, which inspired that saying, presidents and Congresses have flinched from action that might entail confrontation with current beneficiaries. Most of the proposals and all of the enacted efforts to cut federal spending in the last two decades exempted Social Security.

Changes to ensure Social Security's long-run solvency could have been made then, giving all concerned ample time to adjust. They were not. Fear of the political cost imposed paralysis.

Realistic observers warn that the longer action is deferred, the more difficult it will be. That is, our procrastination is exacerbating Social Security's troubles. Our task grows more necessary, difficult, painful and politically dangerous every year. Yet nothing happens.

A deep root of this predicament is a crucial but under-examined aspect of Social Security: the misleading manner in which the program has been depicted to the public from 1935 on. Specifically, Social Security is "retirement insurance" under which taxpayers pay "insurance premiums" or "contributions" to "buy" protection from destitution in old age, with their "contributions" being "held" in a "trust fund" which will pay "guaranteed" benefits which, being "paid for," will be theirs "as a matter of earned right," as America keeps its "compact (or contract) between the generations."

The entire previous sentence is demonstrably, documentably false. Sometimes Social Security officials even admitted as much. To gain public acceptance of the program, they depicted Social Security as insurance—but argued just the opposite before the Supreme Court, to ensure Social Security's constitutionality (*Helvering v. Davis,* 1937) and to uphold their prerogative to deny beneficiaries their "earned right" to benefits (*Flemming v. Nestor,* 1960). Moreover, they never informed the public about Section 1104 of the Social

Security Act: "The right to alter, amend, or repeal any provision of this Act is hereby reserved to the Congress." Congress has repeatedly exercised this right, and has eliminated, cut, delayed or taxed benefits or denied them to various classes of people, belying the vaunted "guarantee" and "earned right." Yet the foregoing myths have been assiduously propagated to this day. Social Security's reliance on payroll taxes for revenue lends them strong *prima facie* plausibility: having paid these taxes, Americans think they have an "earned right" to benefits, that they have bought "insurance protection." In fact, as shall become clear, they have not.

The misleading depiction of Social Security has had extremely pernicious consequences already, and is likely to have far worse ones in the future, some ramifying far beyond Social Security itself.

Conduct is determined by perceptions and beliefs. Much, perhaps most, communication seeks to influence the perceptions and beliefs, and thus the actions, of others. Social Security's legitimacy, its performance, and its very existence depend decisively upon how taxpayers, politicians and beneficiaries understand it. As an intergenerational redistribution, Social Security depends especially upon the willingness of younger Americans to pay its taxes—which in turn rests on their beliefs about it.

Social Security's architects and promoters were keenly aware of the decisive importance of beliefs. Indeed the psychology of belief was a central concern of theirs. Both their depiction of the program to the public, and key decisions about its structure and finance, were made in order to foster a certain set of beliefs, so as to make Social Security accepted, popular, and politically invulnerable.

They succeeded. Social Security's depiction and financing mechanism, and the sense of entitlement that they foster, created a powerful and pervasive false consciousness about Social Security.

Let us pause to address some possible conceptual difficulties. Coined by Marxists, the term "false consciousness" has potentially confusing ideological and historical connotations. They used it to mean an ideology that appeals to a social class but does not accurately reflect its interests and needs, and therefore distracts it, thus reinforcing the existing regime. As Irving Louis Horowitz has aptly pointed out to me, using this term risks muddying the waters, since the Marxists never advanced a theory of accurate consciousness. However, that Marxists coined a term and used it for ideological ends is no reason why another author cannot rehabilitate it as a useful analytical tool by using it to legitimately indicate the gap between understanding and reality.

Let me emphasize that I use it for purely descriptive, not ideological (let alone Marxist) purposes. By "false consciousness" I mean simply an understanding significantly at variance with reality but which is taken as true and governs conduct. "False perception" is inadequate, because perception can be discrete and fleeting, while consciousness implies a more comprehensive, ongoing and active state of mind. The prevailing understanding of Social Security is false in *many* respects: its nature (insurance), revenue source (premiums or contributions), funding mechanism (with trust funds), the character of one's claim (immutable earned right, guaranteed by law), and the arrangement the program reflects (compact between generations, implicit contract). Moreover, most Americans, especially the elderly, have accepted these falsehoods as self-evident truths, and formed their opinions and conduct about Social Security accordingly, ever since 1935. Finally, among Social Security advocates and elderly lobbies, this version became a sacrosanct orthodoxy. I opted for "false consciousness" as a handy, compact, and striking way of conveying all this.

The promotion of this false consciousness, and its acceptance by retirees, politicians and the public, decisively shaped the actions taken when Social Security faced financial crisis in the seventies and eighties. The 1977 and 1983 rescue legislation relied on tax increases and reductions in future rather than current benefits. These measures spawned rising disaffection with Social Security among taxpayers. Meanwhile, Social Security's long-term financial outlook steadily deteriorated from 1983 until recently. Successive Social Security Boards of Trustees warned that the program is not in long-term actuarial balance, and asked Congress to take remedial action. However, Social Security's continued high popularity with its thoroughly gulled but politically formidable constituency precluded corrective action, let alone radical reform, and still precludes it now.

Social Security is therefore trapped between the *imperatives of politics,* springing from a deliberately fostered false consciousness, which force policymakers to act as if Social Security's myths are true, thus locking Social Security into a rigid position regarding current benefits, and the *imperatives of economics,* which require the program to be flexible so as to adjust to changing conditions.

And thus it is that the misleading depiction of Social Security, and the resultant false consciousness, are two of the main roots of the coming crisis, and of our continued paralysis as it approaches.

Mindful of the danger of overstating my thesis, I do not maintain that these are the *only* causes. Demographic and other factors certainly operate. But the government's marketing effort and the false consciousness it created have decisively affected how Social Security's history has worked out, and our responses to its problems so far; and will, if they persist, impair future policymaking.

Since a key Social Security myth is that there *is no* crisis, I begin by showing that a crisis is indeed coming, and explaining its threefold nature. The proliferating Social Security literature is engrossed in the program's finances—reflecting a deeper, general American obsession with everybody "getting theirs"—and fails to make clear that the crisis has two other, and worse, aspects: a crisis of affordability and a crisis of confidence, or political legitimacy. To redress that imbalance, these two aspects receive much attention.

The book's second and largest part addresses my main concern: the development and propagation of the false consciousness, and the consequences. Overall, the press uncritically assisted this marketing effort. Meanwhile, elderly lobbying groups arose, steeped in Social Security's myths and disseminating them to their members, thereby mightily reinforcing the false consciousness. This and the rapid increase in the elderly population interacted to create an obstacle to reform that by the eighties proved immovable.

Nevertheless, cracks have appeared in the false consciousness, discontent about Social Security is rampant, and numerous "reform" proposals are circulating. Unfortunately, wishful thinking abounds here: talk of workers putting their payroll taxes into individual retirement accounts and building huge nest eggs, made possible by high long-term real rates of return on stocks—achieved, in many plans, without any loss of current retirees' benefits.

Given Social Security's importance, and the pain that its demise would inflict, the temptation to escapism is powerful. But it must be resisted, lest we embrace some unsound scheme promising a painless ending in which no hard choices are made, no one gives up anything, and everyone gains. If we are to arrive at sound answers, reform proposals must receive close critical scrutiny.

Accordingly, the final section examines them. Their flaws are serious. Most retain the payroll tax, hence preserve the false consciousness which it fosters. Some have huge costs of transition to a new system. Others risk politicizing the stock market. Virtually all ignore the larger economic and political context that threatens to preclude attainment of their goals. I close with proposals of my own.

Social Security's defenders have a bad habit of demonizing its critics. They accuse them of undermining confidence in Social Security,[1] "spooking the Boomers," fomenting intergenerational strife, and advocating privatization to enrich Wall Street.[2] They smear them as "granny-bashers"[3] and "the ideologues and the selfish," and call reform advocate Peter Peterson "an anti-Social Security zealot."[4] The critics, they say, blame our woes on "greedy geezers"; use intergenerational equity as a "battering ram . . . against the elderly"; are "unfeeling"; lack "compassion"; "resent the money and attention old people are receiving"; target "old people in wheelchairs."[5]

Such abuse discourages the approach we need: untrammeled advancing and sifting of proposals to find the best answer. I do not seek further to poison the atmosphere by maligning such figures as Arthur Altmeyer (chairman of the Social Security Board 1937-1946; commissioner of Social Security 1946-1953), Wilbur Cohen (his special assistant; secretary of health, education and welfare 1968-1969), and Robert Ball (commissioner of Social Security 1962-1973). These men (save Ball) created Social Security; they believed in it and loved it. If they and others depicted it misleadingly to make it accepted and popular, this was, if ethically dubious, understandable. If they believed that the end justified the means, that, too, is human.

My aims, rather, are not ideological but explanatory and (I hope) constructive: first, to establish that there is indeed a crisis in Social Security's future; second, to establish that Social Security's architects, promoters and allies did forge a false consciousness, that it was crucial for forming the reality confronting us, and that the consequences have been decisive and disastrous; third, to dispel that false consciousness so the Social Security debate can go forward based on realities, undistorted by misleading perceptions; and fourth, to further the debate by pointing out the dangers of both preserving Social Security essentially as is and "privatizing" it, and advancing what I submit is a more prudent alternative.

Just how pernicious Social Security's false consciousness will prove to be depends on how willing we are to face reality and how we choose to address Social Security. At present, the auguries are not hopeful. If this effort brings some improvement, it will not have been in vain.

Notes

1. Wilbur Cohen made this accusation too many times to enumerate here. See, e.g., Wilbur J. Cohen, "Author's Reply," *Journal of Insurance,* vol. 28, no. 3 (September 1961), p. 98; U. S., Congress, House, "Statement by Wilbur J. Cohen, Under Secretary of Health, Education, and Welfare," in Representative Wilbur D. Mills, "How Secure is Your Social Security," Extension of Remarks, 90th Cong., 1st sess., September 27, 1967, *Congressional Record,* 113:27028-27029; U. S., Congress, House, "White Paper on Social Security," 94th Cong., 1st sess., February 25, 1975, *Congressional Record,* 121:4195, 4196, 4198; "Cohen questions Reagan cuts," *Detroit News,* May 13, 1981, 3A.
2. John Cassidy, "Spooking the Boomers," *New Yorker,* January 13, 1997, pp. 30-35; Theodore R. Marmor, Fay Lomax Cook, and Stephen Scher, "Social Security Politics and the Conflict Between Generations: Are We Asking the Right Questions?" in *Social Security in the 21st Century,* ed. Eric R. Kingson and James H. Schulz (New York: Oxford University Press, 1997), p. 204; Robert Dreyfuss, "The Biggest Deal: Lobbying to Take Social Security Private," *American Prospect,* May-June 1996, pp. 72-75.
3. Dean Baker and Mark Weisbrot, *Social Security: The Phony Crisis* (Chicago: University of Chicago Press, 1999), p. 12.
4. Max J. Skidmore, *Social Security and Its Enemies: The Case for America's Most Efficient Insurance Program* (Boulder, CO: Westview Press, 1999), pp. ix, xi.
5. Marmor, Cook, and Scher, "Social Security Politics and the Conflict Between Generations: Are We Asking the Right Questions?," pp. 206, n. 13, 204; John Judis, "Chicken Little Lamm," *Baltimore Sun,* July 19, 1996, 25A.

Part 1

Social Security's Threefold Crisis

Part I

Social Security's Financial Crisis

1

The Bankruptcy Crisis

Social Security: Some Basic Facts

It will be useful for readers to have at the outset a concise account of the essentials of how Social Security operates. Created by the Social Security Act of 1935, Social Security replaces labor income lost due to retirement, death, or disability, by paying monthly benefits to retired and disabled workers, their dependents, and their survivors. Social Security payroll taxes, called "contributions," are collected from employees' wages or salaries, matched dollar for dollar by taxes on their employers, and paid to the Treasury. Self-employed persons pay taxes ("contributions") on income from self-employment. These taxes on labor income furnish the chief source of revenue to pay benefits under Old-Age and Survivors Insurance (OASI), which pays benefits to retired workers and their families and to the survivors of deceased workers, and Disability Insurance (DI), which pays benefits to disabled workers and their dependents. Although legally separate, these two parts of Social Security are commonly discussed as a combined program—Old-Age, Survivors and Disability Insurance (OASDI).[1] We follow that convention here.

Besides the payroll tax, OASDI raises relatively modest revenues from benefit taxation. The 1983 amendment of the Social Security Act introduced benefit taxation, and in 1993 the benefit tax was raised (we will address these changes fully later).[2] Benefit taxation revenue was $11.6 billion in 1999.[3]

Payment of benefits is not automatic; one must apply at a Social Security office for them, and meet eligibility conditions, such as age, being retired, insurance status (which is based on having earned a certain amount of income in a certain number of calendar quarters, or "quarters of coverage," of employment in a "covered" occupation—that is, an occupation the income of which is taxed for Social Security), and so on. Benefit amounts are determined by complex combinations of factors such as lifetime taxable earnings, age at retirement, income while retired, and so on, which are outside the purview of this book.[4] While Social Security's tax is regressive, falling more heavily on lower incomes, since income above the "maximum taxable income" is not

3

taxed, benefits are progressive, replacing a larger share of labor income for lower-income workers.

Because a crucial criterion of eligibility for benefits is having worked in a "covered" occupation, Social Security says its benefits come to beneficiaries as an earned right. OASDI is called "insurance" to convey the sense that the worker, through payment of payroll taxes, has "bought" the benefits, or the "right" to receive them. However, Social Security serves social purposes (e.g., poverty prevention), as well as paying individuals benefits in relation to their earnings in "covered" employment. Hence OASDI is called "*social insurance.*"[5] This point will receive thorough scrutiny later; the use of insurance terminology to describe Social Security, the reasons for its use, the legitimacy of that usage, and its consequences are core concerns of this book.

Social Security financing is on a "pay-as-you-go" basis. That is, current revenue is used to pay benefits to current retirees and other beneficiaries. Tax rates are set so as to provide enough revenue to cover current costs and build up a contingency fund, a so-called "trust fund," to cover unexpected surges in costs or drops in income.[6] (OASDI's "trust fund" at the beginning of 2000 sufficed to cover about 218 percent of 2000's estimated costs.[7]) Under pay-as-you-go financing, today's taxpayers, in turn, will get their benefits from taxes on future generations—provided future generations are willing to pay the taxes.

The "trust funds" are, in reality, accounts at the Treasury.[8] Social Security's tax revenues are deposited in the Treasury's general fund, and the Treasury credits them to OASI and DI by issuing special nonmarketable Treasury securities to their accounts ("trust funds"). As the Treasury pays out Social Security benefits, it removes equivalent values of securities from the funds. As the Social Security law requires, any surplus of Social Security revenues over benefit outlays and administrative costs (which costs are very modest, usually less than one percent of benefit outlays) is spent by the Treasury, and the "trust funds" hold an equivalent amount in Treasury securities as assets. The Treasury spends this surplus money on general government outlays. Interest on the bonds is paid twice a year in the form of more Treasury bonds issued to the "trust funds."[9]

Since its inception, Social Security has grown to become the largest single program of the United States government and the largest outlay in the budget, exceeding defense and interest on the national debt. In fiscal 1999 Social Security received $453.1 billion in payroll taxes and spent $382.8 billion on benefits ($332.4 billion for OASI, $50.4 billion for DI).[10] That is, Social Security collected taxes at the rate of $1.2 billion a day, and spent $1.04 billion a day on benefits. For another perspective on Social Security's size, 1999 OASDI benefit spending was 22.5 percent of total federal spending and 4.2 percent of Gross Domestic Product (GDP).[11] While the "trust funds" have been small for most of Social Security's history, because Social Security has been running annual surpluses since 1983, the "trust funds'" holdings of Treasury debt have become huge: $854.9 billion as of the end of fiscal 1999, of which $762.2 billion was held by OASI and $92.7 billion by DI.[12]

While originally just about half of the workforce (employees in commerce and industry only) participated in Social Security, today about 96 percent of the workforce participates. Noncovered workers are mostly state and local government employees covered by a public retirement system; federal civilian employees hired before 1984; some students; irregularly employed farm and domestic workers; and members of the clergy and religious orders who choose not to participate.[13] In 1999, about 152 million persons worked in employment covered by Social Security and paid Social Security taxes, while an estimated 44.6 million persons received benefits.[14] Thus, just about all Americans, including those not born yet, the taxpayers and beneficiaries of the future, are significantly affected by Social Security, and therefore have a substantial stake in the program and its financial performance.

Given Social Security's size and importance, it is imperative to watch its current and likely future financial status closely, so as to ensure its ability to continue timely benefit payments and avoid the need for disruptive and hurtful changes in benefits and taxes. Accordingly, every year the Social Security Administration's Board of Trustees issues a report in which Social Security's actuaries evaluate the program's finances and make both short-range (for the next ten years) and long-range (for the next seventy-five years) projections of its future performance. Because Social Security's future costs and income depend heavily on economic and demographic factors such as productivity, unemployment, fertility, and longevity, the actuaries make assumptions regarding the future trends of such factors. Since the future, especially the distant future, is uncertain, they prepare three analyses using three sets of economic and demographic assumptions, so as to furnish a range of possible outcomes. The sets of assumptions are named according to what the impact of their projections, if realized, would be on OASDI's finances: "low cost" (also known as "optimistic"), "intermediate" (which the Board of Trustees regards as the most likely outcome, or "best estimates"), and "high cost" ("pessimistic").[15] From these actuarial analyses, the Office of the Actuary derives projected costs and income (usually expressed as percentages of taxable payroll), projected dates of "trust fund" exhaustion (when a fund will be unable to pay benefits when due because its assets are gone), and so on.

As the Board of Trustees points out annually, projected dates of "trust fund" exhaustion dates, future income and outlays, and so on "are not intended to be precise predictions of the future financial status of the OASDI program," but indicators of the potential future, "under a variety of plausible economic and demographic conditions."[16] Such dates and figures, then, are *estimates,* as are any calculations based on them.

Social Security and the Demographics of Doom

Unfortunately, as the Board of Trustees has warned for years, while Social Security can unquestionably meet its obligations to today's beneficiaries, and its financing is adequate for the short run,[17] demographic forces doom the program in the longer term.

In the first two decades after World War II, the fertility rate (average number of children born to a woman in her lifetime) was very high, for example, 3.03 in 1950, 3.50 in 1955 and 3.61 in 1960, as millions of young Americans took advantage of postwar prosperity to marry and start families, resulting in the huge "baby boom" generation born in 1946-1964.[18] The baby boomers will start retiring about 2010, and Social Security's intermediate actuarial analysis projects that from 1995 to 2030, when the last boomers retire, the population aged sixty-five and over will more than *double,* from 34.4 million to 69.1 million. High-cost assumptions project growth to 72.6 million, an increase of 111 percent.[19] Under either set of assumptions, the elderly will grow rapidly as a share of total population (table 1.1).[20]

Moreover, thanks to modern medicine and nutrition, which have steadily increased life expectancy, these retirees will, on the average, enjoy long retirements, meaning they will collect benefits for many more years than did previous generations of beneficiaries.

Table 1.1

Elderly (Age 65 and Over) as Percent of Total Population, Historical and Projected Values, 1950-2040

Calendar year	Historical data	Intermediate assumptions	High cost assumptions
1950	8.0		
1960	9.1		
1970	9.7		
1980	11.1		
1990	12.3		
2000		12.4	12.4
2010		12.9	13.2
2020		16.0	16.9
2030		19.7	21.6
2040		20.5	23.5

Source: *2000 OASDI Annual Report*

After 1964, the fertility rate collapsed, to 2.88 in 1965 and 2.43 in 1970, and kept falling. The sexual revolution brought widespread availability of contraception, and after abortion became legal in 1973, fertility dropped still lower. By 1975 the fertility rate, at 1.77, was well below the replacement rate—the number of lifetime births needed to replace existing population, 2.1 per woman. As post-feminist American women stressed careers and consumption over marriage and children, and more and more of them postponed marriage until they were past their peak fertility years, fertility stagnated below replacement. In 1989, it finally rose to 2.01. It has since risen modestly, to 2.06—still below replacement.[21] The generation born after 1965, whose taxes will pay the baby boomers' benefits, will thus grow far more slowly than the beneficiary population: under intermediate assumptions, from 159.8 million to 194.4 million in 2030, or just 21.7 percent; and under high cost assumptions, to 187.9 million, a mere 17.6 percent.[22]

This means that the burden of supporting each beneficiary will be spread over ever-fewer taxpayers. In 1945, 42 taxpayers paid into Social Security for each beneficiary drawing money out; in 1950, 16.5 did. Today, 3.4 taxpayers support every beneficiary; under intermediate assumptions this ratio falls to 3.1 in 2010 and just 2.1 in 2030. Under high cost assumptions, the ratio falls even lower: 3.0 in 2010 and 1.9 in 2030.[23]

But as the number of taxpayers supporting each beneficiary declines, Social Security's tax rates mandated under current law will not possibly suffice to pay benefits mandated under current law. Early in this century, therefore, Social Security costs will begin exceeding revenues. When that happens, the OASI and DI "trust funds" will have to start cashing in their Treasury bonds for funds to cover the shortfall. As more and more baby boomers retire, Social Security's cash flow deficits will widen and liquidation of the "trust funds" will accelerate. In 2037 under the intermediate actuarial assumptions used in the Trustees' 2000 *Annual Report,* and in 2026 under the high cost assumptions, OASDI's combined "trust funds" will be exhausted—that is, they will have no assets left to liquidate—and OASDI will be unable to meet its obligations: bankrupt.[24] At that point, tax revenue would suffice to cover only about 72 percent of annual costs.[25]

Some observers argue that this approach is overly pessimistic, because it focuses narrowly on the dependency ratio between the working-age (ages 20-64) population and the elderly (ages sixty-five and up). Instead, they maintain, analysts should consider the overall dependency ratio, between the working age population and everybody else—that is, the sum of the dependent young (those under twenty) and the elderly, divided by the working-age population. This total dependency ratio, they point out, has actually been falling since the sixties and even in 2040, when the baby boomers are all retired, will still be below the sixties' levels. Moreover, while the number of elderly is rising, the number of infant and school-age children is falling even faster, and the dependent young are projected to decline as a share of the total population. Hence resources could be reallocated from the dependent young to the dependent old. Considered in this light, these analysts argue, Social Security's demographics give little cause for alarm.[26]

This total dependency ratio approach is deeply flawed. First, it adds unlike phenomena, lumping together private spending to support one's own young and old family members, which by definition does not burden public finance, and government programs for child and elderly support, which does. Second, as the Congressional Budget Office points out, "for the outlook for the federal budget, the combined share is misleading because federal spending for an elderly person is roughly seven to eight and one-half times that for a child."[27] Most federal programs for children are poverty programs, outlays of which are puny compared to Social Security's, as are outlays for financial aid for college students. Third, this global approach is a red herring, evading the issue of the financial pressure which the impending explosion of its beneficiary population will exert on Social Security. As the Social Security Advisory Board's 1999 Technical Panel of actuaries, demographers, and economists observed in its report on actuarial assumptions and methods, for Social Security "the total dependency ratio is irrelevant; it is only the old-age dependency ratio that matters."[28]

Fourth, this treatment of the dependency ratio itself is tendentious. True, the total dependency ratio did stand at a daunting .904 in 1960 (that is, the population of dependent young plus dependent elderly equaled .904, or 90.4 percent, of the working-age population in 1960), and had fallen to .708 in 1995. True, the projected total dependency ratio in 2040, at .802 under intermediate assumptions and .800 under high-cost assumptions, is substantially less than 1960's figure. But it is also true that after falling until 2020 or so, the total dependency ratio then marches steadily upward, in 2075 hitting .846 under intermediate assumptions, and .936 under high-cost assumptions. Moreover—and this is decisive—as the population ages in the same period, the *composition* of the total dependency ratio changes, with the share of near-universally entitled, high-cost elderly in the total dependent population rising, while the share of selectively entitled, low-cost children declines. Whereas 1960s total dependency ratio of .904 consisted of .173 dependent aged and .731 dependent young, a relatively low-cost mix of dependents, the intermediate .802 ratio for 2040, for instance, consists of .370 dependent aged and .432 dependent young, a mix which puts a far, far greater burden on federal finances.[29] Even with the total dependent population equaling a lower share of the working population in 2040 than in 1960, the high-cost elderly population equals a much larger share of the working population and the low-cost young population is a much smaller share. The overall effect, obviously, is for far higher costs to the federal government, and to Social Security (and Medicare) in particular.

Then, too, it is incredibly, even suicidally, wrongheaded to take the shrinkage of the dependent young's population share as good news for the long-term viability of a program of transfer payments from young to old. In 1960,

38.4 percent of the population was under twenty; in 1995, 29.0 percent. In 2075, under intermediate assumptions, 23.7 percent of the total population will be under twenty, and under high-cost assumptions, just 18.6 percent. Meanwhile, the share of population aged 20-64 will remain roughly stable, going from 52.5 percent in 1960 and 58.4 percent in 1995 to 54.2 percent in 2075 under intermediate assumptions and 51.7 percent under high cost ones.[30] But where will *their* benefits come from, with the cohort of youth which will support them shrinking?

Social Security's Worsening Prospects

Moreover, Social Security's future has darkened dramatically until very recently. The projected "trust fund" exhaustion dates from the Trustees' 1990-2000 *Annual Reports* display an ominous trend: as we have gone forward in time, *projected "trust fund" exhaustion dates have been creeping back toward us.* In 1990, exhaustion of OASDI's fund under high cost assumptions was thirty-three years away (2023); under intermediate assumptions, fifty-three years off (2043). In 1997, the Trustees projected that under high cost assumptions, OASDI would run out of assets in only twenty-one years (2018); under intermediate ones, in just thirty-two years (2029)—a serious deterioration in just seven years (table 1.2).[31]

Beginning in 1998, there has been a reversal of this unfavorable trend—but only a modest one, due primarily to higher economic growth than the 1997 analysis foresaw, resulting in more favorable economic assumptions for the longer-term analysis.[32] It should be noted too that the year 2000's projected date of OASDI "trust fund" exhaustion under intermediate assumptions, 2037, is only a modest improvement over the 1993 projection (2036), and that in terms of the number of years out, it is substantially *worse*—thirty-seven years away instead of forty-three. And in any case, the intermediate projections for 2000 are weaker than the 1990 ones.

Moreover, for prudence's sake, we should beware of mistaking a spell of better weather for a permanent climate shift. Should a recession occur, which is likely given our expansion's age and its current slowdown, the optimistic development driving the recent improvement in exhaustion dates would be reversed. Social Security's financial outlook would worsen accordingly.

Most of the deterioration in Social Security's actuarial position occurred in 1991-1994, when OASDI's projected exhaustion date under intermediate assumptions shifted from 2041 to 2029 and the actuarial deficit as a percentage of taxable payroll jumped from -1.08 to -2.13. Significantly, about half of this was due to improvements in methods of projecting costs and income.[33] That is, the more accurate a view of OASDI's future the actuaries achieved, the worse that future appeared.

Back in 1981, in his superb *The Coming Revolution in Social Security,* A. Haeworth Robertson, who was Social Security's chief actuary in 1975-1978,

Table 1.2

Social Security's Bankruptcy: Coming Closer

Year of Report	Projected Year of "Trust Fund" Exhaustion (# years out)			ACTUARIAL ASSUMPTIONS
	OASI	DI	OASDI	
1990	*	*	*	Low cost
	2046 (56)	2020 (30)	2043 (53)	Intermediate
	2027 (37)	1998 (8)	2023 (33)	High cost
1991	*	*	*	Low cost
	2045 (54)	2015 (24)	2041 (50)	Intermediate
	2026 (35)	1995 (4)	2019 (28)	High cost
1992	*	2060 (68)	*	Low cost
	2042 (50)	1997 (5)	2036 (44)	Intermediate
	2026 (34)	1995 (3)	2019 (27)	High cost
1993	*	1995 (2)	*	Low cost
	2044 (51)	1995 (2)	2036 (43)	Intermediate
	2025 (32)	1995 (2)	2017 (24)	High cost
1994	*	1995 (1)	*	Low cost
	2036 (42)	1995 (1)	2029 (35)	Intermediate
	2023 (29)	1995 (1)	2014 (20)	High cost
1995	*	*	*	Low cost
	2031 (36)	2016 (21)	2030 (35)	Intermediate
	2020 (25)	2004 (9)	2016 (21)	High cost
1996	*	*	*	Low cost
	2031 (35)	2015 (19)	2029 (33)	Intermediate
	2020 (24)	2005 (9)	2016 (20)	High cost
1997	*	*	*	Low cost
	2031 (34)	2015 (18)	2029 (32)	Intermediate
	2022 (25)	2007 (10)	2018 (21)	High cost
1998	*	*	*	Low cost
	2034 (36)	2019 (21)	2032 (34)	Intermediate
	2025 (27)	2009 (11)	2022 (24)	High cost
1999	*	*	*	Low cost
	2036 (37)	2020 (21)	2034 (35)	Intermediate
	2028 (29)	2011 (12)	2024 (25)	High cost
2000	*	*	*	Low cost
	2039 (39)	2023 (23)	2037 (37)	Intermediate
	2029 (29)	2012 (12)	2026 (26)	High cost

*"trust fund" exhaustion not projected within Report's seventy-five-year projection period
Source: Social Security Administration, Office of the Actuary; OASDI *Annual Reports*

Table 1.3

**Social Security's Disappearing Cash Flows Surplus
(Intermediate Actuarial Assumptions), Calendar 2000-2015
(dollar amounts in billions)**

Calendar year	Total income	Minus Interest income	Equals Cash inflow	Minus Total outgo	Equals Cash flow surplus	Total surplus	Cash flow surplus as % total
2000	$565.7	$64.9	$500.7	$410.3	$90.4	$155.4	58.2 %
2001	603.7	75.6	528.1	432.2	95.9	171.5	55.9
2002	639.2	86.4	552.8	455.6	97.2	183.6	52.9
2003	674.8	96.8	577.9	480.6	97.3	194.2	50.1
2004	712.8	108.0	604.8	508.2	96.6	204.6	47.2
2005	755.3	120.1	635.1	538.6	96.5	216.7	44.5
2006	798.4	133.3	665.1	571.5	93.6	226.9	41.3
2007	846.2	147.3	698.9	607.2	91.7	239.0	38.4
2008	895.2	162.1	733.1	646.0	87.1	249.2	35.0
2009	947.9	177.5	770.4	689.2	81.2	258.7	31.4
2010	1,004.3	194.0	810.3	737.2	73.1	267.1	27.4
2015	1,315.0	208.5	1,034.5	1,045.2	-10.7	269.8	—

Source: *2000 OASDI Annual Report*

warned presciently that "Only the foolhardy would continue to ignore the longer range financial problems projected for the Social Security program. It is not a question of whether future costs will be higher; it is a question of whether they will be so much higher as to be unaffordable. It is a question of whether we are making promises we will not be able to keep."[34]

Even in the near term, Social Security's finances will start weakening. A superficial look at projections of OASDI's overall income and outgo for the next few years under intermediate assumptions shows that Social Security will continue running substantial, and rising, surpluses, so that seemingly there is no cause for alarm. But if we dig deeper, and break down the composition of OASDI's total income, things start to look troubling (see table 1.3).[35]

If we subtract the "trust fund's" interest earnings from total income, we obtain OASDI's cash inflow. Subtracting OASDI's total outgo from this, we get Social Security's cash flow surplus. When we examine the cash flow surplus and the total surplus together, we see that even under intermediate assumptions, while the *total* surplus remains reassuringly large, the *cash flow* surplus is a dwindling share of it, as the cash flow surplus stagnates at a modest level until 2007, then collapses. After 2003, the majority of the "trust fund's" vaunted annual surplus will be obtained not from new revenue coming in but from interest earnings on Treasuries the fund already holds. In other words, the very heart of Social Security's finances—the payroll and

Table 1.4

Social Security's Disappearing Cash Flow Surplus
(High Cost Actuarial Assumptions), 2000-2015
(dollar amounts in billions)

Calendar year	Total income	Minus Interest income	Equals Cash inflow	Minus Total outgo	Equals Cash flow surplus	Total surplus	Cash flow surplus as % total
2000	$560.4	$64.7	$495.7	$411.8	$83.9	$148.6	56.5%
2001	582.5	74.3	508.2	436.9	71.3	145.6	49.0
2002	625.4	84.4	541.0	465.8	75.2	159.6	47.1
2003	672.9	96.2	576.8	505.2	71.6	167.7	42.7
2004	695.4	107.5	587.9	548.9	39.0	146.5	26.6
2005	744.4	117.7	626.7	585.8	40.9	158.6	25.8
2006	794.3	127.4	666.8	627.4	39.4	166.9	23.6
2007	844.3	137.6	707.2	672.7	34.5	171.6	20.1
2008	895.5	148.4	747.1	721.9	25.2	173.6	14.5
2009	948.4	159.4	789.2	776.7	12.5	171.7	7.3
2010	1,003.0	169.4	833.5	836.7	-3.2	166.3	—
2015	1,294.2	208.0	1,086.2	1,222.5	-136.3	71.7	—

Source: *2000 OASDI Annual Report*

self-employment tax—will be beating ever more feebly even *before* the baby boomers start retiring.

Under high cost assumptions, Social Security's cash flow outlook is even worse. In 2010, just nine years away, the payroll tax will stop generating a surplus over outlays. The cash flow surplus turns negative that year, and by 2015 is a substantial deficit (table 1.4).[36]

The Compelling Case for Pessimism

In fact, Social Security's prospects are almost certainly worse than is generally understood, because while virtually all discussions of Social Security employ the intermediate actuarial assumptions, a compelling case exists for using the high cost ones instead.

Edmund Burke famously maintained that prudence is "in politics, the first of virtues."[37] The history of American governance in recent decades is thickly strewn with imprudence, even recklessness, from—to cite but a few cases— the Vietnam War to the Social Security benefit expansion of the late sixties and early seventies to the gargantuan deficits of 1982-1995. Most of these disasters flowed in large part from overly optimistic assumptions about future events. Too often, policymakers' assumptions have flowed not from their most careful and realistic judgment of what they deemed likely, but from what they wanted to believe. Because the stakes in Social Security are enormous—it affects virtually our entire population, and has enormous economic and political significance—and because unforeseeable future events can decisively affect its finances, forecasting for Social Security cries out for prudence. Social Security has already plunged into crisis twice, due to a combination of excessive benefit generosity and unforeseen adverse economic developments—oil price shocks and inflationary recessions—which necessitated very costly rescues in 1977 and 1983. This is a powerful cautionary tale about assumptions about the future.

Former Chief Actuary Robertson has carefully considered the issue of which set of assumptions should be used. He made the insightful observation that *"Social Security is a program of future promises"* (italics in original). Specifically, Social Security contains two sets of promises, benefit promises and tax promises: "one promise that specified benefits will be paid to the inactive segment of the population; and another promise that specified taxes will be collected from the active segment of the population." These promises, he argued cogently, are equally important, and the tax promises as well as the benefit promises should be honored. Accordingly, the purpose of long-range actuarial analysis and cost estimates is "to provide the information necessary to ensure that we do not make promises we cannot keep. The purpose is to make certain that Social Security is a program of *fulfilled promises,* not a program of *broken promises"* (italics in original).[38]

That is, the point of Social Security's actuarial projections is to tell policymakers what they need to know to enable them to manage the program so as to avoid *both* benefit cuts *and* tax increases, and thereby avoid inflicting trauma and injury on *both* beneficiaries *and* taxpayers. Clearly, Robertson's position is statesmanlike and prudent. For the sake of domestic tranquillity (a goal of our Constitution) and orderly governance, we should ensure that Social Security is managed soundly so as to avoid economically and politically traumatic and costly outcomes.

Given the importance of keeping tax and benefit promises, it follows, Robertson maintained, that the issue involved in deciding which set of assumptions to use is "which set of assumptions should be used to assess whether future income will likely be approximately equal to future outgo—and whether both benefit and taxation promises can be fulfilled?" By that criterion, the high cost actuarial assumptions are "the most appropriate . . . and even they may be somewhat optimistic."[39] Another factor, Robertson wisely observed, is public perception of Social Security. If the public believes that Social Security's promised benefits should be inviolable—as the elderly quite clearly do—then high cost assumptions should be used, "to help ensure that we do not promise more benefits than future generations of taxpayers will be willing to finance."[40] Again, this is a position of prudence, properly concerned for financial soundness and sustainability and with a keen eye on political realities.

As for specific assumptions, Robertson went on to argue that the high cost assumptions for productivity, fertility and mortality rates—the variables which "have the greatest impact on long-range projections of future income and outgo"[41]—are more realistic than the intermediate ones.

Obviously, Social Security's long-run financial soundness varies directly with the fertility rate: the more workers supporting each retiree, the easier it will be for the economy to finance the program and the healthier Social Security's cash flow will be. Observing the long decline in fertility rates here and throughout the developed world, to very low levels in 1988 (1.6 in Western Europe, 1.8 in Northern Europe, and 1.9 in the U. S.), Robertson concluded that the 1990 *Report's* intermediate assumption of 1.9 seemed optimistic and that the high cost assumption of a future fertility rate of 1.6 births per woman "is probably quite appropriate to use as an intermediate assumption, and it could even be optimistic."[42]

Robust productivity growth results in Social Security's tax base—labor income—growing faster than outlays, by causing wage increases, hence payroll tax revenue, to outstrip benefit cost-of-living adjustments. This translates into a healthier cash flow, making it easier for Social Security to meet its obligations. By the same token, stagnant productivity growth means stagnant labor incomes, which means stagnant revenues, which means that Social Security has a harder time paying its way. The 1990 *Report* assumed future long-term average annual productivity increases of 2.2 percent (optimistic), 1.7 percent (intermediate, or "most likely"), and 1.4 percent (pessimistic). Noting that the annual increase for 1968-1988 averaged only about 1.1 percent, Robertson concluded that the "pessimistic" 1.4 percent was a suitable intermediate figure—perhaps even optimistic.[43]

Declining mortality rates mean Americans will live longer after retirement, that is, will collect benefits for a greater number of years, thus increasing Social Security's costs. Thus the faster the decline in the death rate, the worse the outlook for OASDI. As health care, living standards, diet and exercise have improved, death rates adjusted for age and sex have fallen steadily: by an average of 1.2 percent a year in 1900-1989, and 1.4 percent in 1969-1989. Given this, Robertson maintained that the 1990 *Annual Report's* intermediate assumption of a 0.6 percent average annual fall in the death rate in 1989-2064 looked overoptimistic, as did the pessimistic assumption of 0.9 percent.[44]

In effect conceding that Robertson was right, the Trustees' 1994 *Annual Report* revised some intermediate assumptions toward pessimism. The fertility rate was cut slightly for the first fifteen years, reflecting lower-than-expected birth rates in 1992. Male mortality rates were reduced, reflecting mortality rates in 1992 and 1993 which were lower than expected. Also, the Trustees adjusted some economic assumptions, for example, labor force participation rates were lowered to reflect increases in the number of workers expected to receive disability benefits, which slightly worsened OASDI's actuarial deficit.[45] And the new future productivity growth assumptions were sharply revised downward: 1.7 percent (optimistic), 1.4 percent (intermediate), and 1.1 percent (pessimistic).[46] That is, 1990's intermediate assumption became 1994's optimistic assumption, 1990's pessimistic assumption became 1994's intermediate one, and 1994's pessimistic assumption was even lower than 1990's—a complete vindication of Robertson's prudent position.

With newer figures, Robertson is still right. Fertility rate assumptions for the Board of Trustees' 2000 *Annual Report* are 2.2 (low cost), 1.95 (intermediate), and 1.7 (high cost).[47] These are seemingly reasonable, since the fertility rate has recently risen to near-replacement levels. But sexual mores remain "liberated"; contraception is still intensely advocated and widely used; abortions continue in very large numbers; attitudes remain hostile to large families, which are seen in some quarters as unfriendly to the environment; young Americans continue to postpone marriage; and children remain financial liabilities. All of these phenomena militate against numerous children, and no revolution in beliefs is visible which would reverse them. There is, too, a widespread incidence of infertility and impotence. The realistic conclusion from all this is that the recent fertility jump is unlikely to endure, making the high-cost assumption better long-term.

Moreover, a crucial qualitative factor is at work which fertility data do not reflect. Given the illegitimacy and divorce explosions, today's American babies are far less likely than those of previous generations to enjoy the sort of start in life conducive to the sustained high-wage employment which is essential to healthy Social Security revenues. It does not necessarily improve Social Security's revenue outlook to have more lifetime births per woman if a large share of births and upbringings occur under circumstances more closely resembling Hogarth's "Gin Lane" than "Ozzie and Harriet." While there has been a (modest) quantitative improvement in fertility, the qualitative context of childbirth is deteriorating for a rising share of American infants—substantially enough, I submit, to offset the better numbers. Use of the pessimistic fertility assumption would reflect this qualitative deterioration.

As for productivity, in still another vindication for former Chief Actuary Robertson, the 1998 *Annual Report* again revised productivity assumptions downward across the board: to 1.6 percent (low cost), 1.3 percent (intermediate), and 1.0 percent (high cost).[48] The 2000 *Annual Report,* however, revised the productivity assumptions upward: 1.8 percent (low cost); 1.5 percent (intermediate); and 1.2 percent (high cost). This change reflects the surge in productivity growth to 2.9 percent a year since 1995 and revisions in National Income and Product Account (NIPA) data which raised productivity growth figures for the past twenty years—as well as "an assessment that some of recent favorable economic performance, with low unemployment and faster than expected growth in both GDP and employment, will carry through into the early years of the projection period."[49]

But while productivity growth for 1959-1998 averaged 1.9 percent, making the 2000 *Annual Report's* intermediate assumption look appropriate, even conservative, this seemingly healthy overall figure masks a steady decline, revealed by disaggregating 1959-1998 into ten-year periods: 3.0 percent average annual productivity growth in 1959-1968, 1.8 percent in 1969-1978, 1.3 percent in 1979-1988 and an only very modest improvement to 1.4 percent in 1989-1998.[50]

In addition, the length of our current expansion, the recent boom in productivity growth, and the long bull market in stocks have spawned enthusiasm about a so-called "New Economy" of sustained rapid technology-driven growth and prosperity, and a long spell of federal budget surpluses, that risks loss of perspective. Several caveats about the productivity surge are in order. First, it is simply too early to tell whether this is a mere temporary increase or indeed portends a trend of high productivity growth. As Roy H. Hall, vice president and economist at the Federal Reserve Bank of Richmond observes, productivity growth fluctuates with the business cycle, so "it is best to look at a complete business cycle or longer" to ascertain whether the productivity growth trend has really changed.[51] The Social Security Advisory Board's 1999 Technical Panel struck the same note of caution, pointing out that "it is too early to determine if those improvements are more than cyclical" and concluding that slight increases in the assumptions "would be reasonable," with larger adjustments later if recent productivity gains are sustained.[52]

Also, some economists have argued that from a long-term perspective, the rapid productivity growth of the postwar period until 1973 was actually an aberration, and that the post-1973 decline in productivity growth was really a return to the lower growth rates that prevailed for most of the period since 1820.[53] If so, the high cost assumption is more plausible for the long term.

Finally, what really matters for Social Security's future is that higher productivity growth is *sustained long term*. How likely is this to happen? Productivity is determined primarily by investment, which depends on savings.[54] American savings performance has been bad and steadily worsening since the fifties. Net private savings averaged 9.7 percent of GDP in the sixties, 9.8 percent in the seventies, 8.8 percent in the eighties, and 7.3 percent in 1991-1997. The fiscal profligacy of the eighties and nineties drove our net national savings rate—net private savings minus federal budget deficits, that is, the share of Gross Domestic Product actually available for investment—even lower: from an average of 9.8 percent of GDP in the sixties and 8.0 percent in the seventies to 5.4 percent in 1981-1990, and just 4.4 percent in 1991-1996. Since 1997, the federal budget has been running surpluses, reversing this trend; in 1998 net national savings were 6.1 percent of GDP.[55] Should surpluses continue, the higher national savings would make sustaining recent productivity gains plausible. But the projected future surpluses being bandied about may well never materialize; indeed pressures are already building which make resumption of deficits likely. Growth of domestic discretionary spending has accelerated in recent years; actual spending exceeded budget resolutions by $50 billion in fiscal 1999, $47 billion in fiscal 2000, and an estimated $40 billion in fiscal 2001.[56] Also, proposals are circulating to expand Medicare to include prescription drug benefits. In 2000 President Bill Clinton proposed to increase Medicare spending to add prescription drug benefits and provide higher payment rates for health care providers, which the Congressional Budget Office estimated would increase Medicare outlays by $310.4 billion over the next ten years, $167.6 billion of it for the drug benefit.[57] Both Al Gore and George W. Bush proposed during the 2000 election campaign adding a prescription drug benefit to Medicare, so some such expansion is a virtual certainty. As the baby boomers become Medicare beneficiaries, the cost will, of course, explode. Moreover, a recession in the near future will depress revenues, making deficits even more likely. Resumption of deficits will resume the national savings depletion that helped cause the 1973-1995 productivity stagnation, and thereby make sustained faster productivity growth unlikely. The likely future fiscal context thus makes the high cost assumption far more realistic.

Because the stakes in Social Security are so high, we should not lean on luck and pin our hopes on optimistic budget surplus and productivity growth projections. And compelling grounds exist for pessimism, or at least skepticism, about future productivity growth. Given all this, it would be appropriate to use the high cost assumption. Any error would then be in Social Security's favor. Again, Robertson's position is the one of prudent, responsible statesmanship.

For mortality rates, the intermediate assumption does look better *prima facie*. American age- and sex-adjusted death rates fell by an average of 1.1 percent annually in 1900-1997, and 1.2 percent in 1968-1997. But the decline slowed to 0.7 percent since 1982. Hence the 2000 *Annual Report's* intermediate assumption of a 0.7 percent average annual decline in the death rate for 1997-2074[58] reasonably fits the most recent trend.

However, after reviewing the assumptions of the 1999 *Annual Report* and surveying the literature on mortality projections, the 1999 Technical Panel pointed out that the decline in mortality rates in other developed countries is rapid and accelerating, especially at older ages, which "demonstrates conclusively that U.S. mortality can fall a long way without encountering biomedical limits." Hence it is prudent to assume that the recent U.S. slowdown is likely to be only temporary, and the average historical rates of mortality decline "provide a prudent *intermediate* [original italics] forecast." The Panel recommended that the intermediate assumption for mortality decline be raised accordingly, such that projected life expectancy at birth in 2070 be raised from the 1999 *Annual Report's* intermediate 81.5 years to the high cost 85.2 years. It reiterated its belief that this would be the prudent course.[59]

A careful and realistic assessment, then, yields the conclusion that former Chief Actuary Robertson is right to recommend use of the high cost assumptions.

Finally, the high cost analysis alone includes actual business cycles in the near term; its 2000 version forecasts two recessions, in 2001 and 2004. Given the record of recessions in 1975, 1980, 1982, and 1991, and the slowing down of our present expansion, this is far more realistic than the intermediate assumptions' forecast of steady real GDP growth of 2.0 to 2.1 percent annually in 2003-2010.[60] This alone is reason enough for the high cost assumptions. Is it really plausible that the business cycle has been repealed and that the next ten years will see no recession at all?

Exploding the Denials

There is a crisis coming in Social Security, then, and the outlook is probably grimmer than is usually understood. Yet some of the program's defenders scornfully deny that serious trouble is coming. Reports of Social Security's demise have been greatly exaggerated, scoff former Social Security Commissioner Robert Ball, former Chief Actuary Robert J. Myers, Brookings Institution senior fellow Henry Aaron, and others. "There is no need for political palpitations and heavy breathing," Aaron assured us; warnings about Social Security are "myths and misrepresentations."[61] Aaron asserted elsewhere that the crisis atmosphere is "bogus."[62] Similarly, former Chief Actuary Myers asserted that lack of confidence in OASDI's long-run sustainability is due to "myths and misconceptions" asserted by "various prophets of gloom and doom."[63] Six members of the 1994-1996 Advisory Council on Social Security, including former Commissioner Ball, asserted in a separate statement in the Advisory Council's Report that *"Social Security is not facing a crisis"* (original italics).[64] Ball added elsewhere that Social Security's troubles are "being greatly exaggerated. There is no need to make major cuts in promised benefits or to make major increases in contribution rates. . . . There is, in short, no need to panic."[65] *New Republic* senior editor John Judis derided former Colorado governor Richard Lamm, who repeatedly warned of Social Security's coming crisis, as "Chicken Little Lamm."[66] Economic Policy Institute economists Dean Baker and Mark Weisbrot co-authored a book titled *Social Security: The Phony Crisis*.

This line of argument is clearly meant to reassure the public—and forestall efforts to substantially change OASDI. Aaron, for instance, disparaged "privatization" plans and asserted that for basic retirement benefits, "the sure bet of social insurance is preferable."[67]

Some of this is specious. Former Chief Actuary Myers, for example, demolished straw men. One "typical" myth, he wrote, is that Social Security is "doomed . . . a ticking time bomb," and that millions of beneficiaries will not get their benefits. This myth fails to recognize that as the program moves toward bankruptcy, "corrective action can be taken."[68] True—and warnings about Social Security recognize precisely this, and are *meant* to stimulate discussion and enactment of "corrective action."

In any case, scoffers reassure us, "trust fund" depletion is so far away, it hardly merits crisis talk. "Can a problem that does not become immediate for a third of a century be a 'crisis'? In a pig's eye," snorts Aaron.[69] While it is true that there is no crisis today, nor is one likely soon, prudence would dictate early prevention of foreseeable trouble.

These denials rely on the intermediate assumptions, which, as I have endeavored to show, is not prudent and quite possibly not realistic. Since so much depends on the choice of assumptions, that choice is itself debateworthy. Aaron, Ball, and other experts cannot fail to know of former Chief Actuary Robertson's persuasive case for the high cost assumptions. They should defend their use of intermediate assumptions, and explain why they think they are right and Robertson is wrong. That a debate over assumptions is not occurring is, itself, telling. The mere fact that most discussions use the intermediate assumptions is no argument for doing so. Surely Robertson's painstaking argument for the high cost assumptions and his sage counsel to pitch our tent toward prudence merit respectful consideration and thoughtful replies.

The "crisis," the scoffers usually add, could be easily fixed by minor tinkering: increased benefit taxation; accelerating already-scheduled increases in the retirement age which qualifies people for full benefits (a benefit cut); reducing the cost-of-living adjustment (COLA) for benefits by using a smaller measure of inflation (another benefit cut); and bringing new hires in state and local government under Social Security to broaden its tax base and capture additional revenue promptly.[70]

One such recommendation popular in the late nineties was the "2.2 percent solution"—raising payroll taxes by 2.2 percent of taxable payroll. The 1998 *Annual Report's* intermediate analysis projected an actuarial deficit for the seventy-five-year period of -2.19 percent of taxable payroll. The actuarial deficit measures how much the stream of projected OASDI costs through the next seventy-five years exceeds the stream of projected revenues plus current assets in the "trust funds." Put another way, it measures how much taxes would have to be raised, and/or benefits cut, immediately so as to make revenues and assets balance costs over the next seventy-five years. Thus the Trustees added that if we immediately raise payroll tax rates "by 1.10 percent for employees and employers, each, and by 2.20 percent for the self-employed," and kept taxes at this higher level for the entire seventy-five years, this would close that gap, with no benefit cuts.[71] Hence the "2.2 percent solution." Examining this "solution" is a handy way to refute the scoffers. Since it drew on the 1998 *Report,* we use 1998 figures here.

First, this solution is not minor. The 2.2 refers to the change in the tax *rate*, by 2.2 percentage points of taxable payroll, *not* the increase in *dollar amounts of taxes*. It means raising the FICA rate from 6.2 percent of payroll to 7.3 percent each for employees and employers, and the self-employment rate from 12.4 percent to 14.6 percent—an immediate, permanent increase of tax payments by 17 percent, which is substantial.

More seriously, this "solution" gives a misleading impression that this—or other measures sufficient to close the actuarial deficit—will solve everything. It will not. Closing the actuarial deficit will not eliminate the need to tap the "trust fund." The aging of our population will still drive expenditures above revenues eventually. This "solution" would achieve *long-term actuarial* balance, making OASDI's revenue and outlay *streams* balance over the seventy-five-year period 1998-2072 *as a whole*. That is, as Harry Ballantyne, chief actuary of Social Security, himself confirmed to me, it will generate larger surpluses in the near future, building up the "trust fund" enough to cover all projected deficits in the later years—which will still occur—and still leave OASDI with enough assets at the end of 2072 to cover all of 2073's expenses. It will *not* achieve *annual* balance (income matching outgo every year).[72]

Grasping the distinction between long-term actuarial balance and annual balance is crucial to seeing the hollowness of this "solution." Even with the scoffers' tinkering, there will still be large annual deficits in the late years. The 1998 intermediate analysis projected cash deficits of -$433 billion in calendar 2025; -$684 billion in 2030; and -$925 billion in 2035.[73] If we had immediately raised payroll taxes 2.2 percent—or enacted some other mix of measures to close the actuarial deficit—these deficits would be, respectively, roughly -$170 billion, -$350 billion, and -$500 billion.[74] Better, but still huge.

Even with the scoffers' own assumptions and recommendations, then, Social Security would still need to redeem huge amounts of Treasury bonds eventually. The Treasury would have to raise taxes or borrow from the public. The economy would suffer accordingly.

To sum up: Social Security is indeed headed for trouble, and its scoffing defenders are wrong. Social Security is weaker than they think—and the case for pessimism stronger than they'll admit. Second, even if tinkering could avert bankruptcy, Social Security would still eventually pose severe fiscal and economic burdens.

Notes

1. *2000 Annual Report of the Board of Trustees of the Federal Old-Age and Survivors Insurance and Disability Insurance Trust Funds* [hereafter, *2000 OASDI Annual Report*], pp. 1, 6, 7. Two excellent detailed yet accessible overviews of Social Security are U.S., Congress, House, Committee on Ways and Means, *1998 Green Book: Background Material and Data on Programs Within the Jurisdiction of the Committee on Ways and Means* [hereafter, *1998 Green Book*], pp. 1-99, and

A. Haeworth Robertson, *Social Security: What Every Taxpayer Should Know* (Washington, DC: Retirement Policy Institute, 1992).

2. *1998 Green Book*, p. 39.
3. *2000 OASDI Annual Report*, p. 7.
4. *1998 Green Book*, pp. 12-19.
5. Ibid., p. 5.
6. Robertson, *Social Security: What Every Taxpayer Should Know*, p. 79.
7. *2000 OASDI Annual Report*, p. 25.
8. Ibid., p. 33.
9. *1998 Green Book*, pp. 73, 75, 77.
10. *2000 OASDI Annual Report*, pp. 40, 44, 48.
11. *Historical Tables. Budget of the United States Government, Fiscal Year 2001*, table 1.1—Summary of Receipts, Outlays, and Surpluses or Deficits: 1789-2005; table 1.2—Summary of Receipts, Outlays, and Surpluses or Deficits as Percentages of GDP: 1930-2005.
12. *2000 OASDI Annual Report*, pp. 52.
13. *1998 Green Book*, pp. 6-7, 9-10; Robertson, *Social Security: What Every Taxpayer Should Know*, pp. 15-16.
14. *2000 OASDI Annual Report*, p. 2.
15. Ibid., p. 9.
16. Ibid., p. 53.
17. Ibid., p. 15.
18. Ibid., pp. 63-64, table II.D2.—Selected Demographic Assumptions by Alternative, Calendar Years 1940-2075.
19. Ibid., pp. 147-148, table II.H1.—Social Security Area Population as of July 1 and Dependency Ratios, by Alternative and Broad Age Group, Calendar Years 1950-2075.
20. Table 1.1 source: Ibid. Percentage calculations mine.
21. *2000 OASDI Annual Report*, pp. 63-64, table II.D2.
22. Ibid., pp. 147-148, table II.H1.
23. Ibid., pp. 122-123, table II.F19—Comparison of OASDI Covered Workers and Beneficiaries by Alternative, Calendar Years 1945-2075.
24. Ibid., p. 27, table I.G3.—OASDI Trust Fund Ratios.
25. Ibid., p. 30.
26. See, for example, Merton C. Bernstein and Joan Brodshaug Bernstein, *Social Security: The System That Works* (New York: Basic Books, Inc., 1988), pp. 70-73; Theodore R. Marmor, Fay Lomax Cook, and Stephen Scher, "Social Security Politics and the Conflict Between Generations: Are We Asking the Right Questions?" in *Social Security in the 21st Century*, pp. 201, 206 n. 13; Baker and Weisbrot, *Social Security: The Phony Crisis*, p. 32; Robert M. Ball, *Insuring the Essentials: Bob Ball on Social Security*, ed. Thomas N. Bethell (New York: Century Foundation Press, 2000), pp. 74-75, 181-182.
27. "Preparing for an Aging Population," Testimony of Dan L. Crippen, Director, Congressional Budget Office, before the House Budget Committee, July 27, 2000, p. 4 (www.cbo.gov).
28. Social Security Advisory Board, 1999 Technical Panel on Assumptions and Methods, *Report to the Social Security Advisory Board*, November 1999, p. 71.
29. *2000 OASDI Annual Report*, pp. 147-148, table II.H1. Calculations of under-20 dependency ratios mine.
30. Ibid. Calculations of population shares and under-20 dependency ratios mine.
31. Table 1.2 sources: "Projected Year of Trust Fund Exhaustion Under Alternatives I - III" (mailing to author from Social Security's Office of the Actuary); *1992 OASDI*

Annual Report, p. 27; *1993 OASDI Annual Report,* p. 29; *1994 OASDI Annual Report,* p. 24; *1995 OASDI Annual Report,* p. 26; *1996 OASDI Annual Report,* p. 26; *1997 OASDI Annual Report,* p. 26; *1998 OASDI Annual Report,* p. 25; *1999 OASDI Annual Report,* p. 25; *2000 OASDI Annual Report,* p. 27.

32. *1998 OASDI Annual Report,* p. 28; *1999 OASDI Annual Report,* p. 28; *2000 OASDI Annual Report,* p. 29.

33. *1992 OASDI Annual Report,* pp. 134-136; *1993 OASDI Annual Report,* pp. 136-137; *1994 OASDI Annual Report,* pp. 127-129; *1998 OASDI Annual Report,* p. 193, table III.D1.—Long-Range Actuarial Balances for the OASDI Program as Shown for the Intermediate Assumptions in the Trustees' Reports Issued in Years 1988-98.

34. A. Haeworth Robertson, *The Coming Revolution in Social Security* (Reston, VA: Reston Publishing Co., Inc., 1981), p. 91. Robertson repeated this warning in 1992 (*Social Security: What Every Taxpayer Should Know,* p. 110).

35. Table 1.3 source: *2000 OASDI Annual Report,* p. 181, table III.B3.—Estimated Operations of the Combined OASI and DI Trust Funds in Current Dollars by Alternative, Calendar Years 2000-2075. Calculations of cash flow surplus, total surplus, and cash flow surplus as share of total surplus mine.

36. Table 1.4 source: Ibid.

37. Edmund Burke, *Further Reflections on the Revolution in France,* ed. Daniel E. Ritchie (Indianapolis: Liberty Fund, Inc., 1992), pp. 15, 91.

38. Robertson, *Social Security: What Every Taxpayer Should Know,* pp. 129, 135, 136.

39. Ibid., p. 146.

40. Ibid., p. 140.

41. Ibid., pp. 140-141.

42. Ibid., pp. 142-143.

43. Ibid., pp. 143-144.

44. Ibid., pp. 142-143.

45. *1994 OASDI Annual Report,* pp. 126-127.

46. Ibid., p. 147.

47. *2000 OASDI Annual Report,* p. 145.

48. *1998 OASDI Annual Report,* p. 148.

49. Post-1995 productivity growth: *Economic Report of the President, February 2000,* p. 79. Productivity assumption revisions: *2000 OASDI Annual Report,* pp. 12-13.

50. *2000 OASDI Annual Report,* p. 150.

51. Roy H. Hall, "The Statistics Corner: National Productivity Statistics," *Business Economics,* vol. 34, no. 2 (April 1999), p. 31.

52. 1999 Technical Panel on Assumptions and Methods, *Report to the Social Security Advisory Board,* p. 52.

53. Robert Arnold and Robert Dennis, "Perspectives on Productivity Growth," *Business Economics,* vol. 34, no. 2 (April 1999), p. 10.

54. A good discourse on the importance of savings, investment and productivity for national economic health and for the affordability of our retirement entitlements is in Peter G. Peterson, *Will America Grow Up Before It Grows Old? How the Coming Social Security Crisis Threatens You, Your Family, and Your Country* (New York: Random House, 1996), pp. 53-72.

55. *Economic Report of the President, February 2000,* Department of Commerce, Bureau of Economic Analysis data, p. 334, table B-24.—Relation of gross domestic product, gross national product, net national product, and national income, 1959-99, and p. 342, table B-302.—Gross saving and investment, 1959-99. Net

private savings defined as gross private saving less private consumption of fixed capital. Net national savings defined as net private savings less federal surplus or deficit (in National Income and Product Account terms). Percent calculations mine.

56. "Binges Becoming Regular Budget Fare; As Spending Annually Exceeds Congressional Plans by Billions, Hawks Warn That Surplus and Process Are at Risk," *Washington Post,* October 25, 2000, A29; The Concord Coalition, "The Surplus Field of Dreams," Issue Brief, October 11, 2000, p. 2 (www.concordcoalition.org).

57. "Preparing for an Aging Population," Testimony of Dan L. Crippen, Director, Congressional Budget Office, p. 3.

58. *2000 OASDI Annual Report,* pp. 145-146.

59. 1999 Technical Panel on Assumptions and Methods, *Report to the Social Security Advisory Board,* pp. 9, 22, 64-67.

60. Ibid., pp. 57-58, table II.D1.—Selected Economic Assumptions by Alternative, Calendar Years 1960-2075.

61. Henry Aaron, "The Myths of the Social Security Crisis: Behind the Privatization Push," *Washington Post,* July 21, 1996, C1.

62. Henry J. Aaron, "Privatizing Social Security: A Bad Idea Whose Time Will Never Come," *Brookings Review,* vol. 15, no. 3 (Summer 1997), p. 21.

63. Robert J. Myers, "Social Security's Financing Problems: Realities and Myths," *Journal of the American Society of CLU & ChFC,* vol. 47, no. 2 (March 1993), p. 41.

64. Robert M. Ball, Edith U. Fierst, Gloria T. Johnson, Thomas W. Jones, George Kourpias, and Gerald M. Shea, "Social Security for the 21st Century," in *Report of the 1994-1996 Advisory Council on Social Security,* vol. 1: *Findings and Recommendations,* p. 59.

65. Robert M. Ball, "First, the System Is Hardly in Crisis," *New York Times,* January 19, 1997, sec. 3, p. 12.

66. John Judis, "Chicken Little Lamm," *Baltimore Sun,* July 19, 1996, 25A.

67. Aaron, "Privatizing Social Security: A Bad Idea Whose Time Will Never Come," p. 23.

68. Myers, "Social Security's Financing Problems: Realities and Myths," p. 41.

69. Aaron, "The Myths of the Social Security Crisis: Behind the Privatization Push."

70. *1998 OASDI Annual Report,* pp. 23-24.

71. *1998 OASDI Annual Report,* pp. 23-24, 192; and author's telephone conversation with Harry Ballantyne, chief actuary of Social Security, October 7, 1996.

72. *1998 OASDI Annual Report,* pp. 181-182, table III.B4.—Estimated OASDI and HI Income Excluding Interest, Outgo, and Balance in Current Dollars by Alternative, Calendar Years 1998-2075.

73. See, e.g., Aaron, "Privatizing Social Security: A Bad Idea Whose Time Will Never Come," pp. 19-21; Ball, "First, the System is Hardly in Crisis." Aaron offers a menu of such adjustments in Henry J. Aaron, "Social Security: Tune It Up, Don't Trade It In," in Henry J. Aaron and John B. Shoven, *Should the United States Privatize Social Security?,* ed. Benjamin M. Friedman (Cambridge, MA and London: MIT Press, 1999), pp. 89-90.

74. *1998 OASDI Annual Report,* pp. 23-24.

75. *1998 OASDI Annual Report,* pp. 23-24, 192; and author's telephone conversation with Harry Ballantyne, chief actuary of Social Security, October 7, 1996.

76. *1998 OASDI Annual Report,* pp. 181-182, table III.B4.—Estimated OASDI and HI Income Excluding Interest, Outgo, and Balance in Current Dollars by Alternative, Calendar Years 1998-2075.

77. We seek to show that even if the scoffers get their way, OASDI will still run burdensome deficits in the out years. We use intermediate assumptions and raise the income rate in all years by 2.2 percent of taxable payroll, which eliminates the actuarial deficit. Using only a few years' data and generating only very rough figures suffices to make the point.

From table III.A2. of the 1998 OASDI Annual Report, we get estimated income (less interest and miscellaneous transfers from the general fund of the Treasury) and cost rates and balances for OASDI expressed as percentages of taxable payroll—columns 2-4 in the table below. Table III.B4. supplies the estimated OASDI income (less interest), outgo, and balance in current dollars. The dollar-term balance is column 5.

Table 1.5
Even with Actuarial Deficit Closed, Large Annual
Cash Deficits Still Occur in Out Years
(dollar amounts in billions)

(1) cal. year	(2) income rate	(3) cost rate	(4) Balance (+/-)	(5) $ balance	(6) add'l. tax	(7) new inc. rate	(8) new bal. (+/-)	(9) new $ balance
2025	13.02	16.70	-3.69	-$433	2.2	15.22	-1.48	-$170
2030	13.10	17.76	-4.66	-684	2.2	15.30	-2.46	-350
2035	13.15	18.17	-5.02	-925	2.2	15.35	-2.87	-500

The income figures differ in that the rate figure excludes miscellaneous transfers from the Treasury and the dollar figure does not, but these transfers are negligible—only a few million dollars—and do not affect the issue.

To arrive at new OASDI cash deficits, first generate new income rates (column 7) by adding existing cost rates (column 2) and 2.2 percent of payroll (column 6). Since we assume no benefit cuts, we do not change the cost rates, which we subtract from the new income rates to get new balances as shares of taxable payroll (column 8). Next, we translate rate terms to dollars (column 9), which can be done with proportions. In 2025, for example, -$433 = -3.69 % of taxable payroll. $x (the dollar-term deficit we want) = -1.48 %. Set up a proportion and solve for x:

$$-433/x = -3.69/-1.48$$
$$x = (1.48)(-433)/(3.69)$$
$$x = -174 \text{ (rounded to -170 to reflect the rough nature of this operation)}$$

The same result would obtain from *any* mix of measures that reduced the actuarial deficit by 2.2 percent of payroll.

Again, this is a *very* rough-and-ready approach. But since all these projections are after all estimates, that is all right. And the answers suffice to demolish the scoffers' claim.

2

The Affordability Crisis

"My father made your yoke heavy,
and I will add to your yoke."

—*I Kings 12:14*

The OASDI cash deficit figures mentioned in debunking the "2.2 percent solution," and the allusions to the budget deficit, indicate that there is far more to Social Security's crisis than OASDI being unable to pay full benefits on time. While the possibility of program bankruptcy dominates discussion, a far more serious problem is largely being ignored: Social Security will become unaffordable, and inflict economic ruin on America, *even if it does not go bankrupt.*

The Historical Burden of Social Security Taxes

Social Security's taxes have already become seriously burdensome for both the individual taxpayer, and the economy as a whole.

To give some sense of just how much the Social Security tax burden has grown for individuals, table 2.1 shows how the Social Security tax on a taxable income of $20,000, and the maximum Social Security tax, have risen since the tax began in 1937.[1] The employee's payroll tax, or Federal Insurance Contribution Act (FICA) tax, was originally just one percent of taxable wage or salary income, and only the first $3,000 of income was taxable, making an initial maximum tax of $30 a year.

But costs necessarily rose as the population aged. Moreover, Social Security was expanded, and benefits liberalized, repeatedly. To preserve solvency, revenues had to rise accordingly, and every liberalization was accompanied or followed by a tax increase. There are three ways to increase revenue: widen the tax base by extending Social Security to more occupations; raise the maximum taxable income; and increase the tax rate. Congress repeatedly did all three.

Table 2.1

Social Security's Soaring Burden on Taxpayers, 1937-1999

Calendar year	Maximum taxable income	Employee FICA tax rate*	Self-employm't (SE) tax rate	FICA tax, $20,000 taxable income**	SE tax, $20,000 income	Maximum employee FICA tax
1937-1949	$3,000	1.000	—	$30.00	—	$30.00
1950	3,000	1.500	—	45.00	—	45.00
1951-1953	3,600	1.500	2.250	54.00	$81.00	54.00
1954	3,600	2.000	3.000	72.00	108.00	72.00
1955-1956	4,200	2.000	3.000	84.00	126.00	84.00
1957-1958	4,200	2.250	3.375	94.50	141.75	94.50
1959	4,800	2.500	3.750	120.00	180.00	120.00
1960-1961	4,800	3.000	4.500	144.00	216.00	144.00
1962	4,800	3.125	4.700	150.00	225.60	150.00
1963-1965	4,800	3.625	5.400	174.00	259.20	174.00
1966	6,600	3.850	5.800	254.10	382.80	254.10
1967	6,600	3.900	5.900	257.40	389.40	257.40
1968	7,800	3.800	5.800	296.40	452.40	296.40
1969	7,800	4.200	6.300	327.60	491.40	327.60
1970	7,800	4.200	6.300	327.60	491.40	327.60
1971	7,800	4.600	6.900	358.80	538.20	358.80
1972	9,000	4.600	6.900	414.00	621.00	414.00
1973	10,800	4.850	7.000	523.80	756.00	523.80
1974	13,700	4.950	7.000	653.40	924.00	653.40
1975	14,100	4.950	7.000	697.95	987.00	697.95
1976	15,300	4.950	7.000	757.35	1,071.00	757.35
1977	16,500	4.950	7.000	816.75	1,155.00	816.75
1978	17,700	5.050	7.100	893.85	1,256.70	893.85
1979	22,900	5.080	7.050	1,016.00	1,410.00	1,163.32
1980	25,900	5.080	7.050	1,016.00	1,410.00	1,315.72
1981	29,700	5.350	8.000	1,070.00	1,600.00	1,588.95
1982	32,400	5.400	8.050	1,080.00	1,610.00	1,749.60
1983	35,700	5.400	8.050	1,080.00	1,610.00	1,927.80
1984	37,800	5.700	11.400	1,140.00	2,280.00	2,154.60
1985	39,600	5.700	11.400	1,140.00	2,280.00	2,257.20
1986	42,000	5.700	11.400	1,140.00	2,280.00	2,394.00
1987	43,800	5.700	11.400	1,140.00	2,280.00	2,496.60
1988	45,000	6.060	12.120	1,212.00	2,424.00	2,727.00
1989	48,000	6.060	12.120	1,212.00	2,424.00	2,908.80
1990	51,300	6.200	12.400	1,240.00	2,480.00	3,180.60
1991	53,400	6.200	12.400	1,240.00	2,480.00	3,310.80
1992	55,500	6.200	12.400	1,240.00	2,480.00	3,441.00
1993	57,600	6.200	12.400	1,240.00	2,480.00	3,571.20
1994	60,600	6.200	12.400	1,240.00	2,480.00	3,757.20
1995	61,200	6.200	12.400	1,240.00	2,480.00	3,794.40
1996	62,700	6.200	12.400	1,240.00	2,480.00	3,887.40
1997	65,400	6.200	12.400	1,240.00	2,480.00	4,054.80
1998	68,400	6.200	12.400	1,240.00	2,480.00	4,240.80
1999	72,600	6.200	12.400	1,240.00	2,480.00	4,501.20

*Equivalent tax rate applied to employers. **Employer pays equivalent amount.
Source: *2000 OASDI Annual Report*

For example, the 1950 Social Security amendments liberalized eligibility standards and increased benefits by 77 percent. They also extended the program to nonfarm self-employed (except some professionals), and increased the maximum taxable income to $3,600 and the payroll tax rate to 1.5 percent. The 1954 amendments extended coverage to self-employed farmers and others not covered by the 1950 law, and raised benefits 13 percent— while lifting the taxable income ceiling to $4,200, allowing a scheduled increase in the payroll tax rate to 2 percent, and mandating higher future tax rates. When Disability Insurance was added in 1956, the tax rate was raised again to cover it.[2]

More benefit and tax increases followed. The evidence is clear that Social Security's architects and advocates cavalierly assumed that private enterprise would keep producing an abundance for them to redistribute, and that the program's taxes would never become burdensome. Thus on December 3, 1959, Wilbur Cohen, "Mr. Social Security," told the American Public Welfare Association,

I believe that during the next ten years the productivity of our nation will continue to grow due to automation, research, inventions, new processes, products and services. It will be possible, therefore, for our country to afford significant improvements in our Social Security system from these increased resources so that every aged, disabled person, and every widow and orphan will have sufficient income to enable him to live in health and decency.[3]

Similarly, economist Paul Samuelson, a staunch Social Security supporter, said in his February 13, 1967 *Newsweek* column, in a subhead tantalizingly titled "Something for Nothing?" that

The beauty about social insurance is that it is *actuarially* [italics in original] unsound. Everyone who reaches retirement age is given benefit privileges that far exceed anything he has paid in. And exceed his payments by more than ten times as much (or five times, counting in employer payments)!

How is this possible? It stems from the fact that the national product is growing at compound interest and *can be expected to do so as far ahead as the eye cannot see* [italics added]. Always there are more youths than old folks in a growing population. More important, with *real incomes growing at some 3 per cent per year* [italics added], the taxable base upon which benefits rest in any period are much greater than the taxes paid historically by the generation now retired . . . .

Social security is squarely based on what has been called the eighth wonder of the world—compound interest. A growing nation is the greatest Ponzi game ever contrived. And that is a fact, not a paradox.[4]

Reflecting this hubris, benefits were recklessly expanded, by 13 percent in 1968, 15 percent in 1969, 10 percent in 1971, and a staggering 20 percent, in a politically inspired bidding war between President Richard Nixon and congressional Democrats, in 1972, for a total benefit surge in 1967-1972 of 71.5

percent. Annual cost-of-living adjustments (COLAs), insulating benefits from inflation, also enacted in 1972, began in 1975.[5]

In a context of a surging elderly population, soaring inflation, falling fertility, and a weakening economy, this benefit explosion overwhelmed OASDI's cash flow. Automatic adjustments raised the maximum taxable income $13,700 in 1974 to $17,700 in 1978 (table 2.1), but it wasn't enough. In 1977, with OASDI's bankruptcy imminent, Congress enacted both higher tax rates and much larger increases in the maximum taxable income: to $22,900 in 1979 (up $5,200); $25,900 in 1980 (up $3,000); and $29,700 in 1981 (up $3,800).[6] Even this couldn't keep the program solvent. The 1979-1981 inflation drove up benefit costs, while rising unemployment in 1980-1982 slowed revenue growth. Bankruptcy was projected for 1983. Congress rescued OASDI again that year, raising both tax rates and the maximum taxable income, which now rises automatically every year, based on increases in average wages.

The simultaneous increases in the *amount* of taxable income and the tax *rates* applied to it interacted powerfully. Social Security taxes rose rapidly, especially after 1977. In 1979, a taxpayer earning $20,000 saw his entire labor income become subject to the Social Security tax. While in 1970 he paid only 1.6 percent of his income ($327.60) in Social Security taxes, in 1979 he paid 5.08 percent ($1,016), and now pays 6.20 percent ($1,240). After 1977, too, as the maximum taxable income soared, more and more middle class Americans found their entire employment incomes subject to Social Security tax. The maximum tax rose accordingly (see table 2.1).

Heavy as Social Security's tax has become for employees, these figures probably understate it. Many economists argue that the worker pays the employer's share of the FICA tax in the long run, in the form of lower wages— or higher prices, if businesses pass the tax on to consumers. Painstaking empirical analysis by Brookings Institution senior fellow John Brittain supports this position.[7] If the employer absorbs the cost, retained earnings and returns on stock fall accordingly—and workers who are shareholders or whose pension plans are invested in stocks pay indirectly this way, too.[8]

For the self-employed, the tax has become even heavier. When they were brought into the program in 1950, a self-employment tax was imposed that was smaller than the sum of the employee and employer shares of the FICA tax. It remained so until the 1983 legislation raised the self-employment tax rate, until beginning in 1989 it matched the total FICA tax rate.[9] Moreover, while for employees the employer's share of the FICA tax is an indirect and seldom-perceived cost, for the self-employed the total tax is explicit.

The Social Security tax is now many taxpayers' heaviest tax, far exceeding their federal income tax. Exemptions, the standard deduction, and other deductions lessen the federal income tax, but the Social Security tax has no such mitigation.

Social Security taxation has also become a substantial drag on the economy as a whole. The repeated tax increases, especially since 1965, have transformed Social Security from a trifling exaction into one of the federal government's most formidable extractors of resources (see table 2.2).[10] Social Security's tax take has far outpaced both economic growth and inflation. In 1970-1980, OASDI revenue more than tripled; since 1980, it has more than quadrupled again. In the 1970-2000 period, OASDI revenue rose by a staggering 1,323 percent. Social Security tax revenue is now about 50 percent of personal income tax revenue, about double its 1960 share. Twenty-four cents of every dollar collected in federal taxes is raised by Social Security. And since 1950, Social Security taxes have risen from 0.7 percent of GDP to 5.0 percent, an increase of 614 percent.

Table 2.2

Bigger and Bigger Bites: OASDI's Resource Extraction, 1950-2000
(dollar amounts in billions) (2000 figures estimates)

Fiscal year	OASDI tax revenue	Federal income tax revenue	Total federal tax revenue	Gross Domestic Product (GDP)	OASDI tax revenue as %		
					of federal income tax revenue	of total federal tax revenue	of GDP
1950	$2.1	$15.8	$39.4	$273.6	13.3	5.3	0.8
1955	5.1	28.7	65.5	395.3	17.8	7.8	1.3
1960	10.6	40.7	92.5	519.8	26.0	11.5	2.0
1965	16.7	48.8	116.8	688.2	34.2	14.3	2.4
1970	33.5	90.4	192.8	1,013.7	37.1	17.4	3.3
1975	62.5	122.4	279.1	1,559.2	51.1	22.4	4.0
1980	113.2	244.1	517.1	2,731.8	46.4	21.9	4.1
1985	186.2	334.5	734.1	4,141.6	55.7	25.4	4.5
1990	281.7	466.9	1,032.0	5,738.4	60.3	27.3	4.9
1995	351.1	590.2	1,351.8	7,322.6	59.5	26.0	4.9
2000	476.8	951.6	1,956.3	9,571.9	50.1	24.4	5.0

Source: Office of Management and Budget

One might argue that resources extracted by OASDI taxes are put back in as benefits, so Social Security puts no such burden on the economy as a whole. By this logic, even total confiscation of income would not be a burden, since every penny collected would be spent. But obviously, the more money is taxed away, the less is available for employment, savings and investment, the more work and enterprise are discouraged, and the more the economy suffers. The international retreat from high taxes in the eighties recognized this.

As an exaction on labor income, Social Security's tax is a labor disincentive. The high self-employment levy discourages enterprise and independent effort. The employer's FICA tax discourages both starting new businesses and hiring more workers in existing ones, thus discouraging production and job creation. It also confiscates monies that employers could have invested productively. High payroll taxes also drive many taxpayers into the underground economy of barter and cash transactions, which not only impose inefficiencies (e.g., time lost in searching out parties to barter) but lose tax revenue. (Forcing people into tax avoidance and evasion is also corrosive to the country's morality.) Finally, Social Security finances consumption, not investment. It stands to reason that Social Security shifts the mix of economic activity away from work, saving and investment and toward unemployment and consumption.

Social Security Taxes vs. Savings

Social Security's advocates argued that it would provide a floor of retirement security and encourage the retirement-minded person to go further and make his own retirement provision out of savings and investments.[11] This may have been so in the program's early years, but there is a strong case that Social Security is now actually making it increasingly difficult for him to do so.

The economist Martin Feldstein argues that Social Security has retarded savings and capital formation, because "Social Security wealth," or the present value of benefits to which current workers and retirees are entitled, leads workers and retirees to expect that the program will provide retirement income, hence they need not save as much as they would without Social Security. So they save less. Feldstein claims that his econometric analysis of 1930-1992 data implies that Social Security reduces personal saving by over 60 percent.[12] The argument does make sense; as Robertson points out, it is reasonable that workers and employers make less provision for retirement with Social Security present than they would without it.[13]

However, this depends decisively on people's perceptions of Social Security. If they are confident that they will get benefits—that is, if they believe that "Social Security wealth" does exist for them—then the program might have the savings-depressing effect Feldstein posits. This may have been true in the forties, fifties, and sixties, when confidence in Social Security was high. For those who still believe that Social Security will be there when they retire, this "Social Security wealth effect" may well operate. But for those without faith in Social Security, it is unlikely. Given the rising doubt over Social Security, the pervasive belief that "it won't be there when I retire," many Americans probably now see "Social Security wealth" as a fiction. They may very well *increase* their saving for retirement to compensate for OASDI's anticipated demise—or try to.

In that climate of belief, any lowering of savings by Social Security will be due to its tax, which reduces income available for saving. Indeed, the Social Security tax is a much stronger explanation of any negative effect on savings. The high Social Security tax is among the factors making it increasingly difficult for Americans to save. The argument rests not on ideology but on simple logic and common sense. One's income has three destinations: taxes, consumption, and savings. The more income is taxed away, the less remains for savings and consumption. Since Americans assign high priority to consumption, it stands to reason that they will meet higher Social Security taxes by reducing saving. Since saving is the source of retirement investment, if the Social Security tax is reducing total personal saving, it is necessarily reducing saving for retirement.

In Social Security's initial years, this was not an issue; individuals had little or no savings in the Great Depression, and the payroll tax was low. After World War II, however, the Social Security tax increasingly competed with personal savings. In 1959, actuary Ray Peterson pointed out that in 1951-53, Social Security taxes averaged 20 percent of personal savings, which were then running about 7.8 percent of disposable income; and in 1954-58, the tax averaged 31.5 percent of personal savings, then just 6.9 percent of disposable income. Had 1969's scheduled payroll tax rate of 9 percent been levied in 1959, he added, estimated Social Security taxes of $17.3 billion would have been 78 percent of $22 billion in estimated personal savings. Peterson raised the possibility that Social Security taxes were significantly reducing the amount of disposable income available for personal savings.[14] The tax has become far heavier since, especially since 1977. Given the upward march in OASDI revenue as a share of federal tax revenue, income tax take, and GDP, the Social Security tax is surely the real source of any fall in savings due to Social Security since the mid-seventies.

Federal tax receipt data support the idea that the Social Security tax has contributed substantially to the decline in private savings. Total tax receipts' share of GDP has risen steadily and is now 4.3 percentage points above its 1950 level (table 2.3).[15] Decomposing this reveals that on-budget receipts' share fluctuated around the 1950 level in subsequent years. But the share for off-budget OASDI taxes rose steadily, and since 1975 has been over five times its 1950 level. Clearly, the decisive factor driving up federal taxes' share of GDP has been the huge increase in OASDI taxation.

Moreover, well over half of Social Security revenue—half the FICA tax revenue and *all* self-employment tax revenue—is extracted directly from personal incomes. Hence the great rise in Social Security taxes has worked powerfully to skew the composition of federal tax revenues lopsidedly toward taxes paid directly by individuals. In 1960, 23.2 percent of total federal tax revenue came from corporate income taxes, 44.0 percent from individual income taxes, and 11.5 percent from Social Security taxes. Ten years later, the

Table 2.3

Total, On-Budget, and Off-Budget (OASDI) Federal Tax Receipts as Share of
GDP, 1950-2000

Fiscal year	Total receipts	On-budget receipts	Off-budget (OASDI) receipts
1950	14.4	13.6	0.8
1955	16.6	15.3	1.3
1960	17.7	15.7	2.0
1965	17.0	14.5	2.4
1970	19.0	15.7	3.3
1975	17.9	13.9	4.0
1980	18.9	14.8	4.1
1985	17.7	13.2	4.5
1990	18.0	13.1	4.9
1995	18.5	13.7	4.8
1996	18.9	14.1	4.8
1997	19.3	14.5	4.8
1998	19.9	15.1	4.8
1999	18.7	15.2	4.9
2000 (est.)	18.7	15.5	5.0

Source: Office of Management and Budget

corporate income tax yielded 17.0 percent of total revenue, the individual income tax 46.8 percent, and OASDI taxes 17.4 percent. In 1980, the corporate income tax's share of total revenue was 12.5 percent, the personal income tax brought in 47.2 percent, and Social Security accounted for 21.9 percent. In 1990, the corporate income tax generated only 9.1 percent of total revenue, the individual income tax 45.2 percent, and the Social Security tax 27.3 percent.[16]

During most of the eighties and nineties, personal saving was the source of two-thirds or more of net private saving, the rest coming from undistributed corporate profits.[17] So the rise in Social Security taxes has worked decisively to put the bulk of the federal tax burden on the selfsame individual incomes which generate the bulk of net private savings. The conclusion is inescapable: insofar as rising federal taxes have contributed to reducing net private savings, the causality traces to the run-up in the Social Security tax.

This notion gains further support when we view matters from another angle. The private savings rate collapsed simultaneously with the huge increase in Social Security taxes after 1977. With the maximum taxable income engulfing more and more of the middle class, rising from $16,500 in 1977 to $35,700 in 1983, more than doubling in just six years, and rising afterward, the tax rate also rising, the OASDI tax hit ever harder at higher incomes—precisely those which have more discretionary income available for saving.

Research by economist Alicia Munnell on Social Security's effect on personal saving gives some further support. While some economists, she noted, argued that Social Security reduced saving since its benefits would reduce the need to save, others said it increased saving by allowing earlier retirement. Munnell investigated Social Security's impact on both total personal savings and savings for retirement (one of the chief motives for saving). After regressing retirement saving on Social Security taxes and labor force participation, she observed, "Ignoring the 1946-1971 estimates [for which the tax coefficient, while large and negative, was not statistically significant], Social Security contributions seem to have been responsible for a $47-$64 decrease in per capita personal saving," while "the decline in the labor-force participation of the elderly has led to an increase in per capita personal saving of between $31 and $44." This yields, we note, a net decrease in personal saving for retirement of $16-$20. And this *before* the post-1977 tax explosion. Munnell also pointed out that the Social Security tax had "a large, negative and often significant" coefficient in most versions of the total personal saving equation.[18] And while Munnell was using Social Security taxes as a proxy for one's future benefits, her results can with equal legitimacy be interpreted as measuring the impact of one's Social Security *taxes* on one's current savings.

We must be careful to skirt the fallacy of *post hoc, ergo propter hoc* (after this, therefore because of this). It would be too much to claim that the post-1977 run-up in Social Security taxes explains *all* of the collapse of savings, since the 1978-1982 period was also a time of both recession, which obviously reduced saving, and runaway inflation, which penalized saving (and pushed people into higher tax brackets before income tax indexation). But surely the huge OASDI tax increase explains *some* of it, perhaps a lot of it.

One might object that the United States is the one of the least heavily taxed industrialized countries, and that Europeans are taxed far more heavily than Americans, yet save more, so Social Security taxes do not prevent saving.[19] This criticism is plausible *prima facie,* but international comparisons that cite only economic statistics and ignore the cultural and historical differences underlying them are adding apples and oranges. Having experienced numerous wars, revolutions and other political crises, social upheavals, hyperinflation (e.g., Weimar), and so on, Europeans tend to be far more prudent than Americans. Hence they save more, and respond to higher taxes by curtailing consumption rather than savings. Americans, by contrast, have enjoyed a much more stable political context (contrast, for example, the histories of France and America since 1787), and had have since World War II given consumption a much higher priority. They therefore tend to meet higher taxes by saving less.

Draining "Trust Funds," Busted Budgets, and Worse

Such is the yoke that Social Security lays on the private sector now. When OASDI encounters financial trouble, that yoke will get catastrophically heavier.

When OASDI's cash flow surplus disappears, OASDI will have to use interest earnings to pay benefits. Since the interest is a charge on Treasury general revenue, at this point, *even before it starts running deficits,* Social Security will no longer be paying its own way, and will start extracting monies from the budget.

Under intermediate assumptions, this will begin in 2015. In 2025, benefit costs will exceed not only tax revenue but interest income, and the "trust fund" will start cashing in its bonds, which will be gone twelve years later (2037). Under high cost assumptions, the cash flow surplus will vanish in 2010, bonds will start being cashed in 2017, and they will be gone just nine years later (2026).[20]

Well before the actual exhaustion date, then, OASDI's "trust fund" will start making claims on general revenues and then running actual deficits. As the number of beneficiaries soars, so will these deficits (table 2.4).[21] After benefit costs absorb all interest income, the cash deficits will equal the "trust

Table 2.4

OASDI Cash Deficits, Intermediate and High Cost
Actuarial Assumptions, 2000-2050
(billions of dollars)

Calendar year	INTERMEDIATE ASSUMPTIONS			HIGH COST ASSUMPTIONS		
	Income excluding interest	Outlays	Balance	Income excluding interest	Outlays	Balance
2000	$501	$410	$90	$496	$412	$84
2005	635	539	97	627	586	41
2010	810	737	73	834	837	-3
2015	1,034	1,045	-11	1,086	1,223	-136
2020	1,310	1,491	-182	1,405	1,790	-385
2025	1,650	2,066	-416	1,807	2,562	-755
2030	2,078	2,762	-684	2,318	3,549	-1,231
2035	2,620	3,572	-951	2,969	4,762	-1,793
2040	3,299	4,491	-1,191	3,785	6,220	-2,435
2045	4,138	5,618	-1,481	4,793	8,056	-3,263
2050	5,177	7,060	-1,883	6,044	10,435	-4,391

Source: *2000 OASDI Annual Report*

fund" deficits. Intermediate assumptions generate OASDI deficits of -$416 billion in 2025 and -$684 billion in 2030. The more likely high cost assumptions yield deficits of -$136 billion in 2015 and -$385 billion in 2020.

To cover these deficits, OASDI will present bonds from its "trust funds" in these amounts to the Treasury for redemption. These deficits, then, are how much the Treasury will have to pay OASDI in those years. Another way of grasping the magnitude of the Treasury's burden is to note that the peak amount of Treasury debt in the "trust fund," before liquidation starts, will be about $6.0 trillion under intermediate assumptions, or about $3.27 trillion under high cost assumptions.[22] "Trust fund" exhaustion means that all that debt will be cashed in. These, then, are the total sums the Treasury must raise, over a about a decade, to honor its obligations to Social Security. Where will the Treasury get all that money?

One option will be to cut other spending in the budget to release money. But Congress is a notoriously reluctant budget cutter. Except for slashing defense in 1946-1950 and after 1989, Congress has made no serious cuts since World War II. Nor has any president sought deep domestic cuts. Is it realistic to expect that any Congress will cut spending by $3.27 to 6.0 trillion in just ten years? Raising taxes by that amount is equally unrealistic. Most or all of the money will almost certainly be raised by borrowing from the public.

This necessarily means that as Social Security's "trust funds" drain, the budget deficit will explode, by amounts roughly equal to these cash deficits. The huge elderly population will meanwhile make heavy demands on Medicare, Medicaid, and other programs.[23] Given all this, budget deficits of -$500 billion or more by 2025, and larger ones later, are all but certain.

Such large deficits would, of course, enormously increase interest on the debt. But that in turn would push federal spending still higher, creating still larger deficits, meaning still higher interest costs. The budget would thus be caught in a vicious circle.

So would the economy. Indeed, three interacting vicious circles would operate, one for Social Security, one for the budget, and one for the economy. Financing such mammoth deficits out of domestic credit would necessarily result in what economists call "crowding out": the federal government would be absorbing credit that would otherwise be available for business and consumers. With the modern economy enormously credit-dependent, economic activity and employment would suffer accordingly.

Table 2.5 shows the link between budget deficits and federal borrowing in the domestic credit market.[24] In 1965, the federal government did only 5.8 percent of total net borrowing. Twenty years later its share had more than quadrupled. This substantial draining of credit to finance deficits came at the expense of private investment, and thus contributed to the collapse in productivity growth since the sixties. Crowding out was especially severe in the

Table 2.5

Federal Deficits and Borrowing In Domestic Credit Market, 1965-1996
(dollar amounts in billions; fiscal years)

ITEM	1965	1970	1975	1980	1985	1990	1995	1996
On-budget deficit	-$1.6	-8.7	-55.3	-72.7	221.7	-277.8	-226.4	-174.1
OASDI surplus/def.	$.2	5.9	2.1	-1.1	9.4	56.6	62.4	66.6
Unified budget def.	$-1.4	-2.8	-53.2	-73.8	-212.3	-221.2	-164.0	-107.5
Total net borrowing in credit market	$66.8	88.2	169.6	336.9	829.3	704.1	720.4	727.1
Federal borrowing from public	$3.9	3.5	51.0	71.6	200.3	220.9	171.3	129.7
—as % of total	5.8	4.0	30.1	21.3	24.2	31.4	23.8	17.8

Source: Office of Management and Budget

high-deficit eighties and early nineties. In 1991, the federal government did 55 percent of net domestic borrowing; in 1992, 59.2 percent.[25] This huge diversion of credit from private use was a major cause of the 1990-1992 recession and "credit crunch."

On-budget deficits have been offset by surpluses in Social Security, which is off-budget, making deficits in the unified budget (which combines on-budget spending and taxes with Social Security) smaller. When Social Security's surpluses become deficits, federal deficits and borrowing will necessarily soar, and inflict even worse crowding out. The resulting economic stagnation would depress tax revenues, meaning deficits would grow from the revenue as well as the spending side. This would lower Social Security's revenues, driving the program deeper into debt, which in turn would worsen the burden on the budget. It would also increase federal borrowing, meaning still more crowding out, and still more spending to pay interest on the debt, swelling both budgets and deficits. Investment, employment, and productivity growth would decline, of course, making matters still worse for Social Security, the budget and the economy, and driving all three still further on a downward spiral.

As for borrowing overseas, foreign creditors would soon balk at continuing to lend to a government sliding toward bankruptcy, and either demand ever-higher interest rates or stop lending altogether. Barring austerity budgeting, the only remaining option would be debt monetization, risking hyperinflation and economic implosion.

Thus, even *before* the "trust funds" are exhausted, Social Security's financial weakness will be creating simultaneous fiscal crisis and economic calamity. Since this point is too seldom grasped, it bears driving home: *The lurking menace in Social Security's economics is not the bankruptcy of the program, but the wreckage of our public finance and our economy.* Moreover, these outcomes do not require Social Security bankruptcy. *Mere substantial partial liquidation of the "trust funds" will suffice.* Under intermediate assumptions, OASDI's assets will shrink from $6.0 trillion in 2025 to $1.7 trillion in 2035—a liquidation of $4.3 trillion over just ten years.[26] That large an addition to publicly held national debt in that short a time cannot fail to be disastrous.

Given all this, the obsession with "saving Social Security" or "privatizing" it so as to improve its "money's worth" for young Americans is dangerously misdirecting our attention, thought, and effort. The most urgent need from the general welfare perspective is not, repeat *not,* to "save Social Security," ensure that current beneficiaries "get theirs," restore intergenerational equity, or rework Social Security so as to give the young a fantastic retirement deal. Rather, *it is to prevent Social Security from becoming a catastrophic burden to the Treasury and the economy.* Protecting the Treasury and the economy must be the highest priority of prudent and responsible statesmanship regarding Social Security.

Sustaining Current-Law Benefits after Bankruptcy

After the "trust funds" are exhausted, Social Security's deficits will be even deeper, and there will no longer be a stock of Treasury debt on hand to cash in to help cover them. In 2040, OASDI's deficit under intermediate assumptions is projected at -$1,191 billion, and under high-cost assumptions at -$2,435 billion. In 2045, the respective figures are -$1,481 billion and -$3,263 billion (table 2.4). Closing such deficits by borrowing from the public would be catastrophic, obviously. Equally obviously, something would be done, would have to be done, to ensure that this did not happen.

If it had not already done so, Congress would have to cut benefits deeply, raise taxes substantially, or both. Paying all benefits under current law would require much higher tax rates (see table 2.6).[27] Under these tax rates, an employee making $20,000 in taxable income would pay FICA taxes of $1,936 in 2030, $2,093 in 2040, and $2,211 in 2050. If self-employed, he would pay $3,872 in 2030, $4,186 in 2040, and $4,422 in 2050.

What such taxes will do to incentives, employment, savings, and investment is obvious. An exodus of taxpayers into the underground economy would be inevitable, and the least of the consequences. Moreover, these taxes are for Social Security alone. Paying for everything else in the budget will mean far higher total taxes. So heavily laden an economy could hardly carry the enormous debt incurred from liquidating the "trust funds."

Benefit cuts sufficient to prevent or at least mitigate such huge deficits and taxes, and their baleful economic effects, would devastate millions of

Table 2.6

**Social Security Payroll Taxes Needed After "Trust Fund" Exhaustion,
with No Benefit Cuts, Under High Cost Assumptions
(as percentage of taxable payroll)**

CALENDAR YEAR	OASDI COST RATE	MINUS BENEFIT TAX RATE	EQUALS REQUIRED TAX RATE
2030	20.17	.81	19.36
2035	21.27	.90	20.37
2040	21.88	.95	20.93
2045	22.47	1.00	21.47
2050	23.17	1.06	22.11
2055	24.12	1.12	23.00
2060	25.18	1.19	23.99
2065	26.26	1.26	25.00
2070	27.31	1.32	25.99
2075	28.29	1.39	26.90

Source: *2000 OASDI Annual Report*

persons. There would still be massive economic pain—only it would be felt by millions of beneficiaries and their families, not in credit markets, investment, and employment. And with the huge baby boom generation in retirement, fierce resistance would be inevitable. But this anticipates our next chapter.

Social Security's defenders will dismiss this as scare-mongering. We'll never see these apocalyptic outcomes; Congress will make timely adjustments inflicting minor pain, and prevent economic ruin.

But as we saw, while their solution would avert "trust fund" exhaustion, it would still entail partial liquidation. OASDI's deficits in 2030 and after would still be huge and worsening; so, therefore, would its claims on the Treasury, and so would budget deficits or tax increases, and so would damage to the economy. The differences between the outcome under their "minor adjustments" and the foregoing are only matters of timing and degree. With their proposals, the ruinous drain on the Treasury and the economy would happen a bit later, and be a bit smaller. But it would still happen.

Notes

1.   Table 2.1 source: *2000 OASDI Annual Report,* pp. 34-35, table II.B1.—Contributions and Benefit Base and Contribution Rates. Calculations of FICA and SE taxes on $20,000 taxable income, and maximum employee FICA tax, mine. For self-employed, we assume that $20,000 is the net taxable income for Social Security purposes, after the currently permitted deduction of 7.65 percent of net income.

Since the permitted deduction varied widely over the 1937-1997 period, we make this assumption for simplicity's sake.

2. Martha Derthick, *Policymaking for Social Security* (Washington, DC: The Brookings Institution, 1979), pp. 430, 431.

3. Ray M. Peterson, "Misconceptions and Missing Perceptions of our Social Security System (Actuarial Anesthesia)," Discussion, *Transactions of the Society of Actuaries,* 11 (November 1959), p. 918.

4. Paul A. Samuelson, "Social Security," *Newsweek,* February 13, 1967, p. 88.

5. Derthick, *Policymaking for Social Security,* p. 432. A good concise account of the benefit explosion is Peter G. Peterson and Neil Howe, *On Borrowed Time: How the Growth in Entitlement Spending Threatens America's Future* (New York: Simon & Schuster, Touchstone Books edition, 1990), pp. 278-283.

6. Derthick, *Policymaking for Social Security,* p. 432.

7. John A. Brittain, *The Payroll Tax for Social Security* (Washington, DC: The Brookings Institution, 1972), chapter 3, *passim.*

8. Dean R. Leimer, "A Guide to Social Security Money's Worth Issues," *Social Security Bulletin,* vol. 58, no. 2 (Summer 1995), p. 7.

9. Robertson, *Social Security: What Every Taxpayer Should Know,* p. 81.

10. Table 2.2 sources: *Historical Tables. Budget of the United States Government. Fiscal Year 2001,* table 1.2—Summary of Receipts, Outlays, and Surpluses or Deficits (-) as Percentages of GDP: 1930-2005; table 2.1—Receipts by Source: 1934-2005; table 2.4—Composition of Social Insurance and Retirement Receipts and of Excise Taxes: 1940-2005. Percentage calculations mine.

11. See, for example, U..S. Congress, House, Mary Dewson, "Fifty Years' Progress Toward Social Security," in Representative Matthew J. Merritt, "Fifty Years' Progress Toward Social Security," Extension of Remarks, May 31, 1938, *Congressional Record,* Appendix, 83: 2266.

12. Martin Feldstein, "Social Security and Saving: New Time Series Evidence," *National Tax Journal,* vol. 49, no. 2 (June 1996), pp. 151-164.

13. Robertson, *Social Security: What Every Taxpayer Should Know,* pp. 231-232.

14. Peterson, "Misconceptions and Missing Perceptions of our Social Security System (Actuarial Anesthesia)," p. 833.

15. Table 2.3 source: *Historical Tables. Budget of the United States Government. Fiscal Year 2001,* table 1.2—Summary of Receipts, Outlays, and Surpluses or Deficits (-) as Percentages of GDP: 1930-2005.

16. Ibid., table 2.1—Receipts by Source: 1934-2005. Percentage calculations mine.

17. *Economic Report of the President. February 1998,* p. 318, table B-32.—Gross Saving and Investment, 1959-97.

18. Alicia Haydock Munnell, *The Effect of Social Security on Personal Saving* (Cambridge, MA: Ballinger Publishing, 1974), p. 64.

19. I am indebted to an anonymous referee for raising this criticism.

20. *2000 OASDI Annual Report,* pp. 25, 108, 179.

21. Table 2.4 source: *2000 OASDI Annual Report,* pp. 183-184, table III.B4.—Estimated OASDI and HI Income Excluding Interest, Outgo, and Balance in Current Dollars by Alternative, Calendar Years 2000-2075.

22. *2000 OASDI Annual Report,* p. 181, table III.B3.—Estimated Operations of the Combined OASI and DI Trust Funds in Current Dollars by Alternative, Calendar Years 2000-2075.

23. For a handy concise survey of these woes, see Phillip Longman, *The Return of Thrift: How the Collapse of the Middle-Class Welfare State Will Reawaken Values in America* (New York: The Free Press, 1996), pp. 8-11.

24. Table 2.5 sources: *Historical Tables. Budget of the United States Government. Fiscal Year 2001,* table 1.2—Summary of Receipts, Outlays, and Surpluses or Deficits (-): 1789-2005; *Analytical Perspectives. Budget of the United States Government. Fiscal Year 2001.* p. 282, table 12-7. Federal and federally guaranteed participation in the credit market. Percentage calculations mine.
25. *Analytical Perspectives. Budget of the United States Government. Fiscal Year 1998,* p. 228, table 12-7: Federal Participation in the Credit Market; *Analytical Perspectives. Budget of the United States Government. Fiscal Year 1999,* p. 256, table 13-7: Federal and Federally Assisted Participation in the Credit Market. Percentage calculations mine.
26. *2000 OASDI Annual Report,* p. 181, table III.B3.—Estimated Operations of the Combined OASI and DI Trust Funds in Current Dollars by Alternative, Calendar Years 2000-2075.
27. Table 2.6 sources: *2000 OASDI Annual Report,* pp. 119-120, table II.F17.—Components of Annual Income Rates by Trust Fund and Alternative, Calendar Years 2000-2075; and p. 171, table III.A2.—Comparison of Estimated Income Rates and Cost Rates for OASDI and HI by Alternative, Calendar Years 2000-2075.

3

The Crisis of Confidence

*"Widespread understanding of the Social Secu-
rity program may result in a certain amount of
trauma and even disruption among the public,
but even more disruption will result if the current misunderstanding is allowed to continue."*

—A. Haeworth Robertson[1]

The third aspect of the coming crisis is political. Faith in Social Security
has been dwindling for decades, and the coming worsening financial pressure
on Social Security, its economic consequences, and disillusion about Social
Security will create a crisis of confidence, not only in the program, but in our
political system itself.

Cracks in the Walls

Social Security enjoyed enormous popularity in the forties and fifties. Its
taxes were low, and the first generation of beneficiaries, who had paid those
taxes for only a few years, were enjoying fantastic windfalls. Benefits were
being liberalized, and more and more of the population was being covered by
the program. Both the government and the popular media, as future chapters
shall show, were extolling Social Security as a retirement insurance bargain,
and it received only scattered criticism. Aside from some conservatives and
actuaries, few people thought, much less worried, about the program's future
cost.

Then, too, the times were on Social Security's side. Contrasting the re-
membered privations of the Depression with their new prosperity, most
Americans were content and confident about the country and its future.
President Dwight Eisenhower was an enormously popular and reassuring
father figure. Confidence in the nation, its government, and its institutions was high.

But in the mid-sixties, cracks began appearing in the masonry. As the Social Security tax began jumping—and in the context of rising inflation, as the economy quickened and the deficit finance of the Vietnam War and Great Society exerted rising inflationary pressure—Americans began grumbling. It dawned on some observers that while Social Security was still a great deal for those already old, the younger generations weren't going to do anywhere near as well. Colin Campbell, professor of economics at Dartmouth College, and his wife Rosemary pointed out in 1965 that under existing law, people then thirty-eight years old or over would get back more in old-age benefits than they paid in taxes, but people under thirty-eight would pay in more than they would get back.[2] In 1967 the *New York Times* reported that "After hearing for years that Social Security benefits are too low . . . Congressmen are now deluged with complaints that Social Security taxes are becoming burdensome."[3]

Several factors combined to further erode public confidence in and approval of Social Security in the seventies. The OASDI tax kept rising, and with the steady increase in the maximum taxable income, more and more Americans found their entire labor incomes subject to the tax rate, which was also rising. In 1937, 96.9 percent of all participating workers had total annual incomes below the $3,000 maximum taxable. With the addition of the self-employed, many of whom had higher incomes than wage earners, and the postwar growth in incomes, this share trended downward, until in 1965 just 63.9 percent of workers had total incomes below the then current maximum taxable of $4,800. But then the trend reversed, and by 1975, 84.9 of workers had annual incomes below the $14,100 maximum taxable.[4] It added up to higher and higher taxes on more and more people, which meant driving more and more Social Security taxpayers toward their threshold of pain, and it hit especially hard at higher-income Americans, who are the citizens best-informed and most articulate about public policy.

Moreover, more critical voices were being raised. And in the mid-seventies, the first genuine crisis in Social Security's history occurred.

In their 1974 *Annual Report,* the Board of Trustees wrote complacently that income was projected to exceed outgo in the 1974-1978 period, and although the latest population and fertility projections would seriously affect long-range cost estimates, "they will not have a significant effect in the short run. According to present short-range cost estimates, action to increase the combined income of the OASDI and hospital insurance systems for the next 5-10 years is not necessary right now." Noting that a newly formed Advisory Council on Social Security was studying Social Security's long-run finances, "The Board believes that there is ample time to await the Council's findings and recommendations before making specific proposals."[5] Incredibly, it seems not to have occurred to them that the inflationary recession America was experiencing would bleed OASDI through adverse changes in both income and outgo.

On February 10, 1975, responding to newspaper and magazine articles criticizing Social Security, Wilbur Cohen led a group of former Social Security and Health, Education and Welfare chiefs and other experts in issuing a white paper and holding a press conference to reassure the public that while Social Security had some long-term financial problems needing attention, it was basically sound and benefits weren't in danger.[6] Just two days later, a panel of experts headed by Harvard professor William Hsiao, a former deputy chief actuary of Social Security, reported to the Senate Finance Committee that Social Security's finances were worse than previously believed, and that "the benefit structure of Social Security should be overhauled in the near future along with additional financing. Unless this is done the present trust fund will be seriously eroded in the years immediately ahead, and will be exhausted by the late 1980s."[7]

Then, on May 6, in its 1975 *Annual Report,* the Board of Trustees frantically announced that OASDI would run a $3 billion deficit in 1975 and faced ruin soon unless something was done:

> It is apparent that without legislation to provide additional financing, the trust funds' assets will be exhausted soon after 1979. . . the assets of the disability insurance trust fund will be exhausted in 1980, and the assets of the old-age and survivors insurance trust fund will be exhausted shortly thereafter. The expected substantial decline in the assets of the trust funds, which was not anticipated in the 1974 annual report, is attributable primarily to (1) the reduction in contribution income resulting from lower levels of employment and taxable earnings due to the current recession, and (2) the greater-than-expected upward movement in the CPI [Consumer Price Index], with the result that automatic benefit increases assumed herein are larger than were previously assumed.[8]

The Trustees recommended "prompt action" to strengthen OASDI's short-term financing. Since OASDI was also projected to run a deficit every year through 2049, they also recommended that development of plans to strengthen Social Security's long-range financing "be pursued immediately."[9]

The news threatened Americans' faith in the program. Social Security Commissioner James B. Cardwell promptly stated that the Trustees' projections were "cause for concern but not alarm," because the "trust funds" would tide OASDI over for several years.[10] A few days later, a front-page *Washington Post* news analysis obligingly reassured readers that Social Security was "not about to go broke. Congress will not let it. Your elderly relatives are not going to lose their benefits. You are not going to lose yours, either; when you retire, they will be there waiting for you."[11] On April 14, Paul Samuelson weighed in with a *Newsweek* column pooh-poohing fears of coming bankruptcy and pronouncing Social Security "A-OK," giving it a "clean bill of health." The Social Security Advisory Panel and the Panel on Social Security Financing chaired by Professor Hsiao had found Social Security sound, he reported. "The clinical findings are favorable. The patient is sound with a life expectancy that can be measured in the centuries." While he noted that both panels had warned of trust fund depletion by the end of the eighties if benefits and taxes weren't adjusted, Samuelson added that "For the present, nothing *has* [Samuelson's italics] to be done."[12]

But the damage was done. More and more articles appeared in popular magazines, reporting that trouble was coming in Social Security; asking whether "the Social Security bubble" would burst; referring to "hard choices" as Social Security faced a "massive flow of red ink," and so on.[13] For the first time, there was widespread unease and speculation about Social Security's soundness.

In 1977, Congress finally enacted a large tax increase to save Social Security. During the debate over it, Republican Senator Carl T. Curtis of Nebraska put his finger on Social Security's true foundation, and on its problematic nature:

> Some years ago when Commissioner [Wilbur] Cohen appeared before our committee, he and I disagreed on many items of social security, but he would always give you an answer. He was honest as he saw it. I said:
>
>> What assurance do the future beneficiaries have that they will ever get their benefits?
>
> He said:
>
>> The assurance is that a particular generation of taxpayers will tax themselves to pay it.
>
> And that is honest.
> Now we have reached a point where people say, "We do not want to pay it any more."[14]

They were not, indeed. The tax increase applied powerful bellows to the flames of discontent. No sooner was it enacted in December 1977 than angry mail began streaming to Congress. The March 13, 1978 *U. S. News & World Report* gave its readers samples of the letters lawmakers were getting. Not only were many constituents enraged, but some even questioned Social Security's legitimacy, and argued—the ultimate heresy—that private arrangements would give them a better deal:

> Since mid-1969, I have contributed $5,380.04 (not including interest) to the Social Security program. I might as well have used the money to light cigars . . . .
>
> I currently pay almost $1,000 per year into the program. The way things look I will get a very poor return for my investment even if the program doesn't go bankrupt. If I personally invested that money at 8 percent, I could have almost $200,000 at age 65 and enjoy almost $1,200 a month from interest alone.

I am 30 years old and will consider it miraculous if I ever see a dime of the money I have put into that turkey [Social Security]. Most of the other people my age feel as I do. I am taking steps to terminate my employment and rehire as an independent consultant so I can get out of that ripoff.

Criminal confiscation! Those are the only words to describe the 227-billion-dollar increase in Social Security taxes. To endanger the entire economic system in a vain attempt to rescue the bankrupt Social Security system is insane.

Each citizen should have the right to decide for himself whether or not he wants the government to provide so-called security for his retirement years. The same amount of money invested in an insurance policy would provide benefits worth three or four times that of Social Security.[15]

What the letters revealed was repeatedly corroborated by polling. In August 1978, Louis Harris and Associates conducted a survey which found that many working Americans had more faith in private pensions' ability to keep their benefit promises than they had in Social Security, which was "a dramatic reversal of the situation of a decade or so ago," when polls found much distrust of private pensions. The Harris survey found that while 87 percent of workers expected to get Social Security retirement benefits, 80 percent had doubts that full benefits would be paid, and more than half of them had virtually no confidence in Social Security. Moreover, about one-third of the workers surveyed said they would leave Social Security if given a chance.[16] The maximum income subject to the Social Security tax rose in a huge $5,200 jump in 1979, anger and bitterness rose apace—and so did disenchantment with Social Security. Over and over, published letters to editors raged against the rising tax as a "ripoff" of working people and expressed lack of faith in Social Security.[17] In late 1979, a survey by Peter D. Hart Research Associates found only 18 percent of respondents fully confident that Social Security would provide future benefits; 24 percent had a great deal of confidence; 31 percent harbored only a little confidence in Social Security; and 17 percent had no confidence in it at all.[18]

In 1980, just five years after Samuelson had pronounced Social Security "A-OK," the Board of Trustees reported that OASDI, which had been running deficits annually since fiscal 1975, had a deficit of nearly $2 billion in fiscal 1979; that by 1982 at the latest, OASI would be unable to pay benefits when due; and that the combined OASDI fund would be exhausted by calendar 1985. Emphasizing that OASI's projected depletion was "an immediate problem that requires early attention by the Congress," the Trustees recommended provision of interfund borrowing authority to keep Social Security afloat through the eighties and buy time for the administration and Congress to craft another rescue.[19]

The news drove the public's morale about Social Security lower. Most Americans now had heavy Social Security tax loads. In 1980, 91.2 percent of workers had total labor incomes below the maximum taxable income, which was now a formidable $25,900; in 1981 it jumped $3,800, to $29,700, engulfing still more workers; now 92.4 percent of workers had all their income below the cap.[20] Yet now it appeared that all this pain wasn't enough. In the summer of 1981, a *New York Times*/CBS News poll found that 54 percent of Americans no longer believed that Social Security would be able to pay them all retirement benefits then mandated by law. The loss of faith was worst among the young: 70 percent of respondents under age 25, 75 percent of those aged 25-34, and 64 percent of those aged 35-44 said they doubted Social Security would provide full benefits for their retirement. Moreover, a majority of those under 34 said they preferred benefit cuts over tax increases to shore up Social Security.[21] What they got instead, in the 1983 Social Security legislation, were more tax increases—and cuts in the benefits they would draw in the future.

Worsening Discontent

Despite the 1983 rescue, and Social Security's return to near-term soundness, public unhappiness over Social Security, and loss of confidence in its future, have kept worsening.

Whereas a 1975 survey for the American Council of Life Insurance found that 63 percent of the public had confidence (22 percent very confident, 41 percent somewhat confident) in Social Security's long-term existence, a 1984 update disclosed a striking reversal of sentiment: only nine percent of respondents were very confident and 23 percent somewhat confident that Social Security would exist for their retirement, with 43 percent not very confident and 25 percent not confident at all. This reversal has endured; in 1998 only 7 percent of respondents in the ACLI survey were very confident that Social Security would be there for them, 28 percent somewhat confident, 33 percent not too confident, and 26 percent not confident at all.[22] Such loss of faith in Social Security being there for them when they retire compounds taxpayers' unhappiness over their Social Security tax, as it creates a sense that their taxes are a useless sacrifice.

Recent economic developments have also made Americans more sensitive to, and resentful of, the OASDI tax. As more and more Americans opt for self-employment or are forced into it through layoffs, they find themselves paying the 12.4 percent self-employment tax rate rather than the employee's 6.2 percent FICA rate. Thus if their income is the same, self-employment almost doubles their Social Security tax on it. Half this tax is deductible from income subject to federal income tax, which does offset somewhat the higher OASDI tax—but it also helps make many taxpayers' OASDI tax larger than their income tax. Where the employer's share of the FICA tax had once masked half of their tax burden for employees who aren't aware that they ultimately pay that share too, self-employment brutally thrusts home just how heavy the OASDI tax really is. However it makes itself felt, the soaring tax burden has made Americans more disposed to listen to Social Security's critics.

The continuing rapid proliferation of literature criticizing Social Security, calling attention to its worsening deal for young people, stressing its coming financial collapse, and advocating privatization, has also intensified discontent. As never before in history, commentators and public policy scholars are attacking Social Security. Both the quantity and the quality of criticism have become formidable. The accumulation of a body of sophisticated, scholarly and well-argued literature, such as Peter Ferrara's *Social Security: The Inherent Contradiction* (1980), Haeworth Robertson's *The Coming Revolution in Social Security* (1981), Carolyn Weaver's *The Crisis in Social Security* (1982) and Peter Peterson's and Neil Howe's *On Borrowed Time* (1988), to name just four key titles, has lent the critics impressive intellectual respectability. Then, too, "Mr. Social Security," the indefatigable Wilbur Cohen, who made it his business to answer Social Security's critics and rally its defenders, is no longer alive to do so. All in all, the balance of power and prestige in the debate, which until 1980 had lopsidedly favored Social Security's partisans, has since shifted toward its critics.

One aspect of the critical literature merits special mention: the intergenerational inequity argument, that Social Security is an ever-worsening deal for younger Americans.[23] Extensive exploration of this controversy is not germane to our purpose. Suffice it to say that reflection on the history of Social Security in the light of common sense makes it clear that complaints about intergenerational inequity are justified. When Social Security was young, tax rates and the income subject to tax were quite low. Hence the first generation of retirees, who had paid very modest taxes for only a short time, received huge windfalls; Ida Fuller, Social Security's first beneficiary, paid $22 in taxes and collected over $20,000 in benefits.[24] But as Social Security matured, benefits were liberalized, the beneficiary population grew, and taxes soared, succeeding generations spent their entire working lives paying rising taxes on a rising maximum taxable income, especially after 1977. It stands to reason that each generation gets a smaller return on its Social Security taxes than the previous one. The tax increases and benefit cuts advocated by Social Security's defenders to close OASDI's actuarial deficit will, of course, worsen the "deal" Social Security offers the young.

Moreover, being a tax-transfer program, Social Security is necessarily a zero-sum game between current taxpayers and current retirees: the latter's gain is the former's loss. The only compensation current taxpayers have is the prospect of being supported in turn by the next taxpaying generation. Intergenerational tension is the ineluctable consequence of Social Security's zero-sum nature.

Another inequity of Social Security is that it forces one to play what might be called a "longevity lottery." If one works and pays Social Security taxes all one's active life, but dies before or shortly after retirement, he is a "loser," since Social Security inflicts a net financial loss on him, whereas one who enjoys a long retirement is a "winner"—his benefits exceed the taxes he paid out.[25] This was not a problem under the original Social Security Act, which contained a money-back guarantee. But with the money-back guarantee removed, this problem is serious, especially for unmarried persons (who have no survivors to receiver survivors' benefits) and persons with lower longevity, such as the poor and minorities.

Arguments about Social Security's inequities, especially intergenerational ones, are falling on receptive ears. Today's young Americans are among the most politically aware and skeptical generations of youth in our history, far less willing than their predecessors of the forties and fifties to accept on faith the assurances of authority figures. The formation of advocacy groups such as Third Millennium to agitate for intergenerational equity for young taxpayers is without precedent in Social Security's history, and still another factor in sharpening political conflict over the program.

The larger political context has also played its part in unsettling the public over Social Security. In the wake of Vietnam, Watergate, the widespread perception of ineptitude in the Ford and Carter administrations, a sour distrust and cynicism about government pervaded America by the late seventies. Like Cinderella's carriage, the renewal of confidence in public institutions in the eighties (much of it due to Reagan's optimism, likeability and thespian skills—necessarily transitory phenomena) reverted to a shriveled pumpkin of sourness, as a costly bailout of the savings and loan industry ensued amid reports of reckless deregulation, regulatory laxity and incompetence; George Bush broke his promise not to raise taxes; Congressmen bounced checks at the House Bank; a painful recession occurred; and federal government floundered haplessly in "gridlock." Glumness and cynicism about government, reflected in low voter turnouts and the popularity of term limits, helped predispose many, especially younger people, to believe the worst about Social Security.

The seemingly intractable high deficits of the eighties and nineties, and the failure of presidents and Congresses to deal with them created a general unease about federal finance and the sustainability of entitlements. In such circumstances it was only natural that people began to wonder if government could ever get its financial house in order again, and keep Social Security solvent.

After twenty years, these faith-corroding factors have done their work. Once almost monolithically supportive of Social Security, Americans are now split into three groups: First, younger Americans and others who are well-informed about Social Security's weakness, cost and inequities, understandably critical of it, and want substantial changes. Second, probably the majority, those who have little accurate knowledge of OASDI but do know that it's headed for trouble, have scant faith in it, and think that "something," they aren't sure what, ought to be done. Third, elderly Americans and others who believe the official depiction of Social Security and know little else about it, and those who expect to depend on it. These persons, just as understandably, want the current program preserved.

Indeed, perceptions of the program differ sharply by age. An April 1998 Zogby poll found that just 37 percent of respondents aged 18-29 believe that there is no need to make significant changes in OASDI, that its long-term solvency can be achieved with some minor adjustments—but 67 percent of respondents aged 65 and over do.[26]

Social Security's expansion to almost universal coverage—meaning that almost all elderly Americans now get benefits and that almost all working Americans now pay Social Security taxes and will likely qualify for benefits in turn—has created a very dangerous political situation. Just about *everyone* now has a compelling stake in Social Security, hence will suffer substantially if it goes bankrupt or is rescued through large tax increases and/or benefit cuts. Never before has almost all of our population been compellingly involved in a single government program which will, under very plausible demographic and economic conditions, collapse in the next few decades, with traumatic personal consequences. The upshot is that Social Security has vast potential for pitting not only the elderly beneficiary and younger taxpaying generations against each other, but virtually the whole population against the government, and creating a political crisis without precedent.

Political Consequences of OASDI'S Collapse

As we saw, liquidation of OASDI's "trust fund" will have damaging, possibly ruinous, budgetary and economic consequences, even if OASDI does not go bankrupt. Such a fiscal crisis would be utterly unprecedented and a terrible shock. As to the attendant inflation and recession, rightly or wrongly, governments are punished for holding office in hard times, and doubly punished if they are deemed responsible, either for causing the misery or for failing to remove it. Hard times toppled Herbert Hoover, Jimmy Carter, and George Bush, and the first two cases resulted in historic shifts of power between parties in Congress as well.

When the "trust fund" is exhausted, OASDI will be able to finance only 72 percent of costs—and therefore unable to pay full benefits mandated under current law. What would happen next is problematic. One possibility is that Social Security taxes would be raised to cover all benefit costs. Another is that benefit outlays would be cut by about 28 percent to lower them to what Social Security's tax can cover, which would probably mean a proportional cut in benefits across the board. Still another is that checks would be held up until enough revenue accumulated to pay full benefit amounts.[27]

Should OASDI become unable to pay benefits, and either delay checks or cut them 28 percent, it is likely, given modern Americans' penchant for litigation, that beneficiaries will sue for "their" benefits, which they have been led to believe are "guaranteed by law," and, since they paid their Social Security taxes, "an earned right." They will get a traumatizing shock, for as we shall see, the Supreme Court has ruled (*Flemming v. Nestor,* 1960) that paying Social Security taxes does not generate accrued property rights to benefits.

This will quite naturally drastically weaken confidence not only in this program, but in the government itself. This, in turn, will very likely destroy the perceived legitimacy of the American system, and with it, the federal government's ability to govern.

Political Consequences of a Draconian Rescue

As Social Security's partisans always assert, the government will eventually take "corrective action" to avert bankruptcy. But if the actual bankruptcy of Social Security would be politically unacceptable, this "corrective action" will be equally so. Recall Robertson's keen insight that Social Security consists of a set of benefit promises and tax promises. Since the problem is one of cash flow, the "corrective action" Social Security's defenders have in mind ineluctably works out to increases in taxes, decreases in benefits, or both. In Robertson's words, "It is indisputable that some of Social Security's promises will be broken. The questions are which promises, when, how, and for what group of the population."[28]

As one might imagine, Americans are unenthusiastic about their government breaking its tax and benefit promises to them. Abundant evidence indicates that while most Americans have little faith in Social Security's future, they have set their faces like flint against both higher taxes and benefit cuts.

In 1985, a poll conducted for *U. S. News & World Report* found that 69.2 percent of respondents opposed cutting benefits for current beneficiaries, 63 percent opposed cutting benefits for future beneficiaries, 57.7 percent opposed higher payroll taxes for both workers and employers, 58.9 percent were against higher taxes for employers only, and 56.3 percent rejected an increase in the minimum retirement age for collecting full benefits.[29]

This overwhelming opposition persists today. A nationwide poll in March 1997 by Harvard University, the *Washington Post,* and the Kaiser Family Foundation found between half and three-quarters of respondents opposed to raising the payroll tax, gradually increasing the retirement age at which people qualify to receive full Social Security benefits, or cutting future benefits across the board.[30]

Similarly, a July 1998 *USA Today* poll conducted by the Gallup Organization found 85 percent of respondents opposed to cutting Social Security benefits (65 percent "strongly opposed"); 70 percent opposed to raising the retirement age to 70 years (52 percent "strongly opposed"); 62 percent opposed to raising Social Security taxes.[31] Significantly, the greatest resistance here is to benefit cuts.

Numerous other polls disclose the same overwhelming opposition to raising payroll taxes or cutting benefits. The March 1999 NBC/*Wall Street Journal* poll found 74 percent of respondents opposing benefit cuts (49 percent strongly opposed, 25 percent mildly opposed) and just 22 percent in favor (16 percent mildly, a mere 6 percent strongly). Another poll found 85 percent of respondents opposed to taxing retirees' Social Security benefits just like ordinary income, instead of letting a portion be tax-free. Lopsided majorities still reject raising the retirement age, even when told that doing so would help save the program or enable current workers to get their benefits without tax increases or benefit cuts.[32]

Two observations emerge from all this. First, Americans long ago hit their threshold of pain for the Social Security tax. Second, an overwhelming majority of Americans regards Social Security benefits, particularly for current retirees, as sacrosanct.

Hence we may safely say that another attempt to stave off disaster by the favorite expedients of raising taxes and/or trimming benefits would be extremely traumatic, almost as much so as OASDI's actual demise. That trauma will be compounded because despite the oceans of ink spilled about the budget and Social Security in the past twenty years, ignorance about them remains widespread. The *Post*-Harvard-Kaiser survey found, for example, that 64 percent of respondents thought foreign aid is the most costly area of government, whereas in reality foreign aid accounts for barely one percent of federal spending—and only 27 percent of respondents believe, correctly, that Social Security is the costliest federal program. And only 28 percent knew that most retirees get more money in benefits than they paid in taxes.[33]

Lacking real knowledge about Social Security, many Americans lean on a Reaganesque fantasy that eliminating waste, fraud, and abuse will solve the problem. While the *Post*-Harvard-Kaiser poll found that most Americans believe the gloomy forecasts about Social Security and Medicare,

the action most favored by respondents is for Congress to eliminate perceived waste, fraud and abuse in the programs.

"It's the beliefs that people hold about how the entitlement programs are being managed that is driving the views that we don't have to come to grips with the hard decisions," said Robert J. Blendon, a professor of health policy and political analysis at Harvard University and a leading expert on public opinion about entitlements.[34]

My own experience in monitoring the man in the street's knowledge of Social Security by reading letters to newspapers, listening to ordinary people's assertions about Social Security, and talking with them bears this out. Over and over, I encounter populist misunderstandings, some of them very dangerous:

"If they'd kept Social Security the way it was originally set up, we'd be all right." False. As we shall see, Social Security's creators intended the original system to be merely the first step toward a comprehensive scheme of "social insurance." Moreover, the original program, which paid very modest old-age benefits for retired workers only (survivors' benefits were added in 1939, disability benefits in 1956), would be far more austere than people today would accept. And since Social Security originally covered only employees in commerce and industry, many of those who think we should have kept to the original program would be outside it, receiving no benefits at all.

"Those cheats who are ripping off the system are the problem." False. Lurid stories of people with multiple Social Security cards may make good sensational journalism, but there aren't enough of them to make any difference. Social Security pays about a billion dollars in benefits every day, and will pay far more when the boomers retire. If all fraud cases were cleaned up, it would be a mere tiny ripple in so massive a cash flow. As for waste and high administrative costs, two other favorite populist bugaboos, Social Security is one of the most efficiently and honestly managed programs the federal government operates, with operating costs a paltry sliver of outlays. Waste, fraud, and abuse are red herrings diverting attention from real problems, and creating a mistaken belief that the program's essential nature is sound, hence radical change is not necessary.

"The politicians are robbing the trust fund. If they'd kept their hands out of the till, Social Security would be in good shape." Probably the most widespread populist grumble about Social Security, this assertion bears no resemblance to reality. As we shall see, the original Social Security Act mandated using surplus Social Security revenues to purchase government debt. Those revenues, it was understood, would be available for general use. This charge, then, is unfair to Congress, which is only doing what the law *requires.* It does reveal that the popular mind equates Social Security's "trust fund" with a private-sector trust fund. As we shall see when we examine the "trust fund" in detail, that is the impression this term was intended to give, but it is fallacious. For now, note that this use of the term "trust fund" has had the very dangerous unforeseen consequence of giving an impression that Congress is guilty of malfeasance, even embezzlement, and encouraging an explosive sense of outrage at betrayal of trust. It therefore has the potential to greatly exacerbate any political crisis that ensues.

All too clearly, most Americans' thinking about Social Security is vague, impressionistic, ill-informed, and dangerously removed from reality. Most Americans have no idea just how large the tax and/or benefit sacrifices necessary to prevent Social Security's collapse would actually have to be. Unfortunately, it stands to reason that the greater the distance between the public's understanding of Social Security and the reality, and the more abruptly that distance is closed, the greater and more traumatic the resultant shock will be.

It should be clear by now that the tax increases necessary to avert Social Security's bankruptcy will be substantial—far more than advocates of minor adjustments would have us believe. Such taxes would probably trigger a tax revolt.

The alternative to putting the entire burden of saving Social Security on taxpayers is cutting benefits. The benefit cuts, which would have to be of roughly similar magnitude, will understandably terrify and infuriate the elderly, many of whom are counting on the benefits, have planned their retirement around them, and will find adjustment on short notice difficult or impossible. Robertson observed that breaking the benefit promises

> could have another serious ramification: namely, the complete loss of faith in the government itself. Social Security is probably the last major government program in which the public still has any significant degree of confidence.
>
> Without the confidence and support of the public, the institution of orderly government cannot long survive. If a major default occurs in Social Security benefit promises, anarchy may not be far off.[35]

Any politically palatable effort to save Social Security would have to mix tax increases and benefit cuts—that is, break *both* the tax *and* the benefit promises. But Social Security's zero-sum character inexorably means that the more Congress tries to limit the increase in the burden on taxpayers, the more sacrifices it will have to compel from retirees. Hence a tax increase-benefit cut mix would only spread the pain and trauma, and anger and alienate *both* groups—which now means, due to near-universal participation, virtually the entire adult population.

And the longer such rescue measures are delayed, the larger they will have to be when finally made, the more pain they will inflict, and the greater political turmoil and anger they will create.

Either Social Security's collapse or a painful rescue will create a climate favorable to demagoguery. Fiscal crisis, and a return to "gridlock" over how to cope with it, will give a strong impression that democracy is not capable of solving urgent national problems, and call into question not only Social Security but the very legitimacy of the democratic process and the democratic form of government. The Great Depression is a disturbing precedent. The Depression's privations prompted calls for a dictator. Demagogues such as Huey Long, Father Charles Coughlin, and Gerald L. K. Smith gained impressive followings; Long's popularity gave the Roosevelt administration a bad and thoroughly justified scare.[36] Such characters could very likely afflict us again. And our population, already badly fractured over race, abortion, and other issues, is already dangerously vulnerable to demagoguery and polarization; hard times will greatly worsen that vulnerability.

Riding a Tiger

And one of the worst sources of trauma, bitterness and fury will be the abrupt revelation of the yawning discrepancy between the reality of Social Security and our government's depiction of it, disseminated for over sixty-five years, as "insurance" collecting "premiums" paying benefits as an "earned right" out of a "trust fund." This is still widely believed. The persistent lopsided opposition to benefit cuts reflects a pervasive sense that Social Security benefits are indeed an earned right, owed to the country's elderly, and that it would be simply unconscionable to deny seniors what they've "got coming to them." Other evidence that the insurance and trust fund myths still grip the minds of many over sixty years after their inception is afforded by this sample of letters to newspapers:

Social Security is not an entitlement program, but a savings system.

When the government sends a Social Security check to an individual, it is not giving him anything; it is paying him back a portion of the money he has saved for his retirement through a special government plan. The money belongs to the individual, money owed him, money systematically and forcibly taken from his paycheck as security against a time when he will be too old to work.[37]

Social Security is an insurance program to finance retirement. Money has been taken from the working man and woman to be put into the Social Security fund since the 1930s. . . .

That money would have multiplied a couple of times had it been left where it belongs [i.e., in the trust fund].[38]

The way to save Social Security immediately is to transfer the administration of this [Social Security trust] fund to a private administrator. The government has been borrowing and stealing from this lucrative fund.[39]

But when the "trust funds" are liquidated and the government turns to taxing and borrowing from the public to make good on its Social Security obligations, the true nature of the "trust funds" will become apparent. Significant benefit cutting will abruptly reveal to tens of millions of Americans that Social Security's "guarantee" of benefits as an "earned right" is a fiction, and the backlash from substantial OASDI tax increases will reveal that Henry Aaron's vaunted "sure bet of social insurance" is merely a bet on Americans' willingness to pay ever higher taxes for the benefit of total strangers. Social Security, it will abruptly become clear, is not "insurance" after all, but a system of taxes and transfers, the rules of which Congress can rewrite at will.

Put another way, it will be abruptly, brutally made clear to Americans that their understanding of Social Security is, in fact, a false consciousness.

As Social Security has become a secular religion thanks to the Social Security Administration, American Association of Retired Persons, and others, the disillusion and demoralization will be devastating. It will be a shattering breach of faith, especially because the personal stakes will be so high for so many—in many cases, the difference between decent living and privation. The potential political crisis ensuing from this mass shock of disillusion, and the resulting rage and bitterness, is well-nigh inconceivable.

This danger might be mitigated if the government were making an effort to educate people about Social Security's true nature, so as to give Americans ample time to prepare for the shocks to come from breaking the tax and benefit promises, especially the latter. But the government dares not do this, since continued acceptance of Social Security by Americans paying its taxes depends on their continued belief in the insurance myth and continued faith that Social Security will be there for them when they retire.

For example, the 1994 edition of *Understanding Social Security,* the basic information booklet issued at Social Security offices, responded to public concerns for Social Security's future by affirming Social Security's soundness over and over in its first three pages:

> Before we get started explaining the program, we think it's important to answer the first question many people have about Social Security. . . . "Will Social Security be there when I need it?"
> The simple and logical answer is, "Yes it will." . . . .
>
> . . . we . . . will honor your investment [sic] in Social Security. It will be there when you need it!
>
> Now that we've answered your first question and told you that Social Security will be there when you need it . . . .
>
> Here's one final message about Social Security's future, your future, and this booklet: Social Security will be there—**whenever** [SSA's emphasis] you may need it.[40]

Perhaps sensing that they were overdoing it, the Social Security Administration's writers switched in the 1995 edition to conveying a soothing sense of time well in hand: "The latest [Board of Trustees] report indicates that the Social Security system, as currently structured, will be able to pay benefits for about thirty more years. This means Congress has the time it needs to make changes to safeguard the program's financial future."[41] As we shall see, the language of private insurance and investment persists in OASDI: "contributions," "coverage," "fully insured status," "insurance," and so on. And Part I of the 1996 edition of the successor to *Understanding Social*

Security, called *Social Security: Understanding the Benefits,* is titled, "Your Investment in Social Security," meaning your Social Security taxes.[42]

Yet the longer the Social Security myths persist, the longer the misinformed public will resist reforming Social Security, the longer the government will procrastinate, and the more drastic and painful the eventual crisis and corrective actions will be. Former Chief Actuary Robertson put the situation well:

> It is unfortunate that the public perception of Social Security has been allowed to grow so far apart from the reality. This has created a serious dilemma for Social Security. If public misunderstanding is allowed to persist, confusion and disappointment will worsen because Social Security will continue its failure to match most of the public's expectations; and this will result in a frenzied cry for change. On the other hand, if the misunderstanding is eliminated it is probable that the public will not like what it sees and thus will demand significant revision.[43]

In short, Social Security is riding a tiger that it dares not dismount. Since Social Security bulks so huge in our national life, America itself is riding that same tiger. The long-term economic and political rewards of dismounting— that is, publicly, officially dispelling the false consciousness and radically reforming Social Security—are very high, but the short-term political risks of doing so are terrifying. The long-term costs of continuing to ride the tiger are even worse, but the short-term political costs are very low. A calculation of political risks and rewards focusing on the immediate short run, the one politicians routinely make, thus favors postponing action. So we go on, deeper into the dark forest, clinging to the tiger's neck, half-fearing that those reporting bones littering the ground ahead are right, half-hoping the scoffers saying there is ample time for a hunter to arrive are right, spinning fantastic "reform" schemes for jumping off the tiger without getting mauled, and ending up doing nothing.

We are caught in a gruesome predicament. And some of the deepest roots of our predicament, and the coming crisis in Social Security, lie in the way Social Security was crafted and in the way its advocates have presented it to the public since 1935.

Notes

1.   Robertson, *Social Security: What Every Taxpayer Should Know,* p. 127.
2.   Colin D. And Rosemary G. Campbell, "You'll Never Get Back All Those Old-Age 'Contributions,'" *Washington Post,* November 7, 1965, E3.
3.   "Malaise in Congress," *New York Times,* March 20, 1967, 15.
4.   *1999 Annual Statistical Supplement, Social Security Bulletin,* p. 168, Table 4.B.4.— Percent of all workers and self-employed workers with total annual earnings below annual maximum taxable, by sex, 1937-96.
5.   *1974 OASDI Annual Report,* pp. 22, 38.

6. "Ex-officials back pension system," *New York Times,* February 11, 1975, 23; "Social Security Is Defended; Attacks Called a Disservice," *Washington Post,* February 11, 1975, A1, A7.
7. "Social Security Fund Seen Facing Long-Term Problems," *Washington Post,* February 13, 1975, A3.
8. *1975 OASDI Annual Report,* p. 32.
9. Ibid., pp. 36-37, 44.
10. "'75 Social Security Deficit Now Estimated at $3 Billion," *Washington Post,* May 6, 1975, A2.
11. "News Analysis: Social Security Benefits Not in Danger," *Washington Post,* May 12, 1975, A1.
12. Paul A. Samuelson, "Social Security: A-OK," *Newsweek,* April 14, 1975, p. 74.
13. See, e.g., "Social Security: Trouble Ahead," *Newsweek,* March 25, 1975, p. 75; R. T. Gray, "Will the Social Security Bubble Burst?" *Readers Digest,* May 1975, pp. 147-151; "Fresh scare over Social Security," *U.S. News & World Report,* February 16, 1976, pp. 68-70; "Hard choices for Social Security; massive flow of red ink," *U.S. News & World Report,* June 7, 1976, p. 71.
14. U.S., Congress, Senate, Senator Carl T. Curtis, *Congressional Record,* 95th Cong., 1st sess., November 2, 1977, 123:36470-36471.
15. "Dear Lawmaker: 'It's a Lousy Deal'," *U.S. News & World Report,* March 13, 1978, p. 73.
16. "A growing disillusion with Social Security," *Business Week,* March 12, 1979, p. 26.
17. See, for example, "Letters to the Editor," *U.S. News & World Report,* March 27, 1978, p. 5; "Letters to the Editor," *U.S. News & World Report,* January 22, 1979, p. 3; "Letters to the Editor," *U.S. News & World Report,* March 12, 1979, p. 5; "Letters to the Editor," *U.S. News & World Report,* May 14, 1979, p. 5.
18. "Poll Shows Americans Losing Faith In Future of Social Security System," *New York Times,* July 17, 1981, A12.
19. *1980 OASDI Annual Report,* pp. 2-3, 57-58.
20. *1999 Annual Statistical Supplement, Social Security Bulletin,* p. 168, Table 4.B.4. The share of workers with total incomes below the taxable maximum has continued to creep up; as of 1996 it was estimated at 94 percent. (Ibid.)
21. "Poll Shows Americans Losing Faith In Future of Social Security System."
22. "A Social Cornerstone Shaken," *Journal of American Insurance,* vol. 60, no. 4, 1984-85, p. 18; Karlyn Bowman, "Social Security: A Report on Current Polls," American Enterprise Institute Papers and Studies, p. 9, Table 1: Counting on Social Security (www.aei.org).
23. The pioneering work on generational accounting and intergenerational equity in general is Laurence Kotlikoff, *Generational Accounting: Knowing Who Pays, and When, for What We Spend* (New York: The Free Press, 1992). Kotlikoff, an economics professor at Boston University, criticized Social Security specifically on grounds of intergenerational inequity (*Generational Accounting,* chapter 8, *passim*) and has since advocated privatization. See, e.g., Laurence Kotlikoff, "Rescuing Social Security," *Challenge,* vol. 39, no. 6 (November-December 1996), pp. 21-22; and Laurence J. Kotlikoff and Jeffrey Sachs, "Privatizing Social Security: It's High Time to Privatize," *The Brookings Review,* vol. 15, no. 3 (Summer 1997), pp. 16, 18, 20, 22. Popular-level literature on the worsening return Social Security gives its taxpayers is proliferating; see, for example, Michael J. Mandel, "From New Deal to Raw Deal," *Business Week,* April 3, 1993, pp. 68-69.
24. Peterson and Howe, *On Borrowed Time,* p. 268.

25. For formulation of this point I am indebted to Irving Louis Horowitz.
26. Bowman, "Social Security: A Report on Current Polls," p. 7.
27. 1999 Technical Panel on Assumptions and Methods, *Report to the Social Security Advisory Board,* p. 35; The Concord Coalition, "What Happens to Benefits When Social Security Goes Bankrupt?" April 19, 2000 (www.concordcoalition.org).
28. A. Haeworth Robertson, *The Big Lie: What Every Baby Boomer Should Know About Social Security and Medicare* (Washington, DC: Retirement Policy Institute, 1997), p. 116.
29. "Social Security at 50 Faces New Crossroads," *U.S. News & World Report,* August 12, 1985, p. 41.
30. "Americans Oppose Cutting Entitlements to Fix Budget," *Washington Post,* March 29, 1997, A4.
31. "Poll: Don't hike retirement age," *USA Today,* July 27, 1998, 1A; "System is face-to-face with change," *USA Today,* July 27, 1998, 7A.
32. Bowman, "Social Security: A Report on Current Polls," pp. 7-8 and p. 16, table 4: Recent Questions on Familiar Social Security Issues.
33. "Americans Oppose Cutting Entitlements to Fix Budget."
34. Ibid.
35. Robertson, *The Big Lie,* p. 119.
36. William E. Leuchtenburg, *Franklin D. Roosevelt and the New Deal 1932-1940* (New York: Harper & Row, Publishers, 1963), pp. 27-30, 99-103, 114-117, 180-183.
37. "Letters to the Editor," *Wall Street Journal,* March 28, 1994, A13.
38. "Letters," *Detroit News,* May 7, 1998, 16A.
39. Ibid.
40. Social Security Administration, *Understanding Social Security,* SSA Publication No. 05-10024, January 1994, pp. 4-6.
41. Social Security Administration, *Understanding Social Security,* SSA Publication No. 05-10024, January 1995, pp. 4-5.
42. Social Security Administration, *Social Security: Understanding the Benefits,* SSA Publication No. 05-10024, January 1996, p. 4.
43. Robertson, *The Coming Revolution in Social Security,* p. xxi.

Part 2

False Consciousness and the Roots of Crisis

4

The Beginnings

"An error crowned with prestige always will be
more powerful than a truth without prestige."

—*Gustave LeBon[1]*

Social Security is generally described as a "social insurance" program. Isaac Rubinow, a pioneer in social insurance, defined it in 1913 as "the policy of organized society to furnish that protection to one part of the population, which some other part may need less, or, if needing, is able to purchase voluntarily through private insurance."[2] In chapter 7 we shall extensively examine the issue, once bitterly controversial and still crucial, of whether "social insurance," Social Security specifically, really is insurance. For now, let us simply present the essential idea, as propounded by one of its founding fathers, and address arguments about its validity later.

The basic idea of insurance, Rubinow maintained, drawing on the *Encyclopedia Britannica*, is a provision by a group of persons, each in some danger of an unforeseeable loss, that if any one member of the group suffers that loss, the whole group will bear the cost, the share of cost borne by each member thereby being small. Workers face serious risks, such as injury on the job or destitution in old age, but cannot afford to protect themselves from such risks through private insurance. Providing such protection, Rubinow argued, was "the concern of the modern progressive state." The state may provide voluntary insurance, lowering the premiums by eliminating profits, administering the insurance itself, and using subsidies; it may go further and make workers' payments compulsory. Money thus collected would be used to pay benefits compensating for the risks.[3] Such, in essence, is "social insurance."

Intellectual Origins: Revolution from Above

Arthur Larson, under secretary of labor under Dwight Eisenhower and a Social Security supporter, observed that compulsory social insurance operated by a national government "did not come in on a great wave of popular demand from the mass of people . . . It came largely because of the efforts of farsighted individuals."[4] That is, it was imposed from the top down by politicians and intellectuals, for pragmatic and philosophical reasons.

The first such "social insurance" system was the handiwork of Germany's Chancellor Otto von Bismarck, who hated and feared socialism, which was gaining strength in Germany. Bismarck's anti-socialist strategy was two-pronged: suppression of socialist agitation, and paternalistic legislation to better the lot of German industrial workers, thereby rendering them less susceptible to socialism. In 1881, he proposed programs compensating workers for income loss due to sickness and accidents, with disability and retirement benefit bills to come later. Germany already had many organizations providing such benefits, some voluntary, some compulsory; some local, some national; some associated with specific businesses (e.g., railways) or trade unions. Bismarck's contribution was to create a national system controlled and administered by the national government, financed by compulsory worker and employer contributions collected and spent by the state. His Sickness Insurance Law was passed in 1883, followed by the Accident Insurance Law (1884) and the Old Age and Disability Insurance Law (1889).[5] Other European countries followed with similar programs for sickness, old age, and other benefits. Great Britain's National Insurance Act (1911), pushed through by Chancellor of the Exchequer David Lloyd George, besides providing compulsory sickness insurance, set another precedent: the first national compulsory unemployment insurance, covering 2.5 million workers.[6]

The United States was slower to adopt social insurance. Until well after the Civil War, its traditional political economy, despite Alexander Hamilton's "American system" of a national bank, protective tariffs, and internal improvements like canals and railroads, was essentially one of laissez-faire: the national government should eschew interference in the economy. The federal government dispensed no welfare benefits. Care of the elderly, disabled, and unemployed fell to family, private charity, and such local poverty relief as existed.[7]

In the latter half of the nineteenth century, however, an increasingly influential viewpoint appeared in America, arguing, as sympathetic historian Sidney Fine put it, that "the state could best promote the general welfare by a positive exertion of its powers," and calling for antitrust laws, railroad regulation, public health programs, labor legislation, and poverty relief.[8] Belief in socialism, Fine argued, had little to do with it; rather, most proponents of this view found "a good deal of truth in the socialist critique of the existing order," and sought to both answer this critique and avert socialism by advancing reforms that, they believed, "would correct the inequities of the capitalist regime without destroying its essentials."[9]

The "social gospel" was an important strain in this movement. Social gospelers stressed salvation not of individual souls but of society. Environment, they argued, was an important cause of sin, hence social reform was imperative. Society had to be Christianized if the individual was to lead a Christian life. The social gospel movement increasingly looked to the State as the only sure means of effecting the needed reforms. Government, argued economist John R. Commons, a prominent social gospeler, is "the key to all social reforms and the Christianization of society."[10]

A specialist in labor economics who joined the University of Wisconsin faculty in 1904, Commons was a key figure in developing and implementing the "Wisconsin Idea," that government was obliged to promote its citizens' welfare through social and economic reform, and that academe should provide experts to advise politicians and government on policies to do so. Wisconsin's progressive legislation for civil service, public utilities regulation, labor conditions, and social insurance owed much to Commons. Arthur Altmeyer, one of his students and research assistants, and an architect of Social Security, believed that "in a sense," the Wisconsin Idea was "the forerunner of the Rooseveltian New Deal."[11]

The Wisconsin Idea, however, was only one stream in a progressive movement that became very broad in the first three decades of this century. Several states enacted various "social insurance" measures in this period, such as unemployment and old-age benefits. Agitation by academics such as Commons and Eveline Burns, labor unions, social workers, "progressive" intellectuals and social insurance advocates such as Isaac Rubinow and Abraham Epstein for nationwide social insurance, drawing on the examples of European countries, was rising.[12] It was unavailing, however, until the agony of the Great Depression created circumstances mightily favoring their cause.

Unemployment during the Depression fell as heavily on the old as on the young. Moreover, many Americans who had saved for their old age saw those savings wiped out by the collapse of the stock market and the failures of thousands of banks, or were forced by unemployment to liquidate their savings to meet rent, mortgage, and other expenses. Roughly 750,000 elderly persons were receiving direct federal relief by the end of 1934.[13]

Traditionally, elderly Americans were supported by their relatives, especially their children. Already in 1928, an estimated 30 percent of persons aged sixty-five and over depended on others, in the majority of cases their relatives, for support. The Depression drove the share of dependent aged persons to an estimated 40 percent in 1930 and 50 percent in 1935. But the traditional means of supporting them were foundering. As Abraham Holtzman observed, "With unemployment well over the twelve million mark in the depth of the depression, the support of aged relatives became impossible for many families. Private charity and pension plans proved useless in the face of the magnitude of the task; many of the plans collapsed utterly."[14]

Many states responded to the plight of the elderly by passing old-age pension laws requiring mandatory participation, and those which already had voluntary old-age pension laws made them mandatory. However, state tax revenues were collapsing due to high unemployment, and pensions were extremely meager, when they were paid at all. Could not the national government take a hand?, some observers wondered. At the same time, sentiment was growing in favor of unemployment compensation.[15]

The new president, Franklin Roosevelt, was already familiar with, and supportive of, Social Security's core idea. Running for governor of New York in 1928, he advocated study of old-age insurance, and, once elected, called for creation of a commission to present proposals to the state legislature. Specifically, he wanted benefits paid for by worker and government contributions. A Commission on Old-Age Security was created, but the resulting old-age pension legislation did not go as far as Roosevelt wanted. Seeking reelection in 1930, he called for old-age insurance financed by "premiums" paid by young workers, supplemented by "premiums" paid by employers and the state government. Reelected, he sought unsuccessfully to get such a program through the New York legislature in 1931 and 1932.[16] Roosevelt's progressivism owed much to the influence of Theodore Roosevelt and Woodrow Wilson. They, and Roosevelt himself, Altmeyer claimed, were "thoroughly familiar" with the Wisconsin Idea and its resultant legislation.[17] During the 1932 campaign, Roosevelt again proposed old-age insurance.[18]

Even before taking office as president, Roosevelt endorsed prompt investigation of methods to create a national system of unemployment and old-age insurance. Accordingly, in 1933 Roosevelt undertook a major effort to sell social insurance to his administration, the Congress, and the country. To familiarize Congress with unemployment insurance, he encouraged Senator Robert Wagner (D-NY) and Representative David Lewis (D-MD) to introduce a bill they had prepared for this measure. Secretary of Labor Frances Perkins, at his encouragement, made a point of pushing social insurance at Cabinet meetings, and later traveled the country making speeches to promote social insurance as a solution to the problems of unemployment and destitution in old age.[19]

The Wagner-Lewis bill made little headway, and the administration decided to try again. On June 8, 1934, President Roosevelt informed Congress that next winter the government would likely undertake to promote "the security of the citizen and his family through social insurance." He would, he said, pursue a comprehensive package providing protection against "several of the great disturbing factors in life—especially those which relate to unemployment and old age."[20] Three weeks later, he issued an executive order creating the apparatus for developing an economic security program: a Cabinet Committee on Economic Security to study social insurance and recommend legislation; an executive director for the Committee; a Technical Board, a panel of federal government experts to advise the Committee and help the executive director develop an actual program; and an advisory council. Besides Perkins, who was chairman, the Committee contained Secretary of the Treasury Henry Morgenthau, Attorney General Homer Cummings, Secretary of Agriculture Henry Wallace, and Federal Emergency Relief Administrator Harry Hopkins. The advisory council contained five employers, five labor leaders, and thirteen "persons," as Altmeyer put it, "interested in social welfare."[21]

As one student of Social Security has pointed out, the Advisory Council's membership was "carefully stacked" by the administration to include only "individuals sympathetic to the cause"; groups known to oppose social insurance, such as the National Association of Manufacturers and the U.S. Chamber of Commerce, were passed over.[22] While this approach ensured that the administration's social insurance advocates got the answers they wanted, and was thus self-serving, it is also quite understandable, especially given the mutual antagonism that existed between business and the New Dealers. One cannot, after all, reasonably expect anyone endeavoring to obtain anything to seek advice from his critics and enemies on how to get it. Conservative and libertarian complaints on this aspect of Social Security's creation, at least, seem unpersuasive.

Because the administration had decided to create a comprehensive economic security package, the number of expert advisors proliferated. Besides the Advisory Council, the Committee on Economic Security created seven specialized advisory groups containing altogether seventy-two prominent figures in their fields: dental, hospital, and public-health advisory committees; a medical advisory board; a committee of actuarial consultants; a child welfare committee; and an advisory committee on employment and relief. Also, suggestions from hundreds of organizations were considered.[23]

Altmeyer, who had become assistant secretary of labor the month before because of his role as secretary of the Wisconsin Industrial Commission and because he hailed from Wisconsin's school of "institutional economists," was picked to head the Technical Board.[24] Interestingly, his economic thought drew not only on the Wisconsin Idea but on the French utopian socialist Claude Henri de Saint-Simon, who, Altmeyer wrote, "laid down the dictum: From each according to his ability and to each according to his need. A society successfully built on that foundation would be a rather fine one in which to live. Nor does a competitive economy necessarily have to reject Saint-Simon."[25]

(Perhaps attempting to legitimize Social Security with conservatives, Under Secretary Larson made a point of noting that social insurance originated as "an antisocialistic measure," courtesy of "the Iron Chancellor himself," and that social insurance's architects were "as often as not . . . those who would be called politically conservative."[26] Given Altmeyer's endorsement of Saint-Simon, this is dubious. There was nothing conservative about Lloyd George, and one may wonder what Bismarck did to merit the mantle of conservative, at least as thinkers such as Russell Kirk understood it.)

Altmeyer recommended University of Wisconsin professor, Edwin Witte, who had succeeded Commons as chairman of the economics department, to be the Committee's executive director. Dr. Witte accepted and, in turn, hired Wilbur Cohen, who had studied under both Commons and Witte at Wisconsin, as an assistant.[27] Thus, the Wisconsin Idea, though of course not the only source of Social Security, inspired several of Social Security's creators, hence did play, as Altmeyer proudly claimed, a substantial role.

Social and Political Origins:
Pressure from the Left—and from Below

Meanwhile, agitation was rising on the political left for radical changes in income and wealth distribution and for sharp departures from established practice regarding provision of government assistance for the poor, the unemployed, and the elderly.

Huey Long, Louisiana's governor, senator, and virtual dictator, was a colorful demagogue whom Roosevelt deemed one of the most dangerous men in America, and a radical redistributionist. In January 1934, he launched a national political organization promising to confiscate large fortunes above a certain amount and redistribute the money so everyone could have a car and a house, old-age pensions, a national minimum wage, public works, and more. By spring 1935, Long's "Share Our Wealth" program had immense appeal nationwide, which worried Roosevelt badly, since Long would apparently be a formidable third-party threat in the 1936 election.[28]

At the same time, the famous Townsend Movement was underway. Dr. Francis Townsend, an elderly California physician who claimed to be outraged by the extreme poverty of the elderly which he witnessed personally, concocted a plan to pay every American aged sixty and over a monthly pension of $200 (his initial figure was $150), financed by a "revolving pension fund" of revenues from a 2 percent sales tax, provided the pensioner retired from employment and spent the pension within a month. Townsend first proposed his plan in September 1933, and he and his former employer, Robert Earl Clements, created Old Age Revolving Pensions, Ltd., in January 1934 to promote it.[29] Simple, specific, in tune with the experimental, discontented climate of the times, and holding out hope for rescuing them from destitution, the Townsend Plan was wildly popular with the elderly. The first Townsend Club was established in July 1934. By the end of the year, Townsend claimed to have 1,200 Clubs; by April 1936, there were 7,000 Townsend Clubs with a total membership of roughly 1.5 million elderly persons. The movement generated an intense crusading spirit, and even published its own weekly tabloid, which first appeared in January 1935. Petitions signed by millions reached Congress urging enactment of the Townsend Plan; Congressmen received hundreds of thousands, perhaps millions, of letters urging the same.[30]

While some of this enthusiasm flowed from anticipations of a windfall,[31] that the Townsend Plan got the response it did is an indicator of the genuine destitution and desperation of many elderly Americans. The Townsend Movement provided a means of giving this phenomenon expression, and translating it into political pressure.

The Roosevelt administration felt the pressure. When, shortly before the Committee on Economic Security's final report was due, the Committee found itself stymied over how to finance old-age insurance, President Roosevelt warned them that including old-age insurance in the economic security bill was necessary:

> We have to have it. The Congress can't stand the pressure of the Townsend Plan unless we have a real old-age insurance system, nor can I face the country without having devised at this time, while we are studying social security, a solid plan which will give some assurance to old people of systematic assistance upon retirement.[32]

To what degree was the Social Security Act an attempt to steal the radicals' thunder, and fend off their proposals? Certainly the Townsend Plan competed directly with Social Security; Congressman John McGroarty (D-CA) introduced a bill for the "Townsend Old Age Revolving Pension Plan" on January 16, 1935, the day before the Social Security bill was introduced.[33] Abraham Holtzman, who made a definitive scholarly study of the Townsend Movement, maintained plausibly that

> The Townsend Plan and the Social Security Act are inextricably linked together, the inclusion of an old-age insurance provision within the Act representing a direct response to Townsend pressure. The Townsend Movement must be credited with having crystallized tremendous popular sentiment in favor of old-age security. And the threat posed by the plan weakened conservative opposition to the more moderate proposals encompassed in the Social Security Act.[34]

Paul Douglas, a University of Chicago economics professor and a member of the Advisory Council on economic security, argued similarly that the Townsend Movement's popular support "probably did weaken the diehard opposition to the security bill."[35] While acknowledging Roosevelt's concern about the Townsend Plan, Altmeyer maintained that his greater concern was about Huey Long, whose voter appeal, so a poll for the Democratic National Committee indicated, was sufficient that he might divide the liberal vote enough to elect a Republican president in 1936.[36] Altmeyer's point is cogent. Whereas the well-meaning but badly incoherent[37] Townsend was not remotely a threat to Roosevelt, Long indeed offered genuine competition for the White House.

Against the thesis of Social Security being concocted under duress, how-ever, recall that Roosevelt's belief in compulsory, contributory, government-administered old-age insurance preceded his accession to the presidency. Then, too, the administration's elaborate preparatory apparatus of numerous advisory bodies of experts à la Commons, which necessarily entailed thor-ough and time-devouring deliberation, is hard to square with being hustled by Long, Townsend, or anybody else. Probably the most judicious assessment is that while the Townsend Movement did dramatically call attention to both a genuine problem of old-age indigence and to a broad demand for some sort of government help for the elderly, the pressure exerted by Townsend, Long, and their ilk did not force President Roosevelt to propose Social Security but rather prompted him to undertake sooner rather than later what he clearly already wanted to do anyway, and made it substantially easier for him to do it.

The Payroll Tax: "Politics All the Way Through"

As the administration's preparations advanced, President Roosevelt aired his views on what the social insurance system should be like. He wanted a very simple system, covering everyone "from the cradle to the grave," with benefits for old age, unemployment, sickness and disability. (Indeed he later claimed credit for the concept of universal, comprehensive social insurance advanced by Sir William Beveridge.) Secretary Perkins, worried about the political climate, financing, and administration, thought this was too ambi-tious, and Roosevelt approved the far more limited plan that finally emerged as the best he could get from Congress.[38]

On one thing Roosevelt was adamant: the old-age insurance program must be self-financed, by payroll taxes on employees matched by excises on em-ployers. "If I have anything to say about it," he remarked, "it will always be contributed, and I prefer it to be contributed, both on the part of employer and the employee, on a sound actuarial basis. It means no money out of the Trea-sury."[39] As the last sentence indicates, Roosevelt's complicated and even contradictory economic thinking included a strain of genuine fiscal conser-vatism.

But this consideration occupied only a corner of Roosevelt's mind on the matter. The primary, deeper motive of his insistence on self-financing lay elsewhere. When Perkins, Rexford Tugwell, and others criticized the payroll tax as regressive, falling on those least able to afford it, Roosevelt turned a deaf ear. Years later, he explained to one such complainant,

> I guess you're right on the economics, but those taxes were never a problem of economics. They were politics all the way through. We put those payroll contribu-tions there so as to give the contributors a legal, moral, and political right to collect their pensions and their unemployment benefits. With those taxes in there, no damn politician can ever scrap my Social Security program.[40]

Roosevelt's words reveal the payroll tax as one of the main roots of the Social Security myth, and therefore of Social Security's crisis. It created—and was intended to create—a powerful sense of entitlement to benefits, which, being "paid for" out of taxes, were an "earned right." The payroll tax was not about financing a program, but about creating a climate of belief. The reason invariably given by Social Security's defenders for the payroll-tax financing method and its consequence of benefits received as a "right" is a desire to spare the feelings and self-respect of beneficiaries from the stigma of taking a dole, which went so bitterly against the grain for so many in individualistic post-Victorian America, and to spare them the humiliation of a means test.[41] Perhaps so; but Roosevelt's words reveal that beneath this humanitarianism lay a self-serving political calculation as insidious as it is brilliant. Giving every appearance of benevolence, the payroll-tax method actually enlists the self-interest of taxpayers. With his usual shrewd grasp of psychology, Roosevelt divined that just as a loan gives the lender a stake in the survival and prosperity of the borrower, so would requiring people to pay payroll taxes for Social Security give them a compelling stake in its survival with its taxation and benefit provisions intact, so as to be able to get "their" money back, and thereby create a highly motivated *permanent constituency*, not only among retirees but among *taxpayers*, fervently committed to Social Security and ferociously resistant to any attempt to tamper with benefits. Each generation of Social Security taxpayers, having been compelled to participate through payroll taxes, would, upon entering the elderly cohort, see to it that their benefit checks arrived and that the *next* generation pay *their* taxes to finance those benefits. That taxpaying generation, in turn, having sunk *their* money into Social Security, would, upon attaining old age . . . and so on. The demonstration effect of Social Security appearing to work as advertised for the first cohorts of beneficiaries would powerfully reinforce this mechanism. So would the incessant assertion that beneficiaries were receiving their benefits as "an earned right." The ultimate effect, as he foresaw, would be to make Social Security politically untouchable.

That this is indeed the true underlying reason for the payroll tax was confirmed in the 1970s when proposals were floated to have all or part of Social Security's costs financed out of general revenue. Former Chief Actuary Robert Myers and others opposed general revenue financing on the grounds that the need to raise payroll taxes to pay for more liberal benefits made the benefits' costs visible and thus imposed a discipline on Social Security spending, which would disappear if general revenue financing were adopted.[42] Yet Commissioner of Social Security Stanford G. Ross did not mention this argument when he told the *U. S. News & World Report* why he opposed repeal of the payroll tax and shifting to general-revenue financing. Had this argument been the main factor in the Social Security Administration's thinking, surely Commissioner Ross would have made it. Instead, he upheld the payroll tax solely on psychological grounds:

It has been an important aspect—*maybe the genius of the system* [italics added]—that workers who pay in feel that they've earned the benefits they get, and their feelings about Social Security are different from what they would be if this were a system financed solely out of general revenues.

It's the difference between the way the public feels about Social Security and the way it feels about welfare payments.[43]

When asked how sensible it was to finance the large welfare, as opposed to retirement benefit, element of Social Security with a regressive payroll tax, Ross added that "a payroll tax means that workers are contributing, and there is a definite connection between workers' wages, contributions and benefits, which makes people feel more like it is their retirement or insurance system."[44] Revealing, again, the importance of psychological factors.

What Roosevelt did not foresee was that the payroll tax would contribute mightily to trapping Social Security in a position in which any substantial benefit reduction for current retirees was unthinkable, forcing presidents and Congresses to meet projected financial crises first by relying chiefly on massive payroll tax increases, driving taxpayers over their threshold of pain and thereby creating serious taxpayer disaffection with Social Security, with ominous implications for the future, and then by simply evading the matter altogether until too late.

The Administration's Proposal

The Committee on Economic Security finished its work and reported its recommendations to President Roosevelt on January 15, 1935. Two days later, the bill was introduced in both the House (H.R. 4120) and the Senate (S. 1130), again by Wagner and Lewis. This original version drafted by the administration had nine titles, most of which we need not address in detail. Title I covered appropriations for "old age assistance"—pensions for needy people aged sixty-five or older, who, never having paid into a contributory old-age insurance system, obviously could not qualify for its benefits. Thomas Eliot, who had drafted the bill, cleverly put this title first because he considered it the most popular proposal in the package. This move, Dr. Witte wrote, diminished opposition to other, less popular titles. Title II set up aid to dependent children. Title V created annuity certificates, which individuals could purchase from the government if they wished. The longest, most complicated title in the bill, Title VI, created unemployment insurance. Title VII appropriated money for providing maternal and child health care, particularly in rural and distressed areas, while Title VIII covered appropriations for public health.[45]

Titles III and IV contained the original Social Security proposal. Title III, Earnings Taxes, covered the taxes to be used to finance old-age insurance: a payroll tax on workers and a matching "employment excise tax" on their employers. Title IV created a "Social Insurance Board" in the Department of Labor to study and make recommendations regarding the most effective way of promoting economic security through "social insurance" and legislation and administration of "old-age insurance," to supervise payment of "old-age annuities under a national contributory old-age insurance system," and so on. It also created an "old-age fund" in the Treasury for the purpose of paying "old-age annuities." The fund or any part of it could be invested in U. S. Treasury debt instruments or in any debt instruments the principal and interest of which were guaranteed by the U. S. government. The annuities, proportional to the worker's average monthly wage, were to be paid to persons who were no less than sixty-five years old when receiving them; had had taxes under Title III paid on their behalf before they turned sixty, for at least two hundred weeks in no less than a five-year period; and were not gainfully employed by others. Interestingly, the administration bill contained a money-back guarantee: "In no event shall the actuarial value of an annuity paid to a person under this section be less than the amount of taxes paid on his behalf together with interest accretions as determined by the Social Insurance Board."[46]

What Titles III and IV did not say, in any manner, was that the taxpayer or beneficiary had a contract with the federal government giving him a contractual right to receive old-age insurance benefits. These titles had no contract language whatsoever.

Moreover, Title IX contained a reservation of power clause routine for legislation: "The right to alter, amend, or repeal any or all provisions of this act is hereby reserved to the Congress."[47]

The following narrative shall not cover all aspects of the Social Security bill's journey through Congress, nor all of the considerations, such as benefit size, burden of taxation on struggling enterprises, and so on, which were discussed. Rather, it shall confine itself to the threads in the tapestry relevant to our theme—namely, the administration's efforts to secure passage by influencing perceptions of the program.

Getting Through Congress: The First Misrepresentations

Secretary of Labor Perkins, Dr. Witte, and other key figures in the preparation of the Social Security bill gave extensive testimony to the House Ways and Means Committee and the Senate Finance Committee. The administration was in a hurry; Roosevelt's message transmitting it urged that it "be brought forward with a minimum of delay."[48] He had designated the Wagner-Lewis bill "must" legislation in 1934, and impressed on Perkins his desire to have the economic security bill passed quickly.[49] Accordingly, hearings started before the Ways and Means Committee on January 21 and before the Finance Committee on January 22.

Consistently, the administration's witnesses described Social Security as a unified system, with the payroll taxes creating a fund from which annuity benefits would be paid. Tax payments and benefit payments were explicitly linked. Dr. Witte, for example, described old-age insurance to the Ways and Means Committee as "a self-supporting system of old-age annuities."[50] Regarding the tax on employees and employers, Witte told the Committee, "The purpose really is to provide the money to pay the annuities," and added that "Contributory annuities are something that the man with the matching contributions of his employer builds up for himself. The primary purpose of the tax is to build up the annuity so that when he reaches old age he has this annuity to fall back on."[51]

This was straightforward enough. However, Perkins, Witte, and others also propounded Social Security's first misrepresentations. They repeatedly described Social Security not only as "insurance," but as creating a "contractual right" to "contractual annuities"—*despite the absence of any contract language in the administration's bill*. Secretary Perkins, for example, while describing the old-age insurance proposal to the Ways and Means Committee on January 22:

> . . . for the probable old-age dependency for persons not now old, we can hope to put that structure upon a relatively self-supporting basis, and to consider it as a type of insurance. . . .
> . . . an effort to provide a secure and systematic method of providing for the old-age necessities of persons who are young and of middle age . . . therefore theoretically able to contribute to the funds which will be used in the future, as a matter of *contractual right* [italics added], and provide them with some small but certain income when they are old . . . .[52]

> When we come into the program of old-age insurance, . . . we begin with persons who are taking their first jobs . . . and who . . . make a small contribution, a small percentage of their pay, to a fund which will later be used to pay them an insurance benefit which they have *as a contractual right* [italics added] when they become 65 years of age. . . their contribution will be matched by a contribution of their employer's.
> So that the proposal here is to begin to collect 1 percent of the pay roll in the case of every employed person, one-half of it being from the employed person and the other half from his employer, and that percentage should be raised gradually over every 5-year period until after 20 years the contribution is 5 percent . . .
> . . . if people who are now under 30 years of age, and who begin to contribute in 1937 . . . work regularly and steadily to the age of 65, [they] will have made a substantial contribution and will have built up an insurance reserve in a great fund which will entitle [them] to collect this benefit.[53]

Similarly, Witte told the Committee that "These annuities will be contractual and free from any means test."[54] And Princeton economics professor J. Douglas Brown, who advised the Committee on Economic Security about the old-age provisions of the bill, testified that "It is insurance not relief. It is contributory and contractual and affords an annuity as a matter of right. . . . The amounts paid to the aged are related to contributions made to the fund, not to need." Among the reasons he and his colleagues recommended worker contributions, Brown added, was that "By contributing, the individual worker establishes an earned contractual right to his annuity through his own thrift."[55]

The gravity of this cannot be overstated. Testifying in congressional hearings is a serious matter; witnesses are routinely put under oath. Secretary Perkins had behind her a career in government dealing with labor legislation and labor relations, and Drs. Witte and Brown were prominent economists in, respectively, labor and industrial relations, and they surely knew what a contract is: a legal and binding document spelling out legally enforceable rights and responsibilities of all parties, who enter into it voluntarily. Probably Perkins and Witte, at least, had seen the text of the bill before testifying; if not, certainly they had a good grasp of the bill's substance. Their prepared statements and their performance under questioning by committee members afterward are lucid and articulate and give every evidence of solid preparation. They could hardly have failed to know that the bill contained no contract and created no contractual rights. It strains credulity to think that they had no idea that what they were saying was not true. The members of the Ways and Means Committee and Finance Committee had doubtless all read the bill already, and likewise must have known that it created no contractual rights. Then as now, most members of Congress were lawyers, so they too surely knew what a contract is. And the committee members, like the administration's witnesses themselves, must have known that the reservation of power clause, giving Congress "the right to alter, amend, or repeal any or all provisions of this act," nullified all this talk of contractual annuities and contractual rights. Yet one searches the printed transcripts of the hearings in vain for any challenge to Perkins or anyone else on this, by anyone on either committee.

Another of the deepest and most formidable roots of Social Security's crisis had its origin here. Americans are an intensely and uniquely rights-conscious people. Our very existence as an independent nation springs from our colonial forebears' passionate sense of grievance at the purported flouting of inalienable rights by Great Britain. Many Americans retain a very zealous sense of property rights; indeed a very bitter battle is shaping up between environmental protection bureaucrats and advocates on the one hand and property owners on the other.[56] The great political movements of our history were, and still are, propelled by fervent belief in rights: the right of black people to be free, the rights of women, the rights of labor, a "right to privacy," an unborn child's "right to life," a woman's "right to choose," and so on. To assert or deny the existence of rights is a most serious matter in America, arousing sentiments which, once engaged, are apt to intensify to the point of making rational discussion or compromise difficult and perhaps even impossible. And once a right becomes entrenched in Americans' minds, abridging or trammeling it becomes very risky, especially if the persons involved are organized and politically powerful. In asserting that Social Security's benefits would come as a matter of earned right, its proponents were taking a momentous step. This endlessly reiterated assertion bought Social Security immense public support, but the long run price, as we shall see, was to lock it into a rigid position about paying benefits, and seriously impair its ability to respond to changing economic circumstances.

Meanwhile, the administration was selling its economic security proposal to the public. On March 16, 1935, the Columbia Broadcasting System broadcast a symposium entitled "The Economic Security Program," reviewing the administration's proposed system, and later published as a pamphlet. Among the participants was Murray W. Latimer, chairman of the Railroad Retirement Board, who spoke on the subject of "Security Against Old-Age Dependency" and described the proposed compulsory old-age insurance system thus: "Under this system men and women, with the aid of their employers, will, through their own contributions, build up the right to an annuity of their own *on an inalienable contractual basis* [italics added], which will enable them to retire from gainful employment when they become old."[57] So now members of the public, as well as the House and Senate committees originating the bill, were receiving assurances of inalienable, contractual rights that did not exist.

Again, the point is not intended to impugn motives or malign characters. Perhaps these persons sincerely believed that they were acting for the best, perhaps out of concern at the extreme suffering the Depression inflicted. Regarding the administration's attempt to pack the Supreme Court, Joseph Alsop and Turner Catledge observed,

> That the end justifies the means has always been a great point of belief with the more intellectual members of the President's inner circle. Convinced as they are of the vital necessity and wisdom of their schemes, these men have rarely boggled at expedients promising to bring them closer to their goals . . . [58]

Perhaps that same lack of scruple drove the administration figures' conduct regarding Social Security, beginning with inaccurate testimony before Congress; perhaps not; but whether that is true or not is immaterial. The crucial facts are that Social Security was being presented and promoted at the very beginning in a way that was highly misleading on crucial points—and to both the Congress and the public. Deliberately or not, a false consciousness about Social Security was already being created.

Averting Trouble with the Supreme Court: Semantic Cleansing and Other Tactics

In the meantime, the Ways and Means Committee was working on the bill, and making numerous changes. Treasury Secretary Morgenthau, acting with

President Roosevelt's approval, insisted in his testimony that the tax rates be raised sufficiently to create a large reserve fund, projected to reach $50 billion by 1980; the Committee adopted Morgenthau's proposed higher rates.[59] Title V, providing for voluntary old-age annuities to be purchased from the government, was dropped.[60] Most importantly for our purposes, the bill was purged of insurance language, and the tax and old-age benefit titles were physically separated.

This was done because both the administration and its supporters in Congress were deeply worried that the compulsory old-age program would be ruled unconstitutional by the Supreme Court. While the Constitution unquestionably gave the federal government a taxing power, it was by no means clear that the Constitution gave it the power to distribute benefits or create a compulsory social insurance scheme. When preparing the bill, the administration had rejected a pure federal unemployment insurance system for a mixed federal-state one for that very reason; the attorney general's office, Perkins recalled, "repeatedly advised us that it was a doubtful constitutional point and that we should be very careful."[61] As Witte wrote later, "It was understood that the validity of a federal old-age insurance system was doubtful, but it was thought that it might be possible to set up such a system under the taxing power of Congress."[62]

It was no idle concern; on January 7, 1935, just ten days before the Social Security bill was introduced, the Supreme Court, voting 5-4, ruled against the administration in the so-called "hot oil" case. To help restrict oil production, the National Industrial Recovery Act (NIRA) gave the president authority to prohibit interstate transport of oil in amounts greater than those allowed by state laws. This, the Court held, was an unconstitutional delegation of authority rightly belonging to Congress, and the oil provision was struck down. With this decision, the NIRA itself, one of the centerpieces of the New Deal legislation enacted thus far, seemed in jeopardy.[63]

The drafting of the economic security bill was going forward at that very same time. Thomas Eliot, the administration's draftsman, had drafted some provisions of the bill in October and November, but most of the work had to wait until the Committee on Economic Security had nailed down policy decisions in December.[64] So it is quite likely that the Supreme Court peril was prominent in Eliot's mind as he worked in late December and early January.

Eliot tried to present a federal old-age insurance scheme "in as constitutionally plausible form as possible."[65] To lessen the resemblance to an insurance program, he separated the tax and benefit provisions of the old-age insurance program into two titles. However, the two titles, III and IV, were physically adjacent, and having the old-age benefit and taxation provisions in adjacent titles gave a strong appearance that the taxes and benefit payments did in fact form a single, unified system of insurance—which of course they did, as the testimony of Perkins, Witte, and others cited above made unmistakably clear. Moreover, Title IV, Section 403 appropriated proceeds from taxes imposed under Title III, "to be allocated to the old-age fund established under this title," and Section 405 repeatedly referred to taxes paid on one's behalf "under Section 301 of this Act" as a condition for receiving benefits.[66] All too clearly from those cross-references, the two titles did indeed create a unified insurance system. And the original administration bill, as we saw, was full of insurance language. Clearly, this could mean trouble with the Court.

Moreover, while the Ways and Means Committee was working on the bill, during March and April 1935, the New Deal suffered defeats in the lower courts, and the National Industrial Recovery Act was under fire in lower courts and headed for a Supreme Court test. And a case involving the Railroad Retirement Act of 1934, which had created a compulsory, contributory retirement pension program for railroad employees in many respects similar to the bill's old-age insurance provisions, was before the Supreme Court. If the Court found against the Railroad Retirement Act, what would it do to old-age insurance? In fact, just a few weeks later, on May 6, it would in fact find the Railroad Retirement Act unconstitutional.[67] The threat from the Court was very much alive, and no doubt very much on the Congressmen's minds.

It was necessary, then, to destroy anything that could give the Supreme Court grounds for deciding that Social Security was an insurance program. Accordingly, Ways and Means Committee chairman Robert Doughton instructed Middleton Beaman, chief draftsman of the House, to redraft the bill. Beaman went over it meticulously, conferring with Eliot for hours on specific phrases.[68] In the Committee's bill (H.R. 7260), all references to "old-age insurance" and "old-age annuities" disappeared; the "Social Insurance Board" became the "Social Security Board."[69] The Committee created a new Title II containing the benefit provisions, and a new Title VIII, Taxes With Respect to Employment, to create an impression that they were unrelated, and enable the bill to survive Court scrutiny. In addition, neither Title II nor Title VIII contains a single cross-reference to the other, nor does the new Title VII, establishing the Social Security Board, refer to either of them.[70]

Seemingly, the three titles are as isolated and unrelated as so many islands. Yet there is a tip-off that the dissociation is spurious: the definitions of "wages" and "employment" given in Section 210, used to describe the basis for old-age benefit payments in Section 202, are identical with those given in Section 811, used to describe the basis for income tax on employees in Section 801.[71]

Eliot admitted long afterward that the seemingly "awkward arrangement" of having the old age insurance tax in one title with the benefit provision "in a separate title many pages distant," much criticized in the press for its seeming poor draftsmanship and disorganization, was indeed deliberate. "It was designed to make it easier for the Supreme Court to sustain the measure's validity—not to fool the court but to give the justices a technical peg on which to hang their hats if they so desired."[72] Given the enormous effort the administration had put into preparing the original bill; its deep anxiety about the constitutionality of its provisions, even going so far as to adopt a clumsy federal-state system of unemployment insurance rather than risk seeing the bill struck down; the rising concern about the reception the bill would get from the Supreme Court, which was showing increasing hostility to the New Deal even as the bill was in committee; and the semantic cleansing by the Committee, Eliot's explanation is weak and disingenuous. Clearly, the physical separation of the titles was meant in fervent hopes of enabling the legislation to tiptoe past a deeply feared Court.

This interpretation is strengthened by what Paul Douglas, a sympathizer but an honest man, wrote regarding the Act's unemployment-insurance titles, Title III (unemployment insurance grants to the states) and Title IX (employer payroll taxes to pay for them), likewise widely separated. Title III has no reference to the source of the grants and treats them as if funded out of general revenue, for fear that if the payroll tax been earmarked specifically for defraying unemployment insurance costs, the constitutionality of the program would have looked dubious. To shore up the constitutionality of unemployment insurance, then, the two titles were widely separated, and

> a legal fiction is maintained that they have no connection with each other. The legal theory which is built up is that the added revenue which will flow into the possession of the federal government will then merge with the general funds of the government and hence will not be the separate source from which the expenditures authorized in Title III are derived. It can then be argued that these revenues are derived from the general resources of the government into which the various sources of revenue have been inextricably mixed and which by this process will have lost their separate identities.
>
> All this may be sound from a legal standpoint but in terms of reality it must frankly be recognized that the act as a whole commits the government to certain expenditures in Title III and then in Title IX gives to the government sufficient added revenue from which these expenses can be met. . . . it is clear from a logical point of view that the outlay under the earlier title was in fact intended to be met from the revenues provided by the latter.[73]

This is a confession that this flow of revenues levied for a specific purpose into a general revenue pool and out again as "general revenues," all taint of earmarking washed away, to that specific destination where they were intended to go all along, is a scheme of what can fairly be called money laundering. Replace "Title III" with "Title II" and "Title IX" with "Title "VIII, and all of the foregoing describes the Social Security titles. Indeed, Douglas admitted that "as in the unemployment features of the bill," the old-age tax and benefit titles were separated "because of the belief that this will enable the act better to run the constitutional gamut."[74] Moreover, despite the formal distinction between the two titles, "there is in fact a close and immediate connection between them. The individual benefits to be paid are computed upon the basis of the contributions or taxes levied and upon nothing else."[75]

This maneuver did not deceive the minority members of the Ways and Means Committee. Their section of the Committee's Report protested that

> These titles are interdependent, and neither is of any consequence without the other. Neither of them has relation to any other substantive title of the bill. Neither is constitutional. . . .
> The Federal Government has no power to impose this system upon private industry.
> The best legal talent that the Attorney General's office and the Brain Trust could marshal has for weeks applied itself to the task of trying to bring these titles within constitutional limitations. Their best effort is only a plain circumvention. . . . The separation is a separation in words only. There is no separation in spirit or intent. These two titles must stand or fall together.[76]

Nor did this separation escape notice in the House debate that followed. Allen Treadway (R-MA), a minority member of the Ways and Means Committee, reiterated the Report's minority views on April 12 and elaborated that the Constitution does not authorize federal taxation "for any other purpose than the raising of revenues for public uses. . . . The money raised by the tax is not intended for the support of the Government but to pay the benefits provided under Title II to the same employees who are taxed under Title VIII." Congressman Treadway also pointed out that the exemptions from the tax under Section 811 (b) and the exemptions from benefits under Section 210 (b) were identical.[77] On April 15, his colleague Thomas Jenkins (R-OH), likewise a member of the Committee, raised the same objections.[78]

A few other alert members of Congress made some other damaging observations. Congressman Daniel Reed (R-NY) argued that Titles II and VIII were an unconstitutional takeover of governing rights which properly belonged to the states, and informed the House that Franklin Roosevelt himself, when governor of New York, had said in a radio broadcast on March 2, 1930, that the states' governing rights were all those which the Constitution or its amendments had not granted to the national government. Whereas the Constitution and its amendments had given Congress the power to legislate about prohibition, "this is not the case" with "other vital problems of government," including such things as insurance and social welfare. "In these," Governor Roosevelt had added, "Washington must not be encouraged to interfere."[79] And Senator Daniel Hastings (R-DE) observed that the creation of an old-age reserve account for future generations "is not a contract that can be enforced by anybody. What we do here is merely to pass an act of the Congress, which may be changed by any Congress in the future, and has in it nothing upon which American citizens can depend."[80]

All of this was true, but to no avail. The House contained over three hundred Democrats, most of whom, like Representative John McCormack (D-MA), accepted and reiterated the administration's line that the old-age benefits were an "earned annuity . . . as a matter of right,"[81] and were not swayed by the unconstitutionality argument. Moreover, the old-age assistance and unemployment compensation provisions were widely popular in Congress. And most Democratic Congressmen were intensely loyal to Roosevelt. The administration wanted the bill, and that was enough for them. Social Security passed each house by lopsided margins: 372-33 in the House on April 19 and 77-6 in the Senate on June 19. Most of the Republican critics voted for Social Security, including Treadway and Jenkins.[82] After a conference committee resolved differences between the chambers' versions of the bill, final approval by the House and Senate occurred on August 8 and 9, respectively, and President Roosevelt signed it on August 14.[83]

The 1935 Social Security Act

The Social Security Act of 1935 (H.R. 7260, Public Law No. 74-271) contained eleven titles, most of them not germane for our purposes. Those which are, are worth examining in detail, as much as for what they did not say as for what they did. Title VIII, Taxes With Respect to Employment, levied taxes on wages received after December 31, 1936 on employees in employment other than agricultural labor, domestic service in a private home, casual labor outside the employer's line of work, service on an American or foreign vessel, work in state or local government, and work in any nonprofit organization. Maximum taxable annual income was $3,000. The rates were scheduled to rise gradually: one percent a year in calendar 1937-1939, 1.5 percent a year in 1940-1942, 2 percent in 1943-1945, 2.5 percent in 1946-1948, and 3 percent thereafter. Employers were to pay matching excise taxes.[84]

Title II, Federal Old-Age Benefits, created an "Old-Age Reserve Account" in the Treasury to which, every fiscal year, funds were to be appropriated sufficient to pay benefits, based on accepted actuarial principles and assuming an interest rate of 3 percent compounded annually. The secretary of the treasury was required to invest amounts credited to the Reserve Account and unnecessary for current benefit outlays in interest-bearing U.S. government debt (including special unmarketable debt issued exclusively for this account for this purpose) and debt whose principal and interest were guaranteed by the U.S. government.[85] There was, however, absolutely nothing in the Act which stated that the money in the Reserve Account belonged to the taxpaying employees or was being held for them in a trust fund, or creating individual savings or annuity accounts for the employees.

Beginning January 1, 1942, monthly benefits were to be paid to qualified individuals—persons at least sixty-five years old who had received wages for employment on at least five days between December 31, 1936 and attaining age sixty-five, each day in a different calendar year, and who earned no less than $2,000 in that period in employment other than the exceptions mentioned in the tax title. However, the beneficiary had to be retired; if he received wages from such employment, he would lose his benefit for each month in which this occurred (this provision is known as the "retirement earnings test"). Benefits were based on total earnings from December 31, 1936 to attainment of age sixty-five, the smallest benefit being $15, the largest $85. If the individual died before reaching age sixty-five, his estate would receive a lump sum equal to 3.5 percent of his total wage income since December 31, 1936. If he died after he began collecting benefits, his estate would get a lump sum sufficient to bring his total receipts to 3.5 percent of total wage earnings since 1936. If he had worked in a covered occupation and reached sixty-five without qualifying for benefits, he would receive a lump sum of 3.5 percent of total wage earnings since 1936.[86] Thus, under the original Act, the worker would always get back at least as much as he had paid in.

However, the Act, like the original bill, contained no contract language whatsoever. The closest it came was to state in Section 202 that "Every qualified individual . . . shall be entitled to receive . . . an old-age benefit."[87] Nor was there any mention of an insurance policy being written for, or issued to, any individual.

Title VII created a three-member Social Security Board to oversee administration of Social Security, study, and make recommendations for the best means of "providing economic security through social insurance," and report regularly to Congress on administration of the program.[88] The first Social Security Board was chaired by John G. Winant, a former Republican governor of New Hampshire, and also included Altmeyer and Vincent Miles, former Democratic National Committeeman from Arkansas.[89]

Significantly, the Act, like the original bill, also included, in Title XI, General Provisions, a reservation of power clause, Section 1104: "The right to alter, amend, or repeal any provision of this Act is hereby reserved to the Congress."[90]

In his speech at the signing of the Social Security Act, President Roosevelt described the law as "a cornerstone in a structure which is being built but is by no means complete."[91] In light of Roosevelt's earlier expressed desire for universal, comprehensive "cradle to the grave" social insurance, this was a strong hint that sooner or later, the Act would be expanded in some fashion.

Marketing after Passage

Perkins, Winant, and Altmeyer promptly set about promoting Social Security intensively in articles and radio broadcasts. This promotional campaign drew heavily on the notion of benefits as an earned right and depicted Social Security as insurance.

Just four days after President Roosevelt signed the bill, an article by Secretary Perkins appeared in the *New York Times* Magazine giving a comprehensive description of the Social Security Act's purposes and provisions. Its "old-age annuities," she wrote, "will not be granted as a matter of charity" but will be "earned annuities to which the recipients are entitled as a matter of right." Like Roosevelt, she made it clear that the Act was just a beginning and that further developments would follow.[92]

On September 2, 1935, speaking over the radio on CBS, Perkins again described the unemployment and old-age insurance provisions of the Act, telling her listeners that monthly old-age benefits would go to individuals who had "contributed to the insurance fund" with "contributions" proportional to wages, thus linking tax payments and benefits, but without mentioning rights.[93] Altmeyer followed her onto the air the next day and informed his listeners that benefits under "the Federal old age insurance system will be paid as a matter of *right* [Altmeyer's emphasis] to qualified individuals who have been paying their contributions into the Federal Treasury."[94] A few minutes later, he stated that benefits would go to "qualified individuals" in proportion to wages earned after January 1, 1937, when "they must commence making contributions to a Federal fund" and drove the point home:

> It is most important to again emphasize that these payments will be made as a matter of right and not on the basis of showing a need. That is to say, qualified individuals will receive these benefits regardless of the amount of property or income they possess, just as they would receive benefits from a private insurance company to which they had paid premiums.[95]

Chairman Winant did his bit, too, in both speeches and articles. Like Altmeyer and Perkins, he told his audiences that benefits would come as a right.[96] Speaking before the New York City Control, Controllers' Institute of America on March 30, 1936, he pointed out that "insurance implies some form of contractual protection."[97] Winant did not add that the Act contained no contracts at all; it was left to former Secretary of the Treasury Arthur Ballantine to tell the ninth conference of the American Association for Social Security a month later that the Act placed old-age protection "on the basis of contract—although a moral rather than a legal contract,"[98] a distinction which no one else in the Social Security camp had bothered to make.

Thus, within a year of the bill's first being introduced, Social Security's creators and administrators had already repeatedly acted in a misleading and manipulative fashion. This was manifest already by the Roosevelt administration in its initial approaches to the two other branches of the federal government. Concerned about the Supreme Court declaring Social Security an unconstitutional scheme of government insurance, the administration had placed the tax and benefit provisions in two separate albeit physically adjacent titles in its bill, so as to give the Court the impression that Social Security was not an insurance program. Yet, as the printed transcripts of the hearings reveal, administration officials told the congressional committees that the program was insurance, obviously to win their support.

The second, and much more serious, instance concerned how Social Security was depicted to the Supreme Court and to the public. The administration's allies in Congress, working with the administration, had taken the anti-Court precaution much further, physically separating these titles and very carefully picking the text of the bill clean of insurance language so as to lessen the likelihood of the resultant legislation's being found unconstitutional. Yet in their promotions of Social Security to the public, the administration's spokesmen were leaning very heavily on that selfsame insurance language. The evidence is clear that two diametrically opposed versions of reality were being concocted, each crafted not for the purpose of accurately depicting reality, but for the purpose of shaping the beliefs and behavior of its intended audience. The administration wanted the public to believe that Social Security was insurance, so that the public would accept and support Social Security. It emphatically did not want the Supreme Court to even suspect that Social Security was insurance, lest it find the program unconstitutional.

Given the time and effort that went into each of these two endeavors, it is clear that the administration knew what it was doing. That this was so, and that the administrators of Social Security were well aware of the danger if the Supreme Court caught on to the very different version peddled to the public, is confirmed by how Social Security's publicity effort responded to the the the Supreme Court decision in early 1936 striking down the Agricultural Adjustment Act. Before the Court killed the AAA, Thomas Eliot, who was now Social Security's general counsel, had told Louis Remnick, head of Social Security's Informational Service, not to worry about how publicity statements might affect the Supreme Court's view of Social Security's constitutionality. Eliot thought the Court would confine itself to the language of the Act itself and disregard publicity materials. After AAA was struck down, Eliot reversed himself, and the Informational Service was instructed "to play down the use of such terms as insurance and not to allow, in any official reports or publicity material, the coupling of the tax titles (VIII and IX) with the two insurance titles (II and III) lest the Court take judicial notice when considering the constitutionality of the act." Indeed, "every public statement relating to these titles was checked and double-checked to see that the language used was sufficiently opaque."[99]

A sympathizer could call all this clever tactics justified by the imperatives of politics. A critic could call it cynical, mendacious, and duplicitous. But the important points for the history of Social Security are that the administration was laboring mightily to affect the climate of belief—and that the understanding of Social Security it was striving to create was at variance with reality. That is, a false consciousness.

The Early Media Reception

On the whole, the mainstream media reception to the Social Security Act was friendly and respectful, not to say supine. The vast majority of media reporting of the Act's passage and provisions simply repeated the administration's depiction of the program.

Thus even while the Act was still wending its way through Congress, *Time* wrote that "The U. S. government will in effect become a great U. S. Insurance Co."[100] Reporting on August 15 that Roosevelt had signed the bill the day before, the *New York Times* told its readers that Social Security was "an annuity plan sponsored by the government," under which workers would get "earned annuities regardless of other income" out of "a fund built up by joint contributions of employers and employees."[101] *Newsweek* obligingly used language even the administration's allies in Congress had thought best deleted, referring to "Old Age Insurance," with taxation to supply "insurance premiums."[102] So for that matter did the *Literary Digest* and the *Independent Woman*.[103]

Editorial comment was lopsidedly favorable. *Collier's*, bitterly complaining that America had been "incredibly laggard in establishing social insurance," hailed the Act as "a good job well done."[104] According to the *United States News*, 63 percent of commenting newspapers approved of passage of the Social Security Act, many very warmly, the St. Paul *Daily News* calling it "an act of historic importance"; the Altoona, Pennsylvania *Mirror* saw it as the administration's "greatest achievement"; the Canton, Ohio *Repository* deemed it "the greatest social experiment ever conducted." The dissenting 37 percent, such as the Charlotte, North Carolina *Observer*, voiced fear that its taxes would cripple industry.[105] The New York *World-Telegram*, the Norfolk *Virginian-Pilot*, and the Syracuse *Post-Standard* praised the Social Security Act in similar terms, while the Council Bluffs, Iowa *Nonpareil* scourged Congress for "supinely" passing a bill that would eventually turn America into a "Socialistic State."[106] In a brief, quiet editorial, the *Detroit News* voiced the earnest hope that the bill's main provisions would be successfully implemented.[107]

Like the early accounts, the magazine articles that appeared later, elaborating on how Social Security would operate, the taxes workers would pay and the benefits they would receive, uncritically accepted the administration's version. Use of insurance language was routine; John T. Flynn went so far as to describe Social Security as "the great old-age insurance system . . . with its 25,000,000 customers."[108] Benefits, these writers also told their readers, would come as a right.[109] One piece, which argued that Social Security was incomplete and in need of amendment because it didn't cover death and disability, did point out that "pensions" and "insurance" were "misnomers and misrepresentations of the facts"—only to maintain instead that the employer was paying an "annuity" and the employee was engaged in "the purchase of an annuity for himself."[110]

Columbia University economist Eveline Burns, a prominent social insurance advocate, went even further when she wrote a book expounding the problem of insecurity and the need for progressive legislation to tackle it, presenting a detailed explanation of how the Social Security Act worked, and speculating on its future and constitutionality. In it she committed the same misrepresentation as Perkins, Witte, and Brown had before the congressional committees. The Act's old-age benefit program, Professor Burns wrote,

> gives cash payments (called annuities) as a contractual right to all workers who have contributed toward their cost in the past. . . .
> The annuity, being paid as part of a contract between the contributing worker and the federal government, belongs absolutely to the annuitant . . . .
> The essence of the contributory plan is that it gives people a contractual right to an income in the future.[111]

The Act gave people, of course, no such thing.

Figures on the left, such as muckraking novelist and socialist Upton Sinclair, assailed Social Security for not going far enough and paying niggardly benefits.[112] Social insurance advocate Abraham Epstein grumbled that the administration had neglected to canvass social insurance experts for their advice, and that the Social Security Act was sloppy, economically unsound, and violated the essential principles of social insurance.[113]

Only two serious and penetrating conservative criticisms appeared in the popular press at this point, both of them in the *Saturday Evening Post*. Both merit mention, because they fingered serious flaws in Social Security and some of the issues they raised persist to this day. In a long, well-informed, two-part article which appeared in March 1936, Frank Parker Stockbridge, besides pointing out the payroll tax's regressivity, the burden of taxes on industry, and other problems, observed, rightly, that Social Security contained no contract and that its promise to pay benefits in the future rests solely on "the good faith of the Federal Government and the good will of future Congresses."[114] He went on to demolish the assiduously promoted analogy with private insurance:

> . . . the payments required from employers and employees are compulsory . . . They are taxes, not premium payments. There is, therefore, no contractual relation between the individual who expects to receive his annuity in due time, and the Government which collects taxes from him for that purpose. The . . . taxes . . . create no vested rights. They become part of the general revenue of the Federal Government. And that Government may, whenever the Congress wishes to, increase or reduce those taxes, pay annuitants at a lower or—more probably—at a higher rate than originally contemplated; or even refuse to pay expectant beneficiaries anything at all.[115]

Stockbridge, who had studied the text of the Social Security Act and conversed with Dr. Witte on the law, contrasted the situation of the insurance policyholder who had a contract, and the Social Security taxpayer who had nothing but a revocable promise.[116]

For his part, Garet Garrett opened his September 1936 piece with a scathing attack on Social Security's paternalism that would cheer a privatization advocate's heart: a dialogue between an individual who wanted to do as he liked with his own money and make his own provision for old age and a government which retorted that he couldn't be trusted to save or invest his money himself and would too often lose it if he did so. Social Security, Garrett went on, would necessarily mean that the young would support the old since there was no one else to do it. The reserve fund, moreover, would be bogus, since nobody can earn interest investing in his own debt. He concluded that perhaps all the economic criticisms of Social Security were beside the point; as an instrument for extending government's power over the population and extracting resources, Social Security was, in fact, a colossal success.[117]

But that was all. Perhaps the conservatives were stunned into silence by the overwhelming majorities Social Security had won in both houses of Congress, including the votes of most Republican members. When Social Security's opponents finally acted, it was in the worst possible way.

The 1936 Election: "Cruel Hoax," Pay Envelopes, and Lots of Insurance Talk

During the 1936 presidential election campaign, Social Security burst into prominence in the national consciousness amid bitter controversy. On September 26, Republican nominee Alfred "Alf" Landon, in a major speech in Milwaukee, Wisconsin, proclaimed his "firm belief" in old-age pensions but denounced Social Security as "unjust, unworkable, stupidly drafted and wastefully financed." Social Security, Landon elaborated, wouldn't start paying pensions until 1942, covered only about half the workers, and would pay very modest pensions, yet beginning in January 1937 would impose "the largest tax bill in history." Landon pointed out—rightly, as subsequent economic analysis has confirmed—that "the whole tax will be borne either by the employee or by the consumer through higher prices," because the employer would simply shift his share of the burden. Calling this tax Social Security, he said, was "a fraud on the working man." Moreover, while the administration said the taxes would go into a reserve fund and be invested at interest, which would help pay the old-age benefits, in fact, Landon maintained, the Treasury would use the worker's cash to buy government bonds, and spend the money on "current deficits and new extravagances." It was as if a father took deductions from his children's wages to invest for their old age, "invested" it in "his own IOU," and spent the money, leaving the children, in their old age, with nothing but those IOUs. Hence, Landon asserted, its forced savings were "a cruel hoax." Finally, he raised the peril of intrusive and cumbersome federal record keeping.[118]

For reasons known only to himself, Landon did not raise the key issue of Social Security's dubious constitutional status—at a time when the Supreme Court had invalidated several New Deal laws, and the Court and constitutionality were on people's minds. He was likewise silent on the absence of a contract, on whether or not Social Security was really insurance, on Social Security's paternalism, and on the possibility of future unaffordable tax burdens. The opportunity to criticize Social Security in terms of fundamentals, as Stockbridge and Garrett had done, was thrown away. As Republicans are wont to do, Landon conceded the fundamentals (i.e., philosophy and goals) to his Democratic opponent; confined his objections to concrete practicalities, questions of dollars and cents; complained that the Democrats' policy was a bad means to a good end; and maintained that the Republican alternative was better.

Nevertheless, Landon's speech did raise legitimate issues, and was so recognized at the time. A *New York Times* editorial two days later lauded it as "a genuine analysis" of Social Security and "a real contribution to public understanding," and found Landon's criticism of the old-age reserve fund "sound." The reserve invested in the government's own securities would be, the *Times* wrote bluntly, "fictitious."[119]

Suddenly Social Security was a hot election issue. But rather than seize the chance to raise serious, substantial matters that Landon had muffed, the Republicans opted for sensationalism. A group of Detroit industrialists resentful of the excise tax which they would have to start paying in January, and the record keeping burden Social Security would impose, hit on the idea of using pay envelopes to convey attacks on Social Security to their workers, and asked the Republican National Committee to implement the idea. In October, the RNC shipped to employers, at their request, millions of anti-Social Security posters, pamphlets, and inserts to be put in workers' pay envelopes. Numerous employers in Illinois, Michigan, Ohio, Pennsylvania and Indiana went along, and printed on or inserted in their workers' pay envelopes for the next payday a notice that read,

PAY DEDUCTION — Effective January 1, 1937, we are compelled by a Roosevelt "New Deal" law to make a 1% deduction from your wages and turn it over to the government. Finally, this might go as high as 4% [including taxes to finance unemployment compensation]. You might get this money back in future years . . . but only if Congress decides to make the appropriation for this purpose. There is NO guarantee. Decide before November 3—Election Day, whether or not you wish to take these chances.[120]

The Republican National Committee chairman, John Hamilton, and the Hearst newspapers also charged that Social Security would require each worker to wear a dog tag for identification purposes; on November 1 the Hearst papers ran photographs of a man wearing a dog tag. (A company had in fact proposed to furnish nameplates for people to wear or carry—a suggestion which, incredibly enough, Social Security Board planning officials had recommended for acceptance, but which Altmeyer had wisely turned down.)[121]

Strictly speaking, the pay envelope notices didn't say anything that wasn't true. But they told only half-truths, neglecting to tell workers that their employers would pay matching taxes and that Social Security did pay benefits. The dog tag scare, however, was deplorable, in the same class as the TV scare commercials used against Barry Goldwater in 1964. Worse, an excellent opportunity for searching, serious criticism of Social Security and a national debate on the program was being squandered. Another such chance would not appear for about half a century. And these gambits provoked a response with equally bad consequences. From the long perspective of history, Landon, the Republicans, and the employers did not only their cause but their country a grievous disservice.

Because Social Security did, after all, require payroll taxes, the pay envelope notices left the Democrats stuck for a reply, and at first they parried weakly, telling workers that the American Federation of Labor endorsed Social Security. The administration tried to shrug off the attack. But not for long: "Democratic headquarters began to hear unnerving stories of Roosevelt buttons thrown away in front of plants, of Roosevelt stickers ripped from automobiles, of Roosevelt posters in industrial towns spattered or torn down."[122] The "pay envelope scare" was drawing blood.

Acting quickly, the Social Security Board issued a rebuttal on October 25, written by Altmeyer, denouncing the anti-Social Security propaganda as misleading. Under Social Security, "workers will build up rights to the payment of regular monthly benefits," which will be "larger than he could purchase from any private insurance company with the taxes he will have paid the government." Moreover, the benefits "are paid as a matter of right" regardless of the worker's income or property.[123] Social Security mounted an intense promotional campaign. Fifty million copies of an explanatory leaflet about Social Security and assignment of Social Security numbers were distributed at factory gates, with union cooperation.[124] A film, *We the People and Social Security*, had been prepared and was not scheduled for release until after the election. At the White House's suggestion, Altmeyer ordered it distributed immediately and as widely as possible. By November 3, some four million people had seen *We the People and Social Security*.[125] What they saw in this thirty-five minute film, included animated cartoon footage depicting dollars trotting into the hands of elderly persons.[126] It was a powerful and simple device, well calculated to play upon the fear of destitution in old age that was making the Townsend Plan so attractive. A four-page pamphlet, *Security in Your Old Age*, of which eight million copies were printed, also received widespread distribution before the election. Social Security sent at least 3.3 million copies to the American Federation of Labor and thousands more to the Democratic National Committee. The pamphlet's text was also sent to two thousand newspapers as a press release. Wilbur Cohen and others went to New York to write speeches for Democratic candidates, and provide information for the Democrats to use to respond to the pay envelope campaign.[127]

Democratic politicians joined in the counterattack, stressing Social Security's safety and leaning heavily on the analogy with insurance. Senator Wagner, understandably enraged at the attack on the bill that bore his name, denounced the Republicans bitterly and said that Social Security guaranteed benefits and was "an absolutely safe system" because it was supported by taxes.[128] His colleague from Connecticut, Francis Maloney, gave two long radio broadcasts on Social Security in late October. Senator Maloney, who had been active in the insurance industry, denied charges that Social Security, which he described as "an insurance policy against a living future and the adversity of old age," would harm the insurance business. Rather, it would make people more annuity-insurance minded. (This, indeed, turned out to be true.) As for the much-maligned payroll tax, "there is no pay cut in this bill, nor any pay reduction, nor a pay-roll tax." On the contrary, "it is a pay increase," since the employer contributes a matching amount. "This pay-roll deduction is not a tax. It is an insurance premium of a few cents a week to be put away by the powerful Federal Government, and to be returned to American workmen . . ."[129]

President Roosevelt himself entered the fray on October 21 near the end of a speech in Worcester, Massachusetts. He briefly reminded workers that Social Security was collecting equal shares of tax money from employers and workers. "And both shares—yours and the employer's—are being held for the sole benefit of the worker himself." Two days later, he mentioned the issue in passing again, in a radio broadcast to businessmen's dinners held all over the country. Noting that "a few employers are spreading half-truths" about Social Security, he pointed out that both the employee's and the employer's tax dollars "are held in a Government trust fund solely for the social security of the workers."[130]

The Republican National Committee retaliated quickly, calling the president's assertion "a complete misstatement." Worker and employer contributions, said the RNC, would go into the Treasury's general fund, not the old-age reserve account, and Congress, not compelled to appropriate them to the old-age reserve account, could spend them "to build warships, roads, or to pay Professor [Rexford] Tugwell's salary [Tugwell was a key member of the New Deal's Brain Trust]." Workers, they added, had no guarantee that any money would be there for them in their old age.[131] And Roosevelt's glancing references did not dispose of the pay envelope matter, which was now giving Democrats and their allies a real fright. Pennsylvania's governor, George Earle denounced employers for spreading "half truths and deliberate falsehoods," in a letter to U. S. Attorney General Homer Cummings, and asked the Justice Department to stop them. On October 27, urgent messages reached President Roosevelt from Michigan's governor, Frank Murphy, Labor's Nonpartisan League, and others telling him that he had to speak out promptly to counter the pay envelope campaign.[132] Accordingly, two days later, in Wilkes-Barre, Pennsylvania, Roosevelt weighed in again. This time, he went much further in portraying Social Security as insurance:

> Why do these employers seek to repeal the Social Security Act? Because under the Act they have to pay far more than half of the insurance given to the workers.
> Get these facts straight.
> The Act provides for two kinds of insurance for the worker.
> For that insurance both the employer and the worker pay premiums, just as you pay premiums for any other insurance policy. Those premiums are collected in the form of the taxes you hear so much about.
> The first kind of insurance covers old age. Here the employer contributes one dollar of premium for every dollar of premium contributed by the worker; but both dollars are held by the Government solely for the benefit of the worker in his old age.
> In effect, we have set up a savings account for the old age of the worker. Because the employer is called upon to contribute on a fifty-fifty basis, that savings account gives exactly two dollars of security for every dollar put up by the worker.[133]

Roosevelt also lashed the employers for "the contemptible, unpatriotic suggestion that some future Congress will steal these insurance funds for other purposes." If they believe that, they have no confidence in American government, he added, suggesting that they emigrate "to some other Nation in which they have more faith." In Camden, New Jersey that same day, he said much the same thing. He took the matter up yet again in his famous fighting speech in Madison Square Garden on October 31, at greater length, and with a much nastier attack on the patriotism of reserve fund critics. The president referred to both old-age insurance and unemployment insurance as an "insurance policy," and added that "the insurance policy that is bought for him is far more favorable to him than any policy that any private insurance company could afford to issue."[134]

There was, in fact, no "insurance policy" or "savings account" in Social Security, and no dollars were being "held" in a "trust fund," as the financial industry, in which Roosevelt himself had worked,[135] understands the term. Surely he must have known that much of what he was saying was not true. Perhaps his false statements were calculated. Perhaps his rage at the attack on Social Security simply blotted considerations of accuracy out of his mind— along with the need to be careful so as not to arouse the Supreme Court. Besides, he already had an unpleasant surprise in mind for the Court.

As his landslide victory a few days later demonstrated, Roosevelt's credibility and prestige with the people were colossal, not only because he was president, but because of the kind of president he was, radiating confidence, strong leadership, warm sympathy, and a desire to help to a people desperate for them. To tens of millions of Americans, many of whom had stared the void of utter destitution in the face and had been pulled back from the brink by one New Deal program or other, Franklin Roosevelt was not merely a president, but a kind of messiah, and they greeted him during the campaign with a fervent, almost hysterical gratitude in which even Roosevelt himself found something terrible. "He saved my home," people in the crowds cried. "He gave me a job."[136] Hence his pronouncement that Social Security was insurance lent it enormous, unassailable credence.

Two weeks after the election, Social Security's administrative machinery went into action to collect information on millions of employees, assign them identification numbers, and set up a record keeping system to keep track of their earnings and taxes. Three million persons received application blanks for Social Security numbers. Another 24 million blanks were delivered beginning on November 24. Social Security shorts were shown to audiences in hundreds of movie houses, announcing that "November 24 marks the beginning of a new era in American life."[137] That evening, Vincent Miles went on the air in New York to tell his listeners that completing the application forms they had received would be the first step to establishing for them "a right to a retirement annuity," and explaining how to fill out the one-page form, item by item. He then explained how the benefit provisions worked. "This old-age benefits plan," he said, "is something like insurance."[138] Miles's listeners probably found such talk reassuring, familiar, and believable. Had they not been told it over and over, from government figures and the media alike, for well over a year now? Had not the president—*their* president, whom they trusted implicitly and loved and believed in as they loved and believed in no one else—himself said the same things just a few weeks back?

Reporting the distribution of application forms for Social Security numbers, *Newsweek* embraced insurance language wholly, referring to "old-age annuities," "premiums," "contributions," "26,000,000 insurance accounts" (this though the Act created no individual accounts); captioning a photograph of a postman holding an account number application blank out to the reader "Insurance agent"; announcing that Social Security's purpose was to provide the elderly with regular income "as a matter of right, not of charity."[139] It is a mark of the triumph of the administration's depiction of Social Security in shaping Americans' understanding of and thinking about the program that even the *United States News* (today's *U. S. News & World Report*), whose editorial page was routinely scathing in its criticisms of Roosevelt and the New Deal, used this insurance terminology in its reporting on the distribution of the application forms and the collection of Social Security taxes that would start in January 1937. It spoke too of the payroll and employer taxes going into "the worker's savings account," of the revenue being "credited to the individual workers of the nation," of funds that "belong to the individual workers, but are held by the Government at interest, until the workers retire and start to draw their annuities."[140]

By the end of 1936, then, the administration's depiction of Social Security had become the version of reality adopted and disseminated by the mainstream media for public consumption. Thus transmitted, the administration's semantics were already determining the national frame of reference, thereby determining the very language in which Americans thought about Social Security. The Republican attack, as the program's administrators shrewdly realized, actually redounded to their advantage, because it gave Social Security free publicity and handed them a matchless chance, which they had the wit to seize, to shape that publicity favorably.[141] Moreover, it infuriated Roosevelt and goaded him to give Social Security the benefit of his matchless prestige and anoint it publicly as insurance. "Short-sighted," the *New York Times* had called the employers' and Republicans' rough tactics,[142] and the author of that editorial was righter than he knew. Social Security's enemies had succeeded only in tightening its grip on the public mind.

Notes

1. Gustave LeBon, *Gustave LeBon: The Man and his Works*, ed. Alice Widener (Indianapolis, IN: Liberty Fund, Inc., 1979), p. 274.
2. I. M. Rubinow, *Social Insurance: With Special Reference to American Conditions* (New York: Henry Holt and Company, 1913; reprint ed., New York: Arno Press, 1969), p. 3.
3. Ibid., pp. 3, 10-11.
4. Arthur Larson, *Know Your Social Security* (New York: Harper & Brothers, Publishers, 1955), pp. 10-11.
5. Edward Crankshaw, *Bismarck* (New York: The Viking Press, 1981), pp. 359-360, 378; Rubinow, *Social Insurance*, pp. 13-16.
6. Rubinow, *Social Insurance*, pp. 21, 24.
7. Sidney Fine, *Laissez Faire and the General-Welfare State: A Study of Conflict in American Thought, 1865-1901* (Ann Arbor: University of Michigan Press, 1956), pp. 10-16, and "The Argument for Laissez Faire," *passim*. Fine's book is a solid work of scholarship, but its statist bias is very clear, even in its semantics, and it must be approached with care.
8. Ibid., pp. 167-168, and "Laissez Faire Under Attack: Emergence of the Concept of the General-Welfare State," *passim*.
9. Ibid., p. 329.
10. Ibid., pp. 170-171, 180-181.
11. Arthur J. Altmeyer, "The Wisconsin Idea and Social Security," *Wisconsin Magazine of History*, vol. 42, no. 1 (Autumn, 1958), pp. 19-21.
12. Gerald D. Nash, Noel H. Pugash, and Richard F. Tomasson, eds., *Social Security, the First Half-Century* (Albuquerque: University of New Mexico Press, 1988), pp. 4-7.

13. Paul H. Douglas, *Social Security in the United States: An Analysis and Appraisal of the Federal Social Security Act*, 2nd ed. (New York: McGraw-Hill, 1939), pp. 5-6.
14. Abraham Holtzman, *The Townsend Movement: A Political Study* (New York: Bookman Associates, Inc., 1963), pp. 22-23.
15. Douglas, *Social Security in the United States*, pp. 7-20.
16. Daniel R. Fusfeld, *The Economic Thought of Franklin D. Roosevelt and the Origins of the New Deal* (New York: Columbia University Press, 1956), pp. 158-161.
17. Altmeyer, "The Wisconsin Idea and Social Security," p. 21.
18. Fusfeld, *The Economic Thought of Franklin D. Roosevelt and the Origins of the New Deal*, p. 244.
19. Frances Perkins, *The Roosevelt I Knew* (New York: The Viking Press, 1946), pp. 278-279. Agitation for social insurance was not confined to the administration. Under the auspices of the Rockefeller Foundation, two English advocates of social insurance, Sir William Beveridge and Sir Henry Steele-Maitland, spoke to business groups, church groups, and others, and "did a great deal to allay the fears and doubts of the business and conservative part of the community" (Ibid., p. 279).
20. Arthur J. Altmeyer, *The Formative Years of Social Security* (Madison: The University of Wisconsin Press, 1966), p. 3.
21. Ibid., pp. 7-8.
22. Sheryl R. Tines, *Turning Points in Social Security: From "Cruel Hoax" to "Sacred Entitlement,"* (Stanford, CA: Stanford University Press, 1996), pp. 46, 59.
23. Committee on Economic Security, *Report to the President* (Washington, DC: U. S. Government Printing Office, 1935), pp. vi, 52-53.
24. Altmeyer, "The Wisconsin Idea and Social Security," p. 21.
25. Arthur J. Altmeyer, "Ten Years of Social Security," *Survey Graphic*, September 1945, p. 369.
26. Larson, *Know Your Social Security*, pp. 10, 11.
27. Edward D. Berkowitz, *Mr. Social Security: The Life of Wilbur J. Cohen* (Lawrence: University Press of Kansas, 1995), pp. 20-24.
28. Leuchtenburg, *Franklin D. Roosevelt and the New Deal*, pp. 96-100.
29. Holtzman, *The Townsend Movement*, pp. 35-36.
30. Ibid., pp. 41-49, 88, 56-58, 71-72; Douglas, *Social Security in the United States*, p. 72.
31. Leuchtenburg, *Franklin D. Roosevelt and the New Deal*, p. 104.
32. Perkins, *The Roosevelt I Knew*, p. 294.
33. Holtzman, *The Townsend Movement*, p. 91.
34. Ibid., p. 87.
35. Douglas, *Social Security in the United States*, p. 73.
36. Altmeyer, *The Formative Years of Social Security*, p. 10.
37. Townsend's plan went through numerous revisions, the tax shifting from a sales tax to a transaction tax, the $200 pension amount being replaced by whatever amount the tax revenue would be able to pay, and so on, which served only to reveal the Plan as ill-considered and half-baked. New Dealers such as Frances Perkins and Edwin Witte went out of their way to attack the Townsend Plan as inflationary, burdensome and unworkable in their 1935 testimony on the Social Security Act and on McGroarty's Townsend bill. In testifying before the House Ways and Means Committee regarding his Plan during the Committee's hearings on the 1935 McGroarty bill and the 1939 Amendments to the Social Security Act, Dr. Townsend cut a poor figure, personifying irresponsibility and muddled thinking (Holtzman, *The Townsend Movement*, pp. 37-40, 92-93, 113-115. See also

Townsend's testimony in the 1939 hearings.). Had Townsend challenged Roosevelt in 1936, or fielded a candidate against him, Roosevelt would unquestionably have demolished the challenge.
38. Perkins, *The Roosevelt I Knew*, pp. 282-284.
39. Arthur M. Schlesinger, Jr., *The Age of Roosevelt,* vol. 2: *The Coming of the New Deal* (Boston: Houghton Mifflin, 1958), p. 308.
40. Ibid., pp. 308-309.
41. See, for example, Larson, *Know Your Social Security*, pp. 18-20; Derthick, *Policymaking for Social Security*, p. 231.
42. For opposition to general revenue financing by Myers and others on grounds of financial discipline, see, for example, "Runaway Expansion of Social Security?" *Nation's Business*, March 1970, pp. 60-63; "Is it true what they say about Social Security?" *Nation's Business*, June 1973, pp. 53-55; Derthick, *Policymaking for Social Security*, p. 419.
43. "Does Social Security Need an Overhaul? Interview with Stanford G. Ross, Commissioner of Social Security," *U.S. News & World Report*, January 8, 1979, p. 62.
44. Ibid.
45. Department of Health, Education and Welfare, *Social Security Administration, Social Security Act of 1935: Reports, Bills, Debates, Act, and Supreme Court Decisions* [hereafter, Social Security Administration, *Social Security Act of 1935*] (Washington, DC: U. S. Government Printing Office, n. d.), 2 vols., vol. 2, in Appendix, at "Administration Bills," H.R. 4120 text, pp. 1-15, 32-63; Edwin E. Witte, *The Development of the Social Security Act* (Madison: University of Wisconsin Press, 1962), p. 79, for Eliot and Title I.
46. Social Security Administration, *Social Security Act of 1935*, vol. 2, H.R. 4120 text, pp. 15-32.
47. Ibid., H.R. 4120 text, p. 63.
48. U.S., Congress, House, Committee on Ways and Means, *Economic Security Act: Hearings before the House Committee on Ways and Means on H.R. 4120*, 74th Cong., 1st sess., 1935, p. 13.
49. Perkins, *The Roosevelt I Knew*, pp. 279, 281.
50. *Economic Security Act: Hearings*, p. 8. Secretary Perkins, Dr. Witte, and others made the same points before the Senate Finance Committee, often using virtually identical words in their opening statements. To avoid needless redundancy and length, only their testimony before the House Ways and Means Committee, which suffices to establish my point, is presented.
51. Ibid., p. 109.
52. Ibid., pp. 173-174.
53. Ibid., pp. 177-178.
54. Ibid., p. 6.
55. Ibid., pp. 240, 241.
56. See James V. DeLong, *Property Matters: How Property Rights Are Under Assault—And Why You Should Care* (New York: The Free Press, 1997).
57. Harry J. Hopkins, Arthur J. Altmeyer et al., *Toward Economic Security: A Review of President Roosevelt's Economic Security Program* (Washington, DC: President's Committee on Economic Security, 1935), p. 6.
58. Joseph Alsop and Turner Catledge, *The 168 Days* (Garden City, NY: Doubleday, Doran & Co., Inc., 1938), p. 95.
59. *Economic Security Act: Hearings*, pp. 897-900, 903; Witte, *The Development of the Social Security Act*, pp. 150-151.
60. Witte, *The Development of the Social Security Act*, pp. 93-94.
61. Perkins, *The Roosevelt I Knew*, p. 291.

62. Witte, *The Development of the Social Security Act*, p. 146.
63. Basil Rauch, *The History of the New Deal 1933-1938* (New York: Capricorn Books, 1963), pp. 192-193.
64. Witte, *The Development of the Social Security Act*, pp. 76-77.
65. Ibid., p. 146.
66. Social Security Administration, *Social Security Act of 1935*, vol. 2, in Appendix, at "Administration Bills," H.R. 4120 text, pp. 23, 24, 25, 28, 29.
67. Douglas, *Social Security in the United States*, pp. 172-176; Arthur M. Schlesinger, Jr., *The Age of Roosevelt*, vol. 3: *The Politics of Upheaval* (Boston: Houghton Mifflin, 1960), pp. 274-275.
68. Witte, *The Development of the Social Security Act*, p. 92.
69. Author's comparison of texts of H.R. 4120 and H.R. 7260. The text of H.R. 4120 may be found in Department of Health, Education and Welfare, Social Security Administration, *Social Security Act of 1935*, vol. 2, in Appendix, at "Administration Bills." The text of the Committee's version of H.R. 7260 may be found in Ibid., vol. 1, at Section I, "Reported to House." Amusingly, the Committee's semantic cleansers missed a reference to "social insurance" regarding the duties of the Social Security Board; it survived in Title VII, Section 702 of the final version signed into law.
70. Author's examination of H.R. 7260 text.
71. Ibid., at pp. 14, 46.
72. Thomas H. Eliot, "The Social Security Bill 25 Years After," *Atlantic Monthly*, August 1960, p. 73.
73. Douglas, Social Security in the United States: An Analysis and Appraisal of the Federal Social Security Act, pp. 146-147.
74. Ibid., p. 157.
75. Ibid., pp. 280-281.
76. U.S., Congress, House, *The Social Security Bill*, House Report 615 to accompany H.R. 7260, 74th Cong., 1st sess., 1935, p. 43.
77. U.S., Congress, House, Representative Treadway speaking on the Social Security bill, 74th Cong., 1st sess., April 12, 1935, *Congressional Record*, 79:5530.
78. U.S., Congress, House, Representative Jenkins speaking on the Social Security
79. U.S., Congress, House, Representative Reed (NY) speaking on the Social Security bill, 74th Cong., 1st sess., April 17, 1935, *Congressional Record*, 79:5892.
80. U.S., Congress, Senate, Senator Hastings speaking on the Social Security bill, 74th Cong., 1st sess., June 17, 1935, Congressional Record, 79:9419.
81. U.S., Congress, House, Representative McCormack speaking on the Social Security bill, 74th Cong., 1st sess., April 17, 1935, *Congressional Record*, 79:5871.
82. U.S., Congress, House, 74th Cong., 1st sess., April 19, 1935, *Congressional Record*, 79:6069-6070; U.S., Congress, Senate, 74th Cong., 1st sess., June 19, 1935, *Congressional Record*, 79:9650.
83. Witte, *The Development of the Social Security Act*, p. 108.
84. Social Security Administration, *Social Security Act of 1935*, vol. 2, at VI, "Public— No. 271—74th Congress," text of Social Security Act of 1935, pp. 19-20, 22.
85. Ibid., pp. 3-4.
86. Ibid., pp. 4-7.
87. Ibid., p. 4.
88. Ibid., pp. 18-19.
89. Altmeyer, *The Formative Years of Social Security*, p. 45.
90. Social Security Administration, *Social Security Act of 1935*, vol. 2, at VI, "Public— No. 271—74th Congress," text of Social Security Act of 1935, p. 32.

91. Franklin D. Roosevelt, *The Public Papers and Addresses of Franklin D. Roosevelt*, vol. 4: *The Court Disapproves 1935* (New York: Random House, 1938), p. 324.
92. Frances Perkins, "Social Security: The Foundation," *New York Times Magazine*, August 18, 1935, pp. 2, 15.
93. Frances Perkins, "The Social Security Act," *Vital Speeches of the Day*, September 9, 1935, pp. 792-794.
94. A. J. Altmeyer, "The New Social Security Act," *Vital Speeches of the Day*, October 7, 1935, p. 8.
95. Ibid., pp. 8-9.
96. John G. Winant, "The Social Security Act," *Vital Speeches of the Day*, May 4, 1936, p. 488; John G. Winant, "An Approach to Social Security," Atlantic Monthly, July 1936, p. 70, 72.
97. Winant, "The Social Security Act," p. 490.
98. Arthur A. Ballantine, "Promoting Social Security," Vital Speeches of the Day, May 18, 1936, p. 528.
99. Charles McKinley and Robert W. Frase, *Launching Social Security: A Capture-and-Record Account 1935-1937* (Madison: University of Wisconsin Press, 1970), p. 453.
100. "The Congress: Hustling Homeward," *Time*, July 1, 1935, p. 11.
101. "How Security Bill Aids Aged and Idle," *New York Times*, August 15, 1935, 4.
102. "Social Security," *Newsweek*, August 17, 1935, p. 5.
103. "Topics of the Day: Giving Hostages to Posterity," *Literary Digest*, August 24, 1935, p. 3; Ruby A. Black, "At Last a Weary Congress Quits," *Independent Woman*, September 1935, p. 326.
104. "A Good Job Well Done," *Collier's*, August 3, 1935, p. 50.
105. "Social Security Bill Widely Approved: Nearly Two-thirds of Editors Commend Passage of Measure," *United States News*, August 19, 1935, p. 12.
106. "Topics of the Day: Giving Hostages to Posterity," *Literary Digest*, p. 4.
107. "Social Security Signed," Detroit News, August 16, 1935, 16.
108. "Look Ahead," Literary Digest, May 2, 1936, p. 9; "Social Security," *Literary Digest*, November 7, 1936, p. 8; George Creel, "What You Pay For," *Collier's*, January 23, 1937, p. 17; Eveline M. Burns, *Independent Woman*, April 1937, p. 108; John T. Flynn, "Fixed for Life," Collier's, August 8, 1936, p. 13.
109. John Janney, "When You and I Are Old, Maggie," *American Magazine*, January 1937, p. 95; Burns, Independent Woman, p. 108.
110. Henry E. Jackson, "Our New Social Security Act," *Review of Reviews*, October 1935, pp. 25-26.
111. Eveline M. Burns, *Toward Social Security: An Explanation of the Social Security Act and a Survey of the Larger Issues* (New York: McGraw-Hill Book Co., 1936), pp. 14-15.
112. "Topics of the Day: Giving Hostages to Posterity," *Literary Digest*, p. 4.
113. Abraham Epstein, "'Social Security' Under the New Deal," *Nation*, September 5, 1935, pp. 261-263.
114. Frank Parker Stockbridge, "Social Security, Or De Levee Done Bust, Part I," *Saturday Evening Post*, March 7, 1936, p. 10.
115. Frank Parker Stockbridge, "Social Security, Or De Levee Done Bust, Part II," *Saturday Evening Post*, March 14, 1936, p. 27.
116. Ibid., pp. 37, 40.
117. Garet Garrett, "Security," Saturday Evening Post, September 19, 1936, pp. 33, 102, 104.

118. Alfred M. Landon, "I Will Not Promise the Moon," *Vital Speeches of the Day*, October 15, 1936, pp. 26, 27, 28.
119. "Landon on Social Security," *New York Times*, September 28, 1936, 18.
120. "Industrialists Fighting Roosevelt By Tax Warning on Pay Envelopes," *New York Times*, October 24, 1936, 1, 6.
121. Altmeyer, *The Formative Years of Social Security*, p. 69; Schlesinger, *The Politics of Upheaval*, pp. 635-636.
122. "Industrialists Fighting Roosevelt By Tax Warning on Pay Envelopes," *New York Times*, October 24, 1936, 1, 6; Schlesinger, *The Politics of Upheaval*, pp. 636-637.
123. "'Pay Cut' Warnings on Pension Issue Assailed as Deceit," *New York Times*, October 26, 1936, 1, 3; Arthur J. Altmeyer, "What the Worker Will Get From the Payroll Tax," *United States News*, November 2, 1936, p. 2.
124. Altmeyer, *The Formative Years of Social Security*, p. 69.
125. McKinley and Frase, *Launching Social Security*, p. 358.
126. "Here Come Those Payroll Taxes," *Business Week*, October 31, 1936, p. 40.
127. McKinley and Frase, *Launching Social Security*, pp. 358-359.
128. "Wagner Sees Plot to Wreck Social Security Act; Says Landon Forces Work in Devious Ways," *New York Times*, October 30, 1936, 11.
129. U.S., Congress, Senate, Senator Francis T. Maloney, "Campaign Radio Addresses by Senator Maloney," Extension of Remarks, 75th Cong., 1st sess., July 15, 1937, *Congressional Record*, 80:1793, 1792, 1794.
130. Franklin D. Roosevelt, *The Public Papers and Addresses of Franklin D. Roosevelt*, vol. 5: *The People Approve 1936* (New York: Random House, 1938), pp. 528-529, 536.
131. "Error on Security Laid to Roosevelt," *New York Times*, October 26, 1936, 3.
132. "Government Asked to Act On Pay Check Propaganda," *New York Times*, October 25, 1936, 27; Schlesinger, *The Politics of Upheaval*, p. 637.
133. Roosevelt, *Public Papers and Addresses*, vol. 5: *The People Approve 1936*, p. 548.
134. Ibid., pp. 549, 556, 569-570.
135. Fusfeld, *The Economic Thought of Franklin D. Roosevelt and the Origins of the New Deal*, pp. 108-116.
136. Leuchtenburg, *Franklin D. Roosevelt and the New Deal 1932-1940*, p. 193.
137. "Security," *Newsweek*, November 28, 1936, p. 28.
138. Vincent M. Miles, "Explaining Social Security," *Vital Speeches of the Day*, December 15, 1936, pp. 149, 151.
139. "Security," *Newsweek*, November 28, 1936, pp. 28-29.
140. "Payroll Taxes to Take $2,800,000,000 From Worker-Employer First Three Years," *United States News*, October 23, 1936, p. 1; "Half of Workers Outside of Pension Plan: Pay No Tax But Entitled to Some Benefits," *United States News*, November 23, 1936, p. 1; "Social Security Program Shifts to High Gear," *United States News*, November 23, 1936, p. 4.
141. McKinley and Frase, *Launching Social Security*, p. 359.
142. "Short-sighted Tactics," *New York Times*, October 31, 1936, 18.

5

Helvering v. Davis

*"To the extent that these [New Deal policies]
developed, they were tortured interpretations
of a document intended to prevent them."*

—Rexford Tugwell[1]

Less than two years after the Social Security Act was passed, its constitutionality was challenged in three Supreme Court cases. On May 24, 1937, the Court, ruling on all three, found it constitutional. The *Helvering v. Davis* decision that day established the constitutionality of the act's compulsory old-age insurance program.

The administration's arguments in *Helvering v. Davis* are highly revealing of its efforts to create a false consciousness about Social Security. In large measure, they flatly contradicted both the testimony of administration figures to Congress and the promotion of Social Security thus far given to the public. Yet despite their numerous misrepresentations they prevailed, for the decision for *Helvering v. Davis* did not occur in a vacuum; it was reached when the Court was in the worst crisis of its entire existence, under a threat and a pressure never seen before or since.

The Political Context: Roosevelt versus the Court

The Supreme Court and the Roosevelt administration had been moving toward a confrontation for years. Since 1933, Franklin Roosevelt had had things very much his own way. The Democrats were behind him; the Republicans, who had lost seats in both houses of Congress in 1932 and 1934 and were reduced to pitiful rumps in 1936, were but a pesky annoyance. Only one institution stood between Roosevelt and complete domination of the country: the Supreme Court. The Court then contained four staunch conservatives who believed that the Constitution meant what it said and should be interpreted in a very narrow, strict sense, adhering to the intent of the Framers:

George Sutherland, Willis Van Devanter, Pierce Butler, and James McReynolds. In their view, the federal government had no right to interfere in the economy or in local matters, and the Constitution simply did not authorize the New Deal's legislation. The Tenth Amendment, which states that "The powers not delegated to the United States by the Constitution, nor prohibited by it to the States, are reserved to the States respectively, or to the people," sharply limited what the central government could legitimately do. Opposing them were three liberals, Harlan Fiske Stone, Louis Brandeis, and Benjamin Cardozo, who believed that what the Constitution authorized had to be construed flexibly, in response to changing economic circumstances and national needs, some of which, such as a general depression and associated social problems, the Framers had not foreseen. In particular, Article I, Section 8, Clause 1 of the Constitution, "The Congress shall have Power to lay and collect Taxes, Duties, Imposts and Excises, to pay the Debts and provide for the common Defence and general Welfare of the United States"—the taxing power and "general welfare" clause—could be construed as providing authorization for New Deal measures. In between were Chief Justice Charles Evans Hughes and Owen Roberts, who usually, but not always, sided with the conservatives.[2]

Beginning with the "hot oil" ruling in January 1935, the Court rendered a series of decisions ruling many major New Deal laws unconstitutional. The Court invalidated the Railroad Retirement Act on May 6, 1935. Three weeks later, on May 27, known to New Dealers as Black Monday, the Court made three unanimous decisions against the administration: it voided both the National Industrial Recovery Act and the Frazier-Lemke Farm Bankruptcy Act; and ruled that President Roosevelt had wrongly removed a Federal Trade Commissioner who had opposed his policies. On January 6, 1936, the Agricultural Adjustment Act went down by a 6-3 vote. The AAA levied a processing tax on cotton textile factories; this, the Court held, was unconstitutional, since it was not a true tax; its purpose was not revenue raising, which the Constitution authorized, but obtaining funds from one group of citizens (processors) to benefit another (farmers), to purchase compliance with an agricultural regulatory scheme, which the Constitution did not. The Court issued on April 6 a 6-3 decision against the Securities and Exchange Commission, which, while not challenging its constitutionality, was marked by a ferociously critical majority opinion written by Justice Sutherland. The Guffey Coal Act went down 5-4 on May 18. Finally, on May 25, the Court voided both the Municipal Bankruptcy Act and a New York State law setting minimum wages for women. In little more than a year, the Court had demolished much of the New Deal. The New York minimum wage law decision made a federal minimum wage law, one of the administration's goals, unlikely. Two major New Deal laws, Social Security and the Wagner Labor Relations Act, seemed vulnerable.[3]

The Court's decisions, especially those on the NIRA and the New York minimum wage law, enraged liberals and "progressives." "We have been relegated to the horse-and-buggy definition of interstate commerce," Roosevelt complained after the NIRA decision. "Nine old men," Drew Pearson and Robert Allen tarred the justices, in a poison-pen book by that title. Some time in 1936, Roosevelt decided to settle accounts with the Court. On February 5, 1937, he sent Congress a proposal to bend the Court to his will. Claiming that the Court was overburdened and badly behindhand in its work because of "aged or infirm" judges, he proposed to appoint one new justice for every justice who reached the age of seventy and did not retire, for a maximum of six, enlarging the Supreme Court from nine justices to a maximum of fifteen.[4]

Roosevelt's proposal touched off an uproar. Although presented as a reform, it was promptly christened by opponents as a Court pack, intended to overpower its opposition to the New Deal—precisely what it was. In a radio speech on March 9, Roosevelt himself revealed the allegation of infirmity of aged justices making them incapable of doing their jobs as a mendacious rationalization; he fulminated at length about how the Court majority had decided to "thwart the will of the people" and had "improperly set itself up as . . . a super-legislature," cited specific rulings that had gone against him, and in only two sentences mentioned his desire "to make the administration of all Federal justice speedier and, therefore, less costly," and for "quicker and cheaper justice."[5] The broadcast cut little ice. Even liberals unhappy with the Court's decisions balked at packing it. Opposition burgeoned all over the country and in the Senate, where Roosevelt's own party was deeply divided. On March 22, Senator Burton K. Wheeler (D-MT), leading opposition to the Court pack, read out to the Senate Judiciary Committee a letter from Chief Justice Hughes demolishing all of Roosevelt's assertions that the Court was incapable of meeting its workload without new blood.[6]

Roosevelt's proposal threatened to destroy the Supreme Court's integrity and independent existence as a separate branch of government. It thereby put immense pressure on the Court to act in self-preservation, by refraining from handing down decisions that would make the pack look justified. Perhaps intimidated by Roosevelt's landslide, the Court had in January already upheld the Silver Purchase Act of 1934 despite its use of taxes, even retroactively, to regulate a market rather than raise revenue. Now, on March 29, 1937, the Supreme Court handed down four pro-administration decisions. Reversing itself, it upheld a Washington State law providing for minimum wages for women; the way was now clear for the administration to propose a federal minimum-wage bill. A revised Frazier-Lemke Act was upheld; so was the National Firearms Act, which, taxing firearms dealers, was using taxes to regulate a market rather than raise revenue, and was seemingly vulnerable to the Court conservatives; and so was the Railway Labor Act, which promoted collective bargaining. Small wonder the New Dealers called it White Monday.[7] The Court wasn't being so obstructive after all. With these decisions, the case for packing the Court was much weakened.

But not demolished altogether, for the Court now faced cases involving two laws of immense importance to the administration: the Wagner Labor Relations Act, which created the National Labor Relations Board and asserted the right of workers to form unions and bargain collectively, and the Social Security Act. Besides the old-age benefits program of Titles II and VIII, which was being challenged, Social Security created an unemployment-compensation system, whereby the federal government imposed an excise tax, initially of one percent of wages, on employers of eight persons or more. Employers could, however, get a credit of up to 90 percent of the tax against their payments to a state fund for unemployment compensation, provided the state's unemployment compensation system met certain federal standards. The effect was to use the tax to induce the states to set up unemployment compensation programs; and the states complied. This provision was under attack in the courts, too.[8] Joseph Alsop and Turner Catledge ably depicted the stakes for the Court, and its dilemma:

> On the Court's decisions on these two laws hung the whole future of the court fight. Each law implied a great extension of the powers of government; each drew the issue squarely between the liberals and the conservatives. The Wagner Act . . . ran directly counter to the Guffey Coal Act [decision] holding that labor relations were of local concern only. The Social Security Act was a far more striking example of that "coercion" of the states which the Court had seen in the AAA. To sustain the Wagner Act the Court would have to abandon its . . . interpretation of the interstate commerce clause. To sustain the Social Security Act the Court would have to allow some real meaning to the general welfare clause. Yet if the Court balked, the court bill would surely pass.[9]

Thus the Court did a great deal more to relieve the pressure on it when on April 12 it ruled, 5-4, that the Wagner Act was constitutional.[10] A string of further administration victories followed. Two weeks later, in a case involving a black Communist, the Court struck down a Georgia statute making insurrection criminal. Then on May 3, the Court unanimously upheld a 1934 law levying a processing tax on coconut oils.[11] The New Deal had not lost one Supreme Court decision since the Court pack plan was unveiled. All across the board, the Court was giving in.

Then on May 18, Justice Van Devanter, seventy-eight, one of the four Court conservatives, announced that he would retire effective June 1. Roosevelt, who had yet to have an opportunity to do so, could now nominate a justice for the Supreme Court. The case for his Court plan suffered accordingly. That same day the Senate Judiciary Committee reported his bill unfavorably. But Roosevelt refused to compromise; the fight was still on.[12]

Such was the situation when the Supreme Court found itself confronting the issue of Social Security's constitutionality.

The Case: The Court under the Gun Again

Two of the three Social Security cases concerned the constitutionality of the unemployment compensation program, hence will go unexamined here. The third originated on November 12, 1936, when a George Davis, a stockholder of Edison Electric Illuminating Company of Boston, filed a suit in the U.S. District Court for the District of Massachusetts alleging that the taxes on employees and employers under Title VIII of the Social Security Act were unconstitutional, that he had asked the company not to pay them, to no avail, and that the taxes threatened to inflict irreparable injury. Davis asked that the Edison Electric Illuminating Company be prevented from paying them. The District Court upheld the constitutionality of the taxes, but the Circuit Court of Appeals reversed the decision on April 14, 1937. Guy Helvering, Commissioner of Internal Revenue, and William Welch, collector in internal revenue for the district of Massachusetts, intervened and asked that the case be brought to the Supreme Court for a determination on the validity of the taxes.[13]

So far, the Court's strategy of winning by losing had done much to remove the pretext for the Court pack. With its string of decisions favorable to the administration, particularly upholding the Wagner Act, prized by both the administration and congressional Democrats alike, it had created a momentum in its favor. Now the sword of Damocles was over its head again. Social Security had been passed by lopsided votes by the very same people who held the Court's fate in their hands; most of the senators who were opposing Roosevelt on the pack had voted for it; and it was popular in the country. The Republicans and employees had harvested much odium with the pay envelope campaign and other anti-Social Security scare tactics; the phenomenon of imputing guilt by association would make a Court repudiation of Social Security doubly dangerous. Should the Court strike down Social Security, there would doubtless be an outcry: the president is right, the Court really is thwarting the will of the people and the Congress, maybe there's something to this Court reform scheme after all; maybe packing the Court wouldn't be such a bad idea—these nine old men are really asking for it. By invalidating Social Security, the Court could revive Roosevelt's campaign to pack the Court and squander all the gains it had made. Indeed, Alsop and Catledge reported, some of the president's circle were hoping that although the Court had refused to commit suicide by voiding the Wagner Act, it would do so on Social Security.[14] Unquestionably, all of that was in the back of the Justices' minds as they considered the brief filed by the attorney general, his assistants, and the Social Security Board's general counsel, Thomas Eliot.

The questions to be decided, the government's brief maintained, were whether the tax on employees was at issue; whether the taxes on employers and employees were valid exercises of the taxing power granted to Congress by Article I, Section 8, Clause 1 of the Constitution (the taxing power and "general welfare" clause); whether a Social Security taxpayer had standing to question the old age benefits provided under Title II of the Social Security Act; whether providing those benefits was a valid exercise of Congress' authority provided by foregoing passage of the Constitution; whether Titles VIII and II, taken together, are an exercise of powers not granted to Congress by the Constitution; and finally, whether the taxes violated the Fifth Amendment, which forbade, among other things, depriving individuals of "life, liberty, or property, without due process of law" and taking private property for public use "without just compensation."[15]

False Consciousness Exposed: The Administration Brief

The administration went on to describe the legislation. Most of that material need not be examined, but a few passages command attention. The old-age benefits provided by Title II, the administration's brief stated, "are gratuities (not based on contract, but based on a Congressional direction expressly subject to amendment or repeal [Section 1104])."[16] Two pages into its brief, and the administration was contradicting the public record already. Hadn't Secretary Perkins told the House Ways and Means Committee two years earlier that benefits would be paid "as a matter of contractual right"? Hadn't Dr. Witte referred to "contractual" annuities?

As for the taxes, "Collections under Title VIII are not earmarked for any special purpose."[17] Moreover, "These are true taxes, their purpose being simply to raise revenue. No compliance with any scheme of Federal regulation is involved. The proceeds are paid unrestricted into the Treasury as internal revenue collections, available for the general support of Government."[18]

If one confines one's attention strictly to the text of the bill itself, this is true enough; the Social Security Act contains not one word to indicate a specific purpose for the taxes. But this is disingenuous, since the testimony before Congress by Secretary Perkins, Dr. Witte and others had it that the purpose of the taxes was to build up a fund to pay old-age annuities, and explanations of the taxes made to the public after the bill was signed into law said the same thing. Moreover, both Congress and the public had been given to understand that payment of the taxes would give the taxpayer an "earned right" to his benefits. Paul Douglas had admitted that the separation was a "legal fiction" and that in reality the benefits in Title II were based on the taxes in Title VIII and that the latter were intended to pay for the former. Given all that, this claim that the purpose of the Social Security taxes is merely to raise revenue and finance general government operations is simply not true.

But if the payroll taxes *are* "true taxes"—and they are, in the sense of being levied coercively by the government, with penalties for nonpayment—then they are neither "contributions" nor "insurance premiums," as they had been consistently described to the public since 1935. Calling the payroll and employer taxes "true taxes," "not earmarked in any way," was tantamount to admitting that all those references to "contributions" and "insurance premiums" had been mere marketing devices.

Obviously, the motive for claiming that the Social Security Act's exactions are "true taxes" was to enable the administration to argue that they were valid exercises of the taxing power of Congress under the Constitution, and this was done.[19] Turning its attention to Davis's standing to challenge the appropriations, the administration argued, among other things, that a taxpayer could not attack the expenditure of Treasury funds except in cases where tax revenues were earmarked for a specific purpose—and that the Social Security Act was not such a case. The administration invoked the money-laundering scheme of routing the revenues raised under Title VIII to the pool of general revenues and then putting them in the Old-Age Reserve Account by appropriations:

> The operation of the taxes under Title VIII is in no way conditioned upon the expenditures provided for in Title II. The rates of tax are fixed, and *the proceeds are commingled in the general Treasury* [italics added]. And no money which has been covered into the Treasury can be paid out except pursuant to an appropriation. . . . But Title II does not contain any appropriation, it merely *authorizes* [italics in original] appropriations. Future acts of Congress are necessary to make the appropriations.[20]

It was true that the letter of the law did not earmark anything, and the money-laundering method alluded to gives further *prima facie* support for that view. But the spirit of the law, and all the testimony and promotion heretofore, was that the revenues *were* for a specific purpose. The brief then argued that in making their appropriations, future Congresses might not elect to follow Title II's provisions, and "A future Congress may not even make any appropriation in a given year"[21]—a breathtakingly specious argument. Did the brief's authors really believe that in a given year Congress would take the money levied under Title VIII yet capriciously vote no appropriation to pay the benefits mandated by law under Title II?

The government then argued at great length that indigence in old age was indeed a national problem, not a local one, and that private charity and state government resources were not up to coping with it, and that old age benefits were therefore valid expenditures to promote the general welfare of the United States. Since the two titles were valid separately, their combination, the government's brief maintained, was valid too.[22]

The next issue was whether Titles II and VIII, taken together, constituted "an invalid regulatory scheme," either "a regulation of employment in that it requires or induces retirement from employment," a regulation of wages, or a compulsory insurance scheme invalid under the Tenth Amendment.

Regarding regulation of employment, the administration flatly denied it. "It is obvious from the face of the Act that it in no way constitutes a regulation of employment. The Act not only does not require retirement from employment, but it has no significant tendency to induce it." In fact, because neither employee nor employer tax is levied after age sixty-five, "the employment opportunities of elderly people will be increased." Someone who reaches age sixty-five and keeps working in employment covered under the Act will, of course, lose his benefits while he's working, *"but he suffers no reduction whatever in future benefits"* (italics in original), hence can keep working as long as he likes. And since benefits are small, "they constitute little if any incentive to retire."[23]

In the oral arguments on the case before the Court on May 5, Charles Wyzanski, Jr., special assistant to the attorney general, added that the tax is not levied on employment after sixty-five, "[i]n order that there may be no inducement for a man when he reaches the age of 65 to retire. The employer is encouraged to keep him at work, and the employee is encouraged to stay at work."[24]

All of this flies in the face of the testimony of Murray Latimer, chairman of the Railroad Retirement Board and chairman of the old-age security subcommittee of the Technical Board on economic security, before the House Ways and Means Committee in 1935. Recommending the bill's compulsory, contributory old-age insurance which would supplant, as quickly as possible, the old-age pensions provided in Title I of the bill, Latimer dwelled at length on the labor-market regulatory aspect of old-age insurance. Overall social welfare would be higher, he maintained, "if we made some arrangement whereby there would be continuously a clearance of the aged persons from among those who seek jobs." For one thing, large numbers of elderly workers in the labor force tend to depress wages. To offset this, labor unions set up annuity systems to get their elderly members out of the labor market. But they found it impossible to get enough funds to keep their annuity schemes going, hence had to raise their dues, which in turn, by making membership less attractive to workers, hindered many unions in organizing. Hence old-age insurance would be "of very great assistance" to trade unions, since it would enable them to lower dues. For another thing, large numbers of elderly workers are detrimental to efficiency and to morale among younger workers, who see the elderly as blocking opportunities for promotion. So "if they could be removed from employment at an annuity or an income which would be sufficient for support," efficiency and younger workers' morale would improve. Moreover, the Title I pensions, even if set above existing standards, "would not be high enough to induce any considerable voluntary withdrawals from the labor market." All in all, labor-market regulatory considerations made a strong case for old-age insurance, in Latimer's view. Moreover, annuity *levels* should be set not just to benefit retirees, but "with the purpose of inducing as many as possible to withdraw from the labor market, so as to be rid of the depressing influence on wages, to provide for the re-absorption of the unemployed, the ordinary absorption of the younger generation as they begin to seek employment," and to promote organization of labor "by enabling trade unions to lower their dues." The annuities in the administration's proposed bill were "a minimum standard" for such an insurance program.[25]

Latimer touched specifically on the matter of continued employment past sixty-five, making it plain that the administration hoped that the old-age annuities would *reduce* such employment:

> Mr. HILL. The chances are that a man who is in good health and in vigor, upon reaching the age of 65, if he still has an opportunity to work at his job at a higher rate of compensation than he would get simply from an old-age annuity, would continue to work at it, or even try to supplement his old-age annuity.
>
> Mr. LATIMER. Not always. Experience with voluntary retirement in industry has shown that there will be very considerable numbers who will retire even though in good health on their own volition.[26]

As if all this were not enough, Professor J. Douglas Brown, who was on the staff of the Committee on Economic Security, testified that he and his colleagues on the CES staff recommended worker contributions because, among other things, "Through increasing the amount of annuities, worker contributions encourage the displacement of superannuated workers . . . from the labor market, with resulting increase in wages and earlier promotion." Moreover, a more adequate retirement annuity system encourages employment of middle-aged workers, "since the employer is no longer faced with the need to continue employment after 65," or to pay higher private pension contributions due to the worker's advanced age.[27]

Now, administration witnesses before a congressional committee are plainly speaking for that administration, so it is reasonable to infer that the reasons they give in advocacy of a bill are reasons which the administration considers valid. So if these men defended Social Security's contributory old-age benefits on the grounds that they would ease older men from the labor market and thereby increase openings for younger men, we may infer that one of the Act's purposes was in fact to induce retirement, that is, to regulate the labor market.

Is it really likely that none of this whole labor-market regulatory line of old-age benefit advocacy before congressional committees was known to the authors of the brief?

As for the brief's emphasized statement that employment over sixty-five would not suffer reduction in *future* benefits, this is transparently a dishonest attempt to call attention away from the obvious incentive to retire in the requirement that a beneficiary not be employed in a covered occupation after sixty-five, and from the equally obvious discouragement to work after that age embodied in the mandated loss of benefits during every month of covered employment beyond sixty-five.

Were the titles in combination an invalid regulatory scheme specifically because they create "a scheme for compulsory insurance invalid under the Tenth Amendment"? The brief denied this, in a passage which flatly contradicted the testimony presented to Congress, all the administration's promotion of Social Security after passage, and the campaign speeches of President Roosevelt himself just a few months back:

> Whether or not the Act does provide an insurance plan within the accepted meaning of the term "insurance" is a doubtful question. It is to be noted that the correlation between taxes paid and benefits received is far from complete. As the Executive Director of the Committee on Economic Security [Dr. Witte] has pointed out, the Act favors the workers who at this time are already middle aged or over and those whose rate of pay is small. . . . Thus some of the taxpayers receive benefits greater than the amount of taxes paid with respect to them. On the other hand, some taxpayers will receive benefits smaller than the amount of taxes paid to them, plus interest . . . Moreover, the Act creates no contractual obligation with respect to the payment of benefits. This Court has pointed out the difference between insurance which creates vested rights and pensions and other gratuities involving no contractual obligations.[28]

The administration went on to contrast World War I's War Risk Insurance for servicemen, which had policies which, "being contracts, are property and create vested rights," with pensions and so on, which are "gratuities. They involve no agreement of parties; and the grant of them creates no vested right. The benefits conferred by gratuities may be redistributed or withdrawn at any time in discretion of Congress."[29] The contrast was clearly meant to include Social Security benefits under the rubric of gratuities; recall that these benefits had been described earlier in the brief as "gratuities (not based on contract, but based on a Congressional direction expressly subject to amendment or repeal [Section 1104])." Not possessing the legal properties of insurance, Social Security was not "an invalid regulatory scheme," hence was constitutional.

The government's summary argument was even more emphatic, declaring flatly that the Act "*does not constitute a plan for compulsory insurance within the accepted meaning of the term 'insurance'*" (italics added).[30]

Arguing the case before the Supreme Court, Assistant Attorney General Robert Jackson, in the course of denying any need for judicial review of Title II, reiterated that

> these benefits are in the nature of pensions or gratuities. There is no contract created by which any person becomes entitled as a matter of right to sue the United States or to maintain a claim for any particular sum of money. Not only is there no contract implied but it is expressly negatived, because it is provided in the act, section 1104, that it may be repealed, altered, or amended in any of its provisions at any time. This Court has held that a pension granted by the Government is a matter of bounty, that the pensioner has no legal right to his pension, and that they may be given, withheld, distributed, or recalled at the discretion of Congress.[31]

So the U.S. Assistant Attorney General himself was telling the highest court in the land that Social Security benefits are pensions or gratuities, so not only is there no contractual right to Social Security benefits, there isn't even a legal right either. Yet for two years, prominent administration and Social Security Board officials had been telling the American people that they would get Social Security benefits "as a matter of right." If what the brief and Jackson's oral argument said was true, all the talk of rights was necessarily false. They cannot both be right.

Is it really plausible that Jackson, and the other administration figures preparing the brief, had no idea that for two years the administration had been touting Social Security as "insurance" collecting "contributions" or "premiums" and paying "earned annuity" benefits "as a matter of right"? Presumably they had followed the Social Security controversy in the 1936 election closely. How could they have failed to be aware of President Roosevelt's depiction of Social Security as "insurance" in his responses in his speeches to the pay-envelope scare? Roosevelt used speechwriters, and it is plausible that Social Security's general counsel, Thomas Eliot, whose name is affixed to the brief, had been consulted in preparing those speeches.

The administration's brief went on that whether or not Social Security "may properly be designated as old age insurance" was "completely immaterial." Since the law involved a valid use to the taxing power and a valid spending of benefits for the general welfare with no regulatory aspect, it was valid "whether it be labelled as insurance or not."[32] But Eliot had certainly not deemed the insurance label "immaterial" when drafting the bill, or when helping the semantic cleansing by the Ways and Means Committee, or when advising the Social Security Informational Service, after AAA was invalidated by the Court, to steer clear of any reference to insurance. If the word "insurance" was immaterial to the bill's validity, why was it avoided like the plague?

Oral Argument: Administration Arguments Unmasked

Some of the awkward fabrications of the administration's position were exposed by Edward McClennen, arguing before the Court on Davis's behalf. McClennen challenged the administration's claim that the Social Security tax was levied simply to raise revenue for the general use of government; rather, "there can be no question in anyone's mind but what this levy was made to provide old-age benefits." For one thing, he pointed out, the act was titled the "Social Security Act," not the "Revenue Act of 1935." For another, the sharp-eyed McClennen added, the preamble to the Act began, "An act to provide for the general welfare by establishing a system of Federal old-age benefits," and ended with "to raise revenue; and for other purposes"—the purpose of raising revenue, then, being "the residuary clause."[33]

Then, too, as McClennen rightly observed, taxing the smallest wage earners in the country and exempting all income above $3,000 a year is a peculiar
way to go about it if the purpose is to raise general revenue; suggesting that
as the purpose "flies in the face of all reason." Rather, the tax was levied on
those wages because the workers getting those wages "would be the ones who
were going to have the security of an old-age benefit. That was the only
reason that they did it."[34]

McClennen raised still another point: If the idea is to raise general revenue, why not tax farm laborers, domestic servants, and other laborers exempted from the Social Security tax? "Why, for the obvious reason that this
idea of old-age benefits was one that was to be limited to the same classes of
people."[35] Then he drove home yet another point: Section 210, defining
prospective beneficiaries, and Section 811, defining workers to be taxed,
have identical language except for one part regarding those over sixty-five,

> and it is perfectly obvious that the reason the over 65 is left out in the one clause is
> because they were going to fall at that age into the benefits that were coming in the
> benefit section.
>   If you looked only at the act itself, applying the common knowledge of the
> community, of what was being talked about, no one, I submit, would have any doubt
> but what in the substance of the thing that money was being raised for the purpose of
> creating this security fund.[36]

By now it was an open secret that the separation of titles II and VIII was not
substantive, that their exact similarity of language in these sections was a
giveaway. It had been pointed out by minority members of House Ways and
Means Committee, both in their minority report and, repeatedly, on the floor
of the House. Davis's lawyer had just done so again. The justices could hardly
have failed to grasp the reality.

McClennen went on to note that although men over sixty-five were certainly suffering then, in 1937, the Social Security Act didn't start paying out
any benefits until 1942. If the idea was to provide out of general revenue for
these needy elderly, why the delay? Obviously, because the money raised
under Title VIII was meant to create a reserve fund for paying benefits under
Title II.[37] In making this point, McClennen was doing no more than reiterate
what the administration itself had been saying publicly beginning with the
testimony of Perkins and Witte before Congress.

He then struck yet another blow at the pretense that the payroll and excise
taxes were intended simply to raise revenue for general use, pointing out that
the Social Security Act was essentially the proposal of the president's
Committee on Economic Security, which, he rightly observed, had been
created to propose legislation promoting economic security, not to raise
general revenue. Likewise, when the administration's economic security bodies reported,

In a 50-page report there is no talk about raising revenue for the Government of the United States, and there is much talk about the different subjects dealt with in the Social Security Act, and they propose under the title "Old Age Security" compulsory contributory annuities—compulsory contributory annuities, not annuities furnished by the United States going out and finding . . . general revenue. . . . This was not to be an act for the payment of a tax. It was an act to provide for compulsory contributions. [38]

He quoted the report's assertion that the best way to provide for the old age of the current young was with "a contributory system of old-age annuities" which would allow young workers "to build up a more adequate old age protection" than could have been done with noncontributory, means-tested pensions.[39]

In his penultimate line of argument denying that the exactions under the Social Security Act were taxes, McClennen zeroed in on the language of these preliminary documents:

"The compulsory contributions are to be collected through a tax on pay rolls and wages, to be divided equally between employers and employees." "The compulsory contributions are to be collected through a tax"—they were going to call the contribution a tax, but it was a contribution. It would have been no different if they had not used the word "tax" and had used the word "contribution," and if it had not been for the possibilities envisaged in the taxing clause [i.e., the clause in the Constitution giving Congress the taxing power] they would have spoken in the same language that they speak in the State act, "a contribution."[40]

Then, finally, there was the matter of benefits being given "as a right." McClennen pointed out caustically that nobody who pays *taxes* thinks that by so doing he has obtained a right to be supported by the government in old age, regardless of his means.[41]

In all of these matters, McClennen had seen through the language of the Act to reveal its obvious intent, as divulged by the economic reality of its provisions and passages in other documents, and exposed the separation of the titles and the argument that the taxes were meant merely to raise revenue for general use as shams. It was, in fact, the sort of attack which the administration had earlier given evidence of being afraid of, and tried to fend off with semantic cleansing and other measures. The administration clung tenaciously to the literal language of the Act and to arguments which were logically conceivable but utterly preposterous, e.g., that some future Congress might not vote appropriations for benefits; McClennen pointed doggedly and relentlessly to the substance and reality of what the Act was doing and was clearly meant to do. Though McClennen did not bring out either the administration's misleading use of insurance language and rights talk, or the intent to induce retirement as cited explicitly in Brown's and Latimer's testimony, he had landed sufficiently devastating blows. If any justices wanted to void Social Security as an unconstitutional tax-benefit scheme, they had their opening.

Yet in their questioning of McClennen, the justices did not pursue any of these matters. Nor did Special Assistant to the Attorney General Wyzanski rebut any of McClennen's arguments when he followed McClennen to present the balance of the government's oral argument. Nor did any of the justices, not even any of the diehard conservatives, raise any of McClennen's points in sifting Wyzanski. In fact, reading the oral arguments, one is struck by how perfunctory the justices' questioning was, how seldom they challenged anything said by either side.

One sees in all of this the efforts of the New Dealers to shape perceptions of Social Security, tailoring various versions of reality to fit their audiences: one version for Congress, another for the taxpayers, yet another for the Supreme Court. One sees too a contrived obliviousness, on the part of both Wyzanski and the Supreme Court, to a very formidable attack on Social Security.

The administration had political pressure and a misleading text on its side; Davis had reality on his. On May 24, reality lost.

The Decision: Let it Stand, and Take Off the Heat

By a vote of 7-2, the Supreme Court found Social Security constitutional. Justice Cardozo wrote the opinion for the majority. He was joined by Justices Brandeis, Stone, Hughes, Roberts, Van Devanter, and Sutherland.

The twelve-page *Helvering v. Davis* opinion makes very curious reading. The first three pages or so merely describe Titles II and VIII of the Social Security Act of 1935 and are taken almost verbatim from the administration's brief.[42] Thus, for example, the brief, describing Title VIII's provisions:

Title VIII imposes two distinct types of taxes, each beginning in the calendar year 1937.

It imposes upon *employers, excise* taxes with respect to having individuals in their employ, measured by wages paid during the calendar year [Section 804]. It also imposes upon *employees, income* taxes measured by wages paid to them during the calendar year [Section 801]. . . .

The proceeds of both taxes are required to be paid into the Treasury of the United States as internal revenue collections, and neither tax is earmarked in any way. Section 807.[43]

The *Helvering v. Davis* opinion, on the same topic:

Title VIII, as we have said, lays two different types of tax, an "income tax on employees," and "an excise tax on employers." The income tax on employees is measured by wages paid during the calendar year. § 801. The excise tax on the employer is to be paid "with respect to having individuals in his employ," and, like the tax on employees, is measured in wages. § 804. . . . The proceeds of both taxes are to be paid into the Treasury like internal-revenue taxes generally, and are not earmarked in any way. § 807(a).[44]

There follow about a page and a half of description of Davis's suit and its treatment in the lower courts, then a half-page of discussion of Justice Cardozo's own view that the Court should simply dismiss the case and not determine constitutional questions unless strictly necessary, then another half-page reporting that the majority of the Court disagrees with him and finds in the case "extraordinary features making it fitting . . . to determine whether the benefits and the taxes are valid or invalid."[45] We are halfway through the opinion, and no argument about constitutionality has yet been made. Next come five pages maintaining that Title II's benefit scheme does not conflict with the Tenth Amendment. Of these five pages, there are altogether little over two pages' worth of actual argument, making five points: that Congress may spend money to promote the general welfare; that the concept of the general welfare is not static, but changes with the times, and that the Depression had made indigence in old age a general, national problem, not a local one; that Congress didn't conjure up a judgment that old-age benefits would promote the general welfare out of thin air, but had the benefit of an extensive administration investigation of and report on economic security, plus lengthy committee hearings; and that whether or not Title II's old-age benefits were wise is a matter for Congress to decide, the Court being concerned only with the power to spend money on the general welfare; and that the concept of general welfare is for Congress to decide, not the states. Even the first two of these points, occupying about three-quarters of a page, lean heavily on the administration's brief. Thus, the brief, after arguing that the general welfare clause of the Constitution gives, besides a taxing power, a corresponding implicit power to spend for the general welfare, argues:

> This power of appropriation is not limited by or to the other enumerated powers. Rather, its limits are those implicit in the term "general welfare." It includes, in other words, any expenditure that will by any "reasonable possibility," conduce to the *general* welfare of the United States. [case and literature citations deleted] Though it is true that eminent men, upon whom the respondent relies (Br. 57-58), have at various times in our history asserted a contrary view, it must now be regarded as settled, not only by the *Butler* case, but also by the long continued practice of Congress in expenditures of public funds, that Story and Hamilton were correct.
>
> The determination whether a particular expenditure is for the general welfare is one of governmental policy—of political economy—in the largest sense of the term. In the very nature of this power, that question must be left to the determination of Congress. [citations deleted] If it were otherwise the Court would repeatedly be called upon to decide matters of policy and expediency—matters which it has stated it has no power to review. [citations deleted] In any event, this Court has stated that only when "by no reasonable possibility" can the challenged expenditure be said to fall within the "wide range of discretion" possessed by Congress will the statute be adjudged to be invalid [citations deleted].[46]

The Supreme Court opinion:

Congress may spend money in aid of the "general welfare." [citations deleted] There
have been great statesmen in our history who stood for other views. We will not
resurrect the contest. It is now settled by decision. *United States v. Butler, supra.* The
conception of the spending power advocated by Hamilton and strongly reinforced
by Story has prevailed over that of Madison, which has not been lacking in adher-
ents. Yet difficulties are left when the power is conceded. The line must still be drawn
between one welfare and another, between particular and general. Where this line
shall be placed cannot be known through a formula in advance of the event. There is
a middle ground or certainly a penumbra in which discretion is at large. The discretion,
however, is not confided to the courts. The discretion belongs to Congress, unless the
choice is clearly wrong, a display of arbitrary power, not an exercise of judgment. This
is now familiar law. "When such a contention comes here we naturally require a
showing that by no reasonable possibility can the challenged legislation fall within the
wide range of discretion permitted to the Congress" [citations deleted].[47]

The other three pages or so of these five are further extracts almost verbatim from the administration's brief, almost wholly recapitulations of facts
regarding indigence in old age and the inability of state government to cope
with it.[48] The remainder, less than a page in length, merely ties up loose ends
such as the validity of the tax on employers, referring readers to the compan-
ion decision in *Steward Machine Co. v. Davis,* and announcing that the de-
cree of the Court of Appeals was reversed.[49] So out of twelve pages, there are
altogether almost nine pages of mere description, six of them lifted from the
administration's brief; about a page arguing or disposing of miscellaneous
points; and roughly two pages of actual argument on constitutional issues, of
which about three-quarters of a page, again, is largely lifted from the
administration's brief.

The bulk of the *Helvering v. Davis* opinion, then, is simply a scissors-and-
paste assembly of extracts, mostly merely factual, from the administration's
brief, with in many cases only very minor changes in the wording. Of actual
independent argument the opinion contains next to nothing.

Now, one might maintain that when the Court decides in favor of one side
in a case, it might be natural for the Court to help itself to a few passages in
that side's brief, simply to save time. But so heavy a dependence on a brief as
this is surely curious, especially in light of many key features of this case.

First, regarding McClennen's many telling arguments and pieces of evidence that Titles II and VIII did in fact constitute an invalid old-age insurance
scheme rather than a bid to raise revenue, the opinion is absolutely silent.
Cardozo merely points out that Davis argued that the provisions of Titles II
and VIII "dovetail in such a way as to justify the conclusion that Congress
would have been unwilling to pass one without the other" and that the government, on the other hand, maintained that "the tax moneys are not earmarked, and that Congress is at liberty to spend them as it will." He adds that

"We find it unnecessary to make a choice between the arguments, and so leave the question open."[50] In other words, the Court ducked the whole issue. One must wonder why, given that Davis's argument opens the issue that Titles II and VIII constitute an organic whole, an unauthorized government insurance scheme, and the government, appealing speciously to the lack of ear-marking of taxes, evades that reality. Why did the Court find nothing to say about this key controversy?

Second, given the enormous innovation in federal policy Social Security entailed, the administration's deep fear that the Court would find it unconstitutional, the intense controversy Social Security generated in the 1936 election, and Social Security's vast importance for the country, the decision was an extremely momentous one in our national life. So it seems *prima facie* baffling that the majority opinion argued the decision so perfunctorily, letting so vast a matter turn on roughly two pages of argument.

Moreover, given the numerous telling points raised by Davis's lawyer, one would think too that Cardozo would at least have made some effort to address them. Yet the opinion singled out for rebuttal *only* McClennen's final three paragraphs, which argued a point utterly ungermane to his entire line of attack exposing Social Security as a program of enforced contributions for old-age benefits: that Social Security was regulating the internal affairs of the sovereign state of Massachusetts, which thought it best to have her people make their own provisions for old age, so as to encourage frugality and self-reliance. One who read only the *Helvering v. Davis* opinion by Justice Cardozo would risk gaining the very misleading impression that this was McClennen's main point.

One's bafflement deepens when one notes that the majority included only three liberals—Justices Brandeis, Cardozo, and Stone; the majority of the majority, Chief Justice Hughes and Justices Roberts, Van Devanter, and Sutherland, were not liberals, the former two frequently, and the latter two consistently, taking the conservative side. Yet they all concurred in Cardozo's listless liberal opinion. Moreover, Justices Hughes, Roberts, and Sutherland had been scathing in their attacks on the administration in earlier cases. In the majority opinion on *Jones v. Securities Commission,* the SEC case, for example, Sutherland had thundered that the SEC's investigation of one Jones, a seller of oil royalties, "finds no support in right principle or in law. It is wholly unreasonable and arbitrary," and compared it with "the intolerable abuses of the Star Chamber."[51] Why, one asks, did such outspoken, vigorous critics of the administration concur in such a sketchily argued opinion which scarcely bothered to make an independent effort to sift and evaluate the issues and articulate a position, and consisted mostly of mere regurgitation of the administration's brief, hence amounted to a limp acquiescence in the administration's position, almost an outright surrender? Is it really plausible that these strong-minded men found in Cardozo's scissor-and-paste job an adequate expression of their settled beliefs on the constitutionality of compulsory, contributory federal old-age retirement benefits? That they deemed it convincing and sound enough to attach their names to it?

Only Justices McReynolds and Butler dissented; Cardozo noted that they "are of the opinion that the provisions of the act here challenged are repugnant to the Tenth Amendment."[52] But they did not write any opinions. This, too, is most singular. Did these two stalwart conservatives, arch-defenders of the Framers' original intent, who, one may safely presume, were bitterly hostile to such a radical departure from original intent as Social Security, really have nothing beyond that terse phrase to say about it? Nothing at all?

Or were they, perhaps, anxious not to give the Court's critics anything to work with? Here lies the key to all the mystery: the political context of the decision. The Court was under enormous political pressure, and the justices were well aware of the danger. In saving Social Security, the Court saved itself.

This was widely recognized at the time. The Court's validation of the Social Security Act was big news, reported in the *New York Times* and the *Washington Post* with huge headlines, long articles, and reprints of the full texts of the majority and minority opinions of the three decisions, and greeted by the administration with almost frantic jubilation.[53] The *Post* editorialized the next day that:

> the Supreme Court, by approving the Social Security Act in its entirety, has driven another nail in the coffin of the President's plan to enlarge the court's membership. Coming as this action does after the approval of the Wagner Labor Relations act and the court's reversal on State minimum wage legislation, it removes the last flimsy argument for the appointment of additional justices who could be expected to reflect the President's viewpoint.[54]

The decisions, the *Philadelphia Inquirer* declared, "brush away, as by a cleansing wind, all possible excuses" for Roosevelt's plan to pack the Court.[55] A solid majority of newspapers commenting on the decision, reported the *United States News,* concurred.[56]

Most editorials had it that the Court had sincerely come around to a more permissive interpretation of the Constitution regarding government measures for the general welfare. But some papers asked whether the pro-Social Security decisions would have come about had the president's Court proposal not been exerting pressure.[57] And one keen observer, writing to the *Washington Post,* argued that certain things about the old-age benefit decision indicated that the Court "acted under pressure rather than through conversion to a new point of view." The May 1935 voiding of the Railroad Retirement Act had been done on the grounds that that Act was not a regulation of interstate commerce within the Constitution's meaning. Since railroads were under federal jurisdiction, while genuine doubt existed as to whether other forms of employment were subject to federal regulation, this decision presumably barred general old-age pensions too. The 7-2 validation of Social Security's old-age benefits surely overruled the Railroad Retirement Act decision—yet the majority opinion did not mention the 1935 decision at all, and the minority opinion went unwritten. "Needless to say, a genuine change of view would not have needed the protection of a conspiracy of silence."[58] Indeed it would not.

Roosevelt slogged obstinately on with his Court pack, only to go down to humiliating defeat. How much positive contribution the Court's Social Security decision made to that outcome is unknown; certainly it made the negative contribution of depriving the Court pack campaign of a chance at rejuvenation. Taken together, all the evidence seen here—the retreat all along the line by the Court in the face of the Court pack plan; the misleading nature of many arguments in the administration's brief, so transparently at variance with the public record of testimony and argument; McClennen's sustained exposure of Social Security's true purpose; the complete evasion of that exposure by both the administration and the Court; the perfunctoriness and flaccidity of the Court's majority opinion, so overwhelmingly derivative from the administration's brief; the tame acquiescence of a majority of the Court's ferocious New Deal opponents in so limp a performance; the silence of the dissenting two-justice conservative rump—indicates that the decision could hardly have been reached on its merits. Reading through the oral arguments with all this in mind, one gets a strong impression that even before the oral arguments were heard, the conservative justices, perhaps in informal conclave, perhaps in the privacy of their own minds, had already decided the outcome: they would again win by losing. The conclusion is all but inescapable that the Court, deliberating at the pistol point, found Social Security constitutional for political reasons, to take off the heat.

Notes

1. Quoted in David Boaz, *Libertarianism: A Primer* (New York: The Free Press, 1997), p. 123.
2. Schlesinger, *The Politics of Upheaval,* pp. 455-467.
3. Rauch, *The History of the New Deal 1933-1938,* pp. 192-222; Schlesinger, *The Politics of Upheaval,* pp. 274-283, 470-481.
4. Rauch, *The History of the New Deal 1933-1938,* p. 202; Drew Pearson and Robert S. Allen, *The Nine Old Men* (Garden City, NY: Doubleday, Doran & Co., Inc., 1936); Alsop and Catledge, *The 168 Days,* pp. 17-21; Robert H. Jackson, *The Struggle for Judicial Supremacy: A Study of a Crisis in American Politics* (New York: Alfred A. Knopf, 1941), pp. 329-337.
5. Jackson, *The Struggle for Judicial Supremacy,* pp. 340-351.
6. Alsop and Catledge, *The 168 Days,* pp. 113-127.
7. Jackson, *The Struggle for Judicial Supremacy,* pp. 203-205, 206-213.
8. Ibid., pp. 214-215, 224-226.
9. Alsop and Catledge, *The 168 Days,* pp. 142-143.

10. Ibid., pp. 145-146; Rauch, *The History of the New Deal 1933-1938,* pp. 277-279.
11. Jackson, *The Struggle for Judicial Supremacy,* pp. 219-220.
12. "Judiciary: Justice Retired," *Time,* May 31, 1937, p. 17; Alsop and Catledge, *The 168 Days,* pp. 205-211.
13. "In the Supreme Court of the United States, October Term, 1936, *Helvering v. Davis,* Brief for Petitioners Helvering and Welch," in U.S., Congress, House, Committee on Ways and Means, *Analysis of the Social Security System: Hearings before a Subcommittee of the House Committee on Ways and Means,* 83rd Cong., 1st sess., 1953, Appendix II, Miscellaneous Documents [hereafter, "Brief for Petitioners Helvering and Welch," *Analysis of the Social Security System: Hearings,* Appendix II], pp. 1427, 1431; *Helvering v. Davis,* 301 U.S. 619, at 619.
14. Alsop and Catledge, *The 168 Days,* p. 214.
15. "Brief for Petitioners Helvering and Welch," *Analysis of the Social Security System: Hearings,* Appendix II, p. 1427.
16. Ibid., p. 1428.
17. Ibid., p. 1429.
18. Ibid., p. 1432.
19. Ibid., pp. 1436-1439.
20. Ibid., p. 1439.
21. Ibid.
22. Ibid., pp. 1440-1453, 1453-1455.
23. Ibid., p. 1455.
24. U.S., Congress, Senate, *Oral Arguments in Helvering et al. v. Davis involving the Old Age Benefit Provisions of the Social Security Act before the Supreme Court of the United States, May 5, 1937,* S. Doc. 71, 75th Cong., 1st sess., 1937 [hereafter *Oral Arguments, Helvering v. Davis*], p. 39.
25. *Economic Security Act: Hearings,* pp. 221-224.
26. Ibid., p. 230.
27. Ibid., p. 241.
28. "Brief for Petitioners Helvering and Welch," *Analysis of the Social Security System: Hearings,* Appendix II, pp. 1455-1456.
29. Ibid., p. 1456.
30. *Helvering v. Davis,* 301 U.S. 619, at 24.
31. *Oral Arguments, Helvering v. Davis,* p. 16.
32. "Brief for Petitioners Helvering and Welch," *Analysis of the Social Security System: Hearings,* Appendix II, p. 1456.
33. *Oral Arguments, Helvering v. Davis,* p. 27.
34. Ibid.
35. Ibid., p. 28.
36. Ibid.
37. Ibid.
38. Ibid., p. 33.
39. Ibid.
40. Ibid., p. 34.
41. Ibid.
42. Author's comparison of texts of *Helvering v. Davis,* 301 U.S. 619, at 634-637 and "Brief for Petitioners Helvering and Welch," *Analysis of the Social Security System: Hearings,* Appendix II, pp. 1427-1430.
43. "Brief for Petitioners Helvering and Welch," *Analysis of the Social Security System: Hearings,* Appendix II, p. 1428.
44. *Helvering v. Davis,* 301 U.S. 619, at 635.

45. Ibid., at 637-640.
46. "Brief for Petitioners Helvering and Welch," *Analysis of the Social Security System: Hearings,* Appendix II, pp. 1441.
47. *Helvering v. Davis,* 301 U.S. 619, at 640-641.
48. Author's comparison of texts of *Helvering v. Davis,* 301 U.S. 619, at 640-645 and "Brief for Petitioners Helvering and Welch," *Analysis of the Social Security System: Hearings,* Appendix II, pp. 1441-1449.
49. *Helvering v. Davis,* 301 U.S. 619, at 646-647.
50. Ibid., at 646.
51. Jackson, *The Struggle for Judicial Supremacy,* pp. 148-149. The Star Chamber was an ancient English high court, apparently named for the stars on the ceiling of the chamber where it sat, which could act on mere rumor and apply torture. The parallel does seem overdone, as Cardozo noted in his dissent.
52. *Helvering v. Davis,* 301 U.S. 619, at 646.
53. "Supreme Court Backs Security Act on Job Insurance, 5-4, Pensions, 7-2; Roosevelt Asks a Wage-Hour Law," *New York Times,* May 25, 1937, 1, 24; "Supreme Court Validates Security Act; Roosevelt Urges Wages and Hours Law," *Washington Post,* May 25, 1937, 1, 4. Interestingly, also on May 24, in a wholly unrelated case, the Court beat yet another strategic retreat, ruling 5-4 that under Wisconsin's labor code, a labor union had the right to peacefully picket a nonunion employer. "Right of Labor to Picket Valid In Wisconsin," *Washington Post,* May 25, 1937, 4.
54. "Social Security Upheld," *Washington Post,* May 25, 1937, 6.
55. "With Other Editors: The Social Security Verdict," *Washington Post,* May 30, 1937, sec. III, 7.
56. "Social Security Decision: What Editors Say," *United States News,* May 31, 1937, p. 10.
57. Ibid.
58. "Letters to the Editor: Supreme Court Since Reform Proposal," *Washington Post,* May 29, 1937, 6.

6

Forging a False Consciousness

*"You can convince anybody of anything if you
just push it at them all of the time. They may
not believe it 100 percent, but they will still
draw opinions from it, especially if they have
no other information to draw their opinions
from."*

—*Charles Manson[1]*

After *Helvering v. Davis:* Insurance Again

However the decision was reached, Social Security was quick to take advantage of it. Now that the program was safely past the Court, the denial that it was insurance had served its purpose. The *Helvering v. Davis* decision cleared the way for a massive campaign to fatefully shape public consciousness about Social Security.

The very same day the Court ruled, the Social Security Board abruptly reversed itself. Years later, Wilbur Cohen, who was present with Winant and Altmeyer when the Court's decisions were read out, reminisced about the immediate aftermath of *Helvering v. Davis:*

> I recall walking down the steps of the Supreme Court building in a glow of ecstasy with Mr. Winant and Mr. Altmeyer. We had hoped and prayed for this day. . . . When I got back to the office, I obtained Mr. Altmeyer's approval to send out a memo to the staff stating that because of the decision we could now call the old age benefits program "old age insurance" and we could now call the unemployment compensation program "unemployment insurance." The American public was and still is insurance-minded and opposed to welfare, "the dole," and "handouts."[2]

As Cohen's last sentence makes clear, the prompt reversion to insurance language was meant to gain public acceptance of Social Security by simultaneously tying it to something which enjoyed wide approbation and avoiding the stigma of welfare.

Losing no time, that very day Altmeyer, who had replaced Winant as chairman of the Social Security Board, issued a press release stating, "The decision in the Massachusetts case validated the Federal old-age insurance program contained in the Social Security Act," and repeated himself the next day speaking in Indianapolis.[3]

Social Security's Bureau of Federal Old-Age Benefits was retitled Bureau of Old-Age Insurance. Social Security circulars and other documents were rewritten to insert insurance language. Thus, in Informational Service Circular No. 1, *A Brief Explanation of the Social Security Act,* the section "Federal Old-Age Benefits" was retitled "Federal Old-Age Insurance."[4] Circular No. 3, a question-and-answer format explanation of old-age benefits, *Federal Old-Age Benefits,* became *Old-Age Insurance: Federal Old-Age Benefits.* This in turn was replaced by a new Circular No. 3, *Old-Age Insurance Under the Social Security Act: Some Questions and Answers.* This version, perhaps attempting to convince readers that Social Security is insurance by sheer repetition, used the phrase "old-age insurance" twelve times in the first three pages of text.[5] Circular No. 4, *Federal Old-Age Benefits established by The Social Security Act,* became *Federal Old-Age Benefits (Old-Age Insurance) established by The Social Security Act.*[6]

As they did after passage, leading Social Security officials promoted Social Security in the press. Not only did they employ insurance language, they went out of their way to tell readers that Social Security gave the worker a better deal than he would be able to get in the private sector. Mary Dewson, a member of the Social Security Board, wrote that "it is particularly important to remember" that social insurance can outperform private insurance. The lump-sum payments, being 3.5 percent of wages, would far exceed the worker's one-percent (maximum 3 percent) payroll tax. A worker who qualified for monthly benefits would do still better, getting "higher returns than he would realize if he put an amount equal to his old-age contribution into private insurance." If a man turning sixty-five in 1942 had averaged $900 in annual earnings since 1936, his total tax would be $54, but he would get a monthly benefit of $16.25; with a life expectancy of twelve years at sixty-five, he'd receive more than 40 times his tax payment.[7] John Corson, Director of the Bureau of Old Age Insurance, made a similar argument in *Survey Midmonthly.*[8]

To summarize the administration's efforts thus far in presenting and promoting Social Security: Social Security was introduced in Congress as old-age insurance, a unified system whose contributions were intended to build up "contractual annuities" and a fund for paying those "annuities" to beneficiaries "as a matter of contractual right," though the bill contained no contract language; but to improve the bill's chances of surviving a constitutional challenge before the Supreme Court, it was then meticulously rewritten and scrubbed of insurance language. After passage, the selfsame Social Security Act was promoted to the public by leading officials as "insurance" charging "premiums" to holders of "insurance policies" paying benefits "as a matter of right"; then after the Court struck down AAA in January 1936, Social Security's Informational Service shunned all insurance talk; then President Roosevelt and other Democratic politicians used insurance language heavily for campaign purposes. Then, to win approval from the Supreme Court for Social Security, the administration explicitly denied that the taxes were for any special purpose; denied that the combination of Titles II and VIII constituted insurance; and denied that Social Security benefits were property to which beneficiaries had a contractual right or even a legal right. The very same day the decision went Social Security's way, the robes of insurance were instantly donned again. Not only was Social Security insurance after all, it was the best insurance deal one could get.

The motives of Roosevelt, Altmeyer, Cohen, and others and Social Security's purposes are not the issue. The point, rather, is that the administration made an enormous effort to shape the perceptions and beliefs of the Congress, the Supreme Court, and the public regarding Social Security—and that as the documentary evidence, for example, the numerous discrepancies in the *Helvering v. Davis* case between the administration's presentations and the facts, reveals, the consciousness which Social Security's promoters were striving to build up was greatly at variance with reality.

The popular media had already obligingly accepted the government's insurance analogy for its old-age program, and continued to do so after *Helvering v. Davis*, thereby further disposing Americans to think of Social Security as insurance. A piece in the social workers' journal *Survey Midmonthly* presented the plight of a hypothetical machinist who buys industrial life insurance paying a meager death benefit of $250. Then his Social Security paycheck deductions start. He looks into Social Security and finds that his government is not just providing old-age income but "acting as his life insurance company—and giving him a better break for his money than any insurance company salesman had ever offered him." Delighted, he visits his local Social Security office, where he learns that "I've got a life insurance policy with the government" offering him far better returns than the industrial insurance policy. The author then predicted that as workers realize that "the federal government has become the largest life insurance company in the world," with a total of $1,340,000,000 of "insurance in force" or "amount at risk," with the employer as "premium collector" just as in private group insurance, and as the "implications and guarantees" of Title II become clear to them, the industrial life insurance business would fade away.[9]

In February 1939, *Time* opened an article on Social Security revision thus:

It is an axiom in the insurance business that insurance is not bought but sold. In 1935 Franklin Roosevelt sold Congress and Congress sold the U. S. the Social Security Act, the biggest, most comprehensive, most expensive *mass insurance policy* ever written. Since then, its *purchasers,* the nation's taxpayers, had had occasion to read their *policy* carefully . . . (italics added)[10]

The government's version of Social Security's nature was swallowed uncritically by the media and passed on to the public. It would never occur to anyone reading these pieces to ask whether or not the insurance language was really appropriate for Social Security. The media's acquiescence was as complete as the Supreme Court's had been.

The Reserve Fund Controversy

On one aspect of Social Security, however, a very heated discussion did rage in the press: the Old Age Reserve Account at the Treasury created by Title II. As we shall see, today's controversy over the Social Security "trust fund" is not new. The same issues, criticisms, and defenses were bandied about sixty years ago.

The Social Security Act required that every year, an amount determined sufficient to pay benefits for that year was to be appropriated to the Account, and any amount not needed for benefits was to be invested in interest-bearing U.S. government debt (including special unmarketable debt issued exclusively for this account for this purpose) and debt whose principal and interest were guaranteed by the U.S. government. In a cogent explanation of the Social Security program in April 1936, M. Albert Linton, president of Provident Mutual Life Insurance Company, who had served as an actuarial consultant to the Committee on Economic Security, noted that the Account was estimated by the Senate Finance Committee to be roughly $47 billion by 1980. The securities in the Account were to earn 3 percent interest a year, and eventually, Linton pointed out, the interest would pay roughly 40 percent of the benefit outlays, current payroll tax receipts paying the rest. Of an eventual $3.5 billion in benefit outlays a year, then, interest on the bonds in the Reserve Account would pay $1.4 billion and payroll taxes $2.1 billion. "It is important to keep in mind that the sole function of the Reserve Account is to produce interest," Linton wrote. "It is not contemplated that the principal will ever have to be drawn upon."[11] The interest from bonds bought with earlier surpluses would thus help pay Social Security's way in the out years, meaning payroll taxes would be lower than they would be otherwise, and the plan would be totally self-supporting, requiring no money from the Treasury.

Criticism was not slow in coming. A few months later, Winthrop Aldrich of Chase National Bank held that the analogy behind the reserve, of a private insurance company building up a reserve to meet likely future demands on it, was specious. The reserve is unnecessary, he argued, because the government, unlike a private insurance company, can not only compel citizens to pay "premiums," it can raise them at will. Moreover, the reserve, being invested in the government's own securities, would be fictitious; the government would merely be issuing promissory notes to itself. As to interest on the bonds in the reserve lightening the burden on future taxpayers, this too was specious. The Account would get interest from the government bonds, but the government would get the interest it pays on those bonds from "the only place it could obtain it—the general taxpayer. The whole elaborate reserve set-up would not relieve him of any burden whatever." Finally, the money the Treasury got in exchange for these bonds would be a standing temptation to extravagant government spending.[12]

Candidates Landon and Roosevelt, as we saw, added their bit to the growing controversy, Landon attacking the reserve fund as a sham, Roosevelt bitterly questioning the patriotism of people who speculated that future Congresses might spend the fund. In January 1937, Senator Arthur Vandenberg (R-MI) introduced a resolution to abandon the "full reserve system," by either cutting Social Security taxes or increasing spending through benefit liberalization or extension of coverage. Social Security Chairman Altmeyer testified against the resolution, arguing that without the reserve of government-held Treasury debt, the government would actually have to pay more in the out years, both to defray benefit costs that otherwise would have been paid by interest on the reserve, and to pay interest on Treasury debt held privately rather than by the reserve. Off the record, Altmeyer suggested to Vandenberg that if the growth of government debt due to the Social Security reserve bothered him, he could insert a provision in his resolution requiring surplus Social Security revenues be put into "sound private securities." "That would be socialism," the horrified Vandenberg replied, and the idea went nowhere.[13]   Note that one of today's privatization proposals—government investment of some of the Social Security surplus in the stock market—was raised first in 1937, not by a free-market critic of Social Security, but by its chief administrator, and rejected, not by a passionate Social Security advocate, but by a conservative Republican critic!

General Hugh Johnson, former head of the National Recovery Administration, weighed in in November with a bitter radio speech attacking the Social Security tax and reserve fund. While defending old-age pensions, he pointed out that though the payroll tax "is supposed to be like a premium for life insurance," the analogy was bogus:

> The insurance company invests premiums paid them in mortgages and other property, to be held in trust for those who pay it. From these incomes and increases in values—this great pool of property—they pay losses and pensions. Is the Government doing something like that with these savings of yours? It is not. It is spending them. . . . All that goes into your reserve is a paper IOU. When the time comes to pay, there won't be any more value there than if the workers had paid nothing in taxes all over these years, instead of fifty billion dollars. . . . All your pennies buy is a promise of government to tax your children to take care of you in your age. . . . The Social

Security Tax is a new . . . tax . . . to pay for current spending, levied adroitly on the pay of the poor by fooling them into thinking it is an insurance premium.[14]

Defenders responded that the talk of IOUs was misleading; after all, aren't all private investment instruments, such as stocks, notes and bonds, nothing but pieces of paper, IOUs really, their value depending in the end on the resources and ethics of the firms issuing them? In investing in government bonds, Beulah Amidon argued, the Treasury was behaving just like a bank, which does not hoard its depositors' money as cash but invests it, the safest investment being . . . government bonds. Besides, if the reserve was used to reduce publicly held government debt, that is in fact a savings—a savings of money that in future years would have been used to pay interest on publicly held debt.[15]

There was some point to all this, but much of the defense of the reserve fund was mere specious evasion of critics rather than engagement of them. Regarding the critics' charge that surplus taxes would simply be spent on general government outlays, Social Security's general counsel, Thomas Eliot, retorted that he doubted that a worker would be impressed by "the argument that the money should be buried in the ground for thirty years." (No one, of course, was advocating any such thing.) While realizing that 1960's benefits would have to be paid out of 1960's funds, the worker also realizes, Eliot continued, that they "are much more likely to be paid in full in 1960 if payroll taxes are levied now, and the proceeds wisely spent."[16] Eliot's other arguments seldom rose above the level of this insolent *non sequitur*. Amidon fell back on accusing critics of fear-mongering and undermining public confidence in Social Security: "To say that the money contributed by wage earners and their employers is being 'spent,' to call government bonds 'I.O.U.'s' is to stir up a lot of fear and misunderstanding."[17]

In point of fact, the reserve's critics were right. Of course the Treasury spent the money it obtained in exchange for depositing government debt in the old-age reserve; what else was it to do with it? Of course the government bonds were IOUs; that, after all, is what all debt instruments, public or private, are. Of course the interest would come from the general taxpayer; where else could it come from?

As preparation got underway to amend the Social Security Act, a vigorous essay by journalist John T. Flynn appeared in *Harper's,* criticizing the reserve at length. Any investment beyond strict cash hoarding is in reality a claim against the entity whose investment instrument one purchases. The Treasury bonds in the reserve, then, are just the government's claims against itself, hence have no real value. That being the case, Flynn maintained, the analogies between government old-age insurance and private insurance and between government reserves and private insurance company reserves, break down. "An investment is a means of adding to your own earnings part of the earnings of another person. It is not a device for merely ear-marking part of your own earnings." Claims on outside assets, such as private insurers have, are real; claims on oneself "are no claims at all." Moreover, the interest on the reserve in the out years would have to be paid from taxes levied in those years. Besides the payroll tax, then, there would be a growing tax burden just to pay the interest on the reserve. People would have to be taxed twice. Flynn drew the moral that "A public old-age insurance plan can be financed on a pay-as-you-go basis and in no other way." He proposed reducing the taxes already in the Act for the early years to eliminate the projected reserve, and adopting a pay-as-you-go system, with general taxes to cover whatever benefit costs the payroll tax didn't cover.[18]

Flynn had a formidable reputation as a progressive, a financial columnist, and a foe of investment trusts, and his essay created a sensation. It was repeatedly inserted in the *Congressional Record,* and Flynn testified at length during the 1939 Social Security amendment hearings, into the record of which his essay was also placed. Others were speaking and writing along the same lines, denouncing the reserve as dishonest and arguing that if it were abandoned, the scheduled increases in the payroll tax would not be necessary.[19]

Pressure to Liberalize: Philosophical and Political

While the reserve issue was heating up, pressure was rising to liberalize Social Security.

Among social insurance advocates, calls were appearing for expansion of the program. In one of the great seminal articles in the Social Security literature, Metropolitan Life Insurance Company executive Reinhard Hohaus, an advocate of expansion, observed that Social Security recognized two different principles in its benefit formula: *individual equity,* insofar as benefits were proportional to wages and payroll tax contributions, and *social adequacy,* insofar as those who had lower earnings and contributions received benefits which were *relatively* larger compared to their contributions. In serving the principle of individual equity, Social Security resembled private insurance, which, seeking to protect individuals from risks and being voluntary, must as much as possible make its benefit proportional to the individual's contribution. Social insurance, by contrast, seeks to give people a minimum of protection against a widespread, that is, "social," dependency problem, hence "views society as a whole" and deals with the individual only as "one small element of that whole." Its "first objective" regarding benefits should be that beneficiaries will receive enough income to "prevent their becoming a charge on society." Social adequacy also addresses the proportion of the population participating in social insurance. While considerations of individual equity needn't be totally disregarded, social adequacy should "control the pattern of social insurance" and of the two principles is "the more essential and less dispensable." The existing Social Security program's combination of individual equity and social adequacy, Hohaus complained, "unduly stresses the former."[20] He concluded that

> any social insurance program should be founded on broad social concepts rather than on reasoning centered around the individual. Accordingly, in deliberations on our federal old age benefits system it would seem logical, first of all, to substitute for the present approach stressing private individual insurance ideas one aiming at a substantially social interpretation of values.[21]

Specifically, Hohaus called for larger initial benefits and broadening the scope of coverage to "aged widows of pensioners and other groups not now included." After presenting proposals for achieve that, Hohaus concluded on "an emphatic note of caution," namely that the proposed liberalizations "should be accompanied by reductions in the benefits for primary beneficiaries the present formula would produce for later years. Failure to do this might well lead to an unsound financial basis."[22]

There was also growing press and political criticism of Social Security's benefits as niggardly. Some of this came from critics of the old-age reserve fund.[23] Also, many deemed the old-age assistance program set up under Title I inadequate; due to fiscal pressures, most states could not meet the maximum federal grant of $15 a month per old-age assistance beneficiary, and the 1937-1938 secondary depression further weakened state finances. With states permitted much leeway under Title I, the 1938 elections saw ballot proposals in seven states to set up more-generous old-age pensions. The Townsend movement, still large and active, was a natural outlet for this sentiment, and as a result became very formidable politically in 1938. The Republicans, battling back from near-oblivion, sought and received Townsend support in many congressional races. Thanks to this and other factors, such the secondary depression and anger over the Court pack attempt, Republicans did well in 1938, gaining eighty-one House seats.[24] Once again, the administration was under severe political pressure from the left over old-age benefits.

Finally, there was expansionist sentiment in the administration itself which, recall, had intended the original Social Security Act as just a start toward universal social insurance. In the wake of Vandenberg's resolution, Altmeyer suggested that Congress recommend persons to advise the Social Security Board about the reserve and how to get rid of it through program liberalization. The Board and a subcommittee of the Senate Finance Committee accordingly picked an Advisory Council. To get things going, Altmeyer sent Roosevelt a memorandum asking for advice on what to do with the advisory group (which hadn't yet met) and suggesting that the administration use political attacks—the Republican National Committee was sending material to columnists describing the payroll tax as a way of taxing the poor to finance the government, and John Hamilton had bragged that Republican Congress-

men had forced the Board to start acting on Republican proposals to liberalize benefits and to keep taxes low by scrapping the reserve—as pretexts for "a
socially desirable program" of liberalizing Social Security benefits and adding disability and survivors' benefits.[25]

Roosevelt agreed that the Advisory Council on Social Security should go
ahead. The Council, the members of which included several of the same
persons who had served in 1934 on the various bodies preparing the original
Social Security bill, held meetings and issued a final report on December 10,
1938. Drawing on this report and others and its own cogitations on Social
Security amendment, the Social Security Board itself reported on December
30. The Board recommended starting monthly old-age benefits in 1940 rather
than 1942; increasing the benefits payable in early years; paying supplementary benefits for aged dependent wives of retirees; using average wages rather
than lifetime wages as the base for calculating benefits, permitting an increase in early benefits; expansion to include survivors' insurance, paying
benefits to widows and orphans, since social insurance's "primary purpose
should be to pay benefits in accordance with the presumptive needs of the
beneficiaries," not to make payments to a deceased employee's estate irrespective of such needs; and broadening coverage to include domestic service, some agricultural labor, workers in nonprofit organizations, and others.[26]

For its part, the Advisory Council proposed not only these changes, but
some others, noteworthy chiefly for what they reveal of the gap between
presentation and reality. First, to compensate for the increased cost of accelerating and liberalizing existing benefit payments and adding survivors' benefits, the Council recommended cutting benefits to single individuals, arguing
that "Certainty is more valuable than promises. Only by such readjustment of
benefit schedules does the expansion of the scope of the insurance program
seem financially feasible." Likewise, the survivors' benefits removed justification for large lump-sum death benefits, which should be radically scaled
back.[27] What certainty a beneficiary could have if Congress broke its promises was left unexplained. Too, this proposal made nonsense of the rights talk
of the previous four years.

The Council also recommended creation of an old-age insurance trust
fund, to which Social Security tax receipts should be credited directly through
automatic appropriation, rather than to the Treasury's general fund and then
shifted over by appropriation. When the Act was drafted, the Council noted,
constitutional considerations made legal separation of tax and benefit provisions necessary. "It is believed that in the light of subsequent court decisions
such legal separation is no longer necessary. Since the taxes levied are essentially contributions intended to finance the benefit program," having them
credited automatically to such a fund "is not only logical but expedient."[28]
All of this, of course, being a confession that the title-separation and money-
rerouting aspects of the Social Security Act were, like the avoidance of insur-

ance language, mere tactics to ensure survival of a court challenge, to be discarded when no longer needed.

The 1939 Amendments:
Institutionalizing Appearances with Insurance Language

On January 16, 1939 President Roosevelt sent Congress a message transmitting the Social Security Board's report and requesting amendment of the Act. Reflecting the decision to present Social Security as insurance, he described Social Security as a "Federal old age insurance system" containing "individual accounts covering 42,500,000 persons who may be likened to the policy holders of a private insurance company."[29] By these persons he meant, of course, the workers in occupations on which Social Security taxes were levied. In the course of his short message Roosevelt referred to "old age insurance" five more times and called for paying monthly benefits sooner, liberalizing benefits in the early years, and expanding Social Security to give monthly benefits not only to the elderly but to dependent children of workers who die before they can retire. Signaling yet further expansion to come, he added that "equity and sound social policy require that the benefits be extended to all of our people as rapidly as administrative experience and public understanding permit." At the same time, mindful no doubt of the Townsend Plan, he warned against "turning to untried and demonstrably unsound panaceas."[30]

The administration's bill to amend the Social Security Act (H.R. 6635) was introduced the next day. The House Ways and Means Committee held extensive hearings February 1-April 7, and on June 2 reported the bill favorably without having made any amendments, and recommended passage. The House passed the bill overwhelmingly, by 364-2, on June 10; the Senate, after slight amendments, passed it 57-8. After conference, both houses passed the bill and Roosevelt signed it on August 10.[31]

The administration's bill loaded the text of the Social Security Act—which four years earlier had been scrubbed of even a hint at "insurance" in order to survive Supreme Court scrutiny—with insurance terminology. "Title II—Federal Old Age Benefits" became "Title II—Federal Old-Age and Survivor Insurance Benefits." "Old Age Reserve Account" was now "Federal Old-Age and Survivor Insurance Trust Fund"; "Old Age Benefit Payments" was now "Old-Age and Survivor Insurance Benefit Payments"; "old age benefits" were now "primary insurance benefits"; and so on. Title VI of the new Act took the original Title VIII's Sections 801 and 804, the employee and employer Social Security taxes, into the Internal Revenue Code as the "Federal Insurance Contributions Act."[32]

No administration testimony before the Committee even mentioned the insertion of insurance terminology. In an utter breakdown of congressional oversight and vigilance, the terminology matter was never debated in either house. The Senate made merely minor clerical amendments such as changing "survivor" to "survivors," and the insurance language passed on unchallenged into the final Act.[33]

While many investments, business and financial institutions, and financiers had suffered a sharp loss of prestige during the Depression, the life insurance industry's standing with the public had actually risen. Life insurance companies were lenient to policyholders beyond legal requirements, and promptly paid death claims, matured endowments, and disability benefits when they came due; Shelby Cullom Davis pointed out that insurance was "one type of savings that had not shrivelled up with every death rattle of the stock market." In 1938 Roosevelt appointed a so-called Temporary National Economic Committee to investigate concentration of economic power. The life insurance part of the investigation, handled by the Securities and Exchange Commission, looked into not just insurance companies' investments but their business practices, the hearings continuing until 1940. Though the TNEC investigators often approached life insurance extremely critically, their conclusions were on the whole favorable, and had the effect of enhancing the industry's prestige further.[34] Clearly, the reversion to insurance language in the bill—like the intense marketing of Social Security as insurance after passage—was an attempt to give Social Security legitimacy by association with private insurance.

It was, too, both a reversal of 1935's meticulous semantic cleansing, and a momentous victory for the administration's efforts to shape the public consciousness, for its public-relations language was now written into the law as Social Security's official semantics, the very language in which Americans would think about and refer to the program. Social Security's advocates could now call Social Security "insurance" and retort to critics that it is indeed insurance because that's what Congress calls it. Colloquially put: It is so insurance—it says so right here on the label! This, indeed, is precisely what happened.

"Trust Funds" and "Contributions"

On the recommendation of Treasury Secretary Morgenthau, an Old Age and Survivors' Insurance Trust Fund at the Treasury was created, as proposed by the Advisory Council. Section 201 of the Social Security Act, "Old-Age Reserve Account," was replaced by a new Section 201, "Federal Old-Age and Survivors Insurance Trust Fund." The only substantial difference from the existing Old Age Reserve Account was the elimination of the money-laundering diversion of Social Security revenues to the Treasury's general fund, followed by their transfer via specific appropriation to the Reserve Account. Instead, a sum "equivalent to 100 per centum of the taxes . . . received under the Federal Insurance Contributions Act and covered into the Treasury" "is hereby appropriated" to the Trust Fund for the fiscal year ending June 30, 1941 "and for each fiscal year thereafter"—that is, automatically. The only other new features were a Board of Trustees to manage the Trust Fund and periodically report to Congress, consisting of the secretary of the treasury, secretary of labor, and chairman of the Social Security Board (Section 201(b)); replacement of the old 3 percent interest rate on the bonds with the average rate of interest borne by all interest-bearing U.S. government public debt; and a provision for paying money from the Trust Fund into the Treasury to defray Social Security's administrative expenses.[35]

For the rest, the Trust Fund operated just like the old Reserve Account. Indeed, the Trust Fund *was* the Reserve Account; the initial assets of the Trust Fund were the assets of the Reserve Account as of January 1, 1940, transferred into the Trust Fund under the new Section 201(a). Since the Reserve Account was "an account in the Treasury" and the Trust Fund was "on the books of the Treasury," the transfer was a formality. For all practical purposes, it was as if a shoebox full of bonds labeled "Reserve Account" had a new label reading "Trust Fund" stuck on top of the old one. The exact similarity is borne out further in that paragraph (c) of the new Section 201, regarding the duties of the Trust Fund's "Managing Trustee" (who was the secretary of the treasury) to invest the portions of the Trust Fund not needed to cover withdrawals in only certain types of U.S. government obligations corresponds *verbatim* to paragraph (b) of the old Section 201 re the secretary of the treasury's duty to do the same regarding the Reserve Account, differing only in replacement of Reserve Account language with Trust Fund language, and in the new interest rate provision mentioned earlier. Moreover, paragraphs (d), (e) and (g) of the new Section 201, pertaining respectively to obligations' sale and redemption, crediting of interest on assets and proceeds from asset sales, and availability of credited amounts for making Title II benefit payments, follow the old paragraphs (c), (d), and (e) *verbatim* except for replacement of Reserve Account terms with Trust Fund terms.[36] From this scrutiny of original documents it necessarily follows that Social Security's "trust fund" is nothing more or less than a Treasury account. We may take this matter as settled.

Why was this step taken? It is important to keep in mind that the reserve fund controversy was raging furiously just then. It was aired in Congress before the hearings, during the hearings themselves, and during debate on the bill afterwards. Critics of the reserve bandied about polemical, loaded words like "embezzlement" and repeatedly raised the charge that the reserve consisted of nothing but IOUs, and that the American people would have to be taxed twice, once to put money into the fund to buy IOUs with, and again later to pay off the IOUs and actually pay the future benefits. Defenders fired back that no embezzlement was going on, that there wouldn't be any double taxation, and that the much-maligned IOUs were the safest investment there was—government bonds. They raised, too, a very valid point: the nature of the situation left the Reserve Fund no choice *but* to invest in Treasuries. Leaving the surplus revenue sit idle as cash was pointless and fatuous; investment in private securities was, as Vandenberg put it, socialism; so where else could the surplus revenue go?[37] Going on and on since 1936 without resolution, the reserve fund controversy had become a serious running sore on Social Security's all-important prestige.

As the documentary record makes clear, the Trust Fund was created for the express purpose of solving this bad, and worsening, public-relations problem. In testifying for the Trust Fund, Secretary Morgenthau said the reserve fund administration method should be changed "so that it will be made clearer to everyone that it is a trust fund established for the benefit of the insured who have contributed to it." A trust fund should be set up, "to be held in trust by a board of trustees."[38]

Three months later, testifying before the Senate Finance Committee, Altmeyer made the public-relations motive of the Trust Fund even clearer:

Senator VANDENBERG: What is the purpose of the trust fund?

Mr. ALTMEYER: Well, to allay the unwarranted fears of some people who thought Uncle Sam was embezzling the money.

Senator VANDENBERG: Well, if there was any fear of embezzlement it was unwarranted. The fact remains, does it not, that the creation of the trust fund does not actually change the routine and the formula under which this money comes into the Treasury and goes over to you and then comes back and you get the IOU and the Treasury expends the money?

Mr. ALTMEYER: I think it changes it, but you will have to ask the Treasury Department officials to explain exactly how . . .

Senator VANDENBERG: I think it is a step in the right direction, although it seems to me the process is called by a different name and has a little more favorable window dressing.[39]

So the Trust Fund, like the payroll tax, was driven by the need to influence the psychology of beneficiaries and taxpayers—to shape a climate of belief. As Vandenberg seemed to perceive, it was old wine in a new bottle.

Whether or not it accurately depicted reality was another matter. Just what is a trust fund? Money, investments, or other property held in trust. And what is trust, or a trust? An arrangement whereby one person, called a trustee, holds legal title to property, and typically invests it or manages it, for the benefit of somebody else, who holds the equitable title to that property, that is, a claim that could be sustained in a court of equity—a property right. The formal, legal definition of a trust is: "A fiduciary relationship with respect to property, subjecting the person by whom the property is held to equitable duties to deal with the property for the benefit of another person, which arises as a result of a manifestation of an intention to create it." To be valid, all trusts must have a creator, or "settlor," who sets up the trust and puts property into it; a trustee, who has the legal title to the property in the trust; a "beneficiary," who holds equitable title to the property; property; and terms of trust, spelling out the purpose of the trust, the duties and powers of the trustee(s), and the beneficiary's rights.[40]

Does the Social Security Trust Fund meet these criteria? The crux of the matter is property. A trust is an arrangement for holding property, so no property, no trust.

One might think that Congress, in approving the legislation creating the "trust fund," is the creator (settlor), but strictly speaking this is not so. A settlor is a party who puts *his own* property into a trust. Congress did not own the Treasuries which were the "trust fund's" initial assets, and does not own the bonds in it now.

As for the Board of Trustees, who in a true trust would hold the legal title to the property in the trust, there was nothing whatsoever in Section 201 of the 1939 act giving the secretary of the treasury, secretary of labor, and chairman of the Social Security Board a legal title to anything.

And do the purported beneficiaries—the people for whose sake the trust is being managed, the people who will collect Social Security benefits— actually have any property in the Trust Fund to which they have an equitable claim or title, an enforceable property right, as true beneficiaries of a true trust do? Under questioning by House Ways and Means Committee member John McCormack (D-MA), Altmeyer revealed that Social Security maintains no accounts containing funds earmarked for individuals, and never had:

Mr. McCORMACK: Let us see. Under the underlying law, pay roll is connected with the individual. As each individual pays his share . . . it goes to his individual account. That is true, isn't it?

Mr. ALTMEYER: Yes, sir.

Mr. McCORMACK: . . . . Under this plan there is a pooling of taxes, isn't there?

Mr. ALTMEYER: *There never was a crediting of the contribution to the individual's account.*

Mr. McCORMACK: Isn't the annuity payable to him connected with his payments and payments of his employer?

Mr. ALTMEYER: It is connected with his earnings . . . and indirectly . . . related to the contribution he has made . . . but the relationship between his contribution and his benefits are *not in the nature of a savings account where his contributions are put in a separate pocket.*

Mr. McCORMACK: We don't say the money is actually put in there, but from a bookkeeping point of view, isn't it there?

Mr. ALTMEYER: *No, sir.*

Mr. McCORMACK: Is that money now pooled in a trust fund?

Mr. ALTMEYER: Yes.

Mr. McCORMACK: How can you determine what lump sum an individual was entitled to if they die before reaching the retirement age?

Mr. ALTMEYER: Because we have individual accounts for that individual's earnings.

Mr. McCORMACK: Then you have got individual accounts?

Mr. ALTMEYER: Yes; *but not individual funds.*

Mr. McCORMACK: The fund, of course, is a general fund, but you have each individual's interest in that fund.

Mr. ALTMEYER: We have his individual earnings account, and will continue—

Mr. McCORMACK: Of course, the money isn't set aside into an individual fund for all of these people. [It] goes into a trust fund.

Mr. ALTMEYER: Yes, sir.

Mr. McCORMACK: And each individual's contributions thereunder and his right thereunder are kept separate and are known?

Mr. ALTMEYER: *No, sir.* [41] (italics added)

Clearly, McCormack was under the impression that the Social Security trust fund would operate just like a private-sector trust fund. Equally clearly, Altmeyer was disabusing him. The individual accounts, then, by the Social Security Commissioner's own admission, are mere record-keeping entities for wage records: file folders, not piggy banks. There is, in other words, no property in the Trust Fund belonging to specific individuals. No individual funds necessarily means no individual property.

Recall, too, that in its *Helvering v. Davis* brief the administration contrasted Social Security benefits with War Risk Insurance benefits, which were property and created vested rights, with the clear and intentional implication that Social Security benefits aren't property and don't create such rights.

As for equitable titles, enforceable property rights, if one has no property it follows that one can't have an enforceable property right. And while the new Section 201 which created the Trust Fund did spell out the Trustees' duties, it said nothing whatsoever about property rights of beneficiaries—

and for a very good reason. Assistant Attorney General Jackson's statement in the oral argument of *Helvering v. Davis* before the Supreme Court, repeated here for reader convenience, explicitly denied that any such right exists:

> . . . these benefits are in the nature of pensions or gratuities. There is no contract created by which any person becomes entitled as a matter of right to sue the United States or to maintain a claim for any particular sum of money. Not only is there no contract implied but it is expressly negatived, because it is provided in the act, section 1104, that it may be repealed, altered, or amended in any of its provisions at any time. This Court has held that a pension granted by the Government is a matter of bounty, that the pensioner has no legal right to his pension, and that they may be given, withheld, distributed, or recalled at the discretion of Congress.[42]

And as we shall see, the government's brief for the Supreme Court case *Flemming v. Nestor* (1960) argued explicitly that a current or prospective Social Security benefit recipient does not acquire an interest in the "trust fund"—that is, does not acquire a property right to the assets in the "fund"—and that the belief that Social Security benefits are "fully accrued property rights" is "wholly erroneous."[43]

The individual who will receive Social Security benefits, then, has no property in the "trust fund" and cannot sue to get it. Still another feature of a true trust vanishes.

To be fair, Section 205 of the 1939 Amendments did establish a procedure whereby individuals who believed that their rights had been prejudiced by a decision of the Social Security Board could obtain a hearing; the 1935 Act had not provided aggrieved individuals such a process. The Amendments also allowed, under 205(g), an individual dissatisfied with the Board's decision in such a hearing to begin a civil action within sixty days to obtain a review of the Board's decision in a federal district court, which had the power to affirm, modify or reverse the Board's decision about the individual's claim. However, this provision applies only to *benefit payments,* not to *trust fund assets;* there is nothing whatever authorizing actions to enforce a claim to "property" in the "trust fund," which is something the Social Security "trust fund" would have to have to be a true trust.

Moreover, 205(h) explicitly states that "No action against the United States, the Board, or any officer or employee thereof shall be brought under Section 24 of the Judicial Code of the United States to recover on any claim arising under this title."[44] This would seem to rule out an aggrieved individual suing the government or any official to recover his "property" out of the "trust fund" consisting of the taxes he had purportedly paid into it.

All of this confirms every syllable of the 1995 observations by Suffolk University Law School Professor Charles Rounds, an expert on trusts and a Fellow of the American College of Trust and Estate Counsel, about Social Security's "trust fund":

Despite the term "trust," the Social Security system contains nothing that remotely resembles the common law trust. There is no segregation of assets, no equitable property rights, no private right of enforcement (all characteristics of the common law trust). It is merely a system of taxation and appropriation sprinkled with trust terms to hide its true nature.[45]

Finally, leaving aside the legal questions, the "trust fund" just simply is not operated like a trust fund as the term is commonly understood. Revenues are not used to purchase assets which are accumulated to meet future obligations and credited to individual accounts. Rather, as mentioned in the opening section of chapter 1, the OASI "trust fund" is simply a Treasury account, to which current Social Security tax revenues are credited (as Treasury bonds) before they are paid out as current benefits. Most OASDI revenues are not invested in anything, but spent immediately on benefits (for which the account is debited). Any revenue which happens to be left over gets used to finance government operations, and an equivalent value of Treasury bonds remains in the "trust fund." This stock of bonds serves as a rainy day fund in case a revenue shortfall occurs. And when the time comes to cash in the bonds, the Treasury will get the money from taxing future taxpayers or borrowing. Today's taxpayer will have his future benefits paid out of taxes levied on future taxpayers or borrowing from the public, not out of invested money building up in a "fund" on his behalf.

The Social Security Trust Fund, then, is bogus. Here, again, is a very significant, explicit effort at promoting a false consciousness.

Apparently the administration hoped to dispose of the vexing reserve fund controversy with a combination of two measures. Make a public relations move: adopt the reassuring terminology and trappings of a trust fund, capitalizing on the favorable psychological effect of the concept of holding assets in trust. Meanwhile, change substantive policy: by both reducing the cash inflow by freezing the tax rate and increasing the cash outflow by liberalizing benefits and coverage, get rid of the dread projected large reserve, shift to a pay-as-you-go approach, and ensure that any reserve that did accumulate, just a "contingency fund" to cover temporary cash-flow shortfalls, would be too small to attract controversy.

Until very recently, this maneuver succeeded handily—the reserve fund controversy gradually died—but at the price of spawning yet another insidiously appealing myth with potentially disastrous consequences. As we have already seen, many Americans today harbor the utterly inaccurate but infuriating belief that Congress has been looting the Social Security "trust fund." In the event that the bankruptcy and affordability crises described earlier come to pass, this widespread misunderstanding, the product of the government's own clever public relations gambit, is a recipe for political crisis: scapegoating, recrimination, and discrediting the institution of Congress as a pack of scoundrelly trust fund riflers.

Morgenthau proposed still another public-relations move: "To improve public understanding of the purpose for which the funds are collected, I recommend that the taxes under Title VIII be termed 'contributions' levied under the Government's taxing power."[46] Questioning Altmeyer later, Congressman McCormack pointed out that "this is a tax, no matter what you call it." Altmeyer insisted there was "a significant difference" from ordinary taxes; when McCormack observed that one was forced to pay it, he retorted, "But they get a special benefit by paying it." McCormack said he had no objection to the name; "it has a pleasant sound if you call it a contribution rather than a tax, but it results in the same thing."[47]

Here again, we see terminology quite deliberately being selected not for how accurately it describes reality, but for how it will affect the beliefs and behavior of its intended audience. The levies were likened to "premiums" to promote the program to the public; then labeled "true taxes" to survive a Supreme Court challenge; now, for public relations purposes, they were "contributions." The taxes did indeed get designated "contributions" in the law. This too would play its part in shaping the climate of opinion, and cast long shadows later on.

The 1939 Amendments: Weakening Substance

While writing insurance and trust fund language into the law, thus strengthening the *appearance* of Social Security's likeness to insurance—and thereby sowing, unbeknownst to themselves, seeds of crisis generations later—the administration and Congress made changes greatly weakening the *substance* of that likeness.

Social Security was liberalized to include survivors' benefits ("Survivors' Insurance") to dependent wives, children, widows, and parents, as well as old-age benefits to retired workers. Moreover, benefit payment was moved up to January 1, 1940, the initial benefit size was increased, and the benefit formula was revised to base benefits on average wage rather than total wages since 1936. Finally, the retiree's monthly "primary insurance benefit" was augmented by an increment of 1 percent of the benefit computed by the benefit formula, multiplied by the number of years in which the individual was paid at least $200 in wages.[48]

However, in order to keep the total cost down, certain old-age benefits were cut. The old lump-sum death benefit paid to the estate of persons under sixty-five, of 3.5 percent of total wages since 1936, was replaced by a much smaller lump-sum payment to the widow, widower, child or parent of the deceased, of six times his monthly benefit. And the old provisions of lump-sum payments to individuals who had turned sixty-five and paid taxes but did not qualify for benefits, or to the estates of those who had died after starting to receive monthly benefits—that is, a money-back guarantee for all

Social Security taxpayers—were dropped, effective the day the Amendments were passed, except for payments to the estates of persons who died before January 1, 1940.[49]

Axing the lump-sum benefits and removing the money-back guarantee marked a radical departure from individual equity, thereby greatly weakening Social Security's resemblance to private insurance—at the very same time Social Security was going to great lengths to encourage the public to think of it as just like private insurance. Put another way, the gap was widening between the consciousness the administration was promoting and the reality.

We must also point out that the 1939 Amendments' demolition of the statutory money-back guarantee demolishes some popular beliefs about Social Security. Social Security is *not* a "government savings system"—and hasn't been since 1939. You do *not* merely "get your own money back" or "get back what you paid in." You get whatever Congress chooses to give you.

The effect of these changes, of course, was to injure single beneficiaries for the sake of beneficiaries with survivors. As the minority members of the Ways and Means Committee pointed out in the Committee's report, in some cases the forfeit would be substantial; under the old law, a man who had worked in covered employment for 40 years making an average monthly wage of $250 would have had a lump-sum payment of $4,200 going to his estate. The new lump-sum death benefit was just a few hundred dollars. Moreover, whereas under the old law a man had been deemed to be buying an annuity for age sixty-five with guaranteed return of principal in case of death before sixty-five, now he was merely seen as insuring himself against old age. The Ways and Means minority fingered an even bigger problem: "It puts the Government in the position of changing the terms of a contract after it has been entered into."[50] But how can one break a contract when there is no contract?

Testifying before the Committee, Altmeyer rationalized the proposal. Paying supplementary benefits for aged dependent wives of retired workers "would provide equitable protection to all by recognizing that the presumptive need of a man and wife is greater than that of a single individual." As for the existing 3.5 percent lump-sum benefit, it "recognizes one of the two guiding principles of social insurance—that of individual equity. But it takes no cognizance of the other principle—that of social adequacy."[51]

Moreover, the administration thought that the lump-sum benefit "does not furnish as much by way of protection" as the substitute, the new survivors' benefits for the widow and minor children. When Congressman McCormack posed the case of a hypothetical single man with "no widow, nobody eligible," Altmeyer acknowledged that the money he would have received stays in the fund. Oddly, he added that this was a departure from the savings principle (recall that Social Security had often been presented as a kind of forced savings) toward the insurance principle. "Social insurance,"

McCormack interjected. Altmeyer replied: "No; private insurance; insurance in the basic sense, because that man has more by way of overall protection."[52]

Actually, McCormack, not Altmeyer, was right; social insurance, as Hohaus had pointed out, stresses social adequacy over individual equity, whereas private insurance focuses on the latter. And how can the single man with "nobody eligible" be getting more overall protection? Assuming he dies single, what good do survivors' benefits do *him?* Altmeyer went on to reassure McCormack that "the single man nevertheless would receive as much or more by way of protection than he could purchase with his own contribution from an insurance company, regardless of the length of time he was in the system," at least for the first 25 years.[53]

Later McCormack, a very formidable interrogator of witnesses, returned to the matter, remarking that "I went out and sold the idea that not only was this insurance, but it was a savings account. You are departing from that, aren't you?" Altmeyer admitted that Social Security was—also that the elimination of the lump-sum benefit would add up to a lot of money over the years.[54]

> Mr. MCCORMACK: And of course that lump-sum settlement was associated with the individual.
>
> Mr. ALTMEYER: Yes.
>
> Mr. MCCORMACK: And associated with the rights of the individual under the plan.
>
> Mr. ALTMEYER: Yes.
>
> Mr. MCCORMACK: So to that extent there is that change taking place.
>
> Mr. ALTMEYER: You are right.
>
> Mr. MCCORMACK: But you contend that the change is necessary in order to utilize the fund for the general welfare of the 42,000,000 people covered by the law and their dependents?
>
> Mr. ALTMEYER: Yes, sir.[55]

Under McCormack's pressure, Altmeyer admitted that it was a departure from present law. McCormack went on:

> Using the fund for the benefit of the entire group covered by it, having regard to social questions and the problems involved, and losing the identity of the individual.
>
> Mr. ALTMEYER: Except to this extent; that we believe it is important to retain an element of individual equity, so that no person can be heard to say that he is getting less by way of protection than he could purchase from a private insurance company with his own contributions. . . .
>
> Mr. MCCORMACK: . . . . You talk about benefit protection for the single person in comparison with private insurance. You take ordinary life insurance. I believe it would be difficult to take issue with that. But in private insurance I have the option of taking out any kind of insurance I want to. Under this I have no option.

Mr. ALTMEYER: That is right.

Mr. McCORMACK: If you just want to talk about straight life, that is one thing; but suppose a man wants to take out a 20-year endowment, or something of that kind. Then, of course, the situation is entirely different.

Mr. ALTMEYER: Yes, sir.[56]

McCormack went on to raise the case of a deceased single man who had paid in and left a parent dependent on him. What about him, and his parents? Altmeyer replied that the basic question of social insurance is to create a benefit pattern that will address as much of the problem as possible, but "you cannot take care of each person's individual circumstance." McCormack agreed, but what about a single man who dies leaving a widowed mother? Why wouldn't it be simple to have her classified as a widow to get benefits? When Altmeyer hesitated, McCormack broke in, "We are not dealing with need now. . . . We are dealing now with the question of right." Altmeyer replied that there would be "a small residual number of widows without protection," and that he knew of no social insurance system that took care of widowed mothers. Satisfied, McCormack did not probe further.[57] The Ways and Means minority members, who had exposed and protested the inequity to single men and the wrongdoing in changing the rules in the middle of the game, likewise acquiesced. As the lopsided votes demonstrate, Congress' complaisance was all but absolute.

Social Security was only four years old, and the government was already cutting some people's future benefits—the benefits they had supposedly earned and would purportedly receive "as a matter of right" regardless of need—so as to give more to others whose "presumptive need" was deemed greater. Thus there was a trading off of individual equity and purported "contractual rights" against "general welfare" and the need to hold costs down—which disproved not only all the administration's rights and insurance language that had already gone before, but the massive effort that commenced as soon as the Amendments became law, to promote Social Security to the public as insurance.

The Marketing of Social Security as Insurance

The very first sentence of the September, 1939 pamphlet *Changes in the Social Security Act: Old-Age Insurance,* explaining the amendments read: "Changes have been made in the Social Security Act, especially in the part which provides old-age insurance for wage and salary workers."[58] After discoursing on "your Social Security account," the pamphlet addressed "Your Old-Age Insurance Tax":

With all the changes, however, the old-age insurance part of the Social Security Act remains much the same principle as before. *It is an insurance plan* [italics in original]. You pay a tax, and so does your employer, to help pay the cost of the benefits you will receive. In other words, you pay a sort of premium on what might be called an insurance policy which will begin to pay benefits to you when you are 65 or over, or to your family when you die.[59]

Note the shaky language: "*a sort of* premium on *what might be called* an insurance policy." In reality, of course, as the 1935 Act made clear, Social Security had no policies, no legal and binding contracts with contractual rights, no true premiums buying future benefits. If Social Security really were insurance, this maneuver, this sort of language, would have been unnecessary. Note too an explicit analogy of Social Security to an individual insurance policy.

Two paragraphs later the pamphlet gave readers the same assurance Altmeyer had repeatedly given in his testimony: "Nowhere can you buy the same amount of old-age insurance and the same protection for your family for what you pay for your benefits under the Social Security Act."[60] Clearly meant to leave the impression that in paying payroll taxes one was buying insurance benefits. Note, too, the lauding of Social Security in terms of how good a deal it offered.

Regarding the trust fund: "All the old-age insurance tax money goes into a fund in the U. S. Treasury, which is called the 'Federal Old-Age and Survivors Insurance Trust Fund.' Old-age insurance benefits will be paid out of this fund."[61]

The pamphlet said nothing whatever about the *loss* of the large lump-sum death benefit and the money-back guarantee.

Another pamphlet issued the same month, *Monthly Benefits Begin in 1940,* likewise full of insurance language, opened by reporting that "lump-sum payments to workers reaching age 65 shall immediately stop." It went on to put the best face on the change: "Instead, such workers now have an opportunity to get *monthly benefit payments, for life,* [italics in original] on retiring from work any time after their sixty-fifth birthday. In the large majority of cases, these payments will amount to much more than the lump sums which were all such workers could get before the Social Security Act was amended."[62] The two obvious implications—that workers other than "the large majority" were left worse off by the change, and that one's "rights" under this scheme were malleable—went, for equally obvious reasons, unremarked.

Similarly, an undated 1940s leaflet, *2 Plans for Old-Age Security,* used "insurance" lavishly and said tax money "goes into the Old-Age and Survivors Insurance Trust Fund under the United States Treasury, from which insurance benefits are paid." A 1940 circular described Social Security's taxes as "similar to premiums paid on an insurance policy."[63]

The 1943 *Old-Age and Survivors Insurance for Workers and their Families* both reiterated some of this and explained how the plan works, so as to convey an even stronger impression that one is buying insurance which will pay benefits as a right:

> Wage earners and their employers share the cost by paying taxes levied for the purpose. This makes it possible to provide *much more insurance protection* for the worker and his family *than he could buy for what he pays toward this Government plan. And because the worker has helped to pay for his benefits, they come to him and his family as a matter of right.* (italics added)[64]

None of these publications ever referred to the fact that Congress reserved "the right to alter, amend, or repeal any provision of this Act."

Once again, prominent Social Security officials published articles in print media. Bureau of Old Age Insurance director John Corson extolled the 1939 benefit liberalization in *Survey Midmonthly*.[65] Altmeyer had a detailed exposition of the amended Social Security "insurance" program in *School Life*, the official magazine of the U.S. Office of Education.[66] Writing in 1940 in the life insurance industry trade journal *Dun's Review*, Altmeyer lauded Social Security as good for business and described its taxes as "analogous to the premiums of private insurance." American businessmen, Altmeyer reported happily, were being very cooperative and accepting of Social Security; they want their workers to realize that "their social security accounts are valuable possessions," and businessmen understand that the program "embodies sound insurance principles in its financial base." Defending the contributory approach, Altmeyer asserted "Workers will get the protection, . . . which they pay for. Thus, there is a sense of participation and responsibility . . . a sense of the ownership of something of value." Note, again, the stress on shaping the taxpayer's all-important attitudes and beliefs. Interestingly enough in view of the malleability of benefit "rights" revealed by the demise of the lump-sum benefits, which he himself had recommended just a few months earlier, Altmeyer concluded that "Social insurance must be *certain* [italics in original]. It cannot gamble with the old age of workers, the care of their widows, the education of their children."[67]

Various politicians also helped market Social Security as insurance. On June 5, 1939, Congressman McCormack, participating in the National Radio Forum, explained and lauded the new bill at length. Remarkably, McCormack, whose protracted grilling of Altmeyer surely indicated nagging misgivings, reiterated the whole administration line: beneficiaries will get more protection than they could buy elsewhere; equity and adequacy are increased by recognizing that married persons had greater presumed need than singles; survivors' benefits had been added without increasing Social Security's future overall cost, thanks to elimination of the lump-sum benefits, which would change the program from one "operated along the lines of a private insurance company" into a "social insurance plan"; and, over and over, the old-age benefits will be paid "by right."[68] A month later, Senator David Walsh (D-MA) went on the air to explain the amendments, telling his audience that "The old-age retirement plan is in substance and effect an insurance plan operated by the Government. The benefits paid are the result of the premiums paid and the premiums are the pay-roll taxes."[69]

And, once again, the press uncritically echoed the government's depiction of Social Security as insurance. Reporting on the new Social Security Act, the *United States News* referred to beneficiaries as "policyholders" and wrote of the new Act, "In effect, it writes insurance policies guaranteeing to pay monthly benefits" to eligible retired workers and their dependent wives, widows, children and parents.[70] Here again an explicit analogy to individual policies. Lauding the amended Social Security Act as both a sane, workable alternative to the radical schemes of Townsend and others, and a giant step toward the American Dream of a richer, fuller life, Shelby Cullom Davis described how "the Federal Government entered the life insurance and annuity business on a vast scale," with citizens as "customers" and "clients."[71]

In a telling index of the press's complaisance, a major December 25, 1939 *Newsweek* article reporting the imminent commencement of monthly old-age and survivors benefits lifted material *verbatim* from Social Security's pamphlet *Changes in the Social Security Act: Old-Age Insurance:*

> No matter how it operates, the old-age pension law is not charity; it is similar to other insurance plans and the worker *pays a premium on what might be called an insurance policy.* And it has no strings attached [this ignores the retirement earnings test]. It goes outright to the pensioner, whether he or she receives a state or local pension, has private policy annuities, or possesses a savings account.[72] (italics added)

Similarly, about a week later the *United States News* described the newly begun monthly benefit payments "available as a matter of right."[73] When in October 1941 President Roosevelt proposed a massive liberalization of Social Security, *Newsweek* reported that "At present old-age and survivors insurance . . . covers 47,000,000 persons, for whose insurance $2,740,602,058 in premiums had been paid up to a month ago. Benefits of $114,840,215 already have been paid to 600,000 persons."[74]

From every quarter, then, Americans were being told that Social Security was insurance, paying benefits as a right, and so on. Press reporting was becoming all but indistinguishable from Social Security's own publications. The only frame of reference available to shape Americans' understanding and beliefs about Social Security was the one the government had crafted in order to gain their support. Alternative descriptions or views of the program to provide a basis for questioning or disputing this account simply did not exist.

Issues in Social Security: A Different Version

A 1946 congressional report on Social Security, however, casts a very different light on matters.

In 1945 the House voted to fund research for the Ways and Means Committee on "the need for the amendment and expansion of the Social Security Act." The Committee created a small staff of private- and public-sector experts. Their report, *Issues in Social Security,* appeared for Committee use in January 1946.[75] While conveying a wealth of information about the federal old-age and unemployment programs, it was meant to promote expansion. For example, it presented anomalous, inequitable situations under the current Social Security program due to persons shifting into and out of covered employment, so that those who just barely qualified for benefits were well taken care of, while individuals in similar situations who just barely failed to qualify got nothing—then argued that as long as OASI's coverage was limited, so that one qualified for benefits by work in some occupations but not others, such situations would occur; that the only feasible way to eliminate such problems is "a general extension of OASI coverage to employments now excluded"; and that delaying this expansion would worsen these problems.[76]

In discussing OASI's financing, *Issues in Social Security* pointed out that estimating future costs was difficult. The government's life insurance for servicemen charged premiums based on normal probabilities of life expectancy plus increased mortality due to war casualties, plus an assumption about interest earnings. The individual premiums, then, reflected individual risk. For OASI, by contrast, one's "contributions" depended only on one's receipt of wages from covered employment, and didn't reflect one's age and the size and composition of his family, which of course determined the size of benefits. Hence "there is little or no room for applying orthodox insurance theory to OASI cases in view of the fact that under ordinary insurance the premium is related to the individual risk."[77] But if so, then this necessarily means that the vast promotional campaign already underway was drawing a misleading analogy between Social Security and insurance.

As to whether Social Security should be made voluntary, the report had some other revealing things to say. A voluntary system implies that "you will get about your money's worth at all hazards and that the rules of the game, so to speak, will never be changed to your detriment." Life insurance for members of the armed forces, for example, gave servicemen "rules of the game" fixed by insurance policies giving them contractual rights for specific payments for specific risks as long as they paid the premiums. OASI was "distinctly different," as witness the 1939 amendments, which rewrote the rules and "drastically curtailed" the money-back guarantee in the lump-sum benefits, and also worsened single men's prospects by trimming the monthly annuity they could get from $85 to $60.[78] The report made its approval clear:

Such changes were considered desirable and were part of a series of changes strengthening and improving OASI as a basic social protection. The Congress was properly proceeding to improve the system under the provision that "The right to alter, amend, or repeal any provision of this Act is hereby reserved to the Congress."

Even though voluntary participation may be with an initial understanding that the rules of the game may be changed on the participant, it is inevitable that his voluntary participation in reliance upon statutory provisions will be brought up as an argument against any change in those provisions adverse to his particular interest, however desirable the change may be from broader viewpoints. OASI is young as a system; revisions have already been made, and other revisions must be expected. The effect of voluntary participation on freedom to change the rules of the game is thus one of the considerations as to whether it should be adopted.[79]

In other words, it is good that Section 1104 enables Congress to break its promises. A compulsory system is superior because the government is free to rewrite the rules and injure individuals if from "broader viewpoints" this is "desirable." If Social Security were voluntary, that freedom would be impaired or even lost. So we should think twice about making Social Security voluntary.

Another problem with making it voluntary is "adverse selection." Among OASI's basic principles is that "all must contribute regardless of benefit prospects," and that benefits in many cases must be so liberal as to be "out of line with any commercial concept of their relation to the amount of the contribution." If this benefit structure were pursued with a voluntary program, alas, "few, if any, may be expected to elect coverage who will be a financial asset, so to speak"—that is, those who are likely to pay in more than they take out. "Those who elect coverage will be those who expect to profit by the election." So if voluntary social insurance were introduced for some participants, only those who expected to gain thereby would participate. Other compulsorily covered persons would then press for voluntary participation, generating still more adverse selection. "This is another consideration as to whether the principle of voluntary coverage should be adopted." *Issues in Social Security* added that the voluntary annuities proposed in the administration's original bill in 1935 had been dropped because people who "from a social viewpoint" most need protection don't buy annuities. If government annuities were "made sufficiently attractive—which means, of course, highly enough subsidized," some "wise investors" would buy them. "But voluntary protection—and at good values—is freely available on the open market today." The report concluded that "The justification of OASI as a compulsory system is that if participation were voluntary, its participants would probably be only a small fraction of what they are at present, and it would hardly be worth while as a mechanism of social protection."[80]

From all this we can infer that the reasons for making Social Security compulsory are that compulsion enables the government to rewrite the rules to an individual's detriment if need be, and to compel participation from "financial assets"—persons who will pay more than they will receive. More-

over, if it were voluntary, only those who expected to profit would participate, and there wouldn't be very many of them—meaning that most people,
rationally weighing costs against gains, would conclude that for them, Social
Security is a bad deal. Making Social Security attractive to "wise investors"
would require large subsidies. All this casts doubt on the repeated assertion
that Social Security gave better insurance deals than one could buy privately
for the same money.

So Congressmen and their staffers were being told that the incessantly-
promoted insurance analogy is "in many respects" not true; that one *has no*
contractual rights or protections; that one's "right" to one's benefits is actually a claim contingent on political and financial considerations, which make
it expendable should annulling it be "desirable . . . from broader viewpoints";
that the welfare of the individual beneficiary, supposedly the object of much
solicitude, is explicitly subordinated to social good and expediency—and
that the flimsiness of these "rights," the freedom to break promises, and the
inferior value assigned to the individual's welfare are seen not as necessary
evils, but as *positive goods.* And the claim that Social Security was a good
deal financially was questionable. This was not what the public was reading
in its Social Security leaflets.

Social Security Triumphant

As far as the public could tell, the version of reality presented to it *was*
reality. Benefits began flowing out in 1940, just as the administration's
literature said they would. The 1939 Amendments had frozen the tax rate at
one percent of taxable payroll each for workers and employers through 1942;
subsequent legislation during and after the war repeatedly extended the freeze;
not until 1950 did the rate rise to 1.5 percent each. Everything was going
smoothly; the Republicans' dire warnings in 1936 of unmanageable record-
keeping burdens and onerous government snooping were exploded as Social
Security numbers were assigned and records kept without fuss; to do it justice, Social Security was a marvel of administrative and bureaucratic efficiency. In 1946 President Harry Truman abolished the Social Security Board
and replaced it with the Social Security Administration, headed by a Commissioner for Social Security, to which post Arthur Altmeyer was appointed.[81]

Pressure came from politicians, social insurance advocates, and Social
Security's own top administrators for further expansion. Taking stock of
Social Security's first ten years, Altmeyer wrote in 1945 that the Social Security Board had proposed to Congress that Social Security be expanded to
cover all gainfully employed persons and their dependents; to cover sickness
and disability; to include health insurance. His words give an impression of
a triumphalist mentality that was, perhaps, losing sight of realities such as
cost constraints, and lurching into open-ended expansionism:

I am optimistic enough to believe that progress in this second decade of social
security in the United States will at least equal the progress we have made in the first.
But I am also confident that when these next ten years have rolled by, we shall still be
talking about the inadequacy of the program in achieving minimum well being.

Social security will always be a goal, never a finished thing, because human
aspirations are infinitely expansible—just as human nature is infinitely perfectible.[82]

Substantial liberalization did take place in the next few years. In 1950,
after extensive hearings and debate, Social Security underwent the first
major amendment since 1939. It was extended to cover about 10 million
more Americans, including most of the non-agricultural self-employed (over
half of the new participants); regularly employed farm and domestic workers; and others. Eligibility conditions were much liberalized; all those
aged sixty-two or over could qualify for benefits with only six quarters of
coverage. On the average, benefits were increased about 77 percent, slightly
more than matching the price inflation since 1937. Authorization to use
general federal revenues to help finance the program, passed in 1944, was
repealed. Employer and employee taxes were raised to 1.5 percent of taxable payroll each, and a self-employment tax was introduced for the self-
employed brought into the program.[83]

Yet there was evidence for the discerning eye that Social Security's vaunted
guarantees and rights rested on quicksand. Ever since the original Social
Security Act was passed, the Treasury and the Social Security Board had been
wrestling with the matter of just what an "employee" was. Neither the Act nor
the Internal Revenue Code defined the term, and in 1936 Treasury and Social
Security officials issued regulations addressing the definitions of "employee"
and "employer." The definition of "employer" stressed the legal right to
control performance of an employee's services, but also took cognizance of
other factors like the right to sack an employee, and the provision of tools and
a place to work. There were important tricky borderline areas, such as outside
salesmen, owner-operators of leased trucks, entertainers, newspaper vendors,
filling-station operators, private-duty nurses, and so on. Were they employees, or independent contractors? Beginning in 1941, a series of court rulings
addressed the employer-employee relation. The 1941 rulings took a narrow
view of the relationship, relying chiefly on the legal terms of the contracts
between the employer and the persons performing the actual activities. The
Treasury consequently adopted a narrow interpretation of "employee," stressing the employer's legal right to control performance of services by the alleged employee. Social Security, on the other hand, stuck to the broader
interpretation of employer-employee relationships in the regulations developed before 1941. Some employers took advantage of the Treasury's narrow
view to craft their employment contracts so as to allegedly renounce their
right to control employee performance of services, thus enabling them to
argue that since their employees were independent contractors, they didn't

have to pay the employer's Social Security tax. Numerous court cases ensued, with some decisions favoring the government and some the employers. Finally in 1947, the Supreme Court stepped in with three decisions favoring Social Security, maintaining that the employer-employee relationship should be determined by the realities of the situation, such as how much control is exercised over the "employee's" provision of services, not the technical, legal relationship.[84]

In 1948 Congress intervened, with the Gearhart Resolution amending the definition of "employee" for Social Security purposes to exclude anybody who under common law had the status of an independent contractor. Opponents claimed that this would exclude from Social Security coverage some 750,000 people who had previously been considered employees under the regulations and the 1947 Supreme Court decisions. Though the resolution's final version in fact grandfathered persons who had already paid into Social Security and established wage credits or had started receiving benefits, even under erroneous interpretation of the word "employee," President Truman concurred with the critics and vetoed it. His veto was overridden and the resolution became law.[85] Inclusion of most non-agricultural self-employed persons under the 1950 Amendments rendered the whole matter moot, but the resolution, like the 1939 Amendments, underscored a crucial reality: Congress could take away benefits and entitlements if it so chose.

The enormous liberalization and expansion of 1950 made the tie between "contributions" and benefits far more tenuous, thus further undermining the principle of individual equity and with it, any plausible resemblance of Social Security to private insurance writing individual policies. Yet Social Security kept promoting itself as insurance. In 1947, a Social Security Administration question-and-answer pamphlet described Social Security as "social insurance" which "works on the same principle as private insurance, on the principle of spreading the financial risk." If society collects small amounts of money from each of the many persons exposed to the risk of breadwinner unemployment, retirement or death, "we build a fund from which to provide an income for the worker and his family" when these things occur. It admitted differences between social and private insurance, such as that Social Security benefits are determined by law, "without the strict correspondence between individual protection and value of contributions provided in private insurance."[86] But it made the most of the insurance analogy, repeatedly calling the tax a "premium": "Under our social insurance programs, workers and their employers pay premiums that meet part of the loss of family income . . . "[87] And:

35. Q. Where does the money for benefits come from?

A. It comes out of a trust fund that is built by special *premiums* paid by employers and employees.

36. Q. How much do workers and employers have to pay into the fund?

A. The worker's *premium* (or tax) at present is 1 percent of the wages he receives in covered employment, up to $3,000 a year. . . . The employer's *contribution* (or tax) is 1 percent of the wages he pays each employee . . .

37. Q. How does the worker pay his tax?

A. The worker's *premium* is deducted from his pay every day by his employer.[88] (italics added)

Similarly, a short leaflet briefly explaining OASI described it as "a Government insurance program" financed by the worker's "contribution (or tax)" and equal payment by employers, and paying benefits "as a matter of right." Unlike public assistance, "Old-age and survivors insurance and unemployment insurance are *insurance* [italics in original]. They are paid for like private insurance, and when the time comes the workers draw their benefits according to insurance rules."[89] Again, a very close analogy to private insurance.

Other mass-consumption SSA documents of the forties and fifties offered more of the same, and told the reader to "Treat your [Social Security] card like an insurance policy" and that "Your card is the symbol of your insurance policy under the Federal social security law."[90] These, clearly, are attempts to analogize Social Security to private insurance writing individual policies.

In none of these publications was the reservation of power clause, giving Congress "the right to alter, amend, or repeal any provision of this Act," ever mentioned.

Press treatment of Social Security in these years was overwhelmingly positive. Several lengthy articles explained how the program worked: how much tax was levied, what the trust fund was, how record keeping was handled, and so on, but devoting the greatest attention to the available benefits, typically using numerous hypothetical examples to show how much people in various situations—single, married, widowed, with dependent children—could expect to get. Some authors mentioned that millions of dollars in benefits were going unclaimed and that individuals should find out if Social Security owed them money. Use of insurance terminology was routine.[91]

One question-and-answer piece, which drew on consultation with top experts on Social Security and visits to field offices and Social Security's main office in Baltimore, described Social Security, in words Social Security's own writers might have penned, as "a form of government insurance" paid for by money which is "taken out of your pay by Uncle Sam and placed in a trust fund for you." The money in the fund, readers were assured, is safe, "As safe as your War Bonds are, or any other investment in the Government." It was used "to buy bonds to finance other national projects, such as building dams . . . As a result, the fund has earned about $700,000,000 in interest in the past 10 years." The law, which mandated that money in the fund go only for benefit and administration costs, would keep politicians from "squandering every dime of it."[92] The author raised and dismissed a crucial question:

Q.—But couldn't some future Congress make a new law which would kill Social Security or suspend benefits?

A.—Yes, but it's inconceivable that any Congress in its right mind would commit political suicide by doing so. Too many voters now have an important stake in Social Security, and are growing in number every year.[93]

This was one of the very few acknowledgments in the popular press that the reservation of power even existed. It was an implicit admission, too, that the taxpayer's and beneficiary's only real protection is political. Congress simply wouldn't *dare* cut benefits!

Another common theme was the great "insurance bargains" Social Security was offering its beneficiaries, which were illustrated with several hypothetical examples. The 1950 amendment was giving windfalls, some of them fantastically large, to many people newly brought into the system; also, some enterprising souls were finding ways to continue working and still collect their benefits.[94]   One article described Social Security as "the biggest, cheapest insurance bonanza the citizens of this country ever have had."[95]

When the 1950 amendments brought the self-employed under Social Security in 1951, the press acted almost as an auxiliary Social Security Administration publicity office in hailing this expansion as a boon for Americans. *U.S. News & World Report* showed how Social Security was a fantastic bargain for the self-employed, especially if aged sixty or over. A store owner, sixty-two years old in 1952, paying his maximum self-employment tax of $81 in 1951, 1952, and 1953, and $108 in 1954, when a scheduled tax increase would kick in, would have paid $351 in taxes by the time he retired in December 1954—and qualified for a monthly annuity of up to $120, which would have cost $21,000 had he bought it privately. And since the Internal Revenue Service had ruled that Social Security benefits were not subject to tax, the Social Security advantage was even greater.[96]

As to whether the new self-employment tax was worthwhile, *U.S. News & World Report* argued "Very much so, for older person in particular," due to the generosity of the new benefits; for example, a man who retired after paying the maximum tax of $81 a year on income of $3,600 or more would get $80 a month, for life.[97] *Business Week* gave an explanation of the self-employment tax that could have been written by Social Security itself:

This maximum $81 payment isn't really a tax; it's an insurance premium. It gives you what amounts to a life insurance policy and an annuity contract, both underwritten by the U.S. government. It gives you this coverage at much less than any insurance company can offer, and the return is taxfree.[98]

Note, again, the clear, strong analogy to an individual policy and an individual annuity.

Media complacency over Social Security was not unanimous. Occasionally, a voice of caution and even criticism sounded. Congressman A. S. Mike Monroney (D-OK) published an article in *Collier's* lauding Social Security and describing it as "the largest permanent insurance the world has ever known," but pointing out that several factors threatened to increase Social Security's future liability, such as the aging of the population, the likelihood that Congress would increase Social Security's Depression-level benefits, and extension to include disability benefits. He advocated raising the payroll tax, then frozen at one percent each for workers and employers; opting for a sizable reserve fund instead of pay-as-you-go financing; and, since everyone "should have the same *right* to *buy* old-age income [italics in original]," bringing all occupations under Social Security to capture additional revenue.[99]

In May 1953, Fletcher Knebel pointed out in a powerful article in *Look* magazine that Social Security, giving so many windfalls to new beneficiaries, was "grossly unfair"; that it discriminated against working women; and that its financial base was "no more solid than a quicksand of I.O.U.'s from the Government." Not only would the trust fund's bonds have to be paid off by taxation to pay future benefits, Knebel argued, but the fund encourages Congress to evade the full costs of caring for dependent persons. He concluded with a call for adopting complete pay-as-you-go financing with no "trust fund" and branded the existing program an "experiment in national self-delusion."[100] But such criticisms were very rare, and had no impact.

So loud and explosive in 1936-1939, the reserve-fund controversy dwindled away to the occasional sullen grumble of a retreating thunderstorm. In 1947 John T. Flynn published a short, repetitive piece reiterating some of his 1939 criticisms of the fund, focusing on the government's having levied $9 billion in Social Security taxes since 1936 and spent only $1.5 billion in benefits, the remaining $7.5 billion being spent on other government expenses.[101] Three years later, the Brookings Institution published *The Cost and Financing of Social Security,* a study which pointedly described the program's adoption of insurance language as "a stroke of promotional genius" through which Social Security "capitalized on the good will of private insurance and, through the establishment of a reserve fund, has clothed itself with an aura of financial soundness."[102] It reserved its sharpest criticism for the "trust fund":

> The operation of the OASI Trust Fund is *not* similar in character to that of a private insurance company. Private insurance reserves . . . are usually invested in projects that directly participate in or promote the production of goods and services. These investments are procreative in character and thus "earn" income. Furthermore, they are assets of the insurance company reserve, but they are liabilities of *other* enterprises. The OASI Trust Fund is invested in federal government securities. Since the money is used by the government in meeting its regular expenditure requirement, no real reserve is created. The obligations of the government (liabilities) deposited in a

trust account do not represent assets; they merely record future obligations which can be fulfilled only through the levy of future taxes upon the economy in general. The Trust Fund is thus a fiction—serving only to confuse.[103] (italics in original)

All of this was true, but made no difference. Most people did not, and still don't, read studies by research institutions like Brookings, and the only result was to earn for the study's conservative co-author, Karl Schlotterbeck, the lasting enmity of Social Security's administrators and advocates.[104]

But that was all. Virtually unopposed and unchallenged, the government's semantics became those of the media's treatment of Social Security, hence became the semantics of the American public.

The federal government, then, made a gigantic and deliberate effort to shape public perceptions of and beliefs about Social Security. As the documentary record makes clear, the payroll tax and "trust fund" were crafted to dispose people to support the program—the payroll tax by encouraging Americans to think that they had an earned right to benefits they had paid for, and by giving taxpayers a financial stake in the program; the "trust fund" through its use of reassuring trust terms. The massive publicity effort of Social Security's Informational Service in not merely purveying information but depicting Social Security as insurance—for the most part, as closely similar to *private* insurance writing *individual policies*—bears out conservative philosopher Richard Weaver's observation that many institutions believe "they cannot permit an unrestricted access to news about themselves," so create offices of publicity where "writers skilled in propaganda prepare the kinds of stories these institutions wish to see circulated." The publicity office, he argued, inevitably acts as "an office of censorship, de-emphasizing, or withholding entirely, news which would be damaging to prestige."[105] Such as the reservation of power clause.

The complaisance of the American press, with its prompt, obliging adoption of insurance terminology, even lifting material from Social Security publications, supports Weaver's criticisms of the press as "the Great Stereopticon," an instrument of daily "systematic indoctrination" of the people, presenting "a version of life quite as controlled as that taught by medieval religionists." Newspapers and other media were giving people a highly filtered and edited version of reality, Weaver warned, and credulous dependence on them was dangerous. "The more firmly an utterance is stereotyped, the more likely it is to win credit. . . . Faith in the printed word has raised journalists to the rank of oracles." Modern publication, he added, was using techniques to promote uncritical, unreflective absorption of its contents. One was "the stereotyping of whole phrases," which are "carefully chosen not to stimulate reflection but to evoke stock responses of approbation or disapprobation."[106] Phrases like "insurance premium," "earned right," "as a matter of right," "contract," "guaranteeing . . . monthly benefits" and "trust fund."

One of the fond beliefs of American life is that the press and media, by helping create a well-informed electorate, are bulwarks of freedom and a sound democracy. The media's invertebrate performance in Social Security's formative years did not live up to this hope. Social Security never received widespread, sustained, root-and-branch critical scrutiny in the popular press. Only over the reserve fund was there any real controversy.

With no alternative account of reality to draw their opinions from, thinking about Social Security in the government's language, Americans quite naturally came to believe that Social Security was what the government said it was: old-age and survivors' insurance, bought and paid for by their taxes, which was guaranteed to come to them as an earned right.

Several other factors also helped shape the public's attitude toward Social Security, of course: the terrible suffering of the Depression; the mass turn in desperation to Washington for succor; President Roosevelt's colossal prestige; the popularity of the New Deal as a whole. The Townsend Movement was important, too. In Abraham Holtzman's assessment, it "did more to dramatize the plight of the aged than any other force in American life." For the first time, Americans were vividly aware of the problem of old-age destitution. The movement also helped form "a public opinion favorable to the concepts that old-age protection was a matter of right, not charity or need; that benefits should be ample, not niggardly; that their provision was properly the responsibility of government;" and that pensions served both individual dignity and national economic stability.[107]   But in determining the *specific* version of reality which prevailed—Social Security as insurance paying benefits as an earned right—the design and promotion of Social Security were decisive.

With all these factors operating, public acceptance and approval of Social Security grew steadily. Thirteen national surveys in the 1936-1944 period by three polling agencies revealed a striking embrace of income maintenance programs for the elderly. Whereas a September 1936 survey found that 68 percent of its respondents supported old-age insurance, the figure was 77 percent in January 1937—and a near-unanimous 96 percent in August 1944! Moreover, seven surveys by three agencies in the 1938-1945 period disclosed strong, and growing, support for extending Social Security to uncovered occupations. In January 1938, 66 percent wanted Social Security expanded; by May 1945, 76 percent did, while the share of respondents opposed fell from 23 percent to 10 percent.[108]

The all-important struggle for popular acceptance and support had been won.

Notes

1.   Vincent Bugliosi with Curt Gentry, *Helter Skelter: The True Story of the Manson Murders* (New York: Bantam Books, 1975), p. 655.

2.   U.S., Congress, Senate, Senator Edward Kennedy, 94th Cong., 1st sess., September 16, 1975, *Congressional Record,* 121:28872.

3.   *Analysis of the Social Security System: Hearings,* p. 882.

4.   Social Security Board, *A Brief Explanation of the Social Security Act,* Circular No. 1, July 1937, p. 2; Social Security Board, *A Brief Explanation of the Social Security Act,* Circular No. 1, December 1937, p. 2.

5.   Social Security Board, *Federal Old-Age Benefits,* Circular No 3, May 1937; Social Security Board, *Old-Age Insurance: Federal Old-Age Benefits,* Circular No. 3, September 1937; Social Security Board, *Old-Age Insurance Under the Social Security Act: Some Questions and Answers,* Circular No. 3, October 1938, pp. 3-5. It might be noted that these circulars are small-format documents (4" x 9"), making the impact from this very frequent repetition of "old-age insurance" all the greater.

6.   Social Security Board, *Federal Old-Age Benefits established by The Social Security Act,* Circular No. 4, August 1937; Social Security Board, *Federal Old-Age Benefits (Old-Age Insurance) established by The Social Security Act,* Circular No. 4, November 1937.

7.   U.S., Congress, House, Mary Dewson, "Fifty Years' Progress Toward Social Security," in Representative Matthew J. Merritt, "Fifty Years' Progress Toward Social Security," Extension of Remarks, May 31, 1938, *Congressional Record,* Appendix, 83: 2266.

8.   John J. Corson, "Survivors' Benefits," *Survey Midmonthly* (December 1938), p. 372.

9.   Lee K. Frankel, Jr., "The Twilight of Industrial Life Insurance," *Survey Midmonthly* (June 1938), pp. 204-205.

10.   "Social Security: Pie from the Sky," *Time,* February 13, 1939, p. 14.

11.   M. Albert Linton, "Old-Age Security for Everybody," *Atlantic Monthly,* April 1936, p. 490.

12.   Winthrop W. Aldrich, "Social Security: An Appraisal of the Federal Act," *Vital Speeches of the Day,* August 1, 1936, p. 687.

13.   Altmeyer, *The Formative Years of Social Security,* pp. 88-89.

14.   General Hugh S. Johnson, "A Hokus-Pocus: The Social Security Tax," *Vital Speeches of the Day,* December 1, 1937, p. 116.

15.   Beulah Amidon, "Old Age Reserve," *Survey Midmonthly,* September 1938, p. 284.

16.   Thomas H. Eliot, "Funds for the Future," *Atlantic Monthly,* August 1938, pp. 228-229.

17.   Amidon, "Old Age Reserve," p. 284.

18.   John T. Flynn, "The Social Security 'Reserve' Swindle," *Harper's,* February 1939, pp. 240-242, 243-245.

19.   Flynn: U.S., Congress, House, Committee on Ways and Means, *Social Security: Hearings relative to the Social Security Act Amendments of 1939 before the House Committee on Ways and Means,* 76th Cong., 1st sess., 1939, 3 vols., I:387-396, II:1707-1751. Other critics: Arthur H. Vandenberg, "A Great Adventure in Humanity," *Vital Speeches of the Day,* February 1, 1939, pp. 236-238; "Make Social Security Secure," *Collier's,* March 25, 1939, p. 78.

20.   Reinhard Hohaus, "Equity, Adequacy, and Related Factors in Old Age Security," *Record of the American Institute of Actuaries,* vol. 27, pt. 1, no. 55 (June 1938), pp. 78, 82-85.

21.   Ibid., p. 92.

22.   Ibid., pp. 92, 113.

23.   See, e.g., Flynn, "The Social Security 'Reserve' Swindle," pp. 238, 245-246.

24. Holtzman, *The Townsend Movement,* pp. 102-104; Leuchtenburg, *Franklin D. Roosevelt and the New Deal 1932-1940,* p. 271.
25. Altmeyer, *The Formative Years of Social Security,* pp. 89-91, 295-297.
26. *Social Security: Hearings,* I:3-7.
27. Ibid., p. 36.
28. Ibid., p. 41.
29. Franklin D. Roosevelt, *The Public Papers and Addresses of Franklin D. Roosevelt,* vol. 8 (1939): *War—and Neutrality* (New York: The Macmillan Company, 1941), p. 77.
30. Ibid., pp. 78-79.
31. Altmeyer, *The Formative Years of Social Security,* pp. 99-113.
32. U.S., Congress, House, Committee on Ways and Means, *Social Security Act Amendments of 1939,* House Report 728 to accompany H.R. 6635, 76th Cong., 1st sess., 1939, pp. 81, 84-85, 57, 96-100.
33. Author's comparison of the texts of the original Act of August 14, 1935, in Social Security Administration, *Social Security Act of 1935,* vol. 2, at VI, "Public—No. 271—74th Congress," text of Social Security Act of 1935, pp. 1-32, and H.R. 6635, the Act of August 10, 1939 to amend the Social Security Act, in *Laws Relating to Social Security and Unemployment Compensation,* comp. Gilman G. Udell (Washington, DC: U.S. Government Printing Office, 1958), pp. 32-79.
34. John H. Magee, *General Insurance,* 3rd ed. (Chicago: Richard D. Irwin, 1950), pp. 32-33, 35-36; Shelby Cullom Davis, "Toward the American Dream," *Current History,* December 1939, p. 41.
35. Author's comparison of texts of Title II, Section 201 of Social Security Act of 1935, in Social Security Administration, *Social Security Act of 1935,* vol. 2, at VI, "Public—No. 271—74th Congress," text of Social Security Act of 1935, pp. 3-4, and Title II, Section 201 of 1939 Amendments (H.R. 6635), in *Laws Relating to Social Security and Unemployment Compensation,* pp. 34-35.
36. Ibid.
37. For discussions in Congress of the "embezzlement" charge and the IOU controversy in general, see, e.g., U.S., Congress, House, 76th Cong., 1st sess., February 27, 1939, *Congressional Record,* 84:1954-1961; U.S., Congress, House, Social Security amendments debate, 76th Cong., 1st sess., June 8 and 9, 1939, *Congressional Record,* 84:6854-6856, 6862, 6890-6893. For a defense of the reserve being invested in Treasuries as the only feasible option, see, e.g., U.S., Congress, House, Congressman McCormack speaking on Social Security amendments, 76th Cong., 1st sess., June 8, 1939, *Congressional Record,* 84:6855.
38. *Social Security: Hearings,* III: 2113.
39. U.S., Senate, Committee on Finance, *Social Security Act Amendments: Hearings before the Senate Finance Committee on H.R. 6635,* 76th Cong., 1st sess., 1939, p. 81.
40. Charles E. Rounds, Jr. and Eric Hayes, *Loring: A Trustee's Handbook,* 8th (centennial) ed. (New York: Aspen Publishers, Inc., 1998), pp. 1-2, 5, 79; Gilbert Thomas Stephenson, *Estates and Trusts,* 4th ed. (New York: Appleton-Century-Crofts, 1965), pp. 63-66.
41. *Social Security: Hearings,* III:2205-2206.
42. *Oral Arguments, Helvering v. Davis,* p. 16.
43. U.S. Supreme Court, *Records and Briefs,* October Term, 1959, No. 54, *Flemming v. Nestor,* Brief for the Appellant, pp. 10-11.
44. Title II, Section 205, paragraphs (a), (b), (g) and (h), of 1939 Amendments (H.R. 6635), in *Laws Relating to Social Security and Unemployment Compensation,* pp. 41-44.

45. Professor Charles E. Rounds, Jr., "Will the Institution of the Trust Survive the Clinton Presidency?" *The Advocate,* vol. 25 (Spring 1995), p. 31.
46. *Social Security: Hearings,* III:2113.
47. Ibid., p. 2245.
48. Text of Title II of H.R. 6635, in *Laws Relating to Social Security and Unemployment Compensation,* pp. 35-38.
49. Ibid., p. 39—Section 202(g); p. 76—Section 902(g).
50. *Social Security Act Amendments of 1939,* House Report 728 to accompany H.R. 6635, p. 119.
51. *Social Security: Hearings,* I:59, 60.
52. Ibid., III:2179.
53. Ibid., p. 2180.
54. Ibid., p. 2207.
55. Ibid.
56. Ibid., p. 2208.
57. Ibid., pp. 2209-2210.
58. Social Security Board, *Changes in the Social Security Act: Old-Age Insurance,* I.S.C. no. 35, temporary ed., September 1939, p. 1.
59. Ibid., p. 3.
60. Ibid.
61. Ibid.
62. Social Security Board, *Monthly Benefits Begin in 1940,* I.S.C. no. 34, September 1939, p. 1.
63. Social Security Board, *2 Plans for Old-Age Security,* I.S.C. no. 42, n. d., pp. 1-3; Social Security Board, *What is Social Security? A Brief Explanation of the Social Security Act,* I.S.C. no. 1, July 1940, p. 10.
64. Social Security Board, *Old-Age and Survivors Insurance for Workers and their Families,* I.S.C. no. 35, January 1943, p. 3.
65. John J. Corson, "Advances in Old Age Security," *Survey Midmonthly,* September 1939, pp. 267-269.
66. Arthur J. Altmeyer, "The New Social Security Program," *School Life,* January 1940, pp. 103-104.
67. Arthur J. Altmeyer, "Security is Good Business," *Dun's Review,* March 1940, pp. 5-9.
68. U.S., Congress, House, Representative Frank H. Buck, "Social Security Looks to the Future," Extension of Remarks, 76th Cong., 1st sess., June 6, 1939, *Congressional Record,* 84:2409-2411.
69. U.S., Congress, Senate, Senator David I. Walsh, "Amendments to Social Security Law," Extension of Remarks, 76th Cong., 1st sess., July 6, 1939, *Congressional Record,* 84:3050-3051.
70. "The New Social Security System: Questions, Answers for Workers, Employers," *The United States News,* August 14, 1939, p. 3.
71. Davis, "Toward the American Dream," pp. 41-43.
72. "U.S. Social Security Payoff Starts in New Year for 912,000," *Newsweek,* December 25, 1939, p. 10.
73. "Billions for the Old Folks," *United States News,* January 5, 1940, p. 18.
74. "Social Security Plan: Five-Front Extension of Act Would Add 27 Million to Rolls," *Newsweek,* October 13, 1941, p. 17.
75. U.S., Congress, House, Committee on Ways and Means, *Issues in Social Security: A Report to the Committee on Ways and Means,* 79th Cong., 1st sess., 1946, pp. iii, xvii.

76. Ibid., pp. 26-34.
77. Ibid., pp. 103-104.
78. Ibid., pp. 129-130.
79. Ibid., p. 130.
80. Ibid., pp. 130-131.
81. Altmeyer, *The Formative Years of Social Security,* pp. 278-280, 71-72, 159, 280.
82. Altmeyer, "Ten Years of Social Security," p. 384.
83. Wilbur J. Cohen and Robert J. Myers, "Social Security Act Amendments of 1950: A Summary and Legislative History," *Social Security Bulletin,* vol. 13, no. 10 (October 1950), pp. 3-14; Altmeyer, *The Formative Years of Social Security,* pp. 185, 251; Derthick, *Policymaking for Social Security,* p. 430.
84. Wilbur J. Cohen and James L. Calhoon, "Social Security Legislation, January-June 1948: Legislative History and Background," *Social Security Bulletin,* vol. 11, no. 7 (July 1948), pp. 5-7.
85. Ibid., pp. 8-10.
86. Social Security Administration, *Questions and Answers on Social Security,* I.S.C. no. 60, December 1947, p. 5.
87. Ibid., p. 1.
88. Ibid., pp. 13-14.
89. Social Security Administration, *Federal Old-Age and Survivors Insurance: A Brief Explanation,* I.S.C. no. 64, June 1948.
90. *Analysis of the Social Security System: Hearings,* pp. 907-912.
91. See, e.g., Alexander Griffin, "What Social Security Does for You," *Saturday Evening Post,* July 18, 1942, pp. 28, 51-52; Jerome Beatty, "Will You Get Your Share of Social Security?" *American Magazine,* February 1944, pp. 43, 105-106, 109; Charles Stevenson, "Does the Government Owe You Money?" *Reader's Digest,* November 1949, pp. 108-110; "Social Security: What You Get," *U.S. News & World Report,* September 15, 1950, pp. 24-25.
92. Clarence Woodbury, "Social Security Pays Off," *American Magazine,* vol. 143, vacation issue, 1947, p. 14.
93. Ibid.
94. William Hazlett Upson, "Social Security—It's Wonderful!" *Reader's Digest,* April 1953, pp. 104-106.
95. J. K. Lasser and Walter Ross, "You Are Richer Than You Think," *Nation's Business,* October 1951, pp. 25-27, 84-85.
96. "Bargains in Pensions," *U.S. News & World Report,* October 26, 1951, pp. 52, 54, 56-57.
97. "We've Been Asked: About Tax on Self-Employed," *U.S. News & World Report,* January 11, 1952, p. 57.
98. "More Security," *Business Week,* February 23, 1952, p. 150.
99. Congressman A. S. Mike Monroney, "Protect That Pension," *Collier's,* October 12, 1946, pp. 13, 53, 55-56.
100. Fletcher Knebel, "Will You Be Cheated by Social Security After Paying the Bill?" *Look,* May 5, 1953, pp. 81-83.
101. John T. Flynn, "Our Present Dishonest Federal Old Age Pension Plan," *Reader's Digest,* May 1947, pp. 4-8.
102. Lewis Meriam and Karl T. Schlotterbeck, *The Cost and Financing of Social Security* (Washington, DC: The Brookings Institution, 1950), p. 8.
103. Ibid., p. 155.
104. Derthick, *Policymaking for Social Security,* p. 155.

105. Richard M. Weaver, *Ideas Have Consequences* (Chicago: University of Chicago Press, Phoenix Books ed., 1948), p. 99.
106. Ibid., pp. 93-96.
107. Holtzman, *The Townsend Movement,* p. 208.
108. Michael E. Schiltz, *Public Attitudes Toward Social Security 1935-1965,* Social Security Administration, Office of Research and Statistics, Research Report no. 33 (Washington, DC: U.S. Government Printing Office, 1970), pp. 35-36, 57.

7

The Curtis Hearings
and the Insurance Controversy

"Why do you dress me in borrowed
robes?"
—Macbeth, *Act I, Scene iii.*

"I submit that such actions and
inactions all savor of public immorality."
—*Ray Peterson*

After the 1950 liberalization, Social Security's resemblance to private insurance was problematic at best. Yet, as we saw, the official and media depiction of Social Security as insurance persisted. The gap between the reality of Social Security and the public's understanding of it was widening into a chasm.

The issue of whether or not Social Security really is insurance did not go wholly unnoticed. In January 1950, testifying before the Senate Finance Committee during the hearings on the 1950 amendments (H.R. 6000) to the Social Security Act, Altmeyer told the Committee that Social Security gave lower wage-earners a larger benefit in relation to their wage loss than higher-wage earners got. Senator Robert A. Taft (R-OH) observed, "That is not an insurance principle, of course. That is a social-welfare principle" with "no relation to insurance." Altmeyer retorted that it was "a very sound social-insurance principle." It is so related to insurance, he added, because in some group policies the employer pays a larger share of the cost of benefits for a lower-wage worker.[1]

The next day Taft and Altmeyer sparred again, Taft scoring the weak relation between what one pays and what one gets, and pointing out, rightly, that the beneficiaries then receiving benefits, who had paid only modest taxes, "haven't begun to pay anything like what they are getting back compared to what somebody may pay later on." History has, of course, abundantly borne

159

Taft out, and he made another observation about Social Security's true nature: the Social Security tax is nothing but a tax levied "to pay other people who are not working." Hence "all this talk about insurance and contribution is away beyond anything that is really the fact."[2]

> Mr. ALTMEYER: I am in complete disagreement with you. . . . One, it is insurance because it spreads the risk. That is the definition of insurance. It is not private insurance, where there is a very specific relationship between the individual—
>
> Senator TAFT: Wait a moment. Insurance is to spread the risk? Insurance is paying for something under a contract between two people in which you get something for what you pay equal to what you pay. This does not pretend to give you what you pay.
>
> Mr. ALTMEYER: Of course that is your definition of insurance.
>
> Senator TAFT: That is what I think insurance is.[3]

Admittedly, Taft was somewhat clumsy—while private insurance does indeed involve contracts, insurance is indeed partly about spreading risk, and the amount of insurance in a policy usually well exceeds one's premium outlays, because of the large number of people paying premiums and the actuarial calculations of probability that the risk insured against will eventuate for any given policyholder—but the clashes with Altmeyer had raised the crux of the matter: Was Social Security a social-welfare program or bona-fide insurance? And did the word "insurance" refer to anything in reality, or was its meaning malleable and pragmatic? Underlying this latter question, as we shall see, were profound differences about the nature and role of language.

The Curtis Hearings:
Benefit Terminations and "Vested Rights"

However, the first real challenge to Social Security did not come until 1953, when Representative Carl T. Curtis (R-NE), a staunch conservative and foe of the New Deal and of social insurance, decided to pursue the matter. The Republicans had gained a majority in the House in the 1952 election, and Curtis, a majority member of the House Ways and Means Committee, persuaded the chairman that the House should pass a resolution authorizing an investigation of Social Security. This was done, and Curtis appointed chairman of the Ways and Means investigative Subcommittee on Social Security.[4] For the first time, Social Security would receive searching, sustained critical examination.

Curtis had already criticized Social Security for anomalies in benefit payments, citing several cases in which a beneficiary recovered all his tax payments in just a couple of years and thereafter received a windfall. He had appended "additional minority views" to the minority report of the Ways and

Means Committee for the 1949 version of H.R. 6000, in which he attacked OASI as "grossly unsound and ineffective," causing numerous benefit inequities, and "totally unmoral" in binding future generations to pay benefits in perpetuity. He called for a flat uniform benefit paid to all aged persons without a means test, financed by an addition to the income tax rather than a payroll tax.[5]

The Curtis hearings opened in July 1953 and covered a wide array of topics including U.S. population trends; public assistance; OASI's coverage, benefits, eligibility, and financial position. Much of it is irrelevant to our purpose, but Curtis did obtain testimony from Robert Ball, then Acting Director of the Bureau of Old-Age and Survivors Insurance, regarding benefit terminations and cuts under amending legislation. Ball had the honesty to admit that the original Social Security Act had a money-back guarantee, and that if a worker died before attaining the age of sixty-five, the money he had paid, plus a small consideration for interest, would have been sent to his estate. Curtis drew attention to the reduction in the single man's retirement benefits by the 1939 amendments. Ball protested that "you have substituted for that a type of protection of survivorship and dependents' benefits." Although he objected to the characterization of what happened to single men as a benefit cut, he did at last admit that "it is certainly true that the return on a single man's record upon death has been cut," and that the 1939 amendments did leave some people worse off—"certain people would have been better off if the protection had been left as it was, that is true."[6]

Winding up the penultimate part of the hearings, Curtis and Chief Counsel Robert Winn brought up the character of an individual's rights to benefits. They cited "Pensions in the United States," a 1952 study by the National Planning Association which stated that "The right to retirement benefits under old-age and survivors insurance is vested after meeting the minimum service requirements previously described." Winn then asked Ball, who was staff director for the report, what was meant by "vested."

Mr. BALL: . . . . Under the old-age and survivors insurance program once an individual has met the insured status requirements for his age brackets, and the maximum there . . . is 40 quarters—that is this 25 million people who have worked under the system long enough to be entitled to benefits without having to make any further contribution or without having to perform any more work under the system—they are entitled to those benefits without any additional action on their part, which is comparable to the vesting provisions in civil service after 5 years if the individual does not withdraw his money and so on.

Chairman CURTIS: Subject, of course, to change by Congress.

Mr. BALL: Oh, yes. . . . Congress can, of course, make changes in any of these laws, civil service, or railroad retirement or social security, in the future.

Mr. WINN: The Funk & Wagnalls Unabridged Dictionary defines "vested":

> To confer ownership of, as property, upon a
> person; invest a person with (the full title to
> property); give to a person (an immediate,
> fixed right of present or future enjoyment).

Do you think the word "vested" is a proper word to apply to something which may be taken away either as a result of an act of Congress or as a result of the marriage of this person?

Mr. BALL: It seems to me the term "vested" is proper in this connection, Mr. Winn, yes.

Mr. EBERHARTER: . . . . Are you an attorney?

Mr. BALL: No; I am not.

Mr. EBERHARTER: "Vested" is a legal term . . . It has a legal definition.

Mr. BALL: . . . . I meant the term as used in "Pensions in the United States" to describe generally the situation where, under the law as now written, an individual had certain definite rights without further action on his part.[7]

Here again, Social Security was appropriating terminology that didn't really apply. The reservation of power clause, as Curtis and Winn implied, invalidates Ball's claim that the term "vested" is appropriate. In the *Oregon Law Review* five years later, Elmer Wollenberg gave the issue of vested rights to Social Security benefits meticulous scrutiny, and pointed out that "Congress has, as a practical matter, exercised its powers freely to revise, amend, and perfect the system," and could "reduce established benefit rights and even terminate regular benefit payments on the basis of new Federal policy." Wollenberg concluded that "The OASDI program, as Congress seems to view it in practice, does not involve any contractual obligations binding upon the Federal government. It is even doubtful that there is any point at which OASDI benefits vest in the recipient."[8]

We shall return to Wollenberg's careful treatment of the matter later. The point for now is that Curtis and Winn had succeeded in bringing out a inappropriate use of legal language, which had perhaps been done in order to give its reader the impression of acquiring a solid, unassailable right to benefits.

The Curtis Hearings: The Altmeyer Testimony

But the most important part of Curtis's investigative hearings for our purposes came on November 27, 1953, the day after Thanksgiving, when Arthur J. Altmeyer, who had been Commissioner for Social Security until April 10, testified on the legal status of OASI benefits.

Mutual hostility marked both Altmeyer's testimony and the approach march to it. Curtis wanted Altmeyer to serve as an expert consultant to his committee

and on June 9 wrote him asking him to prepare a statement of OASI's principles, offering to arrange remuneration. Curtis read the letter to Wilbur Cohen
before sending it and asked him to persuade Altmeyer to accept. Instead,
Cohen talked to Democratic Congressmen Wilbur Mills and Jere Cooper,
and, after hearing negative opinions of Curtis, contacted Altmeyer, who, after
consultation with Cohen, decided not to be of any help to Curtis. Altmeyer
wrote a bleak and chilly reply refusing to prepare the requested statement,
enumerating Curtis's criticisms of Social Security and citing "the grave danger to social security which I believe your present views represent." Curtis
repeated his request; Altmeyer refused again. Curtis then had Altmeyer served
with a subpoena, and Altmeyer made plans to appear before the subcommittee in November. He requested that Curtis send him a list of questions he
planned to ask or at least indicate the topics he wanted to discuss; the request
was ignored. Both Curtis and Chief Counsel Winn treated Altmeyer abruptly
and discourteously throughout the hearing, occasionally badgering him.
Altmeyer, for his part, was frequently defiant and testy. He was supported by
two minority members, John Dingell (D-MI) and Herman Eberharter (D-PA),
who, especially Dingell, interrupted constantly and often rudely, taunting
and baiting Curtis, who repeatedly had to gavel them to order.[9]

After some preliminaries Winn told Altmeyer that one of the matters the
committee wanted to investigate was "whether the arrangements provided in
Title II of the Social Security Act are, in fact, insurance." Winn and Curtis then
had Altmeyer read aloud, despite repeated objections from Altmeyer, Dingell,
and Eberharter, excerpts from numerous press releases, articles, radio broadcasts and Social Security publications in which Social Security was described
as "insurance." Among other things, this brought out that the original Social
Security Act did not describe the benefits as insurance; that the
administration's brief in *Helvering v. Davis* denied that Social Security could
be described as insurance; and that the Social Security Board had embraced
insurance language immediately after the *Helvering v. Davis* decision.
Altmeyer objected, reasonably enough, to his not having been furnished with
some idea of what was going to be asked of him, and being asked to read
excerpts out of context "to build up a case of some kind which I do not
understand frankly." He repeatedly affirmed his belief that "Titles II and VIII
together constitute an insurance program."[10]

Winn then brought up references to one's Social Security card in Social
Security publications which left an unmistakable impression that the
cardholder had an insurance policy. *Your New Social Security,* published in
April 1951, advised the reader to "Treat your card like an insurance policy."
*Old-Age and Survivors Insurance for You and Your Family Under the Federal
Social Security Law,* published in 1952, informed the reader that "Your card
is the symbol of your insurance policy under the Federal social security law."
Altmeyer confirmed these wordings.[11]

The issue then arose as to whether there was an insurance contract under Social Security. Altmeyer admitted that "This insurance is established as a matter of statutory right. There is no individual contract between the beneficiary and the Government." Asked if he had ever tried to give the impression that the individual had a contract with the Government, Altmeyer denied it.[12] Curtis probed further:

> Chairman CURTIS: The individual who perhaps was 21 years of age in 1937 and who has been in covered employment since then . . . and will have to continue to pay these taxes until he is 65, has no contract? Is that your position?
>
> Mr. ALTMEYER: That is right.
>
> Chairman CURTIS: And he has no insurance contract?
>
> Mr. ALTMEYER: That is right.
>
> Chairman CURTIS: It is a statutory right?
>
> Mr. ALTMEYER: It is a statutory right enforceable by law.
>
> Chairman CURTIS: Now, could the Congress change that statutory right?
>
> Mr. ALTMEYER: Yes; and it has done so to improve and liberalize the benefits time and again, and it will do so in the future, I am sure.
>
> Chairman CURTIS: And it has taken benefits away; has it not?[13]

Specifically, Curtis asked about the changes in 1939. "Prior to that they had a benefit in there that they no longer have?" Altmeyer replied that "There was more of a savings bank element and less of the insurance element prior to 1939." He also conceded that a statutory right could be changed by a duly elected legislative body.[14]

Curtis pointed out the misleading nature of the official descriptions of Social Security as "insurance" and the Social Security card as an "insurance policy," noting that "a 'policy' to the minds of most people, in the generally accepted meaning of the term, means a contract that cannot be changed by either party."[15] In this observation Curtis was, of course, exactly right; an insurance policy is, indeed, a contract. There was nothing in either the original Act of 1935, or the amendments of 1939, about policies or contracts. In telling people they had policies, and thereby implying that they had contracts, the Social Security Administration was deliberately giving a false impression.

Altmeyer argued that "statutory rights" under Social Security were stronger than contractual rights under some private insurance companies, "for the very reason that you have a responsible legislative body, the Congress of the United States of America." At that time, 90 million Americans had built up wage credits under Social Security. It was "inconceivable," Altmeyer went on, that Congress "would ever think of taking action to prejudice their rights that have developed under existing legislation."[16]

But if there was no contract, Winn asked later, didn't it follow that the benefits under Title II were "merely statutory benefits which Congress may withdraw or alter at any time?" Altmeyer retorted that "statutory rights are about the strongest type of rights," especially for a system affecting 90 million people, and "I think they are not to be impugned by you or anybody else."[17]

Altmeyer's retorts amounted to an admission that Social Security's vaunted statutory rights are indeed malleable and that the taxpayer's only real backstop is political: the sheer number of taxpaying, voting Americans participating in Social Security made it "inconceivable" that Congress would trammel their right to benefits. Put another way, the only real security taxpayers and beneficiaries have is the realization by Congress that tampering with benefit rights would be political suicide. Should a Congress ever muster up the fortitude to run that risk, benefits could indeed be cut. There was nothing in the law to prevent it.

This in turn implies that the crux of the whole matter is psychology—that the real foundation of Social Security is the public's perception of it, its opinions and beliefs about it. From the beginning, the government's actions had been taken with a keen eye to psychology. It was psychology, as Roosevelt himself had admitted, that had governed the decision to use the payroll tax, which was "politics all the way through." Psychology, too, had motivated the adoption of the "trust fund" in 1939 and the euphemism of "contribution" for the taxes. It was psychology that drove the massive promotional campaign since 1935, in which insurance language and rights talk figured prominently. And once the public had formed their consciousness about Social Security accordingly and the program had become a accepted fixture in the their lives, psychology would lock in their "rights" by creating a threat of political punishment for tampering with benefits. The taxpayers' and beneficiaries' political backstop was not statutory but psychological.

After a protracted presentation by Altmeyer of the history and basic ideas of Social Security from 1935 to 1950, and scores of angry clashes with Dingell and Eberharter, Winn raised the issue of the psychology of the people regarding Social Security benefits, and read a statement Altmeyer had made in the hearings before the Senate Finance Committee in 1939, which observed that even though Social Security was a compulsory system, "it is dependent upon the acceptance of the people, and the continued acceptance of the people." He followed with a 1952 statement by Robert Ball that people's attitude about the payment they would receive was "a matter of the first importance," that a security system can't really give security "unless people know they can count on the payment and feel good about the conditions under which the payment is made." Asked if he subscribed to those statements, Altmeyer replied angrily, "I do, and I think you are doing more to destroy the confidence of the American people in this system than anybody else except the chairman of the committee."[18] This was to be a stock response to criticism: angrily accuse the critic of trying to destroy the American people's confidence in Social Security. Roosevelt had done it in 1936 in response to Republican criticisms of the reserve fund; Beulah Amidon had done it in response to talk of IOUs in the fund; Social Security's defenders would continue to do it from now on. Here again is an admission that public opinion is all-important.

Winn read out from court cases several definitions of insurance, all of them defining it as a contract. Altmeyer retorted that all of those definitions pertained to private insurance, not social insurance. Winn went on to ask whether the presence of Section 1104, the reservation of power clause, made it impossible for a contract to exist between the government and the workers paying Social Security taxes. Altmeyer replied evasively that he didn't know whether that was correct or not.[19] It seems obvious that the reservation of power clause does indeed render a contractual relationship impossible.

Curtis and Winn returned again and again to the fact that private insurance has a contract, but Social Security does not. At one point Altmeyer and Congressman Eberharter raised the seeming exception of group insurance, in which the insured individual does not have a contract with the insurer. There is still a contract, Curtis retorted, between the insurer and the employer.[20] Moreover, bringing up group insurance is disingenuous, because as we have seen, Social Security's own publications intended for popular consumption had sought to analogize Social Security very tightly to an *individual* insurance policy, not to group insurance.

In yet another attempt to stress the noncontractual nature of Social Security benefits, Curtis and Winn presented the Internal Revenue Service's rationale for nontaxation of benefits. In response to a request by Curtis for information on the matter, IRS Commissioner T. Coleman Andrews wrote him on August 26 that in 1941 the IRS ruled that OASI benefits should not be reported as income for determining tax liability. While some experts in the IRS deemed the benefits taxable as annuities, Andrews wrote, the prevailing view was that Social Security benefits are not taxable income. The main reason for this decision was that the Supreme Court had ruled in *Helvering v. Davis* that Social Security benefits are payments in aid of the general welfare. Moreover, the Government's brief in *Helvering v. Davis* had argued that Titles II and VIII "did not constitute compulsory insurance within the accepted meaning of the term 'insurance,' or a compulsory addition to wages." Given that and the Court's decision, "it was suggested that it would be inconsistent and improper to take the view that the payments made under Title II were taxable on the ground that they were in the nature of purchased annuities or additional compensation for services rendered." Interestingly, Andrews added that the IRS also considered that making the benefits subject to income taxation "would tend to defeat the underlying purposes of the Social Security Act." The Act intended to tackle the problem of insecurity by paying benefits to reduce dependency. "Benefit payments were small and they would, of course, be further reduced if they were subjected to the income tax."[21]

After digging into the records further, Andrews wrote to Curtis that the IRS had apparently decided that the benefits are exempt from income tax for either one or all of these reasons: "the benefits are in the nature of gratuities and are, therefore, exempt under section 22 (b) (3) of the code"; the IRS had already ruled the lump-sum benefits nontaxable, and Congress hadn't authorized taxation of monthly benefits in the 1939 Amendments; and finally, Congress hadn't intended the benefits to be reduced by being subject to taxes.[22]

Interestingly enough, in 1983 Congress changed its mind, and that year's Social Security legislation authorized the first benefit taxation. In 1993 the benefit tax was raised.[23] Quite apart from the fact that this benefit taxation amounts to a benefit cut, this reversal drives home the insecurity of one's politically grounded and purportedly strong "statutory rights" under Social Security. *Pace* Henry Aaron, Congress has proven over and over again that one's "sure bet" of Social Security is in fact uncertain. If the imperatives of general welfare or expediency require it, one's "rights" go by the boards. They did in 1983 with this benefit taxation. As Winn and Curtis were soon to bring up, they did in 1939 and 1950 too.

Altmeyer shrugged off the issue of benefits' status as gratuities, retorting that gratuity is a "technical expression, and defined rather narrowly." Apparently trying yet again to get him to make a damaging admission about Social Security, Winn cited Congress' attempt in the Economy Act of 1933 to shirk its contractual obligations for World War I War Risk Insurance by repealing all statutes for that insurance, only to be blocked by the Supreme Court, which ruled that the war risk insurance contracts are "legal obligations of the same dignity as other contracts of the United States and possess the same legal incidence," hence Congress' attempt to disavow the contracts was unconstitutional. Winn then asked Altmeyer if he'd ever recommended that OASI benefits be based on a contract between the Government and the workers. "No, sir; I do not think it is necessary to protect them," Altmeyer retorted. "I have more confidence in the Congress than you have."[24]

Asked for his definition of a "right," Altmeyer defined it as "a claim against another person or agency or government which is enforceable in the courts of the land." Curtis and Winn then pointed out that under the 1939 amendments, single persons without dependents would no longer have a 3.5 percent of income lump-sum benefit paid to their estates. Questioned about these "strong" statutory rights, Altmeyer turned evasive:

Mr. WINN: . . . did they have a right, according to your reasoning, Mr. Altmeyer?

Mr. ALTMEYER: Certainly they did.

Mr. WINN: What happened to it in 1939?

Mr. ALTMEYER: It was amended to give them a better right.

Mr. WINN: I see; these rights can be swapped around as you think they should be?

Mr. ALTMEYER: I am confident that the Congress of the United States will continue to improve and increase the rights of the workers.

Mr. WINN: I am talking about the right of a single man, Mr. Altmeyer, to have his estate receive a lump-sum benefit. What was given to him in place of that right which was withdrawn by Congress in 1939?[25]

Altmeyer replied that the single man didn't know he was going to be single all his life; he could have gotten married, in which case he'd pick up survivor's benefits. Yes, Winn replied, but supposing he did and his wife died before he reached sixty-five, and he had no dependents—what about his right to a lump-sum benefit then? Well, it was replaced by the more valuable survivor's benefit in case she hadn't died. Winn then raised the 1950 amendments, which took away the 1 percent annual increment in benefits inserted in the 1939 amendments.

Mr. WINN: . . . What happened then to the rights of those people to receive a benefit which had an increment provision in it?

Mr. ALTMEYER: The persons retiring in the earlier years got more valuable rights. The persons who will be retiring years hence got less valuable rights, and I deplore that . . .

Mr. WINN: You have not answered my question. . . . What happened to the rights which existed prior to 1950? . . . What happened to those rights, Mr. Altmeyer?

Mr. ALTMEYER: Those rights, which of course, as you know, will accrue in years hence, are not as valuable as they would have been under the previous law, but it is going to be many years hence before anyone is going to be disadvantaged by extinguishing this annual increment . . . .

Mr. WINN: But the rights were extinguished, were they not, Mr. Altmeyer, by the 1950 amendments?

Mr. ALTMEYER: Those rights in the future, no rights in the present.[26]

Winn then cited numerous letters by beneficiaries complaining about benefit terminations and other inequities. The first of these, written by a Mr. C. V. Stinchecum of Duncan, Oklahoma to Congressman Harold Ostertag on January 10, 1953, reads in part as follows:

DEAR MR. OSTERTAG: I was agreeably surprised to read in the daily papers a few days ago that there are at least two Congressmen who recognize the injustice which is being perpetrated upon a large number of self-employed persons, of whom I am one.

My position is that Congress has violated the sanctity of a contract, to which I am a party, without my consent, and it is a well-established principle of law that no valid contract can be altered or amended without the consent of both contracting parties.

When the social security system was first inaugurated I was brought into it without any action on my part nor any opportunity on my part to decline.

Since the inception of the plan I have paid my premiums by payroll deductions until April 1947, when it became necessary for me to retire under a retirement plan operated by my employers.

At that time my contract matured, and from that time until January 1951 I received the benefits to which I was entitled. I engaged in business promptly thereafter as a self-employed person and earned a satisfactory profit, as self-employed persons were not covered by the then existing statute. I continued to receive my social-security benefits until the new act.

The new act extended the coverage to self-employed persons, and my benefits were suspended until such time as I definitely retire or reach the age of 75, and to add insult to injury, I was then required to resume payments.

. . . . If this were a pension based upon need and supported out of the Federal Treasury, it is possible that Congress would have been within its moral rights, but it has been repeatedly stated that this plan is entirely self-supporting . . . .

Should any insurance company who might be carrying an annuity policy in my favor decide, when the policy matured, that due to my earnings I did not need the annuity payments and then suspended or reduced same, they would promptly be faced by legal action. . . .

I can live without these benefits, but am angry and disgusted that my Government should take from me what is morally mine and for which I have paid considerable sums of money . . . [27]

The following revealing dialogue ensued:

Mr. WINN: What happened to Mr. Stinchecum's right to receive benefit payments, on January 1, 1951?

Mr. ALTMEYER: He got a more valuable right, so far as protection is concerned, because he probably started developing higher benefit rights.

Mr. WINN: You still have not answered my question as to what happened to his right on January 1, 1951?

Mr. ALTMEYER: There was substituted, in my judgment, a better right.

Mr. WINN: He got no more payments.

Mr. ALTMEYER: But he is building up more benefit rights.

Mr. WINN: He had been receiving benefits from 1947. He stopped receiving benefits.

Mr. ALTMEYER: Well, I am telling you that I think that protection against the loss of income is the end objective of social insurance, and I would like to see more adequate benefits payable to persons who suffer a loss of income than to persons who through happenstance, can continue working in uncovered employment and draw a benefit which has no relationship to the fact of loss of income. [But weren't benefits supposed to come "as a matter of right, irrespective of need"? Hadn't that been Social Security's consistent promotional line for 18 years?]

Mr. WINN: The fact remains, though, that Congress by amending the law in 1950, took away his immediate right to benefits; did it not?

Mr. ALTMEYER: Sir, all I can say is: Why don't you canvas the 5.5 million beneficiaries to see whether they approve or disapprove of the 1950 amendments?

Mr. WINN: I would like an answer to my question.[28]

Similar letters were quoted from several other self-employed persons over sixty-five in the same situation. Many retirees had started small businesses or other self-employment so as to earn more income while drawing Social Security. With self-employment now a "covered" occupation (1950 amendments), it was now subject to the retirement earnings test. So retirees who engaged in it now had their benefits cut off if they earned more than $75 a month from self-employment work, and were required to return benefits already paid them and to resume paying Social Security taxes. Other letters complained of other inequities. Altogether, there were two dozen letters.[29]

We will cite merely representative excerpts. The crucial point is that these letters reveal three things: First, that Social Security's false consciousness had *already* gotten a firm grip on the public mind just eighteen years after the Social Security Act was passed. Many Americans believed, as they were led and intended to believe, that Social Security was "insurance," that benefits were "their money," that they were "entitled" to them "by right." As Curtis observed, "the people have relied upon the statement that this is insurance, as they understand it."[30] Second, that the reality of the retirement earnings means test necessarily collided with the depiction of benefits as an "earned right." Third, that their "rights" were therefore not remotely as secure as they had been led to believe they were.

I am 70 years of age and was collecting social security for 3 years when the Government discontinued it because I earn more than $50 and later $75 per month.

My complaint is—why was the Government permitted to make this change retroactive. When I joined this plan in the beginning we were promised we would collect at the age of 65 with no ifs, ands, or buts.[31]

I was promised by the President of the United States that when I had completed my part of the social-security law I was then entitled to my pension, and laboring under the impression that I was secure in my pension, I failed to make any other provision for my old age. I thought (foolishly, I suppose) that even the Congress of the United States could not annul a contract already complete and fulfilled in every detail. I thought (foolishly, I suppose) the Constitution of the United States would not recognize a new law that was retroactive and that would hurt a good citizen and deprive him of what he was entitled to . . . [32]

The people who get social security paid for it. It is their money, they invested it during all the years to the social-security fund. The social security is not a charity. It is a form of insurance. How has the Government the right to take the money away or to say how much these people can or cannot earn?[33]

Those of us who have contributed to social security since its inception have surely the right to expect that the integrity of the insurance we paid for shall be preserved.[34]

Attached is a page from a magazine which refers to loss of maximum social-security protection for those who have made the maximum contributions to social security since its inception, but whose disability prevents them from maintaining this maximum rate to age 65. No insurance company changes the rules of the game against the players after the contract is accepted, and neither should Federal social security.[35]

Winn made much of Section 1104. But Altmeyer did not share Winn's and Curtis's misgivings about it. When asked if he thought that the consistent reference to benefit payments as a matter of right might have been misleading in view of Section 1104, he denied it, yet later admitted that because of Section 1104 "there are no vested rights."[36] As for informing the public about it,

Mr. WINN: . . . apparently you did not think that it was necessary in discussing the difference between social insurance and private insurance [in Social Security publications for the general public] to point out that there is no contractual arrangement between the Government and the workers in social insurance; is that correct?

Mr. ALTMEYER: That is right.

Mr. WINN: Apparently you never thought it necessary to point out section 1104 of the act and explain its implications.

Mr. ALTMEYER: That is right.[37]

So while it was necessary to tell the American people that Social Security is "insurance" paying benefits "as a matter of right," it wasn't necessary to tell them that their "insurance policy" could be unilaterally rewritten or even torn up at the discretion of Congress. Weaver's words about a publicity office acting as "an office of censorship, de-emphasizing, or withholding entirely, news which would be damaging to prestige," have point and force here.

Altmeyer admitted that all the time he was running Social Security he was aware that Congress could change the benefits at any time, cut as well as raise them, even take them away, but the last possibility never crossed his mind, nor was he disturbed over the possibility that Congress might cut benefits.[38] His faith in Congress, apparently, was absolute.

After more inconclusive sparring, Curtis wound the hearings up. He still wanted the government to meet its benefit obligations, he said, and did not share the stock criticism of Social Security's "trust fund" as worthless Government IOUs; realistically, there was nowhere else for the surplus to go.

However, since there was no contract, Social Security wasn't insurance, and putting insurance language into the statute didn't make it so. He concluded,

> The young people who are paying in money month after month only have a statutory right that a Congress 10 years, or 15 years, or any time might take away from them. Maybe it has to be that way. But certainly we should not tell them that it is insurance, because in the minds of the average American that is something valuable, it is an enforcible policy, and whoever was responsible for conveying this misleading information to the American people and saying such things as "Your card constitutes a policy," certainly was mistaken.[39]

It was a monumental effort. Curtis had in many ways succeeded in establishing the falseness of the false consciousness which had been so assiduously instilled. He had brought out how Social Security had been sold to the country as insurance; pressured Altmeyer into admitting that the taxpayer had no insurance contract with the government giving him a contractual right to benefits; brought out how weak one's "strong" statutory rights really were; established that one's true security in Social Security was political; exposed the one-sidedness of Social Security's self-promotion, in which a dubious insurance analogy was presented incessantly and the reservation of power clause that exploded that analogy went unmentioned; and gotten onto the record Altmeyer's utter unconcern for the need to inform the people of the reservation of power clause, and his unconcern for the possibility that benefits might be cut.

The Aftermath: Steaming as Before

Yet it achieved nothing. What little newspaper reporting there was focused on the sensational aspects: Altmeyer's subpoena; the stormy nature of the hearings; and accusations by Eberharter that Curtis's goal was to destroy Social Security—not the substance of what Curtis had found.[40] The press took almost no notice of Curtis's exposure of Social Security's shaky legal status. Of the major weekly news magazines, only *U.S. News & World Report* reported on Altmeyer's testimony, spelling out Curtis's disclosure that despite the reassuring semantics, there was no contract, but adding that other federal employee retirement plans also lacked contracts and that even private pension plans with contracts were vulnerable if the firms went bankrupt. *U.S. News* asked Secretary of Health, Education and Welfare Oveta Culp Hobby about the possibility that workers wouldn't get their OASI benefits. Secretary Hobby replied that for persons qualified under the law, which only Congress could change, "their benefits, in my opinion, are as safe and sure as the financial integrity of the Government." Politics, the article concluded, provided a beneficiary's real security. The consensus view was that future Congresses "are hardly likely to risk the deliberate political suicide" which would ensue in "reneging on such a firm commitment made for so long to so many people." Such "political realities" would keep Social Security alive.[41]

The only other mainstream magazine to pick up on the hearings' disclosures was *Nation's Business,* the publication of the U.S. Chamber of Commerce. A December 1953 piece stressed the lack of a contract and that Social Security's benefit provisions "have been, and will be, modified from time to time," and pointed out that Social Security is not insurance but "tax-supported social welfare." Social Security's social insurance had had the "insurance" aspect stressed and the "social" aspect played down. But all this was merely a foil to pitch Chamber of Commerce proposals for extending Social Security to unprotected aged and adopting pay-as-you-go financing.[42]

Two months later, *U.S. News* published a long interview with Curtis. But most of it concerned Social Security's finances, anomalies and inequities in qualification for benefits, and Curtis's proposals for a universal old-age pension program, to extend Social Security benefits to all the elderly then outside the program ("blanketing in"); the lack of a contract was mentioned only in passing, neither Curtis nor the interviewer making much of it.[43] And that was that.

The hearings did not affect policy. Curtis's was a minority view even among Republicans. The only tangible result was a report, *Social Security After 18 Years,* which summarized the hearings' findings, stressing the lack of a contract, the insurance language, and the conditional, tentative nature of benefit "rights." In January 1954 he introduced a bill (H.R. 6863) proposing a benefit to all Americans aged sixty-five or over, paying a minimum of $45 a month, and retaining the contributory principle of financing through taxes paid by future beneficiaries, on gross income rather than labor income. Curtis's bill went nowhere, because the Eisenhower administration had a bill in play to expand Social Security.[44]

The resulting 1954 Amendments massively liberalized the program. Effective January 1, 1955, it was extended compulsorily to roughly six million Americans: self-employed farmers; other farm and domestic employees not covered under the 1950 Amendments; certain self-employed professionals (architects, funeral directors, engineers, and accountants); and miscellaneous other occupations. Another four million were brought in on an elective basis: mostly state and local employees who already had retirement systems, plus ministers and members of religious orders who chose to participate. Coverage was thus now extended to almost everyone but federal government workers and various professional groups. Benefits were increased 13 percent for about 6.6 million current beneficiaries. Payroll tax rates for the 1970s were increased to cover the anticipated increase in costs.[45]

In 1956, Social Security was expanded yet again, to add Disability Insurance (DI), which paid monthly disability benefits to workers aged fifty to sixty-four and totally or partially disabled. Dependent children aged eighteen or older who had become totally disabled before turning eighteen would also get benefits. Another "trust fund," the Disability Insurance Trust Fund, was created to pay benefits. In addition, the retirement age for women was cut to sixty-two, although with reduced benefits for working women and wives without child beneficiaries in their care. More professionals were brought under the program: dentists, veterinarians, optometrists, and lawyers. To defray disability benefit outlays, the tax rate went up by 0.25 each for workers and employers, and by 0.375 for the self-employed, these revenues to be paid into the new "trust fund."[46]

It is a measure of Social Security's acceptance as an American institution in the fifties that Congress approved these expansions by colossally lopsided votes. The 1950 Amendments passed by 333-14 (and the final Conference Committee report 374-1) in the House and 81-2 in the Senate. For the 1954 Amendments, the House vote was 355-8, and the Senate approved by voice vote. The House passed the 1956 Amendments 372-31 and the Senate 90-0.[47] Congressional opposition to Social Security, never strong to begin with, had all but vanished. The country was prosperous; Social Security's tax burden was light; the program appeared to be working just fine. Social Security steamed onward in triumph like a battleship, and Curtis and Winn had no more stopping power than a peashooter.

As if Curtis's elaborate hearings had never happened, insurance and trust fund analogies still prevailed in the media. Prominent government officials again helped keep them before the public. Under Secretary of Labor Arthur Larson's 1955 *Know Your Social Security,* seeking to give the reader "everything you need to know about social security," described it as "a combination of old-age pensions and life insurance." Social Security "is based on the same principle as private insurance"; though there are differences, "the general idea is the same." You and your employer make contributions, "in return for which you get certain insured rights" such as death benefits and pensions. Social Security involves "the simple insurance principle" of making small payments while working and getting back a larger sum when needed to face an emergency like death or retirement.[48]

There were only three main differences between Social Security and private insurance, Larson wrote: the system is government-operated; some people, for social-welfare reasons, get more than others relative to their contributions; and while a private insurance beneficiary "has an absolute right to collect the proceeds of the policy with no questions asked," Social Security applies restrictions, such as the requirement for old-age insurance that one be over sixty-five, and retired (the retirement earnings test). This was done to control costs: "A system under which rights as absolute as those of private annuities and private life insurance were provided would cost several times as much as social security." Not to worry; leaving those differences aside, Social Security resembled private insurance and annuities, and "What you get, moreover, is yours as of right, like any other insurance. . . . It bears no relation to relief or public assistance." Larson repeated that "the benefits belong to you as of right. . . . The benefits are yours—bought and paid for."[49] So much for all Curtis's work revealing the malleability of these "rights."

And in disputing the argument that Social Security should be on a purely pay-as-you-go basis, Larson made a crucial revelation about the "trust fund":

> If future years had to pay the full cost of benefits without the help of interest from a trust fund, there would be an increased temptation to cut down the amount of social security benefits. The present arrangement safeguards against that possibility in two ways. The first . . . keeping future cost down to avoid the necessity for reducing benefits. The second has to do with *the public's conception of its vested right in a certain level of benefits* [italics added]. If you are now contributing to a trust fund, *you have the definite sense* [italics added] that it is *your* [italics in original] money that is going into that fund and *staying there to back up your benefits* [italics added] when the time comes to pay them. You feel, *and you are intended to feel* [italics added], that the money you contribute is, at least in part, being paid to support your own ultimate benefits. Therefore, if some future Congress began to toy with the idea of cutting social security benefits, *you and all the other people who had contributed would regard this as a breach of faith* [italics added]. You would insist that the money you had paid in had been contributed on an advance understanding that the benefits would at least not be less than the law called for when you contributed. In these circumstances, it seems unlikely that any future Congress would dare to lower the scale of social security benefits.[50]

Setting aside the awkward fact that there *is no* vested right to benefits, this was both a frank admission that influencing public belief figured highly in how Social Security's "trust fund" operated, and an uncannily accurate prophecy. As we shall see, when the Reagan administration proposed some benefit cuts in 1981 to keep OASDI solvent, the protest—charging breach of faith and much else—stopped it cold. Nothing like that was ever tried again. The psychology of the payroll tax and the trust fund worked just as Larson predicted it would. That through its maneuvers Social Security might some day trap itself between the devil of political suicide and the deep blue sea of financial ruin did not occur to him.

That same year, HEW Secretary Hobby published an article in the *American Magazine* describing Social Security as "a form of insurance to which [beneficiaries] had contributed." She elaborated:

> Its official name is Old-Age and Survivors Insurance. . . . The monthly [benefit] payments come from the Old-Age and Survivors Insurance Trust Fund, which now totals more than $20,000,000,000.
> This fund was built up in two ways. First, regular contributions to the Trust Fund are made by workers, by their employers, and by people who are self-employed. Then, most of the Trust Fund itself is invested in U.S. Government bonds—the safest investment in the world. The interest earned by these bonds goes right back into the Old-Age and Survivors Insurance Trust Fund.

> The Trust Fund belongs to the people eligible for social-security benefits. The
> Government acts as trustee of the fund.[51]

As should be clear, the final part of Secretary Hobby's foregoing statement
is not true. But government officials were not alone in keeping false analogies alive. Freelance journalist Helen Hill Miller opened a long article on
Social Security in *Collier's* by telling the reader that if he is either a taxpaying worker "building up credits under Social Security" or a beneficiary, "you
own a valuable property, amounting to an estate of between $7,000 and
$30,000, invested at 5 per cent."[52] In fact, as the government had argued in
Helvering v. Davis, the 1939 Amendments had proved, and the Curtis hearings had revealed, nobody "owned" anything. The rest of her piece, aptly
reflecting and appealing to Americans' obsession with "getting theirs," was a
question-and-answer discussion of who could qualify how to get how much
of which benefits when. Only once did Miller raise and dismiss a concern
about Social Security, in words uncannily like Hobby's:

> Somebody told me the payments we make for Social Security are used to meet
> current government expenses, so that later when a lot of people are eligible for
> benefits there won't be enough to pay them. Is that true?
>   No. All Social Security tax money is kept [sic!] in a special Trust Fund, admin-
> istered by the U.S. Treasury but kept separate from other Treasury functions. The
> Social Security program meets its own expenses, with no funds coming from the
> public purse. In fact, there is a reserve in the Trust Fund totaling about
> $21,000,000,000. It's invested in interest-bearing U.S. government securities; the
> interest is added to the Trust Fund.[53]

Only one serious criticism emerged in the mainstream press in those years,
by Dillard Stokes in *Commentary.* Drawing on the Curtis hearings, Stokes
argued that Social Security was not insurance as Americans understood it;
that they had no real right to benefits; that Congress had already broken its
word and might do so again; that the benefits were in fact relief, administered
with a means test, the retirement earning test; and that the reserve fund was a
fiction.[54]

Stokes succeeded only in drawing a rebuttal by Wilbur Cohen, then Director of Social Security's Division of Research and Statistics. Cohen asserted
that Stokes's claim that people have no rights under Social Security was not
true; Section 205 of Title II enables them to sue for their "statutory rights."
This neglected, as Stokes replied, the reservation of power clause. Stokes's
statement that Social Security had originally sought to build up a reserve
able to meet the probable liability but was now on a pay-as-you-go basis,
Cohen asserted, was "not true"; in fact it was.[55] Congressman Harold Ostertag
entered Stokes's piece in the *Congressional Record,*[56] but it made no impact.

Stokes expanded his *Commentary* piece into a full-length book, *Social
Security—Fact and Fancy,* which appeared in 1956. Again and again, Stokes

drove home the reservation of power clause and the tenuousness of benefit rights. He also indicated the staggering scale of Social Security's publicity effort. In 1953 alone, Social Security issued 7 million booklets, put up 535,000 posters and 1,300 displays, aired 1,700 TV and 39,000 radio programs, furnished 7,700 radio scripts, gave 16,500 lectures, presented 14,500 motion picture shows, published 2,207 magazine articles, and issued 14,500 news releases. Between 1950 and March 1, 1955, the Social Security Administration issued 86,655,000 copies of booklets and leaflets, in large editions addressed to the general public and to specific audiences such as the self-employed, soldiers and sailors, farm families, and the disabled.[57] One can infer from this how much importance the SSA attached to promoting the false consciousness of Social Security as insurance financed with a trust fund.

Yet Stokes's book, like his article, availed nothing. No storm of controversy broke upon its publication, no groundswell of outrage ensued about a misleading insurance analogy. The checks were going out, the program was steadily becoming more generous, and this tangible evidence that Social Security worked shouted so loudly it drowned out the grumbles of people like Curtis and Stokes.

Is It Insurance or Isn't It? The Academic Controversy

Meanwhile, both insurance educators and the insurance industry were engaged in an intense intramural controversy as to whether social insurance in general and Social Security in particular are in fact insurance.

Just what is insurance? Essentially, insurance is a means of coping with risk, which insurance textbooks usually define as a condition of uncertainty regarding a loss.[58] Insurance combines the risk management tools of *risk pooling* (also called "risk sharing" or "combination") and *risk transfer*. In risk pooling, a large number of persons, each facing an uncertain large loss (death or a home burning down, say), essentially agree to share the loss through the device of charging each member of the group a small premium and thus creating a fund to compensate those group members who do incur that loss in a given time period. The individual's premium is his share of the likely loss to the group and of the insurer's administrative expenses and profit. Instead of facing a large uncertain loss in the absence of insurance, the individual pays a small certain cost (the premium). Moreover, by having very large numbers of persons in very similar situations facing the same risk ("homogeneous exposure units," in insurance jargon) participate in the risk pooling, the insurance company is able to employ the law of large numbers, which in essence states that the larger the sample group being observed for a phenomenon, the closer the observed frequency of that phenomenon is to its frequency among the total population. This enables the insurer to predict how likely a given loss is to occur, and to charge premiums large enough to cover that loss, meet expenses and furnish a profit. By buying insurance, the insured transfers the risk to the insurer. Without insurance, the individual would have to face the possibility of loss himself and meet the cost out of his own resources. With insurance, the financial loss entailed by the risk's eventuating is borne by the insurance company instead, as a "speculative risk," so called because whether the company actually incurs a loss will depend on how well it calculated probabilities. If the insurer calculated accurately, it will in fact suffer no loss, because its premiums will generate a large enough fund to pay off its claims; if the insurer erred, its premiums may be too small and it may lose money, even go under.[59] Under insurance, risk is *shared* by the *insured* and *transferred* to the *insurer.*

I. M. Rubinow defined social insurance as "the policy of organized society to furnish that protection to one part of the population, which some other part may need less, or, if needing, is able to purchase voluntarily through private insurance."[60] Another pioneering social insurance advocate, Abraham Epstein, elaborated that "spreading the risk" over a nation's entire working population of would maximize the gain from risk pooling; making insurance compulsory would cut overhead costs; and spreading costs among workers, employers and the community would bring individual cost within the worker's reach. Hence, Epstein continued, social insurance could be described as "a relatively inexpensive form of insurance, devised by the state to guarantee the wage earner and his dependents a minimum of income during periods when, through forces beyond his control, his earnings are impaired or cut off." Its aim was to establish a minimum floor of sustenance below which one shouldn't fall during unemployment, old age, sickness and disability, "rather than an actuarially perfect system of insurance."[61]

Epstein went on to admit that social insurance is "based largely on financial expediency and social wisdom rather than on strict insurance principles." Hence social insurance puts "greatest emphasis" on having the costs distributed as widely as possible. For social insurance whether the persons bearing the risk pay the premiums themselves "matters little." Rather, what's important is that those with the greatest need receive the most protection. A government social insurance tries to accomplish a social goal, not stay in business like an insurance company, and "The premium rates are dictated by social policy, not by the actuary."[62]

That being so, social insurance and Social Security look suspiciously like welfare programs rather than insurance. Indeed, Altmeyer himself admitted in 1945 that in his view "it seems impossible to draw hard and fast lines between social insurance and public assistance." As for many people's claim that they get social insurance because they paid for it, "they forget that no social insurance program provides precisely what you have paid for."[63] Relief financed out of general taxation, such as mothers' aid, Epstein added, "may be accurately described as social insurance" whenever such aid is based on "predetermined qualifying conditions." Moreover, a means test doesn't necessarily make such benefits welfare, since they are usually given to beneficiaries who meet qualifying conditions for them "and in a dignified manner."[64] Apparently the term "social insurance" could be stretched to cover any welfare benefit short of an outright handout given to all comers without conditions and in an undignified manner—a strong hint that even in the minds of its own advocates, the "insurance" character of the thing was chimerical.

Nevertheless, advocates of social insurance and Social Security insisted, the basic insurance characteristics do exist in both. Some of these claims were clearly untenable. In the summer of 1935, the Wharton School's Professor of Insurance C. A. Kulp argued that social insurance is insurance, and that "unemployment insurance" (although he disliked the term, preferring "unemployment compensation"), as "a pool for meeting risk on a contractual, formal, non-charitable basis," qualifies as insurance. Professor Kulp defined social insurance as "a formal, contractual, non-charitable pooling of risks almost exclusively impersonal in their origin and bringing losses to members of great groups unable to bear them without public assistance." He laid great stress on the (purported) contractual nature of social insurance. If one had to prove need to get benefits, he maintained, the program "is not insurance but charity" and "the system loses insurance status . . . the essence of social insurance is not individual status but individual contract."[65] Accordingly, Kulp embraced Social Security as insurance, arguing that it was simply a government method of buying contractual annuities. Benefits, he declared, would be received "as a contractual right," and the employer's and employee's taxes "are really insurance premiums."[66] But this approach founders for lack of a contract in Social Security. Insofar as insurance entails a contract, which it clearly did in Kulp's view, Social Security cannot be insurance.

Addressing a mutual insurance companies' convention in Grand Rapids, Michigan in October 1937, Arthur Altmeyer took a different tack, one that would recur in defenses of Social Security as insurance. Social Security shared the same purpose as private insurance: "mutual protection against widespread risks"—and the means of doing so: "the pooling of risks and through common contributions."[67] Other sympathizers and scholars elaborated on this, arguing that "social insurance" shares with private insurance a pooling of risk over a large number of individuals, and the transfer of risk from the individuals to the insurer, in this case the government. Moreover, social insurance, like private insurance, is self-supporting, with beneficiaries financing their protection in the form of regular premiums. Benefits are linked both to specific risks and to one's contributions, but do not require demonstration of individual need.[68]

As we have seen, advocates like Altmeyer and Larson conceded that social insurance has significant differences from private insurance in that "social adequacy" served as well as "individual equity," but affirmed that Social

Security is insurance nevertheless because of these common characteristics. Economics professor Domenico Gagliardo lengthily enumerated the differences between private and social insurance—social insurance provides a minimum income, links benefits only loosely to premiums, uses compulsion, has others than the insured pay premiums, and so on—yet insisted that they "should not be permitted to obscure the fundamental fact that social and private insurance have much in common." Social insurance operates on "the same fundamental principle of distributing among the many the losses of the few," and doing it through some form of insurance carrier. Moreover, private insurance was in fact so closely regulated as to be "quasi-public in nature."[69] Some supporters, such as Albert Linton, also maintained that Social Security's much-maligned reserve fund in fact operates just like the reserve fund of a private insurance company.[70] Professor Kulp pointed out that private and social insurance have different objectives, hence standards applicable to one aren't appropriate to the other. Moreover, insurance may be viewed as not just a contract but as a technique for group-budgeting of risks and as a means of social planning, and by these standards social insurance passes muster.[71]

Sometimes the claim that social insurance and Social Security are insurance seemed to rest on little more than vigorous assertion, as if saying something emphatically enough would make it so. When Equitable Life Assurance Society's Vice President and Associate Actuary Ray Peterson argued that private insurance is "the only field . . . .where the word 'insurance,' standing alone, is properly used," Wilbur Cohen blustered in print that "Private commercial insurance has no more right to the exclusive use of the word 'insurance' standing alone than does social insurance. Both are insurance, with more similarities than differences. For the private insurance industry to arrogate to itself the exclusive use of the word is, in my opinion, presumptuous and unwarranted."[72]

On the contrary, critics retorted, the differences between social insurance and private insurance outnumber the similarities, and are so substantial as to vitiate the designation of Social Security as insurance. For one thing, whereas private insurance is voluntary, social insurance is compulsory. Also, while in private insurance the principle of individual equity dominates, social insurance puts more stress on social adequacy, favoring lower income earners and other presumably more needy persons. Individuals may pay the entire cost in private insurance, but the employer usually contributes as much as the employee in social insurance. Unlike private insurance, which uses legally binding contracts, social insurance contains no contract giving beneficiaries contractual rights or property rights to benefits; the programs are open to change by legislatures, which may change both the taxes and the benefits. This political dimension and other imponderables make costs extremely difficult for actuaries to predict, whereas costs in private insurance are far more readily predictable. Moreover, private insurance, closely regulated, is required to operate on a full reserve basis: a private insurance company must have enough financial resources to be able to meet all its commitments to its policyholders even if revenue inflow from premiums ceased. Social insurance, by contrast, need not have a full reserve because it can always extract more resources as needed through tax increases.[73]

Moreover, some observers, not all of them conservatives, faulted "social insurance" as a misuse of insurance language. Fabian socialist Beatrice Webb called Great Britain's Unemployment Insurance "a terrible example of the misuse of technical terms." Since the government could change at will the rates of contributions and benefits and even the conditions of eligibility for benefits, she elaborated, this "takes the matter at once quite outside the category of an insurance policy, as the term has always hitherto been understood."[74] Webb's observation, being a general statement of government's role in such programs, clearly applies to Social Security too. Ray Peterson complained that the use of insurance and trust fund language in the Social Security Act, Social Security publications, and the media was creating a "semantic facade" that hindered rather than promoted public understanding of how Social Security's financing really worked.[75]

Interestingly, in the discussion of Peterson's paper on that subject, George Immerwahr, a private-sector actuary who was on the staff of the Bureau of Old-Age and Survivors Insurance in 1939-1946, provided reminiscences strongly suggesting that Social Security's "insurance" character was contrived rather than real. He mentioned that in Social Security's early years, actuaries were "imported from the Metropolitan and other life insurance companies to give the organization the aura of actuarial respectability." Seeking to exculpate the actuaries from Peterson's apparent implications that they had been derelict in their responsibilities in allowing the misconception of Social Security's financing mechanism to flourish, Immerwahr pointed out that they had clashed with Social Security's economists precisely because they tried (vainly) to teach the economists that Social Security's financing mechanism "is fundamentally different from that of private insurance and pension plans" and that it could be rationalized only by its objective of providing only basic protection from presumed need.[76]

> The economists argued then, just as their successors (such as Robert Ball . . .) argue now, that the social security taxes are *premiums* [italics in original] for the OASI benefits in just the same way as life insurance premiums are for life insurance. At one time, in fact, some of us were instructed [!] to use the word "premiums" in lieu of "contributions" or "taxes" in written material going to the public. Some of us were not always obedient.[77]

This is strong evidence that the insurance analogy did not really spring from the nature of Social Security's economic realities but was imposed on Social Security to foist it on the public. And if the insurance company actuaries balked, surely it must have been because, steeped in the realities of insurance, they knew perfectly well that Social Security taxes were in fact not premiums.

The controversy about social insurance and Social Security really being insurance was complicated by the fact that, as university teachers of insurance acknowledged by the late fifties, insurance terminology was often used imprecisely, a given term often having multiple meanings, making understanding between the industry and the public difficult. Accordingly, in 1958 the American Association of University Teachers of Insurance established a Commission on Insurance Terminology to study insurance language; to create a glossary of words and phrases for which a consensus existed among experts as to their meaning; to make more accurate and meaningful insurance terminology available, and by persuasion and assistance, "gradually bring some order out of the present chaos."[78]

In 1965, the Commission reported that it had defined insurance as: "Pooling of risks of fortuitous losses by transfer of such risks to insurers who agree to indemnify insureds for such losses, to provide other pecuniary benefits on their occurrence, or to render services connected with the risks."[79]

The Commission formed a separate Committee on Social Insurance Terminology in 1961. Chaired by University of Minnesota insurance and economics professor C. Arthur Williams, the committee consisting of several professors in insurance education; Wilbur Cohen; Social Security's chief actuary, Robert Myers; Ray Peterson; and other experts.[80] As the committee bent to its task, Professor Williams pointed out in a scholarly paper, reasonably enough, that the whole issue turned on how one defined insurance, which could be done either to include or to exclude social insurance. Between social insurance and private insurance there existed sufficient similarities and differences to furnish grounds for either approach. However, he maintained, the two systems share risk pooling and risk transfer to an "insurer," and if one believes that only these two elements are necessary for a thing to be insurance, then social insurance and OASDI qualify. Professor Williams ended by requesting that the semantic debate over the term "social insurance" cease. Given the important problems in both private and social insurance, he said, it would waste time and energy to pursue the matter further. However, he insisted that distinctions between the two insurances be "crystal-clear" so neither would be "judged by false standards."[81]

In 1965, the Committee on Social Insurance Terminology promulgated the following definition of "social insurance": "A device for the pooling of risks by their transfer to an organization, usually governmental, that is required by law to provide pecuniary or service benefits to or on behalf of covered persons upon the occurrence of certain pre-designated losses," under all of these conditions: coverage is compulsory; benefit eligibility is derived from contributions to the program by the beneficiary or the person as to whom the beneficiary is a dependent; the individual is not required to demonstrate inadequate financial resources, but may need to establish dependency status; the cost is paid mostly by contributions by covered persons, their employers, or both; the method for determining benefits is prescribed by law; benefits usually aren't directly tied to contributions, but instead redistribute income (e.g., to favor low-income workers or breadwinners with many dependents); the financing system is designed to be adequate for the long run; the plan is government-administered or -supervised; it is not solely for present or former government employees.[82]

While the committee was developing this definition, many of its members wrote to Professor Williams asserting their belief that social insurance is insurance because it is a device for pooling risk, transferring risk to an insurer, or both.[83] Several insurance textbooks, citing this definition, argue the same thing.[84]

The Reality: It's Welfare, Not Insurance

Despite these new rigorous definitions, and assertions by Social Security's partisans and sympathizers, I submit that Social Security is not insurance. Social Security's critics, such as Congressman Curtis, cited the absence of a contract to prove that assertion. The argument that Social Security is not insurance is much stronger, however, if it can be shown that these *defining characteristics,* which deal with *fundamentals*—risk pooling and risk transfer to an insurer—do not exist under OASDI. Social Security's appearance apparently misled even the insurance scholars on the Committee on Social Insurance Terminology (who perhaps, out of sympathy with the program or its beneficiaries, were willing to be misled). However, with all due respect, the reality, Social Security's *essential nature,* is such that Social Security cannot be insurance.

For one thing, with benefit levels determined mainly, and in many instances wholly, by political considerations, the whole notion of Social Security as "insurance" providing protection for "loss" or "risk" clearly becomes vacuous and untenable. A classic case in point is the 13 percent increase in benefits legislated in 1968, which sprang from President Lyndon Johnson's personal desire to be generous to the elderly. When Wilbur Cohen, then Undersecretary of HEW, proposed a 10 percent benefit increase, Johnson goaded him with "Come on, Wilbur, you can do better than that," until the proposal was raised to 15 percent.[85] Another is the election-year bidding war between Republican president, Richard Nixon, and prominent congressional Democrats with presidential aspirations, George McGovern and Wilbur Mills, in 1972, resulting in a benefit increase of 20 percent.[86] (Note that the vagaries of a politician's character and the maneuvers of election-year politics make a mockery even of Social Security's vaunted "social adequacy" principle as determinant of benefit levels.) The hapless taxpayers, forced to shoulder correspondingly higher taxes, could by no stretch of the imagination be said to be paying higher "premiums" reflecting a greater "risk."

Enlarging on this last point, the political and social-welfare considerations driving benefit levels render the notion of Social Security taxes as a "premium" simply absurd. In theory, Social Security insures one against the risk of income loss through retirement or disability, and one's survivors against one's death. Under true insurance, one's "premium" reflects *one's own* risk of income loss, and the cost to the insurer of assuming that risk, and buys one protection against *one's own* loss. But when one's Social Security taxes are increased following a legislated increase in benefits for current beneficiaries—in response, say, to intense pressure by the elderly lobbies—or by increase in the program's costs due to the aging of the population, one's "premium" level is being driven not by one's own "risk," one's own uncertain prospect of loss, nor by the cost of protecting one against it, but by the cost of politicians' and policymakers' decisions to be generous *toward others bringing political pressure to bear.* The link between one's "premium" and one's own risk and benefits may have been plausible in 1935, when the principle of individual equity in Social Security was (as Hohaus complained) quite strong, but with all the expansions and liberalizations which have occurred since, until individual equity has virtually disappeared, that link has become laughably tenuous. To call this redistributive tax an "insurance premium" is simply unwarranted.

This also makes the applicability of risk pooling to Social Security dubious. Under risk pooling, a large number of "homogeneous exposure units," that is, similarly-situated persons facing the same risk, combine, and as a result each person pays a premium which is an aliquot portion of the cost of compensating for losses likely to befall members of that group in a given period (and of the insurer's administrative costs and profit); one's premium varies with one's probability of incurring the insured loss. This becomes problematic under Social Security. For one thing, people in their twenties and people just shy of retirement at sixty-five can hardly be called *homogeneous* exposure units; their situations are radically different relative to the "risk"—income loss due to retirement—being "insured against." While demanding *perfect* homogeneity among exposure units is of course unrealistic and unreasonable, so radical a heterogeneity as that makes the concept of homogeneous exposure units untenable. Yet these disparate units are all "pooled" and bear exactly the same payroll tax rate—a huge departure from the risk pooling of insurance theory. For another, while premiums in private insurance really are the result of risk pooling and calculations of probable loss, in OASDI benefit levels are determined largely by politics, and then the tax rate is set to pay for them; risk, and risk pooling, have absolutely nothing to do with it. With the "exposure units" quite heterogeneous and the size of one's "premium" driven by causality utterly divorced from the risk faced by one's own age cohort, "risk pooling" across "homogeneous exposure units" as a determinant of one's Social Security "premium" falls to the ground—taking one leg supporting OASDI's claim to be insurance with it.

Then, too, as a general rule, the older one is when purchasing a life insurance policy or annuity, the higher one's premium. This of course reflects the greater risk associated with an older entrant into an insurance scheme, and the pooling across homogeneous exposure units. Yet the 1950 Amendments enabled all those aged sixty-two or over to qualify for Social Security benefits with only *six quarters of coverage,* and their "premiums" were not increased to reflect their advanced age. That is, they got insurance for *smaller* total premium outlays than those paid by younger participants—the exact *opposite* of what risk pooling and risk transfer would dictate. That was a pure social-welfare measure; no true insurance grounded in risk and probability considerations could or would do such a thing.

Moreover—and this is absolutely crucial—it is completely false to assert that under Social Security risk is transferred to the insurer. Under true insurance, risk is indeed transferred thus, because the policyholders' premiums essentially *buy claims on the insurer,* which commits itself by legal and binding contract to make good those claims out of its assets. When one qualifies for Social Security benefits, one does not obtain a claim on Social Security itself. Rather, one acquires claims on *other taxpayers,* whose resources are extracted and transferred by Social Security to pay one's benefits. This situation is not modified by OASDI's so-called "trust fund," because the ultimate resource standing behind the "trust fund" is the taxing power of the federal government.

Also, Social Security experiences no true financial exposure, putting its *own* assets at risk with possible negative consequences for itself. An insurance company assumes a true speculative risk; it may end up worse off if its costs exceed their predicted levels. It faces a prospect of potential harm up to and including being forced out of business and ceasing to exist. Social Security assumes absolutely no speculative risk whatsoever, hence has no status analogous to that of a private insurer. Neither OASDI nor the persons administering it owns any property that is at risk of liquidation to meet obligations should insured risks eventuate. Should Social Security's costs exceed revenues and exhaust its "trust fund," it will suffer nothing at all; it will merely turn to the private sector and extract fresh resources through taxes and/or borrowing. Again, *risk is being transferred not to the so-called "insurer," but to the taxpayers. Not one iota of risk sticks to the "insurer"; it is all passed through to other taxpayers.* Social Security is not risking one thin dime.

Note too that the definition's phrase "pooling of risks of fortuitous losses by transfer of such risks to insurers" implies that the transfer of risk to the insurer is the instrument whereby risks are pooled. But it must follow then that if risk is not really being transferred to the insurer, then risks are not being pooled, either.

But if neither risk pooling nor risk transfer to the insurer is in reality operative, Social Security's claim to be insurance, even by the insurance scholars' definitions, collapses. The truth is that Social Security is not insurance at all, but a welfare program—a scheme of taxes and transfer payments dressed in the borrowed robes of insurance language to make it acceptable to the American people. The essence of Social Security is not the application of probability and the law of large numbers to risks and the transfer of those risks to an insurer in the form of his assumption of speculative risk. Rather, Social Security is the coercive extraction of resources from members of one group and their transfer to support members of another group, with the rate of resource extraction (tax rate) and the rate of transfer (benefit amount) determined by politics and ideology. That is income redistribution. That is welfare. It is not insurance.

Objections from the Insurance Industry

Another telling argument against Social Security as insurance is that many individuals and groups in *the insurance industry itself* (as opposed to college instructors in insurance) were bitterly opposed to Social Security's use of insurance terminology from the beginning, and made repeated, if unavailing, protests at this misrepresentation. Along the way, industry figures advanced several sound arguments against Social Security as insurance.

Even before the Social Security Act was sent to Congress, *Best's Insurance News* argued that "insurance" was a misnomer for social insurance schemes. Observing that social insurance plans in Europe were supported mostly by government rather than the beneficiaries' own contributions, the editor maintained that "These plans are not insurance plans at all, which are self-supporting in the group, but are 'benefits' or 'charity' plans. They attempt to support one part of the population at the expense of another part."[87]

After the Social Security Act passed, the industry's trade journals carried repeated denunciations of Social Security's use of insurance terminology, and repeated arguments that Social Security is not insurance. Much, though not all, of the industry's critical interest in Social Security had to do with concern that Americans might jump to the conclusion that with Social Security, they wouldn't need insurance any more. In 1936, John S. Williams III, Commissioner of Insurance of the state of Mississippi, pointed out in a speech that Congress reserved the power to alter the Act, there was no contractual relationship between the government and the taxpayer/beneficiary, and participants acquire no vested interest in the old-age reserve fund, hence have no cash or loan available (unlike purchasers of whole life insurance, who can borrow against their policies). Given all that, he argued, "it was not the purpose of the Congress to offer these benefits as a substitute for life insurance or life insurance annuities in any sense of the word." Williams's point was to reassure his listeners that Social Security posed no competitive threat to the private insurance business—obviously, because it was not insurance!—and that the interest in protection which Social Security would stir up would "increase the demand for and the popularity of life insurance."[88]

The industry's interest in Social Security was renewed during and after the 1939 amendment process. *Best's Insurance News* pointedly noted in February that so far, Social Security's taxes had merely financed current government operations and that nothing had been saved.[89] Albert Hirst, counsel of the New York State Life Underwriters Association, told the Life Supervisors Association of New York that the Act's structure gave it "an altogether superficial but very deceptive similarity to insurance. This is said not as a criticism of the Act but as a statement of fact." Hirst added that the underwriter's job was to make sure people knew accurately both what Social Security would do for them and what it wouldn't.[90] A very detailed account of the amendments of 1939, intended for life insurance agents and the insurance-buying public, repeatedly drew attention to the various benefits' modest size and the political uncertainty of receiving benefits, and argued that people should put their trust primarily in private insurance, and treat Social Security as supplementary.[91]

One of the strongest, most comprehensive and far-sighted insurance-industry criticisms of Social Security was voiced in 1950 by Judd Benson, President of the National Association of Life Underwriters. Benson vigorously opposed the expansion of Social Security under H.R. 6000, warning perceptively about the corrosive effect of benefits on work incentives and the tendency of all government organs to seek to expand their activities and increase their importance, leading Social Security's top administrators to agitate ceaselessly for Social Security's expansion. Over half a century ago, he was prescient about the aging of the population imposing a rising Social Security tax burden, warning that the number of persons aged twenty to sixty-four per person sixty-five and over would decline steadily, and that "40 years hence [i.e., in 1990], the probabilities are that the ratio will be 5 or even 4 to 1" (Benson was right on the nose: it was 4.78).[92] But he was especially scathing about Social Security's misleading self-advertisement as insurance:

> We are of the opinion that Congress acted extremely wisely in passing the Pure Food and Drugs Act which provides that all articles of food and all drugs shall be clearly and correctly labeled in order that the public will in no-wise be deceived. We think it is equally important that the public should not be deceived in the matter of Social Security. We shall, therefore, suggest to the Congress that the name or title of the Section of the Act providing old-age benefits and benefits for widows and dependents should be "Retirement and Dependents Benefits Section of the Social Security Act" rather than "Old-Age and Survivors Insurance Section of the Social Security Act."
>
> We suggest that Social Security is not insurance in the true concept of the word, nor is it insurance as insurance is understood by the American public. The taxes

collected to provide Social Security benefits are in no-wise premiums, despite the fact that the Social Security Administration has been so bold as to so label them in some instances: neither are the benefits, insurance benefits. I am sure that you and I would have considerable difficulty in selling contracts which provided that our companies could adjust the premiums whenever they chose to do so and could likewise juggle the benefits to suit their convenience.[93]

Bluntly insisting on honest language, Benson reiterated his recommendation that the title of the Act providing for old-age and survivors benefits be renamed the "Retirement and Dependent Benefits Section of the Social Security Act."[94]

Four years later Ray Murphy, President of the Equitable Life Assurance Society of the U.S., weighed in with another stiff criticism. He found no fault with the desire for security, and deemed enactment of the Social Security Act "understandable" in light of the uncertainties of modern urban, industrial life and the sufferings of the Depression. But he warned that Social Security was giving people a dangerous sense of getting something for nothing and a misconception, which he traced to Roosevelt's 1936 campaign speeches (see chapter 4) and the subsequent Social Security publicity, that its taxes were "a form of saving being stored up for the future and guaranteeing their future benefits." Murphy added that Social Security's use of the word "insurance" "is very objectionable to those in the insurance business. The words 'social insurance' slip easily from the tongues of many people, but the word 'insurance' suggests an individual equity relationship which simply does not exist in OASI. Neither is OASI based on commonly accepted insurance principles."[95] A. L. Kirkpatrick, manager of the U.S. Chamber of Commerce's Insurance Department, pointed out that in private insurance each policyholder pays his "proportionate share" of the total cost of benefits—but Social Security, rather than being a true insurance system in which "each participant pays the cost of his own benefits," is a tax-transfer system in which, on the average, the employee's taxes pay for roughly 2 percent of his benefits, his employer's taxes pay for about another 2 percent, but 96 percent is paid for with other people's taxes, levied on present workers.[96] This ability to push the cost of one's benefits onto the next generation through taxes, Benjamin Kendrick argued at length, enabled Social Security to offer an illusory "bargain" in insurance.[97]

A research associate of the Life Insurance Association of America who specialized in Social Security, health insurance and such, Kendrick cited Social Security's growing "trust fund" as a source of much of the misunderstanding, giving people an impression that their future benefits have been paid for as they went along. In fact, he pointed out, Social Security's taxes were inadequate to store up assets sufficient to meet future obligations; its unfunded liability was growing much faster than the "trust fund," standing at $200 billion before the 1954 Amendments and rising to $250 billion after. A given generation's "bargains" in Social Security rested squarely on future generations' willingness to pay the taxes to cover their benefits. These intertemporal, intergenerational relationships, Kendrick added, were "entirely different from those of a private pension plan or life insurance policy, where advance provision is made for future benefit payments. The voluntary plans and policies do not expect one man to buy another man's benefits."[98]

It should be noted that the coverage of Social Security in the insurance trade journals was by no means entirely negative. The journals repeatedly gave ample space in their pages to articles by Reinhard Hohaus, for example, in which Hohaus endorsed the concept of social insurance, lauded Social Security, and presented recommendations for its expansion.[99]

The insurance industry's unhappiness with Social Security depicting itself as insurance culminated in repeated resolutions to Congress et al. requesting deletion of insurance terminology from the Social Security law. In 1959 the trustees of the National Association of Life Underwriters (NALU) adopted such a resolution, affirming, among other things, the NALU's opposition to further liberalization of Social Security and its belief that liberalization demands sprang from the "erroneous conception generally held by the public that the Social Security program is an insurance program like those underwritten by private life insurance companies." This misconception, the resolution added, was largely fostered by references to "insurance" in the Social Security Act and by Social Security Administration officials and writers on the program who "have frequently equated the program to *true* insurance programs by such devices as mistakenly likening Social Security taxes to 'premiums' and the Social Security card to an *'insurance contract'* [italics in original]."[100] The NALU went on to argue that

> the Social Security program is not a true insurance program in that, among other things, it confers no contractual rights upon the participants and may be altered, amended or repealed by the Congress at will, and the compulsory contributions thereto are not "premiums" at all but are factually and legally merely additional excise taxes in the case of employers and additional income taxes in the case of employees and self-employed individuals.[101]

Therefore, the NALU recommended that Congress purge the Act of insurance language, change Social Security's name to one that described its nature and purpose accurately, and include in the Act a policy declaration "that the program is not and is not intended to be an insurance program and that it shall henceforth not be represented as such in any way" by any federal employee or official.[102]

Copies went to President Eisenhower, all members of Congress, the Secretary of HEW, the Commissioner of Social Security, all presidents of state and local associations of life underwriters, and presidents of the major life insurance companies. In 1960 the National Association of Insurance Agents, acting in support, adopted a similar resolution.[103] Both were ignored.

One would think that if anyone knows the true nature of a thing it is the people who make their livings by it, who deal with its realities daily. If so many in the insurance industry were so hostile for so long to Social Security depicting itself as insurance, specifically as very closely similar to private insurance, that must in all fairness be taken as a strong sign that that depiction was indeed inappropriate, misleading, and false to reality.

A Self-Serving, "Antisocial" Industry?

Social Security's partisans might discount all this by asserting that the insurance industry was merely being self-serving in its criticisms of Social Security and its opposition to Social Security's calling itself insurance. Wilbur Cohen made this charge quite stridently. He accused the industry of "opposing most major social insurance improvements" since 1945, and warned that this obstructionism caused many to regard the industry as "arrogant" and "antisocial," and issued a threat: "the only alternative may be Federal controls over private insurance policies to assure that private insurance operates in the public interest. As the attacks by the insurance industry against social insurance mount in intensity, the insurance industry must expect a mounting opposition."[104] When Ray Peterson protested, pointing out that private insurance was already regulated and not allowed to misrepresent its products, whereas Social Security operated under no such restriction, Cohen accused Social Security's critics in the industry of trying to subvert public confidence:

> Some members of the industry . . . are permitted to, and do, make misleading and inaccurate statements about social insurance in this country. Apparently some of them regard the old-age and survivors insurance program as a competitor—indeed, as an unfair competitor, for some reason—and feel that any statements they can make that will undermine the confidence of the American people in their basic retirement, life and disability insurance protection and to forestall needed improvements in the program, are legitimate. Private insurance, operating in the public interest, should not try to undermine the people's confidence in their social insurance program.[105]

But the record shows that Cohen's charges are as untenable as they are ugly. Some of the industry's complaints were indeed prompted, as their articulators stated frankly, by concern about Social Security's impact on the insurance business. But this is no more than perfectly natural and understandable human self-interest. What's more, some, as we saw, went on to argue that not only would Social Security, not being real insurance, pose *no* competitive threat, it would likely have the effect of making the public more security- and insurance-minded, hence lead to *greater* insurance and annuity sales. *Best's Insurance News*—which, recall, denied that social insurance was true insurance—observed as much when the Roosevelt administration introduced the Social Security bill in 1935.[106] Dr. S. S. Huebner, a renowned teacher and writer on life insurance and a giant among insurance scholars, though sharply critical of the huge future reserve fund contemplated under the original Act, argued that Social Security presented "no real reason for alarm" to the industry and would, in fact, stimulate life insurance sales.[107] Writing in the *Weekly Underwriter* about the 1939 amendments, attorney William Porteous concluded not only that the amended act's benefits "will not compete with life insurance" but that private insurance and Social Security would complement each other and that an insurance agent who knew the Act and his company's products would be able to sell more insurance.[108] So much for Cohen's charge that private insurance saw Social Security as an unfair, dangerous competitor.

Moreover, as E. J. Faulkner, then president of Woodmen Accident and Life Company and a trustee of the American College of Life Underwriters showed in 1963, the accusation by partisans of Social Security expansion that the insurance industry opposed the establishment of Social Security and its expansion and development was false. Some prominent insurance industry executives and actuaries such as Linton and Hohaus were instrumental in creating and developing Social Security; and a 1945 policy statement on Social Security by the American Life Convention, Life Insurance Association of America, and National Association of Life Underwriters endorsed Social Security as an improvement over earlier methods of helping needy elderly, and argued that Social Security as a provider of a basic floor of protection and the security obtained from personal effort and thrift should complement rather than conflict with each other.[109] Indeed, in 1945 the American Life Convention, Life Insurance Association of America, and National Association of Life Underwriters recommended *extending* OASI coverage to all gainfully employed groups not covered (albeit keeping benefit levels modest, to preserve work incentives), and adding benefits for "total and permanent disability after age 55"[110]—a recommendation which was not carried out for another eleven years. This hardly seems like opposition to Social Security. Clearly, the industry opposed not Social Security, but Social Security's inappropriate insurance language.

A revealing light on the industry's attitude toward Social Security is shed by a 1961 training manual on Social Security for life underwriters. Most of it was devoted to a concise presentation of the main, relevant features of Social Security—coverage; wages and self-employment income; insured status; benefits and how to compute them; loss of benefits due to earnings; Social Security taxes—but it ended with advice on how to use Social Security to sell insurance. OASDI's survivor and retirement benefits were sufficiently large, the manual pointed out, that "Conscientious life underwriters *must* tell prospects about them and include them in *every* client's financial plans" (italics in original). The benefits' size also meant that "We can, with clear conscience," encourage prospects' "natural selfish desires" for what endowment and other private life insurance products had to offer. Also, Social Security benefits would *not* do many things, such as pay off a deceased's mortgage, and could not be borrowed, and these limitations created opportunities for life insurance sale. The manual advised insurance agents to know the law and be able to compute a prospect's approximate benefits.[111] It further advised,

> *Never disregard social security.* We can not pose as qualified, conscientious underwriters while disregarding the estate values of a man's social security benefits. That is as serious as overlooking a large policy of life insurance or the guaranteed income from a $100,000 investment he already owns.
>
> On the other hand, we should be careful to explain the nature of the social security system:
>
> (a) That social security is *not* insurance, but a tax system;
> (b) That social security exists at the will of Congress;
> (c) That benefits are not based on contractual guarantees, like commercial life insurance, but are most often based on political expediency;
> (d) That because social security taxes are invested in government securities, current benefits are paid from current tax appropriations rather than from a true reserve, as in commercial life insurance;
> (e) That the U.S. Government has, through the social security system, promised billions in future benefits without any assurance that future generations of taxpayers will be able or willing to carry the load.
>
> Explain social security factually and without prejudice [!]. *Let your prospect tell you* what importance he wishes to attach to the promised benefits, particularly the retirement benefits. If he wishes to rely on these benefits in his financial planning then act accordingly.[112] (All italics in original)

The manual instructed the agent, among other things, on how to help prospective clients contact Social Security and find out what their status was, and how to help them file their claims for benefits according to Social Security's guidelines so as not to lose any benefits from delays in filing.[113] Granted, there's a self-interested calculation in such helpfulness—but it would have been more self-serving still to instruct insurance agents to ignore the value of a prospect's benefits and offer no such help.

While the manual does manifest the regard for self-interest one would expect in an industry seeking to make a profit, there is a conscientiousness and honesty here, particularly in the injunction to explain Social Security "factually and without prejudice," that contrasts favorably with the government's misleading depiction of Social Security as insurance and its failure to inform the public about the reservation of power clause. (Note too that everything the manual says about OASDI's not being insurance is true.)

In light of all this, it is fairly certain that hostility in the insurance industry to Social Security's self-advertising as insurance flowed not from antisocial self-serving but from honest professional indignation at a government entity pretending to be what it was not and trying to obtain a windfall gain of goodwill from the insurance industry's reputation, won in the teeth of the Depression's hardships, for soundness, dependability, probity, and trustworthiness.

A Dubious Analogy:
Confessions of Social Insurance Partisans

Still another factor undermining Social Security's claim to be insurance is the admission by some leading social insurance advocates that the analogy to private insurance is both tenuous and made with intent to affect belief. I. M. Rubinow, one of the founding fathers of the social insurance movement in America, observed in 1911 that the state, in creating a social insurance program, could furnish different degrees of assistance, to cut the cost or premium of insurance and increase its population of covered persons, ranging from merely providing a safe non-profit organization to full or partial assumption of administrative costs; providing a subsidy; shifting all or part of the premium cost to others, such as employers; and, finally, making participation compulsory.[114] Social Security, of course, entails many of these. Rubinow then admitted that

> every one of the steps enumerated is a step away from the true scientific principles of business insurance, which is based upon distribution of loss among all those subject to the possibility of loss. And, of course, from the point of view of actuarial science, all these steps are subject to severe criticism. But social insurance might almost be defined as *a form of insurance which cannot live up to the exacting laws of insurance science.*[115] (italics added)

This is an extraordinary and damaging admission. Ordinarily something claiming to be a thing while admitting inability to manifest its defining characteristics—a medicine that cannot live up to the laws of medical science, say—would be laughed out of court. One cannot help suspecting that only Rubinow's sympathy for the less fortunate enabled him to call social insurance insurance even as his intelligence honestly admitted that it did not make the grade.

Economist Eveline Burns, another social insurance proponent, wrote in 1944 that social insurance was created to perform a specific task "in a specific economic and social environment," including a certain prevailing set of beliefs, and upheld it as "the ideal instrument for effecting a change in the deterrent treatment of insecure workers, because its apparent analogy with private insurance made the change acceptable to a society which was dominated by business ethics and which stressed individual economic responsibility." When Social Security was proposed and enacted, she pointed out, the prevailing view was individualistic—individuals were responsible for their well-being, and poverty was a disgrace—and apprehensive about government as a tool of redistribution or other social change. Hence it was important at this point "to stress the analogy of social, to private, insurance." In both this beginning period and the second stage of social insurance's evolution, when it begins to be accepted by the public and extended to cover additional groups and provide additional benefits, Burns added, "Earmarked funds and a close tie-up between taxes and benefits [i.e., the financial features which allow social insurance to claim that it works like real insurance] may then be psychologically necessary for two reasons: to afford what appears to be a guarantee of the rights of the contributors, and to serve as a continual reminder that those who benefit have 'earned' their privilege by contributing." Once social insurance coverage became universal, indicating "a change in social attitudes" to a widespread desire for minimum guaranteed security, earmarked payroll taxes are "no longer so necessary in view of the changed attitude," and can be replaced by general revenue financing.[116]

But this is a confession that social insurance's analogy with private insurance was drawn with intent to affect attitudes, not to reflect reality. Moreover, Burns is implicitly admitting that the fiscal features of programs such as Social Security—the payroll tax, the "trust fund," the link of payroll taxes to benefits—are not the ineluctable products of economic realities, unlike the premiums and reserve funds of private insurance, which do spring from and reflect the economic realities of insurance: risk pooling, risk transfer, and giving the insurer the resources to compensate the insured for probable losses. Rather, they were employed to make the program acceptable to the public, and could be dispensed with once the public's psychology changed. But if the payroll tax is psychology-driven and expendable due to *attitude changes,* then it must follow that *it does not reflect or rest on any notion of risk, hence does not have the character of an insurance premium.* It is a psychological tool—as President Roosevelt said, "politics all the way through."

Moreover, as Social Security was liberalized, it became more and more like welfare, and less and less like insurance—as Burns had the honesty to admit. Nine years later she observed that social insurance "has increasingly shed the features which closely paralleled, or even duplicated, those of private insurance." It had been greatly broadened to extend benefits to people who could not have earned those benefits through their contributions, Social Security's 1950 eligibility liberalization allowing elderly people to qualify for full benefits with a mere six quarters of coverage being a case in point. Moreover, reserve financing was abandoned in many programs. Hence in many countries "social insurance has become an institution to which the word 'insurance' can be applied only at the risk of serious distortion of the language." The analogy to private insurance "is no longer appropriate, if it ever was." The analogy kept breaking down, because the purpose of social insurance—the pursuit of social welfare—is basically different from that of private insurance. Where private insurance's benefits are determined by contract, social insurance benefits are driven by public policy and public opinion. Where the beneficiary's premium in private insurance is determined by insurance principles, in social insurance the beneficiary pays a contribution "to establish in the minds of beneficiaries some sense of the relationship between benefits and cost; or to overcome the reluctance of workers to accept public payments at one time identified with the 'poor law'; or to reconcile the rest of the community to a system which makes nondeterrent social security payments, by invoking the familiar procedures of private insurance"—note, parenthetically, that all these flow from psychology, not economic realities— or to raise money, justify paying differential benefits, and so on. Burns concluded that modifications of the "insurance" element in social insurance had been so radical that they made "retention of the word not merely unjustified but misleading," and that abandonment of the analogy was inevitable—and desirable.[117]

Some years later, Burns admitted that if one regards insurance as ordinary life insurance, with benefits being directly, actuarially linked to premiums and "the principle of risk homogeneity in cost apportionment is strictly adhered to," social insurance "cannot appropriately be classified as insurance," because there is little actuarial link between one's contributions and benefits, individuals aren't classified by risk, and one's cost "is not proportionate to the probability of his incurring the risk." Then, too, there is the absence of a contract. Even if regarding social insurance as "insurance" is proper, Burns added, it is clearly "a very different type of insurance from private commercial insurance."[118] The accuracy and legitimacy of a *strong* analogy drawing a *close* parallel to private insurance, especially individual policies, suffer accordingly.

"Public Immorality" and Playing with Fire

Judging whether or not Social Security is insurance entails answering three questions: Is Social Security insurance as academic experts define it: a mechanism of risk pooling and risk transfer? Is it insurance as the *public* understands the term? Finally, is it insurance as Social Security presented itself in its publications—that is, does it live up to its own advertising?

By showing that Social Security does not truly pool risk or transfer it to an insurer, we have answered the first question in the negative. But what really matters for practical and political purposes is how the *general public,* which votes, pays Social Security taxes, and has expectations about benefits, understands Social Security, not professors of insurance. As E. J. Faulkner wisely observed:

> The nice distinctions between 'contractual insurance' and 'social insurance' made by those sophisticated in these matters are without meaning to the man in the street. He can scarcely be blamed for his misconceptions when leading politicians of both parties constantly assure him that social security is 'insurance.' Whether social benefit schemes are or are not 'insurance' and in what sense is of less consequence than that when the advocate of ever-bigger government plans keeps referring to them as 'insurance,' he means one thing while the general public thinks he means another.[119]

Faulkner's last sentence is charitable. As the evidence makes clear, Social Security's publications, the articles and broadcasts by its officials, and the speeches and broadcasts by politicians such as President Roosevelt sought to create a strong impression that Social Security is just like an individual private insurance policy, with its inviolable contract—that it, that it is insurance as the man in the street understands the term. The motive, obviously, was to maximize Americans' acceptance of and faith in Social Security. After Americans had been saturated with this insurance talk for almost thirty years, Faulkner observed that

> As insurance salesmen discover daily, many Americans err by thinking of social security in terms of private insurance. They believe that the social security taxes they pay are a premium to provide a pension for their own old age. They suffer from the delusion that somehow the government can provide life insurance, annuity, and health insurance benefits cheaper and better than can private insurers.[120]

But this "delusion" is what Social Security *wanted* Americans to believe and led them to believe. Americans generally understand insurance as entailing a binding commitment by an insurer manifested in a policy, in which one pays insurance premiums, hence has a legal and contractual right to receive insurance benefits—and Curtis's hearings showed that Social Security lacks a contract. Social Security is not insurance as generally understood, nor is it insurance as advertised.

Faulkner found the widespread misperception of Social Security as closely similar to private insurance alarming, since our democracy depends on a well-informed electorate. To spare future generations a breakdown in Social Security, he added, "certain popular illusions about social security will have to be corrected."[121] While it would be very awkward, to put it mildly, for the same government organ that deliberately created these "popular illusions" to correct them, Faulkner was right. In its insurance talk Social Security was, and still is, playing with fire. Whereas the academic expert has a "fine" understanding of his field, sensitive to fine distinctions, popular understanding tends to be coarse, relying on a rough-and-ready, none too rigorous sense of what words like "insurance" mean. And the popular mind, especially under financial and emotional pressure, tends to be impatient with fine shades of meaning. Should a fiscal crisis require substantial benefit cuts, it will be bootless for Social Security's spokesmen to tell the public that Social Security is *social* insurance, meaning there's no contract, there really isn't much of a link between "premiums" and benefits, and we reserve the right to modify benefits, so— The nuances of "social insurance" that might impress academic or professional colleagues will not impress angry, frightened beneficiaries. The resultant political crisis will be the child of Social Security's self-promotion as insurance.

There are still deeper implications. In a searching criticism of Social Security's self-advertisement as insurance, Ray Peterson raised a disquieting moral problem:

> Are the following consistent with public morality:
>
> (i) To depict the social security system as greatly similar to private voluntary insurance?
>
> (ii) To fail to explain to "the man in the street" that current taxes are largely required to pay current benefits?
>
> (iii) To fail to make clear to "the man in the street" that social security benefits are not a contractual vested right?
>
> (iv) To enact legislation involving greater commitments for future generations than the current one is willing to assume?
>
> (v) To advocate generous expansion of social security benefits with a bland and blind confidence but with no confirmed assurance that an expected great growth of the national product will enable us to afford such benefits?
>
> I submit that such actions and inactions all savor of public immorality.[122]

Truth's Labor Lost

Clearly, Social Security is not insurance. It is not insurance according to the insurance scholars' criteria. It is not insurance as the public understands the term. It is not insurance as it depicted itself. The insurance analogy is misleading and untenable.

Yet this analogy dominated Americans' understanding of Social Security. The June 1958 House Ways and Means Committee hearings on proposals for further liberalization and expansion of Social Security, especially into health care, were very revealing of the analogy's acceptance by politicians. Thus, when Senator William Proxmire (D-WI), author of one such bill, testified on June 17:

> Mr. EBERHARTER: . . . social security taxes are to some extent *an investment by the employee,* an investment to be considered as *buying future security.* That is the social security tax. Whereas, with respect to the income tax all the money is spent by the Government every year. Here we have a *trust fund* to *guarantee to some extent the future security of the employee.* That is the fundamental difference between the two taxes.
>
> Senator PROXMIRE: . . . that is an excellent point. . . .
>
> Mr. EBERHARTER: I think that is the reason I have had the impression that *almost all the employees are willing to pay more taxes on social security* where they are unwilling to pay more taxes in income tax. . . .
>
> Mr. KING: What you mean I believe, . . . is that the average man who insures himself or buys an annuity would not consider his *premiums* in the same category as his taxes . . .
>
> Senator PROXMIRE: That is a perfectly valid and excellent distinction. The fact is that *this is an insurance system. This is a premium that he is paying. His employer is*

paying a part of the premium. It is entirely different from income tax. It is a *benefit that comes back to him.* He is *buying something* for himself.[123] (italics added)

Representative Eugene Siler (D-KY), who wanted to drop the retirement age to sixty, described Social Security as

insurance pure and simple. And insurance benefits always come from insurance premiums. . . . So, all that is now needed for safe social security benefits at age 60 is for *the provision of a suitable premium to be paid by employers and employees* that will be commensurate with the added benefits.[124] (italics added)

Congressman Karl Keating (D-NY) remarked that he had always felt that "since *social security is essentially an insurance system* [italics added], there should be no limit on the amounts which beneficiaries can earn, and still receive benefits."[125]

Some time in the early sixties, the industry's opponents of Social Security's self-advertisement as insurance gave up. The controversy disappeared from the insurance literature and never returned. Perhaps adoption of an "official" definition of social insurance quashed the controversy; perhaps, as Professor Williams's request that the semantic debate cease suggests, it was meant to. In any case, the struggle against the promotion of a false consciousness was over, and lost. The false consciousness was now entrenched in the public mind—and in the minds of politicians. This would affect, decisively, how public and politicians alike reacted when Social Security came under financial stress in the decades ahead.

Notes

1. U.S., Congress, Senate, Finance Committee, *Social Security Revision: Hearings on H.R. 6000, an Act to Extend and Improve the Federal Old-Age and Survivors Insurance System, before the Senate Finance Committee,* 81st Cong., 2nd sess., 1950, p. 39.
2. Ibid., p. 73.
3. Ibid.
4. Carl T. Curtis and Regis Courtemanche, *Forty Years Against the Tide: Congress and the Welfare State* (Lake Bluff, IL: Regnery Gateway, 1986), p. 334.
5. Ibid., pp. 332-334; U.S., Congress, House, Committee on Ways and Means, *Social Security Act Amendments of 1949,* House Report 1300 to accompany H.R. 6000, 81st Cong., 1st sess., 1949, pp. 173-184.
6. *Analysis of the Social Security System: Hearings,* pp. 640-641, 644, 649-650.
7. Ibid., pp. 853-854.
8. Elmer F. Wollenberg, "Vested Rights in Social-Security Benefits," *Oregon Law Review,* vol. 37, no. 4 (June 1958), pp. 357-358.
9. Berkowitz, *Mr. Social Security: The Life of Wilbur J. Cohen,* p. 88; Altmeyer, *The Formative Years of Social Security,* pp. 223, 298-301; *Analysis of the Social Security System: Hearings,* pp. 879-1015. Unlike everyone else who addressed him when he testified at congressional hearings, Curtis and Winn called Altmeyer "Mister" rather than "Doctor." At one point Eberharter proposed, quite reasonably,

that Altmeyer, who had been testifying for four hours and twenty minutes without a recess, be allowed to take a break; the request was ignored. He repeated his request later; it was again ignored. By contrast, Curtis gave Ball five-minute breaks, and Curtis and Winn were warmly courteous to Ball, who reciprocated.

10. *Analysis of the Social Security System: Hearings,* pp. 881-909.
11. Ibid., pp. 911-912.
12. Ibid., p. 918.
13. Ibid., pp. 918-919.
14. Ibid., p. 919.
15. Ibid., p. 920.
16. Ibid.
17. Ibid., p. 968.
18. Ibid., p. 964.
19. Ibid., pp. 967-968.
20. Ibid., pp. 997-998.
21. Ibid., pp. 970-971.
22. Ibid., p. 974.
23. *1998 Green Book,* p. 39.
24. *Analysis of the Social Security System: Hearings,* pp. 979-980.
25. Ibid., p. 980.
26. Ibid., p. 981.
27. Ibid., pp. 982-983.
28. Ibid., p. 984.
29. Ibid., pp. 985-992, 1000-1007.
30. Ibid., pp. 991.
31. Ibid., p. 986.
32. Ibid., p. 989.
33· Ibid., p. 1003.
34. Ibid., p. 1005.
35. Ibid., p. 1006.
36. Ibid., pp. 980, 994.
37. Ibid., p. 995.
38. Ibid., p. 998.
39. Ibid., p. 1014.
40. "Altmeyer Subpenaed in Welfare Study," *Washington Post,* November 26, 1953, 1; "Smashing of Social Security System Goal at Hearings, Eberharter Charges," *Washington Post,* November 27, 1953, 2; "Clash Stirs Hearing on Changes in Benefit Law," *Washington Post,* November 28, 1953, 1; "Pensions Hearing Stirs Up Wrangle," *New York Times,* November 28, 1953, 22.
41. "Your Old-Age Pensions: How Safe?" *U.S. News & World Report,* December 11, 1953, pp. 96-98.
42. "It's Social but it's not Security," *Nation's Business,* December 1953, pp. 34-35, 79.
43. "What's Wrong with Social Security: Interview with Representative Carl T. Curtis," *U.S. News & World Report,* February 19, 1954, pp. 70-74.
44. U.S., Congress, House, Committee on Ways and Means, *Social Security After 18 Years: A Staff Report to Hon. Carl T. Curtis, Chairman, Subcommittee on Social Security,* 83rd Cong., 2nd sess., 1954, especially pp. 37-40, 51-55, 71-72; Altmeyer, *The Formative Years of Social Security,* pp. 235-243; Derthick, *Policymaking for Social Security,* pp. 154-156.
45. Wilbur J. Cohen, Robert M. Ball, and Robert J. Myers, "Social Security Amendments of 1954: A Summary and Legislative History," *Social Security Bulletin,* vol.

17, no. 9 (September 1954), pp. 3-13; Derthick, *Policymaking for Social Security,* p. 431.

46. Charles I. Schottland, "Social Security Amendments of 1956: A Summary and Legislative History," *Social Security Bulletin,* vol. 19, no. 9 (September 1956), p. 3.

47. Cohen and Myers, "Social Security Act Amendments of 1950," pp. 6, 8; Cohen, Ball and Myers, "Social Security Amendments of 1954," p. 16; Schottland, "Social Security Amendments of 1956," p. 11.

48. Arthur Larson, *Know Your Social Security,* pp. xv, 3-4.

49. Ibid., pp. 4-7, 19.

50. Ibid., pp. 40-41.

51. Oveta Culp Hobby, "Are You Getting Your Share of Social Security?" *American Magazine,* April 1955, pp. 109, 21.

52. Helen Hill Miller, "Social Security," *Collier's,* May 13, 1955, p. 28.

53. Ibid., p. 20.

54. Dillard Stokes, "Does Our Social Security System Make Sense? Insurance, Relief, or What?" *Commentary,* June 1954, pp. 566-574.

55. "Letters from Readers," *Commentary,* October 1954, pp. 370-371.

56. U.S., Congress, House, Representative Harold C. Ostertag, "Does Our Social Security System Make Sense?" Extension of Remarks, 83rd Cong., 2nd sess., June 1, 1954, *Congressional Record,* 100: A4077-A4080.

57. Dillard Stokes, *Social Security—Fact and Fancy* (Chicago: Henry Regnery Co., 1956), pp. 175-177.

58. Emmett J. Vaughan, *Fundamentals of Risk and Insurance,* 3rd ed. (New York: John Wiley & Sons, 1982), p. 4; Robert I. Mehr and Emerson Cammack, *Principles of Insurance,* 7th ed. (Homewood, IL: Richard D. Irwin, 1980), p. 18; Herbert S. Deneberg, Robert D. Eilers, Joseph J. Melone, and Robert A. Zelten, *Risk and Insurance,* 2nd ed. (Englewood Cliffs, NJ: Prentice-Hall, Inc., 1974), p. 4.

59. Vaughan, *Fundamentals of Risk and Insurance,* pp. 21-22; Mehr and Cammack, *Principles of Insurance,* pp. 28-31.

60. Rubinow, *Social Insurance,* p. 3.

61. Abraham Epstein, "Social Insurance," *New Frontiers,* March 1937, p. 10, quoted in William Haber, *Social Insurance Course Outline* (Ann Arbor, MI: planographed Edwards Brothers, Inc., 1937), p. 30.

62. Ibid.

63. Altmeyer, "Ten Years of Social Security," p. 370.

64. Epstein, "Social Insurance," *New Frontiers,* March 1937, p. 10, quoted in Haber, *Social Insurance Course Outline,* p. 30.

65. C. A. Kulp, "Social Insurance: What Is It And Do We Need It?" *Journal of American Insurance,* vol. 12, no. 6 (June 1935), pp. 9-11.

66. C. A. Kulp, "Public Provision for Old Age," *Journal of American Insurance,* vol. 12, no. 8 (August 1935), pp. 14, 16, 26.

67. "Grand Rapids Host to Mutual Convention," *Journal of American Insurance,* vol. 14, no. 10 (October 1937), pp. 14-15; "Operation of Social Security Act Explained by Dr. Altmeyer," *Journal of American Insurance,* vol. 14, no. 10 (October 1937), p. 19.

68. Robert M. Clark, *Economic Security for the Aged in the United States and Canada,* 2 vols. (Ottawa, Canada [?]: n.p., 1959), I:30-32.

69. Domenico Gagliardo, *American Social Insurance,* rev. ed. (New York: Harper & Brothers, 1955), pp. 14-21.

70. M. Albert Linton, "The Social Security Outlook, An Address Delivered by M. Albert Linton, University of Michigan, June 3, 1953," *Analysis of the Social Security System: Hearings,* Appendix II, p. 1483.

71. C. A. Kulp, "Social and Private Insurance: Contrasts and Similarities," *Journal of the American Society of Chartered Life Underwriters,* vol. 6, no. 3 (June 1952), pp. 263-272.

72. Wilbur J. Cohen, "Author's Reply," in "Communications: Comments on 'The Challenge of Aging to Insurance' by Wilbur J. Cohen," *Journal of Insurance,* vol. 28, no. 3 (September 1961), p. 99.

73. Clark, *Economic Security for the Aged in the United States and Canada,* I:33-53.

74. Lincoln H. Lippincott, "A General System of Social Insurance is not a Practicable Ideal," *Proceedings of the Annual Meetings of the American Association of University Teachers of Insurance,* vol. 2 (1934), p. 50.

75. Ray M. Peterson, "Misconceptions and Missing Perceptions of our Social Security System (Actuarial Anesthesia)," pp. 826-827.

76. Ibid., "Discussion," p. 885.

77. Ibid., p. 886.

78. Ralph H. Blanchard, "Words," *Journal of Insurance,* vol. 27, no. 3 (September 1960), pp. 73-76; "The Commission on Insurance Terminology," *Journal of Insurance,* vol. 27, no. 3 (September 1960), p. 71.

79. *Bulletin of the Commission on Insurance Terminology of the American Risk and Insurance Association,* vol. 1, no. 4 (October 1965), p. 1, quoted in George E. Rejda, *Social Insurance and Economic Security,* 2nd ed. (Englewood Cliffs, NJ: Prentice-Hall, Inc., 1984), p. 36.

80. "The Commission on Insurance Terminology," *Journal of Insurance,* vol. 27, no. 3 (September 1960), p. 119.

81. C. Arthur Williams, Jr., "'Social Insurance'—Proper Terminology?" *Journal of Insurance,* vol. 30, no. 1 (March 1963), pp. 117-119.

82. "Social Insurance Definitions Are Offered by Terminology Committee," *National Underwriter (Life Insurance edition),* May 22, 1965, pp. 6, 18.

83. Williams, "'Social Insurance'—Proper Terminology?," pp. 120-128.

84. C. Arthur Williams, Jr. and Richard M. Heins, *Risk Management and Insurance,* 5th ed. (New York: McGraw-Hill, 1985), pp. 386-387; Vaughan, *Fundamentals of Risk and Insurance,* p. 54; Rejda, *Social Insurance and Economic Security,* pp. 36-38.

85. Derthick, *Policymaking for Social Security,* p. 342.

86. Ibid., pp. 357-368.

87. "Editor's Note" to Gerhard Hirschfeld, "Social Insurance Abroad," *Best's Insurance News (Life Edition),* January 2, 1935, p. 564.

88. "Social Security," *Journal of American Insurance,* vol. 13, no. 6 (June 1936), pp. 16, 17.

89. "Social Security Act Changes," *Best's Insurance News (Life Edition),* February 1, 1939, p. 670.

90. "Hirst's Views on Effect of Security Amendments," *Weekly Underwriter,* October 14, 1939, p. 820.

91. William E. Jones, "Social Security Amendments of 1939," *Best's Insurance News (Life Edition),* November 1, 1939, pp. 461-465, 475-478.

92. Judd C. Benson, "Social Security—1950 Style," *Best's Insurance News (Life Edition),* February 1950, pp. 14-16, 60; *1998 OASDI Annual Report,* pp. 145-146, Table II.H1.—Social Security Area Population as of July 1 and Dependency Ratios, by Alternative and Broad Age Group, Calendar Years 1950-2075.

93. Benson, "Social Security—1950 Style," p. 58.

94. Ibid., p. 61.

95. Ray D. Murphy, "The Government's Role," *Best's Insurance News (Life Edition),* September 1954, pp. 21-23, 51-52.

96. A. L. Kirkpatrick, "Social Security," *Best's Insurance News (Life Edition)*, December 1954, pp. 28-29.
97. Benjamin B. Kendrick, "Social Security," *Best's Insurance News (Life Edition)*, September 1953, pp. 25-28, 80-81; Benjamin B. Kendrick, "Social Security, Part II," *Best's Insurance News (Life Edition)*, October 1953, pp. 29-33; Benjamin B. Kendrick, "Can We Have Sound Social Security?" *Journal of the American Society of Chartered Life Underwriters*, vol. 9, no. 1 (Winter 1954), pp. 6-9.
98. Kendrick, "Can We Have Sound Social Security?" p. 10.
99. Reinhard A. Hohaus, "Social Security Plans and Developments," *Journal of American Insurance*, vol. 20, no. 10 (October 1943), pp. 15-17, 24; Reinhard A. Hohaus, "Social Security Challenge," *Best's Insurance News (Life Edition)*, January, 1950, pp. 19-22, 86-87; Reinhard A. Hohaus, "Social Security Challenge, Part II," *Best's Insurance News (Life Edition)*, February, 1950, pp. 53-57.
100. National Association of Life Underwriters, "Resolution Against Continued Use of Insurance Terminology in Social Security Act," in William Haber and Wilbur J. Cohen, eds., *Social Security: Programs, Problems, and Policies—Selected Readings* (Homewood, IL: Richard D. Irwin, Inc., 1960), pp. 554-555.
101. Ibid.
102. Ibid.
103. "President, Congress Told About Misuse Of Terms By Social Security Unit," *National Underwriter (Life Insurance edition)*, July 4, 1959, p. 22; "Insurance Language In Social Security Hit By Fire Agents," *National Underwriter (Life Insurance edition)*, June 18, 1960, p. 5.
104. Wilbur J. Cohen, "The Challenge of Aging to Insurance," *Journal of Insurance*, vol. 27, no. 4 (December 1960), pp. 16-17.
105. Ray M. Peterson, "Communications: Comments on 'The Challenge of Aging to Insurance' by Wilbur J. Cohen," *Journal of Insurance*, vol. 28, no. 3 (September 1961), p. 93; Wilbur J. Cohen, "Communications: Author's Reply," *Journal of Insurance*, vol. 28, no. 3 (September 1961), p. 98.
106. "Social Security Program," *Best's Insurance News (Life Edition)*, February 1, 1935, p. 642.
107. "Social Security Act: Huebner's Views," *Best's Insurance News (Life Edition)*, February 1, 1936, p. 682.
108. William A. Porteous, Jr., "Life Insurance and the Social Security Act," *Weekly Underwriter*, October 28, 1939, pp. 928-929, 935.
109. E. J. Faulkner, "Social Security and Insurance—Some Relationships in Perspective," *Journal of Insurance*, vol. 30, no. 2 (June 1963), pp. 198-200. A slightly differently worded version of the policy statement Faulkner cited may be found in "Social Security Program," *Trusts and Estates*, vol. 80, no. 3 (March 1945), pp. 309-310.
110. "Social Security Program," p. 309.
111. National Underwriter Company, *1961 Social Security Manual for Life Underwriters Including the 1961 Amendments* (Cincinnati, OH: National Underwriter Company, 1961), pp. 81, 82-84.
112. Ibid., p. 84.
113. Ibid., pp. 85-86, 93-95.
114. Rubinow, *Social Insurance*, pp. 10-11.
115. Ibid., p. 11.
116. Eveline M. Burns, "Social Security: Social Insurance in Evolution," *American Economic Review, Supplement: Papers and Proceedings*, vol. 34, no. 1, pt. 2 (March 1944), pp. 199, 200, 201, 207, 209.

117. Eveline M. Burns, "Private and Social Insurance and the Problems of Social Security," in *Analysis of the Social Security System: Hearings*, Appendix II, Miscellaneous Documents, pp. 1471-1478.
118. Eveline M. Burns, *Social Security and Public Policy* (New York: McGraw-Hill, 1955), p. 34.
119. Faulkner, "Social Security and Insurance—Some Relationships in Perspective," p. 204.
120. Ibid.
121. Ibid.
122. Ray M. Peterson, "Misconceptions and Missing Perceptions of our Social Security System (Actuarial Euthanasia)," Discussion, pp. 914-915.
123. U.S., Congress, House, Committee on Ways and Means, *Social Security Legislation: Hearings before the House Committee on Ways and Means,* 85th Cong., 2nd sess., 1958, pp. 163-164.
124. Ibid., p. 817.
125. Ibid., p. 1075.

8

Flemming v. Nestor, the Amish, and the Power of the Word

*"When I use a word," Humpty
Dumpty said, in a rather scornful tone, "it
means just what I choose it to mean—neither
more nor less."
"The question is," said Alice,
"whether you can make words mean so many
different things."
"The question is," said Humpty
Dumpty, "which is to be master—that's all."*

*"That's a great deal to make one
word mean," Alice said in a thoughtful tone.
"When I make a word do a lot of
work like that," said Humpty Dumpty, "I
always pay it extra."*

—Lewis Carroll, Through the Looking-Glass

The *Flemming v. Nestor* Supreme Court decision of 1960 and the Internal Revenue Service's penalizing of Amish farmers for nonpayment of their OASDI "premiums" afford further proof that Social Security's self-description as "insurance" is inaccurate and misleading. They also reveal that the popular consciousness contrived by that self-description is indeed a false one—and that what are ultimately at stake are issues of language and truth.

Wollenberg's Warning:
Social Security Gives No Vested Rights—and Can't

In 1958, Elmer Wollenberg of the Oregon State Bar took a long and careful look at the issue of a person's vested rights under OASDI. He began with a clear-eyed view of the realities of Social Security. While OASDI benefits must be supplemented with private old-age provisions, they are for most people the foundation of their retirement planning. To fulfill its social-welfare function of furnishing this foundation, Social Security has to provide predictable benefits under predictable circumstances, and individuals anticipating retirement should be able to nail down their "minimum rights" to OASDI benefits as certainly and quickly as possible. However, Wollenberg observed, OASDI is a huge and growing program entailing enormous and growing financial commitments, in the context of other federal social programs also carrying large costs. Hence the government has to avoid locking itself into "an overextension of fixed commitments that will endanger the nation's finances" should retrenchment ever become necessary.[1]

Wollenberg then put his finger on the tension, and potential for danger, at Social Security's very core:

> Thus, a general Federal social-insurance system must work out an accommodation of these somewhat conflicting interests: the interest of the individual citizen in certainty of retirement income for himself and his family unit and the interest of the Federal government in a future free of too-heavy fixed fiscal obligations. The problem is not entirely a legal one but does have legal aspects.[2]

While noting that some writers tried to "transplant" legal concepts from private, contractual pension plans to Social Security—he cited Robert Ball's misuse of "vesting," brought out in the Curtis hearings—Wollenberg stressed that the individual's "rights" under Social Security were "flexible," due to the reservation of power clause (Section 1104), which has never been repealed. Social Security legislation, he pointed out, gives Congress and the Social Security Administration much power while giving "little legal certainty to the individual." Individuals' rights under Social Security "are statutory rights and nothing more. There is no express *contract of insurance* [italics in original], within the traditional legal meaning of insurance, between the Federal government and the individual payer of a social-security tax." One's Social Security benefit "must, therefore, be considered a gratuity." Federal courts, he added, had ruled that individuals acquire no vested rights to federal gratuity-type benefits (e.g., for veterans), and that the government "has broad powers over its noncontractual benefit programs." In support, he drew on the government's brief and arguments in *Helvering v. Davis,* the Court's opinion, and Altmeyer's testimony in the Curtis hearings.[3]

Exhaustively, Wollenberg reviewed the numerous specific amendments of the Social Security Act in which individuals' rights to benefits were restricted by Congress, "cut down and even abolished upon occasion," stressing the 1939 Amendments, the Gearhart Resolution, and some aspects of the 1950 Amendments. From the evidence he concluded that one's "pre-entitlement" rights, those acquired due to participating in employment covered by the Act, are actually tentative, in view of the Congress' power to revise covered-employment qualifications for eligibility, and that prudent individuals shouldn't lean on them too heavily. As for "entitlement rights," those obtained by applying for benefits and receiving a formal notification of entitlement, these too, the record showed, are open to adjustment by Congress, even, perhaps, retroactively. Post-entitlement rights—the right to receive benefit checks and remain entitled to them—are the most important rights for beneficiaries, being where the program pays off in cash. However, they are also "the most unpredictable. They have been the most subject to change both by Congress and by the SSA." One important change that, as the Curtis hearings brought out, hurt many beneficiaries occurred in 1950 when the self-employed were brought under the program.[4]

Wollenberg then worked through the process, from employment in a covered occupation to after receipt of benefits, to see if there was any point at which, in theory, rights to benefits could vest. He concluded that there probably wasn't.[5]

It must be stressed that Wollenberg was not criticizing Social Security in saying all this. He argued that Social Security was probably the best such program under the circumstances, meeting both the government's need to be free to deal with the future, and the individual's need for *"adequate* (as distinguished from *assured*) income [italics in original]" to offset family income loss due to death, old age or disability. The uncertainty of an individual's rights under Social Security, Wollenberg pointed out, was "inherent in the program." Given Social Security's social-welfare purpose, it was vital to be able to pay claims expeditiously, hence SSA's determinations are necessarily tentative and one gets benefits "under a kind of contingent right." Far from faulting Social Security for not being contractual, Wollenberg argued that "A system of contractual social insurance involves the arrogant assumption that ours is the wisest generation of Americans for some time to come," locking unborn generations into vast legally binding commitments. Moreover, a contractual system would give less scope for experimentation and require slower, stricter benefit claim processing, since legally binding vested rights would be involved.[6]

Wollenberg maintained that Social Security's social-welfare purpose is best served without contracts in another sense. Not having its hands tied by contracts, Social Security "can make some financial gambles on the future" that private insurers "would not dare attempt," paying out higher benefits and making bigger commitments than perhaps could be afforded later. Congress can do this not only because of the government's power to tax, but because "benefit rates can be trimmed if the need should arise." If the country runs into financial trouble with Social Security, Congress need only revise the program. By contrast, if Congress were to lock the country "irrevocably" into contractual social insurance, its benefits and scope would have to be modest.[7]

In short, not only does Social Security *have no* vested rights for individuals, in Wollenberg's view it *can't,* and probably *shouldn't.*

Wollenberg ended by observing that Congress had delegated broad powers to the SSA, and warning the old and economically dependent that if they are counting on Social Security's bargain-priced benefits, "they must anticipate that their own needs for financial security will often be subordinated to other paramount requirements of Federal policy."[8]

Wollenberg had divined the fatal contradiction inherent in Social Security. Harrowed by the Depression, stimulated by the Townsend Movement, and prompted by advocacy in the media and government, Americans were making an unprecedented demand for government-provided security and decency in old age. For their part, the politicians and intellectuals who saw social insurance as an instrument for social reform had their own urgent need to have the program accepted by the public. So on the one hand, for political reasons, Social Security and its defenders had to give the public an impression that it would provide a guarantee of absolute security in a frightening uncertain world, a firm foundation for their retirement, a trustworthy anchor that would not slip. Hence the massive campaign to link Social Security in the public mind with the solid private institutions of insurance and trusts, to capitalize on the assurance those institutions conveyed. On the other hand, to keep the program from breaking the government's finances, the government had to retain the capacity to modify it—as former Chief Actuary Robertson might put it, to break its benefit promises—at will as needed. On the one hand, a manufactured *impression* of certainty which created, as it was meant to create, a *perception* of certainty on the part of taxpayers and beneficiaries. On the other, a need for flexibility—and a capacity for it (Section 1104) which was never conveyed to the public.

Certainty and flexibility cannot coexist; a flexibly certain or tentatively guaranteed benefit is a contradiction in terms. This tension has the makings of a catastrophic dilemma: should Social Security face a financial crisis, would the program live up to its professions of benefit certainty and break its tax promises, alienating taxpayers, afflicting the economy, and perhaps precipitating a political crisis on the tax side—or break its benefit promises, revealing its "sure bet" and "guarantees" as fictive, traumatizing beneficiaries, and precipitating a political crisis on the benefit side? Something would have to give.

With apt timing, just a year later a Social Security case reached the Supreme Court. It fully bore out all of Wollenberg's observations, and epitomized both the false consciousness and its consequences.

The Case: That's My Property, and My Earned Right!

Among the many 1954 amendments of the Social Security Act was a provision that old-age benefits were not to be paid to anyone deported from the

U.S. after August 1954 for illegal entry, conviction of a crime, or subversive activity.[9] On July 7, 1956, Ephram Nestor, a Bulgarian-born alien who had been a member of the Communist Party of the United States in 1933-1939, was deported. Nestor had become eligible for monthly Social Security benefits in November 1955 due to attaining age sixty-five. On December 2, he applied for benefits and began receiving $55 a month as of November. The attorney general notified the Social Security Administration's Bureau of Old-Age and Survivors Insurance in August that he had been deported, and effective September 1956, his OASI benefits were suspended.[10]

On February 26, 1957, Nestor appointed his wife and an attorney to represent him and filed a hearing with the Social Security Administration, to get his benefits reinstated and sent to Sofia, Bulgaria, where he was then residing. The referee of the SSA's Office of Appeals Council upheld the Bureau. Nestor asked the Appeals Council to review the decision, and was denied. So on May 5, 1958, he initiated a suit in the U.S. District Court for the District of Columbia, alleging that the benefit suspension was illegal and unconstitutional.[11]

Among other things, Nestor argued that "throughout the history of the Social Security Act, old age insurance benefits have been referred to as a right of the recipient which he has earned and paid for." He also cited the 1949 Report of the House Ways and Means Committee on Social Security legislation, President Eisenhower's January 14, 1954 message on Social Security, and remarks by Senators Eugene Millikin and Walter George, "all of which," the government's appeal noted, "in effect, state that Social Security benefits are not charity or a 'hand-out,' but rather are paid to the recipient as an earned right" and linked in part to his earnings. Plaintiff Nestor also reasoned, the appeal observed, that the payments he claimed "were, in fact, earned through his work and are assured as a matter of statutory right."[12] That is, he was *appealing to the government's own public-relations depiction of Social Security,* which was by now the general perception in America of how the program worked. Hadn't the public been told all these years that benefits were paid "as a matter of earned right"? Hadn't the government said over and over that in paying his "contributions" or "premiums" the worker was building up a right to benefits in his old age? In short, Nestor was professing his belief in Social Security's advertising and asking Social Security to stand by that advertising. He was in for an unpleasant surprise.

The District Court ruled in Nestor's favor, and found that his benefit termination was repugnant to the Fifth Amendment's Due Process clause, because it had deprived Nestor of a "property right" which had "fully accrued" to him.[13]

Secretary of Health, Education and Welfare Arthur Flemming appealed the decision to the Supreme Court, and in September 1959 U.S. Solicitor General J. Lee Rankin, Assistant Attorney General J. Walter Yeagley, and two federal attorneys filed a brief with the Court on Flemming's behalf—in effect, on the

Social Security Administration's behalf, since the Social Security Administration was part of the Department of Health, Education and Welfare.

The Government's Brief:
No Insurance, No Premium, No Trust

The government brief acknowledged that one of the questions at issue was whether an alien who had begun to receive monthly Social Security benefits "has a vested or 'property' right to the continued receipt of such benefits, of such a nature that their suspension pursuant to statutory direction, following his deportation, deprives him of property without due process of law."[14] Naturally, the government argued that Nestor had no such right—and in the course of its argument, exploded the false consciousness that Social Security had confected and incessantly striven to instill since 1935.

Like the government brief for *Helvering v. Davis,* the brief for *Flemming v. Nestor* described Social Security and its financial mechanism. For this it drew extensively on the efforts of none other than Social Security's resolute scold, Congressman Curtis, citing both the Altmeyer testimony in his hearings and the subsequent report by his staff, *Social Security After 18 Years.*[15] Based on this, the government denied what it had so long asserted:

> The OASI [Old-Age and Survivors Insurance] program *is in no sense a federally-administered "insurance program" under which each worker pays premiums over the years and acquires at retirement an indefeasible right to receive for life a fixed monthly benefit,* irrespective of the conditions which Congress has chosen to impose from time to time. While the Act uses the term "insurance," the true nature of the program is to be determined from its actual incidents.[16] (italics added)

So much for all the broadcasts and mass-produced popular-level literature explaining Social Security to the taxpayers as just like private insurance. The brief later reiterated this and added, regarding the term "insurance," that "in context, it plainly refers to *social security* 'insurance,' not 'insurance' in the conventional sense"[17] (italics in original).

However, as we have seen, the government had long been depicting Social Security as "'insurance' in the conventional sense," appealing to a "coarse" understanding of insurance, in language transparently intended to get the reader to equate Social Security with private insurance—with an individual policy, no less. But to win a case before the Supreme Court, the Justice Department, arguing on the Social Security Administration's behalf, appealed to a "fine" understanding, right down to citing context for proper interpretation of the word "insurance," a nuance which an ordinary American taxpayer—an autoworker, say, or a supermarket cashier—could hardly be expected to grasp and was never informed about.

As for the payroll tax, which Social Security's popular-audience pamphlets had described as "a sort of premium on what might be called an insurance policy" and "similar to premiums paid on an insurance policy," the brief had this to say:

> The "contribution" exacted under the social security plan from an employee in covered employment in the form of payroll deductions made by the employer on behalf of the Government and paid into the general Treasury, is a true *tax* [italics in original]. It is not comparable to a premium under a policy of insurance promising the payment of an annuity commencing at a designated age.[18]

And the Old-Age and Survivors Insurance Trust Fund, which, so Social Security's literature had it, worked just like a real trust fund, in which the taxpayer's money was placed and held for him in trust, the assets of which belonged to him and all the other Social Security taxpayers, and out of which benefits were paid?

> The "Trust Fund" from which OASI benefits are paid is maintained by annual appropriations made by Congress out of money in the Treasury not otherwise appropriated. Unlike private life insurance companies, which essentially require reserves equal to the present value of all benefits, the social security program needs no such reserves since it is assured of continuing participation by the exaction of taxes. The Trust Fund is, therefore, more in the nature of a contingency fund and serves to facilitate the fiscal policies of Congress. *The beneficiary or prospective beneficiary of the OASI program acquires no interest in the fund itself.*[19] (italics added)

In this context, "interest" means a right, share or title—which implies property. The last sentence, then, is a statement that the beneficiary has no property in the Trust Fund. Not only does this contradict the public statements of various high government officials, for example, Secretary Hobby's in the *American Magazine* that "The Trust Fund belongs to the people eligible for social-security benefits," it is an official admission, to the highest court in the land, that the Trust Fund is not a true trust.

All of this was a vindication for Congressman Curtis and the other critics of the insurance myth, such as Ray Peterson, Dillard Stokes, and Judd Benson. The administration was in effect admitting that everything these men had said about Social Security was true.

Now, we may safely presume that when these high Justice Department officials drew up this brief on the Social Security Administration's behalf, they were saying what the SSA wanted said. It is reasonable to presume further that they perused the Social Security law themselves, consulted with experts at the Social Security Administration or both, so as to ensure an accurate depiction of Social Security's nature for the Supreme Court's benefit. This necessarily means that when they wrote that Social Security is "in no sense" federally-administered insurance giving an indefeasible right to benefits in exchange for premiums, that the so-called "contribution" was a tax and not remotely resembling a premium, and that a beneficiary has no property in the so-called "trust fund," *they were describing Social Security as it really is*—a reality in glaring contrast to the "insurance" and "trust fund" talk.

Nestor had appealed to the government's own popular-consumption depiction of Social Security benefits as an earned right, something one had bought and paid for. Hence in arguing that Nestor's understanding of Social Security was wrong, the government was necessarily arguing that *its own depiction of Social Security for public-relations purposes was wrong.* By the government's own admission, then, the understanding of Social Security that it wanted the public to subscribe to was a false one.

And it was a misunderstanding deliberately fostered. The decision by Altmeyer and Cohen on May 24, 1937 to start calling Social Security "insurance" had come immediately after a Supreme Court ruling drawing on a government brief, the contents of which they must have known, *denying* that Social Security was insurance. Altmeyer had testified to the Senate Finance Committee in 1939 that the decision to call a Treasury account a "trust fund" had been taken for public relations reasons, and had testified to the House Ways and Means Committee that same year that some of the key characteristics of a true trust—individual property rights and segregation of assets—did not in fact exist. What Social Security's spokesmen, from Altmeyer and Cohen down, had been telling the public was inaccurate—and they could hardly have failed to know it.

Property Rights? What Property Rights?

Since the core issue was whether Nestor had been denied due process by being shorn of a "fully accrued property right"—that is, "the right to the continued receipt of social security benefits once they have been awarded"—the government understandably devoted considerable effort to arguing that "this view that such benefits are 'fully accrued property rights' is wholly erroneous."[20]

For one thing, the government pointed out, the Supreme Court had frequently distinguished between insurance and annuity programs, which create property rights, and pensions, which, being gratuities, or "bounties of government," do not. The granting of pension benefits by Congress, the Court had ruled, for example in *Lynch v. United States,* didn't create vested rights, and Congress could withdraw benefits conferred by gratuities if it so chose. In other cases the Court had ruled that pensions were gifts and not vested rights.[21]

What's more, the Court had usually seen legislation creating compulsory state government employee retirement programs as not creating any vested rights.[22] Drawing on these principles and precedents, the brief maintained that "the right to federal social security benefits is a statutory, conditional right, which the possessor enjoys subject to all the conditions which Congress has attached and may attach."[23]

Moreover, Social Security has numerous features which make clear the "non-vested and non-contractual character" of benefits. Benefit amounts are based on average earnings in covered employment, not the amount of one's tax payments, and any link between wages, taxed paid, and benefits "is subject to change at any time by Congress." The noncorrelation between taxes and benefits is illustrated by the "work test" whereby benefits are forfeit for retired beneficiaries who earn over a certain amount; by the "wage credit" offered to servicemen in the armed forces though they had paid no taxes; the huge benefits received by beneficiaries in the early years of the program, far exceeding what they would have obtained had their taxes been used to buy private annuities; and by the "new start" for the elderly under the 1950 Amendments, allowing them to qualify for maximum benefits with only six quarters of coverage.[24]

Still another indicator that the benefits are non-contractual is the IRS ruling that monthly benefits are "voluntary payments" to the beneficiary by the government—that is, gifts—not "purchased annuities or additional wages," hence are nontaxable.[25]

As for the reservation of power clause, the brief pointed out, rightly, that "No contractual obligation on the part of the Government and no contractual right of a beneficiary could coexist with this reservation of power."[26]

Not only that, "since Congress has expressly reserved its 'right to alter, amend, or repeal any provision' of the Social Security Act from its very inception in Section 1104," the suspension of Nestor's benefits, while authorized by a statutory provision passed in 1954, "would have been proper and valid" even if the provision authorizing it "had been passed *after* [italics in original] appellee became eligible for and commenced to receive his monthly benefits."[27]

The brief then noted that other cases had come up in which lower federal courts rejected constitutional challenges to other provisions of Social Security legislation which had reduced or cut off benefits to people who had qualified for them and been awarded them *before* those provisions had been enacted. In *Price v. Folsom,* for example, a retired patent attorney had applied for and been awarded OASI benefits in July 1954. At that time, the Social Security Act did not include self-employment income from law practice among the grounds for reducing benefits due to exceeding the permissible earnings ceiling. Subsequently, the 1954 Amendments became law, and went into effect January 1, 1955. In January he opened his own law office. Unfortunately for him, the Amendments included self-employment income from law practice in the occupations whose earnings, if they exceeded the ceiling, would trigger a "deduction" in benefits. The lawyer sued, claiming that this amendment was unconstitutional in his case because he had obtained a vested right to his benefits when they were awarded in July 1954. The District Court of New Jersey disagreed, and ruled that pension funds and payments from them are government gratuities, hence a beneficiary doesn't acquire a vested right to any payments except those which were already due.[28]

Similarly, in *Mullowney v. Folsom,* a beneficiary had started receiving OASI benefits in April 1950, and also worked as a self-employed real-estate broker. Under the 1950 Amendments which took effect in January 1951, his benefits were suspended for each month he earned more than $50 as a self-employed broker. He sued, claiming that this self-employment earnings provision was unconstitutional. But the New York district court decided against him, maintaining that he had not acquired a vested right to his benefits making them immune to further congressional control.[29]

All this necessarily means that if Congress were to pass a law cutting or terminating benefits, the reservation of power clause gives Congress all the authority it needs, and the beneficiaries, in the government's view, wouldn't have a legal leg to stand on.

The District Court ruling in Nestor's favor had cited *Steinberg v. United States,* a Court of Claims case striking down a law cutting off Civil Service retirement benefits to retired civil servants who took the Fifth Amendment in testifying about their government service before courts or congressional committees. However, the brief argued, rightly enough, the District Court was comparing two unlike things, since the salary deductions for contributions to the civil service retirement fund have never been considered taxes, whereas the OASI payroll deductions are "true taxes, and lack the incidents of 'contributions' toward a retirement fund, or 'annuity.'"[30]

Another case cited by the District Court, *Ewing v. Gardner,* decided by the Court of Appeals, involved an attempt by the executor of a deceased wage-earner's estate to obtain for the estate old-age benefits the worker had qualified for before death. The worker had shown little interest in obtaining them, ignoring repeated requests to furnish proof that he'd reached age sixty-five. Nevertheless, the Court of Appeals had ruled in favor of the estate, arguing that his right to benefits was not a gratuity but a property right. This decision too rested on dissimilar things; it invoked two cases, one involving War Risk Insurance, the other annuities under the Civil Service Retirement Act, involving government benefits that were not "pensions" or gratuities like Social Security.[31]

All in all, the government's brief was a thorough and meticulous demolition job. If Social Security indeed isn't insurance and involves no vested property rights—and in light of the Social Security Act's provisions, the government's brief and arguments for *Helvering v. Davis,* our own perusal of insurance, Wollenberg's painstaking sifting of the whole issue of vested rights to benefits, and the legal precedents cited, the brief's arguments seem irrefutable—Nestor's position was untenable. So, necessarily, is the insurance and trust fund advertising disseminated for so long on such a huge scale.

"Distortion of Language" and "Inappropriate Analogies"

The administration summed up:

> In summary, social security must be viewed as a welfare instrument to which legal concepts of "insurance," "property," "vested rights," "annuities," etc., *can be applied only at the risk of a serious distortion of language.* We are dealing with a social instrument by which public action, involving compulsion, is invoked to deal with a social problem. . . . An understanding of the difficult and changing problems of public policy arising out of attempts to eliminate individual or family insecurity . . . *will be obscured by Procrustean efforts to force the social security program into the mold of inappropriate analogies.*[32] (italics added)

Yet this "distortion of language" and application of "inappropriate analogies" was what Social Security itself had been doing for decades. Here we see the same pattern of tailoring language to have the desired effect on the intended audience as emerged in the brief for *Helvering v. Davis.* To get taxpayers to accept and pay the payroll taxes, Social Security is "insurance"—but to win a Supreme Court case to deny benefits to a beneficiary who'd paid his taxes, it's not.

The brief cited the Court of Appeals ruling in *United States v. Vogue, Inc.,* in which the court had pointed out that Social Security was meant to further a public policy "unknown to the common law," hence its application was to be evaluated according to its policy goals, not according to common law rules. Quoting Wollenberg's passage on the unwisdom of locking the country into commitments with contractual social insurance and the advantage of flexibility conferred by a statutory program, the brief added:

> If the privilege under the Social Security Act to benefits is to be called a "right," it is one which—by the very Act which created it—is expressly subject to amendment or repeal as Congress in its wisdom feels will best promote the general welfare. [Wollenberg quotes omitted] We submit, therefore, that the court below erred in applying "vested rights" theory to this case [citation omitted]. Rather, as we have shown, the beneficiary has a statutory "right," contingent upon the continued existence of the law which created it, and subject to the expressly reserved power of Congress to amend or repeal any provision of the law. The only restraint which the Constitution places upon Congress in enacting subsequent amendatory legislation is that such legislation be reasonably related to the ultimate object sought to be attained, i.e., not arbitrary or unduly discriminatory.[33]

The brief then dispatched the objection that Nestor had been discriminated against as an alien and ex-Red. There was no constitutional bar against limiting welfare benefits to citizens only, it pointed out, and such action had plenty of precedents. And so on.[34]

The Decision: No Accrued Property Rights to Benefits

On June 20, 1960, by a vote of 5-4, the Supreme Court decided *Flemming v. Nestor* in the government's favor. Justice John Harlan wrote the Court's opinion. Unlike the *Helvering v. Davis* opinion, it was a substantial piece of original work. Opening the section dealing with the issue of Nestor's purported property right, Justice Harlan came straight to the point: the District Court erred in ruling that paragraph 202(n) of the Social Security Act, regarding deportation, deprived Nestor of an "accrued property right." "Appellee's right to Social Security benefits cannot properly be considered to have been of that order."[35]

Harlan quickly sketched the essentials of Social Security and the criteria for benefit eligibility. "Of special importance in this case," he noted, is the fact that eligibility and benefit amounts "do not in any true sense depend on contribution to the program through the payment of taxes, but rather on the earnings record of the primary beneficiary."[36] (That is correct.) After briefly describing the payroll tax financing method, he cut to the heart of the matter:

> The Social Security system *may be accurately described as a form of social insurance,* enacted pursuant to Congress' power to "spend money in aid of the 'general welfare'," *Helvering v. Davis, supra,* at 640, whereby persons gainfully employed, and those who employ them, are taxed to permit the payment of benefits to the retired and disabled, and their dependents. Plainly the expectation is that many members of the present productive work force will in turn become beneficiaries rather than supporters of the program. *But each worker's benefits, though flowing from the contributions he made to the national economy while actively employed, are not dependent on the degree to which he was called upon to support the system by taxation. It is apparent that the noncontractual interest of an employee covered by the Act cannot be soundly analogized to that of the holder of an annuity, whose right to benefits is bottomed on his contractual premium payments.*[37] (italics added)

Justice Harlan was telling the truth. Social Security is "social insurance"— but the crux of the matter was whether social insurance is insurance; controversy was raging among insurance scholars on that very point even as Harlan wrote, and as of *Flemming v. Nestor,* the issue was not settled. Moreover, Harlan did not undertake to settle it. And benefits had been based from the beginning on wages in covered employment, not taxes. The termination of the money-back guarantee by the 1939 Amendments, the windfalls enjoyed by the first generation of beneficiaries, the further windfalls given by "new start" provisions of the 1950 Amendments, and the repeated benefit increases already voted by Congress, had made any link between taxes and benefits tenuous. As for one's noncontractual relation to Social Security, Arthur Altmeyer himself had already admitted to the lack of contractual rights and to Congress' prerogative under Section 1104 to modify one's benefits and benefit "rights." He had also admitted that there were no vested rights.

Moreover, Harlan's first two sentences make it clear that Social Security taxes are not the source of one's own benefits; rather, they furnish the revenue for redistributive transfers to current beneficiaries. One is later supported "in turn" by redistribution from still others. This is a description of a welfare program, not insurance. His last two sentences are of decisive importance. They demolish the notions that benefits are an "earned right," and that one "buys" one's benefits with one's taxes just as one buys insurance benefits with premium payments. As far as the Court was concerned, Nestor did not have an "earned right" to his benefits because he had paid his taxes, nor had his taxes bought him those benefits. One's benefits flow from one's "contributions to the national economy while employed," not one's contributions to the Social Security program. And while the paragraph opens by accepting the designation of Social Security as "social insurance," the body of the paragraph effectively explodes both the economic and the legal aspects of the long-standing analogy between Social Security and private insurance.

Justice Harlan brusquely dismissed discussion of "earned rights" and "gratuities" as "hardly profitable." In one sense, he admitted, one's "right" to OASDI benefits is "earned," in that the program rests on Congress' judgment that having supported the economy in one's productive years, one might "justly call upon that economy" for protection from destitution in old age. But making that principle operative in practice entailed a very complex legislation and program. Meant to exist "into the indefinite future," Social Security's provisions "rest on predictions as to expected economic conditions which must inevitably prove less than wholly accurate," as well as on decisions and preferences about proper resource allocation which will necessarily be modified due to changes in economic and social conditions.[38] Therefore, Harlan concluded,

> *To engraft upon the Social Security system a concept of "accrued property rights" would deprive it of the flexibility and boldness in adjustment to ever-changing conditions which it demands.* [Wollenberg (!) citation omitted] It was doubtless out of an awareness of the need for such flexibility that Congress included in the original Act, and has since retained, a clause expressly reserving to it "[t]he right to alter, amend, or repeal any provision" of the Act. . . . That provision makes express what is implicit in the institutional needs of the program. . . . It was pursuant to that provision that §202(n) was enacted.
>
> We must conclude that *a person covered by the Act has not such a right in benefit payments as would make every defeasance of "accrued" interests violative of the Due Process Clause of the Fifth Amendment.*[39] (italics added)

The Supreme Court had just confirmed all of Wollenberg's contentions. Social Security *has no* accrued property rights—and *can't,* and therefore *shouldn't.* It simply has to be free to cope with "changing circumstances"— by which was meant, quite clearly, a possible economic downturn, fiscal crisis, or simply a tight budget—hence just can't tie its hands by giving beneficiaries true property rights. Too bad about their "earned rights" and "statutory rights," but if Social Security's solvency ever faced serious danger they could hardly expect Congress to let the Treasury exsanguinate for their benefit. Congress has to leave itself an out, and it did so.

In sober truth, a fair and honest consideration of the matter compels the conclusion that Wollenberg, the government brief, and the Court were right about that. For any "social insurance" program above the most modest and austere, a system of binding contractual obligations is utterly incompatible with maintaining sound public finance and a sound economy, which are crucial for the selfsame general welfare OASDI is meant to serve. Much of Social Security's threefold crisis explained in Part 1 flows from that very fact. We are drifting fecklessly toward a situation in which honoring all of OASDI's tax and benefit promises will break the budget, wreck the economy, or both, risking grave political turmoil. The only way out will be to invoke Section 1104 and break some or all of those promises—which will also risk terrible political upheavals.

(Indeed, in 1993, when concern over Social Security's financial prospects was rampant, Social Security's former Chief Actuary Robert Myers lauded this flexibility for precisely this reason. Rebutting the "myth" that OASDI is "a ticking time bomb" threatening to explode in "a potentially devastating crisis," Myers wrote: "This myth fails to recognize that, if the fund balance is moving toward exhaustion, corrective action can be taken—either to increase contribution rates or to decrease future growth in benefit outgo—or both. The program is flexible and is not set in concrete. Its provisions involve statutory rights, not contractual rights."[40] Not to worry—if Social Security's cash flow hemorrhages, we can just break our promises. We're not tied down. True—but another admission that the prevailing understanding of Social Security is false.)

However, Harlan went on, this doesn't mean Congress can act capriciously, without any constitutional restraint. "The interest of a covered employee under the Act is of sufficient substance as to fall within the protection from arbitrary governmental action afforded by the Due Process Clause." But this was not to undo the foregoing denial of a vested, accrued property right—merely to say that the government couldn't act *arbitrarily*. As long as Congress was within its powers and had an intelligible reason for what it was doing, that was enough: *"Particularly when we deal with a withholding of a noncontractual benefit under a social welfare program such as this,* we must recognize that the Due Process Clause can be thought to interpose a bar *only* if the statute manifests *a patently arbitrary classification, utterly lacking in rational justification* [italics added]."[41] Note, too, the characterization of Social Security benefits as noncontractual.

There followed a concise and cogent argument that there was nothing arbitrary or irrational about the decision to terminate Nestor's benefits. For one thing, one national benefit from Social Security is its support of purchasing power by making transfer payments to the elderly—a benefit which is lost in the case of checks sent overseas. For another, Congress wasn't being irrational in deciding that the public purse shouldn't be used to support deported Communists. Hence "this provision of the Act cannot be condemned as so lacking in rational justification as to offend due process."[42]

So the highest court in the land had settled it: there *is no* accrued, vested property right to Social Security benefits. Social Security *has no* contract for benefits. And there *is no* sound analogy between Social Security and private insurance or annuities. The promotion of that analogy was misleading. The understanding of Social Security flowing from that analogy is necessarily inaccurate. Congress can modify the program at will, just so it has a "rational justification" for what it does. (A need to avoid breaking the budget and the economy easily qualifies. Sound public finance and a sound economy are at least as vital to the general welfare as honoring Social Security's promises.) Whether or not one's noncontractual benefit termination violates due process does not turn on one's having an accrued, vested property right, for no such right exists—it turns on Congress having a "rational justification" for terminating benefits. In short, *Flemming v. Nestor* amounts to a reaffirmation of the reservation of power clause and an authorization for its very broad use.

The Dissents: But It's *Insurance!*

Unlike *Helvering v. Davis,* the *Flemming v. Nestor* opinion drew vigorous dissents. Chief Justice Earl Warren and Justices Hugo Black, William O. Douglas, and William Brennan dissented; Black, Douglas, and Brennan wrote dissenting opinions.

Outraged by Nestor's misfortune, Justice Black cited *Lynch v. United States,* the decision which had prevented the government from reneging on its War Risk Insurance contracts, and deplored how this decision was "cast aside" in the decision against Nestor. Here Black too was adding unlike things, since War Risk Insurance involved actual insurance contracts, whereas Social Security didn't. Black claimed that the Court was misunderstanding Congress' purpose in passing Social Security. Congress meant, he said, that old people shouldn't think of the program as giving them something for nothing. Like the hapless Nestor, he went on to quote Senator George's remarks that Social Security benefits were not charity, relief or handouts but rather "an earned right based upon the contributions and earnings of the individual."[43]

Justice Black then emitted an indignant *cri de coeur* revealing that he, like Nestor, had uncritically accepted Social Security's self-advertisement as closely analogous to private insurance:

> The Court consoles those whose insurance is taken away today, and others who may suffer the same fate in the future, by saying that a decision requiring the Social

Security system to keep faith "would deprive it of the flexibility and boldness in adjustment to ever-changing conditions which it demands." People who pay premiums for insurance usually think they are paying for insurance, not for "flexibility and boldness." I cannot believe that any private insurance company in America would be permitted to repudiate its matured contracts with its policyholders who have regularly paid all their premiums in reliance upon the good faith of the company. It is true, as the Court says, that the original Act contained a clause, still in force, that expressly reserves to Congress "[t]he right to alter, amend, or repeal any provision" of the Act. . . . Congress, of course, properly retained that power. It could repeal the Act so as to cease to operate its old-age insurance activities for the future. . . . But that is quite different from disappointing the just expectations of the contributors to the fund which the Government has compelled them and their employers to pay its Treasury.[44]

Of course no private insurance company could repudiate obligations to policyholders under matured legal and binding contracts—but the whole problem was precisely the invalidity of the analogy to private insurance. The well-meaning Black had failed to grasp what Curtis and Wollenberg had realized: that the reservation of power clause demolishes any analogy to private insurance with its "matured contracts" and obligations to "policyholders." Somehow, he seemed to think that Section 1104, which in his view gave Congress a power "properly retained," and inviolable rights to benefits could coexist.

Justice William O. Douglas had similar difficulties with the realities of Social Security. "Social Security payments are not gratuities," he wrote flatly— and, in light of the government's *Helvering v. Davis* brief and Robert Jackson's oral arguments in that case, wrongly. The taxes, he continued, are placed in the OASI Trust Fund, "and only those who contribute to the fund are entitled to its benefits [not true; covered workers' survivors, who themselves paid nothing, have entitlement to benefits], the amount of benefits being related to the amount of contributions made [not true; they are based on earnings in covered employment]." Like Justice Black, Douglas quoted Senator George about handouts and earned rights.[45]

There is a disturbing air of innocence, even naïveté, here. Black and Douglas were intelligent men. Yet their dissents prove that like Nestor and like millions of their less exalted countrymen, they believed the pronouncements for public consumption by the Social Security Administration and politicians about Social Security, and had apparently made no effort to acquaint themselves with the Curtis hearings, Dillard Stokes's sturdy criticism, or— which is shocking in view of its great relevance and its lavish use by the Justice Department in its brief—Wollenberg's masterful treatment of vested rights to OASDI benefits. Indeed, one sees in these indignant but ill-informed dissents an uncanny prefiguration of the protests ordinary Americans would emit decades later about Reagan's benefit cut proposals and congressional "raids" on the "trust fund."

The Reaction

Astonishingly for such an important case, there was very little reporting. In brief articles buried deep in their front sections, the *New York Times* and the *Washington Post* reported that *Flemming v. Nestor* had held that workers do not have an accrued property right to Social Security benefits.[46] That was all. No big headlines, front-page stories, reprints of the full text of the opinion, or editorials. The mass-circulation news magazines such as *Time* and *Newsweek* did not mention the case. The decision and its shattering, momentous implications went undiscussed in the mainstream press. It was not like the aftermath of *Helvering v. Davis.*

Only the academic and trade journals of the insurance profession discerned the importance of *Flemming v. Nestor.* Even before the decision was handed down, private insurance actuaries were pointing out the discrepancy between the Social Security Administration's public relations depiction of OASDI and the government's brief filed on its behalf.[47]

After the decision, Ray Peterson keenly observed that *Flemming v. Nestor* "may well become a landmark on the road to an understanding of the social security system." He sharply criticized the way Social Security had been presented to the public. "One of the great afflictions of the American people," he wrote, "is social security nescience: that is, lack of knowledge. Never has an economic organism so powerful as social security affected so many and been understood by so few." Both the general public and many prominent figures have "a distorted image" of Social Security: as a close relative of private insurance.[48]

Quoting extensively from both the administration's brief in *Flemming v. Nestor* and the Court's opinion, Peterson demolished that image. He quoted from several Social Security Administration communications to show how that distorted image had been foisted on the country by the SSA. One consequence of the distorted image of Social Security as insurance was a wide misunderstanding of the retirement test. Since Social Security was intended as partial compensation for wage loss due to retirement, it included a retirement test in its benefit eligibility requirements. To qualify for benefits, one had to be substantially retired from covered employment; if one did work intermittently or part-time in a covered occupation, and one's earnings exceeded a certain amount, one lost one's benefits for each month in which that was the case. From the theory of social insurance, the retirement test was sound; benefits were meant to meet presumed need. Also, Peterson pointed out, it helped keep program costs down; without the earnings limitation, benefit outlays would be $2 billion a year higher and the payroll tax would have to be increased by 1 percent of payroll (he was writing, recall, in 1960). As the Curtis hearings disclosed, the retirement test drew bitter protests from beneficiaries. It also drew much wrath from politicians and journalists who argued that because Social Security was insurance, with its benefits an "earned right" bought and paid for by one's "contributions," the retirement test was outrageous and should be abolished. Peterson maintained, quite cogently, that "If the system were properly depicted as a *social* [italics in original] insurance program, with benefits payable to meet social needs, this distorted concept would be less likely to arise."[49]

A few months later Equitable's president, James Oates, likewise observed that the commonly-held view of Social Security as similar to private voluntary insurance had been exploded by *Flemming v. Nestor.* He too dipped into the brief and the Court's opinion for devastating quotes. From this Oates drew the conclusion that "there is no contractual relationship between the individual and his government." One only has statutory rights under Social Security, which can be altered at any time by Congress. "There exists no irrevocable vested contract such as that involved in a private voluntary insurance operation."[50]

In 1961, as controversy rose regarding extension of Social Security to provide medical and hospital benefits, Peterson again laid out the distorted "insurance" image of Social Security and warned that the price of "social adequacy" of Social Security benefits for a given generation of beneficiaries is individual inequity inflicted on somebody else, specifically new entrants into the program, onto whom was pushed the cost of giving current beneficiaries benefits far in excess of their own tax payments. Successive generations of young taxpayers would get an increasingly worse deal under Social Security. Once the young realized what was happening to them, and that the reality of Social Security was very different from its image, Peterson speculated, they might balk amid "a rising clamor of unfairness—a din of inequity." To avert this, he advocated, among other things, no further benefit increases beyond cost-of-living adjustments, and monitoring of the Social Security's statements and publications by an independent government agency to disclose inaccuracies.[51] Elsewhere, Peterson raised the government-promoted distorted image of Social Security yet again, complaining that "the Social Security Administration, in statements of OASDI officials and publications, has for years been presenting to the public an inaccurate and incomplete picture of the nature of social security rights, taxes and benefits."[52]

Wilbur Cohen, ever vigilant for criticisms of Social Security, retorted that

contrary to Mr. Peterson's statements, the issuances of the Social Security Administration have been scrupulously accurate. From the beginning, officials of the Social Security Administration have attempted to explain clearly and accurately the nature of the old-age and survivors insurance program. In order to do this they have . . . drawn analogies between social insurance and commercial insurance. The drawing of an analogy . . . based on points of similarity is not misrepresentation, even though the two things analogized may not be the same in all respects.[53]

In light of the government's failure to inform the public about Section 1104 and its brief for *Flemming v. Nestor,* this is breathtaking. Yet Cohen promptly outdid himself:

> In many respects social insurance has advantages over private insurance. The lack of existence of a contract, for example, in government social insurance is not a disadvantage but an advantage. In the words of the U.S. Supreme Court, "To engraft upon the Social Security system a concept of 'accrued property rights' would deprive it of the flexibility and boldness in adjusting to ever-changing conditions which it demands."[54]

As Ephram Nestor had learned the hard way, the issuances of the Social Security Administration were anything but "scrupulously accurate," and the lack of existence of a contract had certainly not been an advantage for *him.*

Two years later, E. J. Faulkner noted that despite "deplorable political double talk," both the government's brief for *Flemming v. Nestor* and the Supreme Court's decision had authoritatively demolished the analogy of Social Security to private insurance. In light of the government's arguments in both *Helvering v. Davis* and *Flemming v. Nestor,* Faulkner added, "the continued reference to social security as 'insurance' in the publications of the system and the utterances of its officials is inconsistent if not indefensible."[55]

But that was all. Presently, the industry's commentary on the implications of *Flemming v. Nestor,* like its controversy over whether Social Security was insurance, abruptly vanished. Meanwhile, however, another revealing controversy was shaping up.

The Amish: It's Insurance? Count Us Out!

The same 1954 Amendments which created so much grief for poor Mr. Nestor led to a confrontation between the IRS and, of all people, the peaceable Amish farmers. The Amendments extended Social Security coverage to self-employed farmers. But the Amish, devotees of an extremely plain Christian church which rejects many aspects of modern life, refuse to participate in any insurance whatsoever on religious grounds. Their faith teaches that the community is to take care of its own through voluntary charity and mutual assistance. Accordingly, after the Amendments took effect on January 1, 1955, the Amish sought an exemption from participation in Social Security on religious grounds. Congressman Paul Dague (R-PA), whose district contained many Amish, introduced bills in 1955 and 1957 seeking this exemption for them. On June 16, 1958, during House Ways and Means Committee hearings on Social Security, Dague testified in favor of exemption. A week later, Bishop Henry Z. Miller of the Old Order Amish Church testified that "Our churches do not tolerate other insurances," that the Amish had always taken care of their own in obedience to Scripture and Christ's teaching, and that "we feel the present OASI is an infringement on our responsibilities." Bishop Miller asked respectfully that the Amish be exempted from Social Security. When asked if the Amish were willing to pay the tax but not accept the benefits, or if they wanted to be exempted from taxes and benefits both, Bishop Miller replied: "The tax, if it could be paid as a tax, would be one thing. We always pay our taxes if it is a tax. But the insurance is what we object to."[56]

So there it was. The Amish were taking Social Security's self-promotion at its word—that OASDI is insurance. But if OASDI was insurance, they wanted absolutely no part of it.

The IRS tried hard to get the Amish to comply. In the fall of 1956, the IRS District Director in Cleveland, Ohio held meetings with Amish church officials and farmers to try to secure voluntary compliance. "The major point which was stressed at these meetings," IRS Commissioner Mortimer M. Caplin wrote in 1961 to an angry Pennsylvania Congressman, "was that the social security levy was a tax rather than an insurance premium, and that the Revenue Service was responsible for the enforcement of this legislation." Most of the Amish, apparently swayed by this argument, went along.[57]

So to get people to pay the Social Security levy, tell them it's an insurance premium. But if some of them have religious scruples about participating in insurance and don't want to pay this levy on the grounds that it's an insurance premium, tell them it's a tax.

Bishop Miller told the Ways and Means Committee that the Amish had paid the Social Security tax so far in hopes of being exempted. However, he added, "some didn't feel they could pay it. That is where our problems were."[58] They were indeed. In the 1959-1961 period the IRS enforced payment in roughly 130 cases by making levies on bank accounts and on the proceeds from sales of farm produce. This proved impossible in some cases, because the IRS could not locate bank accounts or other income sources to levy. Sometimes this was due to Amishmen closing their bank accounts rather than pay the tax; in other cases, officials (many of them Amish) of cooperatives to whom the farmers sold their milk stymied IRS efforts to attach the farmers' checks by refusing to sign them.[59] When these approaches failed, the IRS came down hard. In the summer of 1959, when the Amish farmers of Wayne County, Ohio refused to pay the Social Security tax, federal agents seized and sold their farm horses. When the sale started, an editorial in the *Indianapolis Times* reported, an Oberlin College student appeared wearing on his back a homemade sign reading "If the government can take these horses today it could take yours tomorrow—Don't bid." "He had hardly walked a dozen steps before two burly sheriff's deputies grabbed him and hauled him off to their car. The Gestapo couldn't have done it more efficiently. The sale went on."[60]

The Amish kept pleading for exemption from participation in OASDI. In April 1960, seventeen Amish bishops sent Congressman Dague, who had introduced still another bill on their behalf, a petition stating that the OASI "is abridging to our faith, and doctrine which is older than this Government" and affirming their intent "to defend and protect these costly pearls, and not trade them for an old-age and survivors insurance." A similar petition went to Congressman John Brademas of Indiana.[61] These entreaties availed nothing.

Farmer Valentine Byler of New Wilmington, Pennsylvania, was one of the "hard core" of Amish holdouts about the OASDI tax. In late 1959 the IRS estimated that he owed $214.43, and requested payment. Byler replied that "We Amish pay our taxes because the Bible says, 'Render unto Caesar the things that are Caesar's.' But our religion forbids insurance." The IRS's argument that the OASDI levy is a tax, not an insurance premium, did not faze Byler, who retorted, "Doesn't the title say 'Old Age, Survivors and Disability *Insurance'?*" He ignored a summons to meet an IRS representative to answer queries about his finances, and was subsequently taken to court for contempt, but the case was dismissed. By April 15, 1961 he owed $308.96 in OASDI self-employment taxes. Three days later, he was notified that some of his property would be seized for tax delinquency. While Byler was plowing his fields a few days later with three of his six horses, IRS agents turned up at Byler's farm, crossed his fields, unhitched his team of Belgian mares, and led them away. On May 1 the IRS sold them at auction, obtaining $460, keeping $308.96 for taxes due and $113.15 to cover feed and auction costs, and sending Byler the remaining $37.89.[62]

The IRS action caused an uproar in the press and Congress. However, it was over the persecution of the peaceful, self-reliant Amish and infringement of religious freedom; the implications regarding Social Security's use of language went unnoticed. After a long conference with several Amish bishops and their lawyer in September, IRS Commissioner Caplin announced a moratorium on further seizures of Amish horses, and that he would seek a tax moratorium for the Amish until Congress or the courts could decide the matter. Byler filed for a tax refund, the Amish went to court, and numerous unavailing attempts were made in Congress to exempt the Amish.[63] Finally, the 1965 amendments of the Social Security Act (which, among other things, created Medicare) included an exemption for the Amish from participation in Social Security.[64]

Essentially, the Amish who suffered levies or property seizures were punished for believing Social Security's self-description—but not doing what its promoters wanted them to do. Note too the use of language, calling the OASDI levy an insurance premium or a tax depending on which term would evoke the desired response in the intended audience. The Amish cases confirm that Social Security's self-depiction as insurance was and is meant to to foster support and financing for the program—not to accurately describe reality.

The Power of the Word:
Social Security, Language, and Truth

From *Flemming v. Nestor* and the Amish incidents flow still deeper implications.

What happened to Nestor and Byler witnesses vividly for what Richard
Weaver called "the power of the word." Words, nouns especially, he observed,
are the means humans use to sort out and order reality. Moreover, words have
an "evocative power" to call forth responses in persons who hear or read
them, to shape belief and thus to govern actions. Definitions, Weaver insisted, must be scrupulously accurate; he attributed much of humanity's con-
fusion of thought to "failure to insist upon no compromise in definition."[65]
Interestingly, one of his examples of words' "power to define and to compel"
was taken from semanticist S. I. Hayakawa's *Language in Action,* whereby
one group of citizens terms payment of cash benefits to unemployed persons
"relief" and another called it "social insurance," the two groups quarreling
bitterly over whether "insurance" was being properly used![66]

Weaver was right. Without words, we cannot sort out reality or even think.
Our choice of words to identify or describe things necessarily is decisive for
determining how we think about them, our beliefs about them, and our actions about them. Nestor's loss of his benefits and Byler's loss of his horses
were ultimately caused by these men's understandings of what the words
"earned right" and "insurance" mean and what Social Security was when
described with these words—a powerful demonstration that from words and
ideas flow physical, real-world consequences. Words matter; the beliefs they
form matter; and they matter a great deal.

Far from being abstruse, pointless quibbles, then, struggles over semantics
are among the most decisive battles a society wages; they are literally battles
over the basic orientation of the mind. The victor controls the choice of words
used think about things, hence has enormous power over our minds and
conduct. Social Security's advocates succeeded in getting their semantics
accepted virtually without opposition; with few exceptions, the media
adopted and complaisantly transmitted them to the public. The acceptance of
Social Security's semantics—its version of reality—was one of the most momentous events in modern American history. The fates of Nestor and Byler
witness for the mighty grip that Social Security's self-promotion had on the
American mind by 1955, just twenty years after Social Security was created.
In 1978, Nelson Cruikshank, one of Social Security's stalwart supporters,
dismissed the semantic controversy over whether or not Social Security is
insurance as "a silly battle."[67] Yet he and other Social Security partisans
certainly took it seriously enough, and as *Flemming v. Nestor* and the Amish
cases show, it was anything but silly. The depiction of Social Security as
"insurance" and its benefits as an "earned right" was decisively affecting how

Americans perceived the program, what they believed about it, and how they acted with respect to it, even unto appeals to the highest court in the land and defiance of the tax gatherer. Social Security's language matters—decisively.

Nestor's and Byler's misfortunes also prove that language must render reality accurately—and that Social Security's language does not do so. One's understanding of reality cannot be accurate unless one's language is accurate. Quite apart from the evidence presented in the foregoing chapters, the discrepancy of Social Security's self-depiction from its reality is proved by the fact that Nestor and Byler, who treated the self-depiction as an accurate descriptor of reality and acted accordingly, suffered for it. Nestor made and lost his case because he believed what he was told, that benefits are an "earned right," when they are not. Byler lost his horses because he believed what he was told, that Social Security is "insurance," and its tax a "premium" or "contribution," when they are not.

Tellingly, the government's brief for *Flemming v. Nestor* explicitly admitted the discrepancy between the program's language and its reality: "While the Act uses the term 'insurance,' the true nature of the program is to be determined from its actual incidents."[68]

All of this justifies, too, Weaver's concern that language be used honestly. In his view,

> language is a covenant among those who use it. It is in the nature of a covenant to be more than a matter of simple convenience, to be departed from for light and transient causes. A covenant—and I like, in this connection, the religious overtones of the word—binds us at deeper levels and involves some kind of confrontation of reality. When we covenant with one another that a word shall stand for a certain thing, we signify that it is the best available word for that thing in the present state of general understanding.[69]

Affirming that language is a means of accurately describing reality, of communicating truth, Weaver was alarmed at the spread of a relativistic philosophy of language—that is, a belief that a word's meaning "will depend upon the time and place in which it is used and the point of view of the user. Meaning is thus contingent and evolving. There is no absolute position from which the application of a word can be judged 'right' or 'wrong.' There can be only shrewd estimates of what the majority of men will accept."[70]

On the evidence, "shrewd estimates of what the majority of men will accept" aptly describes the thinking that lay behind the decision to apply "insurance" to Social Security and "premiums" or "contributions" to its taxes, and "trust fund" to its Treasury account. Such terminology clearly presupposed a belief that language's proper purpose is influencing the consciousness of others in pursuit of one's agenda. Weaver also noted an observation by fire insurance investigator Benjamin Lee Whorf that in his experience people could be misled by "verbal analogies," with accidents sometimes happening because "people behaved in response to the conventional meanings of words," for example, men being careless with matches and cigarettes around "empty" gasoline drums.[71] Nestor and Byler were indeed misled by certain "verbal analogies"—but their response to the conventional meanings of "earned right" and "insurance" was contrived, not accidental.

Once, it was taken for granted that the purpose of words is to sort and order reality and accurately convey information about it—a belief epitomized by the homely but powerful statement of Ulysses Grant's boyhood teachers: "A noun is the name of a thing."[72] But the prevailing Western notion of language's proper function declined over the centuries, in Weaver's view disastrously, from *vere loqui* to *recte loqui* to what he called *utiliter loqui*—from "speaking truthfully to speaking correctly to speaking usefully." Under the last, he added, "language is a tool which will enable you to get what you want if you use it well—and well does not mean scrupulously."[73]

As Weaver's last phrase indicates, there is a grave moral problem, and danger, in a relativist, pragmatic view of language and truth. Such a corrupt conception of language implies a self-authorization to misapply words and use euphemisms in order to advance one's ends or to conceal the nature of what one is doing. It implies too a belief that if such methods work, they are morally right. This in turn presupposes that the end justifies the means.

While our focus is on the false consciousness and its pernicious effect on policymaking, the ethical aspect cannot be altogether ignored. The unfortunate reality, which has to be faced, is that the performance of Social Security's architects and promoters is disturbing from an ethical point of view that values truthfulness. What stands out from our narrative of Social Security's history beginning with the drafting of the original bill in 1935 is a subordination of truth to the imperatives of getting the Congress, the Supreme Court, and the public to accept Social Security and sustaining the public's willingness to pay Social Security's taxes. The Social Security bill was written with titles physically separated and picked clean of insurance language to enable it to survive a possible challenge by the Supreme Court. The people were told that Social Security nonetheless *is* insurance to get them to accept it, while at the same time the Court was told it's *not* insurance to get the Court to accept it. Then the whole country was given an inaccurate picture of Social Security for decades as "insurance" paying benefits "as an earned right." As the fates of Nestor and Byler demonstrate, the effect of all this was not innocuous. In light of what these men suffered because they took the Social Security Administration at its word, and the enormous potential harm which Social Security's false consciousness threatens to inflict on retirees and taxpayers alike, Ray Peterson's charge of "public immorality" is thoroughly justified.

And the power of the word explains Social Security's defenders' reflexive response to critics: the accusation of undermining public confidence in the program. In a compelling sense the charge is accurate. Repeated incessantly over the years from every quarter, the phrases "Social Security is an insurance program," "your payroll tax is really a contribution (or premium)," "benefits are paid as a matter of right/earned right," and so on serve as incantations—phrases endlessly repeated to transform the consciousness of their audience, inducing belief and suspension of critical judgment by the power of sugges-tion and sheer repetition. Incantations work only if they go unchallenged and uninterrupted. The critics, with their dissonant counterpoint "But it's not insurance," *threaten to break the spell*—and thereby to undermine the public's faith.

Subsequent actions by Social Security advocates also bore out Weaver's concerns about language, reality, and truth. Instead of choosing words ac-cording to Social Security's nature, they began arguing as if Social Security's nature is determined by the label given it. Having had Social Security's misidentification as insurance written into the law in 1939, and thus in a sense *incorporated into the reality of Social Security,* Social Security's parti-sans could then cite this "reality" to justify their position.

A striking example occurred when Wilbur Cohen debated Milton Fried-man about Social Security in 1972. Friedman pointed out, rightly, that "so-cial security is not in any meaningful sense an insurance program in which individual payments purchase equivalent actuarial benefits," that it is in-stead a program of taxes and transfers, and that the insurance analogy rested on deliberate propagation of falsehoods. "The very name—old age and survi-vors insurance—is a blatant attempt to mislead the public into identifying a compulsory tax and benefit system with private, voluntary, and individual purchase of individually assured benefits."[74] Cohen's response affirmed the things Weaver deplored:

> [H]is criticism suggests he doesn't know what insurance is. He gives us a Friedman definition, but not the right definition.
>
> Insurance does not mean that you have to have an actuarial relationship between the individual contributions and the individual benefits. No group insurance in the United States would qualify as insurance under his test. [Irrelevant, since OASI was pitched to the public since 1935 as closely analogous to *individual* policies.] .... If he wants to have his definition, let him have it. It is not mine, and *it is not the definition that the Congress of the United States has given. Congress has called social security insurance. . . .*
>
> Mr. Friedman calls a lot of the things he doesn't like about social security rheto-ric. . . . People do live by rhetoric. . . . I believe in rhetoric *because it makes a lot of things palatable that might not be palatable to economists.* [75] (italics added)

That is, insurance rhetoric is good because it makes the program's taxes "palatable." It reflects what Weaver called "shrewd estimates of what the majority of men will accept." Cohen later went on in the same vein:

Mr. COHEN: . . . The other guarantee [of social security], which I know Mr. Friedman doesn't like, is the expectation of future contributions, or taxes as he prefers to call them, from the individuals covered under the system. . . .

Mr. FRIEDMAN: As I prefer to call them! Do you really think that it is a straight, nonrhetorical description to call compulsory taxes "contributions"?

Mr. COHEN: Congress has done so. . . . [76]

And who had proposed the insertion of insurance terminology into the text of the Act? The Social Security Board, headed by Arthur Altmeyer, who was assisted by Mr. Cohen.

Chief Actuary Robert Myers made a like exercise in asserting the reality by appealing to the label, stating in his textbook *Social Insurance and Allied Government Programs* and its successor *Social Security* that "it should be noted that Congress has referred to OASDI benefits as 'insurance benefits' and has designated the part of the Internal Revenue Code that levies the employer an employee taxes to support the OASDI system as the 'Federal Insurance Contributions Act.'"[77] Very much to his credit, however, Dr. Myers had the honesty to admit, beginning in the 1975 edition of *Social Security,* that the Social Security Board "very definitely overstressed the insurance concept in the early days of the program. . . . primarily to build up and maintain public support for the social security program—by drawing upon the good name and reputation of private insurance."[78] This, of course, bears out Weaver's observations.

Social Security's fostering of a false consciousness is a grave danger to the general welfare. All contracts, commitments and agreements, indeed all intercourse between persons, and all civilized life, rest on mutual trust and confidence, which in turn rest on an implicit faith that language is honest and is being used honestly, without intent to manipulate, that one can safely, reliably believe what one hears and reads and act on it. That is, civilization rests ultimately on the covenant of language.

So does governance. The consent of the governed rests not on a pragmatic calculation to leave a state of nature, as social contract theory would have it, but on faith in their government: faith that the government's word is credible, that it can be trusted—ultimately, that the government makes and keeps the covenant of language with the governed. The legitimacy and authority of a regime, especially in a democracy or republic, depends on its perceived fitness and worthiness to rule, which rests on its moral character. And much of that is bound up in its keeping the covenant of language.

Thanks to Social Security's rupture of that covenant, a dangerously wide discrepancy exists between popular understanding of Social Security and the reality. Faith in government has been grievously strained in recent decades; for many Americans, it has collapsed altogether. Should Social Security's projected future financial crisis come to pass, Social Security's rupture of the covenant of language in a matter of vital concern to all Americans threatens to inflict a serious blow to that faith—and with it, to our political and social order.

Notes

1. Wollenberg, "Vested Rights in Social-Security Benefits," p. 299.
2. Ibid., pp. 299-300.
3. Ibid., pp. 300-307.
4. Ibid., pp. 308-351.
5. Ibid., pp. 352-358. See discussion of "vesting" in chapter 7.
6. Wollenberg, "Vested Rights in Social-Security Benefits," pp. 301, 351-352, 359.
7. Ibid., pp. 334, 359.
8. Ibid., pp. 359-360.
9. Cohen, Ball, and Myers, "Social Security Act Amendments of 1954: A Summary and Legislative History," p. 10.
10. U.S. Supreme Court, *Records and Briefs,* October Term, 1959, No. 54, *Flemming v. Nestor,* Brief for the Appellant [hereafter *Flemming v. Nestor,* Brief for the Appellant], pp. 3-4.
11. Ibid.
12. U.S. Supreme Court, *Records and Briefs,* October term, 1959, No. 54, *Flemming v. Nestor,* Appeal from the United States District Court for the District of Columbia, pp. 25-26.
13. *Flemming v. Nestor,* Brief for the Appellant, pp. 4-5.
14. Ibid., p. 2.
15. Ibid., pp. 28-40.
16. Ibid., p. 10.
17. Ibid., p. 40.
18. Ibid., p. 41.
19. Ibid., pp. 10-11.
20. Ibid., p. 53.
21. Ibid., pp. 54-56.
22. Ibid., pp. 56-59.
23. Ibid., p. 59.
24. Ibid., pp. 59-60.
25. Ibid., p. 61.
26. Ibid., p. 14.
27. Ibid., pp. 61-62.
28. Ibid., pp. 62-64.
29. Ibid., p. 64.
30. Ibid., pp. 64-65.
31. Ibid., pp. 66-68.
32. Ibid., p. 68.
33. Ibid., pp. 69-70.
34. Ibid., pp. 70-87.
35. *Flemming v. Nestor,* 363 U.S. 603, at 608. The opinion also addressed the propriety of the single-judge District Court exercising jurisdiction over the case, and whether Nestor's benefit termination amounted to punishing him without a trial, which aspects of the case are ungermane for our purpose.
36. Ibid., at 609.

37. Ibid., at 609-610.
38. Ibid., at 610.
39. Ibid., at 610-611.
40. Robert J. Myers, "Social Security's Financing Problems: Realities and Myths," p. 41.
41. *Flemming v. Nestor,* 363 U.S. 603, at 611.
42. Ibid., at 612.
43. Ibid., at 622-623.
44. Ibid., at 624-625.
45. Ibid., pp. 631-632.
46. "High Court Rejects Pension Plea By Man Deported as Former Red," *New York Times,* June 21, 1960, 19; "High Court Delays Union-Dues Ruling a Year," *Washington Post,* June 21, 1960, A10.
47. Peterson, "Misconceptions and Missing Perceptions of our Social Security System (Actuarial Anesthesia), Discussion," pp. 888-889, 903.
48. Ray M. Peterson, "Social Security Challenges," *Journal of the American Society of Chartered Life Underwriters,* vol. 14, no. 4 (Fall 1960), p. 324.
49. Ibid., pp. 324-327.
50. James F. Oates, Jr., "Social Legislation," *Best's Insurance News (Life Edition),* January 1961, pp. 20-21.
51. Ray M. Peterson, "The Coming Din of Inequity," *Journal of the American Medical Association,* vol. 176, no. 1, April 8, 1961, pp. 118-124.
52. Ray M. Peterson, "Communications: Comments on 'The Challenge of Aging to Insurance' by Wilbur J. Cohen," p. 93.
53. Wilbur J. Cohen, "Communications: Author's Reply," p. 98.
54. Ibid., p. 99.
55. Faulkner, "Social Security and Insurance—Some Relationships in Perspective," pp. 204, 205.
56. U.S., Congress, House, Committee on Ways and Means, *Social Security Legislation: Hearings before the House Committee on Ways and Means,* 85th Cong., 2nd sess., 1958, pp. 41-42, 470-471, 500-502.
57. U.S., Congress, House, Congressman Herman T. Schneebeli, "Persuasion of the Amish (To Join Social Security)," Extension of Remarks, 87th Cong., 1st sess., May 23, 1961, *Congressional Record,* Appendix, 107:A3367.
58. *Social Security Legislation: Hearings,* p. 503.
59. Congressman Schneebeli, "Persuasion of the Amish (To Join Social Security)," A3367; Clarence W. Hall, "Revolt of the 'Plain People,'" *Reader's Digest,* November 1962, pp. 75-76.
60. U.S., Congress, Senate, Senator Alexander Wiley, "What Freedom?" Extension of Remarks, 86th Cong., 1st sess., July 27, 1959, *Congressional Record,* Appendix, 105:A6460-A6461.
61. U.S., Congress, House, Congressman Paul B. Dague, "In Defense of Freedom From Too Much Government," Extension of Remarks, 86th Cong., 2nd sess., April 5, 1960, *Congressional Record,* Appendix, 106:A3019-A3020; U.S., Congress, House, Congressman John Brademas, "Petition From a Plain People," Extension of Remarks, 86th Cong., 2nd sess., May 18, 1960, *Congressional Record,* Appendix, 106:A4615-A4616.
62. Congressman Schneebeli, "Persuasion of the Amish (To Join Social Security)," A3367; Hall, "Revolt of the 'Plain People'," *Reader's Digest,* November 1962, p. 76; "U.S. Sells 3 Mares For Amish Tax Debt," *New York Times,* May 2, 1961, 34; "The Amish and Taxes," *New York Times,* May 22, 1961, 45.

63. See, e.g., Congressman Schneebeli, "Persuasion of the Amish (To Join Social Security)," A3367-A3668; "Embattled Amish Farmers," *Commonweal,* June 2, 1961, pp. 244-245; "Government Seizes Amish Property," *The Christian Century,* June 7, 1961, p. 701; U.S., Congress, House, Congressman James Bromwell, "Of Costly Pearls and Old-Age Survivors Insurance," Extension of Remarks, 87th Cong., 1st sess., September 11, 1961, *Congressional Record,* Appendix, 107:A7122; "Another Round in Amish Fight Against Social Security Tax," *U.S. News & World Report,* September 25, 1961, p. 123; Hall, "Revolt of the 'Plain People'," *Reader's Digest,* November 1962, pp. 76-78.

64. Wilbur J. Cohen and Robert M. Ball, "Social Security Amendments of 1965: Summary and Legislative History," *Social Security Bulletin,* vol. 28, no. 9 (September 1965), p. 17.

65. Weaver, *Ideas Have Consequences,* pp. 148-149, 166, 168.

66. S. I. Hayakawa, *Language in Action* (New York: Harcourt, Brace and Co., 1941), pp. 3-12, cited in Weaver, *Ideas Have Consequences,* pp. 152-153.

67. Nelson H. Cruikshank, "A Philosophy for Social Security," Third Robert M. Ball Lecture, delivered December 12, 1978, National Headquarters of the Social Security Administration, Baltimore, Maryland, p. 4. (www.ssa.gov/history).

68. *Flemming v. Nestor,* Brief for the Appellant, p. 10.

69. Richard M. Weaver, *Language is Sermonic: Richard M. Weaver on the Nature of Rhetoric,* ed. Richard J. Johannesen, Rennard Strickland, Ralph T. Eubanks (Baton Rouge: Louisiana State University Press, 1970), p. 136.

70. Ibid., p. 117.

71. Ibid., p. 127.

72. Bruce Catton, *A Stillness at Appomattox* (Garden City, NY: Doubleday & Co., Inc., 1953), p. 38.

73. Weaver, *Language is Sermonic,* pp. 188-189.

74. Wilbur J. Cohen and Milton Friedman, *Social Security: Universal or Selective?* (Washington, DC: The American Enterprise Institute, 1972), pp. 25-27.

75. Ibid., pp. 53-54.

76. Ibid., p. 84.

77. Robert J. Myers, *Social Insurance and Allied Government Programs* (Homewood, IL: Richard D. Irwin, Inc., 1965), p. 9; Robert J. Myers, *Social Security* (Homewood, IL: Richard D. Irwin, Inc., 1975), p. 13; Robert J. Myers, *Social Security,* 2nd ed. (Homewood, IL: Richard D. Irwin, Inc., 1981), p. 12; Robert J. Myers, *Social Security,* 3rd ed. (Homewood, IL: Richard D. Irwin, Inc., 1985), p. 13; Robert J. Myers, *Social Security,* 4th ed. (Philadelphia: Pension Research Council, Wharton School, University of Pennsylvania, 1993), p. 14.

78. Myers, *Social Security,* p. 14; Myers, *Social Security,* 2nd ed., p. 13; Myers, *Social Security,* 3rd ed., p. 14; Myers, *Social Security,* 4th ed., p. 15.

9

Shoring Up the False Consciousness

*"One of the most constant general
characteristics of beliefs is their intolerance.
The stronger the belief, the greater its
intolerance. Men dominated by a certitude
cannot tolerate those who do not accept it."*

—Gustave LeBon[1]

As if the insurance controversy and *Flemming v. Nestor* had never happened, Social Security and its allies kept promoting OASDI as insurance in the following decades. In a 1963 *Reader's Digest* piece, Michael Belloise, an SSA field representative, pointed out that many persons were eligible for but not getting benefits because they weren't aware of their rights under the program, and that Social Security was trying to find them so they could get their benefits. "But it's your money we're trying to pay you," he ended. "Shouldn't you be coming to *us* for it?"[2]—thereby reinforcing Americans' belief that Social Security benefits are "their money" and that in taking them they are just getting back what they paid in. Interviewed in 1964 by *U.S. News & World Report* in a time of rising concern for the safety of Social Security pensions (future obligations were rising, and the trust fund was dwindling), Commissioner Robert Ball, in what was implicitly an attempt to depict OASDI as a better insurance buy than private insurance, argued that it had been altered to the beneficiary's advantage, whereas private insurance, with its contracts, locks beneficiaries into paying and receiving fixed sums.[3]

Social Security's mass-consumption publications too kept using the insurance analogy. The booklet *Your Social Security* began thus:

> The basic idea of social security is a simple one: During working years employees, their employers, and self-employed people pay social security contributions which are pooled in special trust funds. When earnings stop or are reduced because the worker retires, dies, or becomes disabled, monthly cash benefits are paid to replace part of the earnings the family has lost.[4]

In his *Newsweek* column, economist Milton Friedman called this passage "Orwellian doublethink," citing the labeling of taxes as "contributions," the impression that the "trust funds" were important when they were really small contingency funds, and the misleading impression that one's own contributions financed one's benefits. *Your Social Security* added that "Nine out of ten working people in the United States are now building protection for themselves and their families under the social security program." In fact, Friedman noted, they were supporting current beneficiaries. A taxpaying worker "is in no sense building his own protection—as a person who contributes to a private vested pension system is building his own protection." Moreover, the booklet left readers a sense that benefits are tied to contributions ("building protection"), when in fact the tie between benefits and taxes is weak.[5]

Nonetheless, throughout the sixties and seventies, the SSA used "insurance" and "trust fund" terms. Social Security critic Warren Shore reported in 1975 that in sixty-one publications the SSA referred to its payroll taxes as either "contributions" or "premiums." Social Security pamphlets published in 1974 stated in fifty-three separate places that payroll tax revenues were "pooled" and that "contributions paid to the pool" would later partly replace lost earnings.[6]

Mainstream news media continued to assist Social Security in this. After Congress increased benefits 7 percent in 1965, *Business Week* reported that a man who retired in 1966 at age sixty-five and lived 13.5 years, his life expectancy at sixty-five, would, together with his wife, receive $32,400 in benefits. She would also collect widow's benefits, receiving $6,540 if she lived the expected five more years, making a total of $38,940. This is a great bargain, because assuming he had paid the maximum tax, his "total lifetime premium" would be under $3,000 (matched by his employer).[7] Even while criticizing the liberalization of Social Security the following year, *Business Week* implicitly affirmed "the insurance principle that was intended to guide its expansion."[8]

As the years passed, some of Social Security's great architects and administrators entered private life, from which vantage point they continued to promote the program they loved. The insurance analogy remained prominent in their advocacy. In successive editions of his textbook on Social Security, Chief Actuary Robert Myers, who resigned in 1970, continued to maintain that OASDI is insurance.[9] Commissioner Ball, who retired in 1973, published a chatty, admirably lucid, popular-level book on Social Security in 1978. He took the issue of Social Security as insurance so seriously that he spent an entire chapter on it. OASDI is indeed insurance, Ball stoutly insisted, because "The essence of insurance is risk sharing," and under Social Security, this occurs. Moreover, as with private insurance, one makes a small certain payment to the insurer, who agrees to make specified payments in the event of defined large uncertain loss. As for getting one's money's worth under Social

Security, Ball pointed out, rightly, that under term life insurance or fire insurance, one only gets a payment if the risk actually eventuates; but even if one does not die in the period of coverage or one's house never burns, one still gets one's money's worth, because one was protected against the loss. Hence it is normal in insurance for some to get more out of it than others.[10]

Ball's keen awareness of "the power of the word" showed, too. He argued that the Social Security levy is both an insurance premium and a tax, and maintained that while it was legally a tax, he preferred the term "contribution" to reflect its "special" nature. As for "insurance," he deemed it "important that people view the social security institution as an insurer, with the obligations of the insurer toward the contributor who has paid his premium in anticipation of protection against the specified risks" spelled out in the law. "It is the nature of the program as insurance that gives it much of its stability." For high government officials to regard social security as just another tax-funded government program, as they did in 1975, "is a threat to the security of the whole benefit system." President Gerald Ford had proposed putting a 5 percent cap on the Social Security COLA to help reduce the budget deficit. Ball doubted that Ford would have done so if he had perceived Social Security benefits as "insurance obligations." He concluded tellingly that "we need to promote such a perception if the system is to give true security; we need more emphasis on the fact that social security is insurance."[11] All of this is a confession that the "true security" of the program rests on public perceptions and beliefs, on psychology, on public acceptance of a certain image of Social Security, hence that "fact" must receive "more emphasis"; and that the program has no inherent "true security," but rather that security must be fabricated by using insurance language.

Ball spent another entire chapter wrestling with the retirement earnings test (also known as the "retirement test" or "earnings test"), which, he acknowledged, was "undoubtedly the most unpopular provision" of Social Security. In response to public pressure, the test had been liberalized repeatedly; by 1978 it merely reduced benefits by $1 for every $2 of earnings above $4,000 for beneficiaries aged sixty-five and over (if one was seventy-five or over, the test did not apply). Ball argued, reasonably, that retirement benefits were after all meant to protect against income loss through retirement, and that paying a retirement benefit to someone who had not retired made no sense. He made the equally reasonable points that the test had been much liberalized to address the valid complaint that it hurt work incentives, and that it sought to strike an acceptable balance between competing desirable goals: holding down program costs, and not harming work incentives. However, he never addressed the conflict between the earnings test and the "earned right" to benefits, or acknowledged that in making receipt of benefits depend on income level, the retirement test was necessarily a means test—indeed, his book asserted elsewhere that Social Security has no means test.[12]

Endlessly reiterated, the insurance language had its intended effect. A 1973 *New York Times* national survey found that most Americans believed that they "owned" the money deducted from their earnings through the payroll tax.[13] And when in the following year a reader wrote a letter to the *Times* proposing that Social Security payments be denied to persons with incomes above a certain amount, another reader replied that this proposal "reveals ignorance of the nature of Social Security, which is not welfare but insurance for which premiums are paid."[14]

Rising Criticism, Misleading Replies

Some challenges did occur. In 1960, Henry Hazlitt, a prominent free-market economic journalist, and former New Dealer Raymond Moley published separate columns in *Newsweek* attacking the government's practice of calling Social Security "insurance," Hazlitt observing that the payroll tax worked to make the term plausible, Moley pointing out that the program "has been judged by the Supreme Court to be a gratuity, not the payment of an equity in insurance."[15] Accurate as these attacks were, they fell, like Curtis's and Stokes's before them, on deaf ears.

But as the sixties wore on and the OASDI tax kept rising, more criticisms emerged, including arguments that young people would get a worse deal from the program than their elders.[16] A pattern emerged too of the program's defenders calling critics scaremongers, offering misleading and only half-true rebuttals, and accusing critics of undermining the public's confidence in Social Security.

When an August 1967 *Washington Post* editorial criticized inequities in Social Security, argued that young people then paying payroll taxes would not get their money's worth, and pointed out that OASDI's programs, "contrary to popular belief, are not a system of insurance in which people pay their own way, but a curious mixture of insurance and welfare provisions," HEW Undersecretary Wilbur Cohen replied in a letter to the editor that the editorial "is a compounding of misinformation." Young taxpaying workers "could not buy comparable insurance protection from private insurance companies at anywhere near the amount they pay for their social security protection," Cohen declared, adding that the editorial ignored "the fact that the benefits provided by the present social security law are very much lower than the benefits that will actually be paid" to current young workers when they retire. As wages rise, he pointed out, "benefits can be increased." Cohen apparently took economic growth, making continually increasing benefits affordable, for granted. He berated the *Post* for not understanding what insurance is and asserted that insurance "undertakes to indemnify or guarantee against a loss from a contingent event." (But by this criterion, a transfer payment compensating for losses from the contingent event of becoming poor, such as Aid to

Families with Dependent Children, qualifies as insurance.) Social Security insures against the risk of loss of work earnings, Cohen added, paying "insurance benefits" when earnings stop due to retirement, death or disability, with the loss of income "actuarially evaluated," and "contributions sufficient to cover these costs" levied. Moreover, "The right to these benefits is a legal right enforceable in the courts. These are the characteristics that make Social Security insurance."[17] What of risk pooling and risk transfer to an insurer, the defining characteristics agreed on by the insurance scholars?

In October 1967, *Reader's Digest* ran an article by its Washington editor, Charles Stevenson, titled "How Secure is Your Social Security?" Stevenson opened with the arresting assertion, "Our Social Security insurance is in trouble." After quoting supporting remarks by Republican Representatives John Byrnes of Wisconsin and Tom Curtis of Missouri, he argued that Social Security's publications such as *Your Social Security* and statements by HEW Undersecretary Cohen imply "a genuine insurance setup with guaranteed payment—but there isn't any." He pointed out, correctly, that most of one's Social Security taxes go to pay current benefits for others, the rest financing general government expenses, offset by Treasury IOUs credited to the "trust fund." Quoting extensively from the government brief in *Flemming v. Nestor* denying that Social Security is insurance, Stevenson observed, again correctly, that this "doesn't jibe with the government's assurances that people who invest in Social Security are 'building protection for themselves.'"[18]

Social Security's blanketing-in of millions of persons who did not pay anything like enough taxes to pay for their benefits also received much attention, as did the "squeeze on the young" through a soaring tax burden. Stevenson pointed out that 90 percent of a retiree's benefits are paid by taxes on younger workers, who therefore would get a worse deal than current elderly, and quoted Chief Actuary Myers as saying that "The benefits that a new entrant gets are not equal in value, over the long run, to the contributions that he and his employer pay," and Commissioner Ball as saying that "young employees do not, in those terms, get their money's worth." Comparing Social Security benefit figures and calculations by the National Association of Life Underwriters, Stevenson argued that private insurance could give a worker a better annuity for the money. Moreover, whether OASDI would give younger workers anything at all in their retirement "will depend entirely on the mood of the taxpayers of that later day." Social Security's unfunded liability (excess of promised benefits over projected revenues) was $350 billion—bigger than the national debt. Stevenson asked how much the economy can afford and how willing young people would be to keep paying higher taxes when they realize they'll get back less than they contribute, and raised the problem of rising Social Security taxes reducing people's ability to save for their own retirement. He recommended examining Social Security and restoring it "to its legitimate purposes before it is too late."[19]

This was a far more serious threat to Social Security's prestige than an occasional stray newspaper or magazine piece. *Reader's Digest* is an American institution, with readership in the tens of millions, guaranteeing Stevenson very wide exposure. Moreover, the *Digest,* as is its practice with articles it deems especially significant, made reprints available.[20]

A measure of the danger Stevenson's thrust posed is that no less a figure than HEW Undersecretary Cohen undertook to parry it. House Ways and Means Committee Chairman Wilbur Mills (D-AK) inserted both Stevenson's article and Cohen's reply in the *Congressional Record.* Cohen opened by calling the article "misleading" and creating "anxiety and fear" about Social Security that was "groundless." He disputed Stevenson's claims about Social Security's squeeze on young people and the better deal offered by private insurance, reiterating much of his argument from his letter to the *Post.*[21] He did not refute the quotations of Myers and Ball.

But the worst aspect of Cohen's statement was his treatment of *Flemming v. Nestor.* Cohen pointed out, correctly, that Stevenson had not quoted from the Court opinion itself. But he went on to assert that "the Court decision reversed the contention of the Justice Department brief (prepared in the Eisenhower administration) that the program is not an insurance program" and quoted the paragraph in the decision which stated that Social Security "may be accurately described as a form of social insurance." (Cohen's *en passant* attempt to discredit the brief on partisan grounds, by pointing out that it was prepared in the Eisenhower administration, need not be taken seriously. Recall that the administration shrugged off Curtis's efforts and presided over two massive expansions of Social Security. The Eisenhower administration was hardly hostile to Social Security.) He added, "The fact is that the Supreme Court rejected many of the contentions made in the brief" and quoted the passage that a covered employee's interest "is of sufficient substance to fall within the protection from arbitrary government action afforded by the due process clause."[22]

As Cohen knew perfectly well, having participated in it, insurance scholars were at the time of *Flemming v. Nestor* engaged in a debate as to whether social insurance is insurance—and Harlan's opinion did not settle it. Moreover, as should be clear, Cohen's quotations of the Court's opinion were tendentiously selective. He omitted the passage arguing that an employee's noncontractual interest to benefits "cannot be soundly analogized to that of the holder of an annuity, whose right to benefits is bottomed on his contractual premium payments"; the statement that giving people "accrued property rights" would rob the program of needed flexibility; the explicit invocation of the reservation of power clause; and the statement that "a person by the Act has not such a right in benefit payments" as would make every denial of "accrued" interests a violation of due process. Moreover, as this supply of deliberately-omitted quotes makes clear, it just simply isn't true that the opinion reversed many contentions of the brief. It *upheld* the brief's central point about Nestor's lack of an accrued property right and *upheld* the brief's explosion of the government's own insurance myth.

Cohen concluded by berating Stevenson for "scaremongering" and "a great disservice to the millions" of current and prospective beneficiaries. "A glib and superficial attack on a program so important to millions of Americans is not a contribution to the American people."[23]

Other Democrats joined the attack. Senator Abraham Ribicoff (D-CT) inserted Stevenson's article and Cohen's response in the *Congressional Record.*[24] Congressman Charles H. Wilson (D-CA) excoriated the *Reader's Digest* as "up to its old tricks of slanted rightwing attacks on American institutions" for running "a clever hatchet job on social security," and accused it of meanwhile "constantly dipping into the public till to add to its own profits," since magazine publishers paid less than 30 percent of postal delivery costs.[25] Two days later Congressman Charles Vanik (D-OH) roasted the *Digest* for "a misleading and unfair attack on the social security program . . . . designed to sow anxiety and fear among the 23 million beneficiaries of social security. A more diabolical scheme to unnecessarily worry our senior citizens could not have been conceived." The *Digest* had taken the "even more scandalous and reprehensible step" of running newspaper advertising for the piece showing a Social Security card torn up—"a new low in its unprincipled and vicious attack on the social security program."[26]

Thousands of elderly Americans organized to picket *Reader's Digest* offices in ten cities across the country simultaneously at 11:00 A.M. on December 11, 1967. "The phenomenon of America's senior generation organizing a protest against a magazine which enjoys the largest circulation in America," Congressman James Scheuer (D-NY) rightly observed, "is significant."[27] It was an early demonstration of a political clout that would cow Congress for the next three decades.

By the mid-seventies, Social Security taxes were exerting rising pressure on young workers' incomes, and discontent was growing. More criticisms erupted, provoking the same pattern of response.

In a compact and biting article in the June 1974 *Harper's,* University of Miami law and economics professor Roger LeRoy Miller branded Social Security "the cruelest tax," observing, correctly, that the OASDI payroll tax was not only regressive, but soaring, the fastest-growing tax since World War II. Miller pointed out numerous inequities in Social Security, such as the fact that millions of Social Security taxpayers would never get a penny in benefits because they did not work enough quarters in covered employment to qualify. Noting the government's duplicitous position on Social Security as "insurance," Miller cited the brief for *Flemming v. Nestor* and concluded that "To call Social Security an insurance scheme requires a special skill in deforming the meaning of words in the English language." Rather, benefits are "basically welfare, pure and simple," an income transfer from the employed to the unemployed. Social Security outperforms private insurance only because it can forcibly extract ever-more resources through taxes. However, this implicit compact between generations, he predicted, would likely disintegrate as workforce growth slows and the tax burden becomes unbearable. Miller also predicted—correctly as it turned out—a rapid run-up in the Social Security tax before the year 2000 and a slowdown in the growth of benefits. He called for leveling with the public about Social Security's true nature; ending the regressive payroll tax and financing the program out of general revenues; making Social Security's implicit debt of unfunded liabilities explicit and issuing Federal Reserve bonds to cover it; and allowing anyone who wants to leave Social Security to do so, provided he buys a private annuity and/or survivors' insurance.[28]

Everything Miller said was true, and his piece was a heavy blow to Social Security's prestige. But some responses revealed readers' belief in Social Security's self-advertisement. When his article was reprinted in the *Oregonian,* one reader wrote that Miller was trying to "stir up discontent about something that probably has been of more good for more people than anything that has ever happened in this country." As for Miller's proposal for private insurance, the reader scoffed that it was unlikely that a private plan could give "the service now rendered for the present cost."[29]

By then a professor of Social Security at the University of Michigan, Wilbur Cohen recognized the threat Miller's article posed and took it upon himself to write a reply. When only five publications carried it, Cohen decided to write a white paper rebutting the critics. He drafted a 4,500-word statement, "Social Security: A Sound and Durable Institution of Great Value." It was co-signed by former HEW Secretaries Arthur Flemming, John W. Gardner, Robert Finch, and Elliott Richardson, and former Social Security Commissioners Robert Ball, Charles Schottland, and William L. Mitchell. Issued in February 1975, it received wide publicity; the *Washington Star-News* published a lengthy excerpt, and both the excerpt and the white paper itself were entered in the *Congressional Record* by pleased Democratic Congressmen.[30]

"Attacks on the system designed to create doubts of its soundness and durability are a disservice to the nation," Cohen thundered, pouring scorn on "current destructive attacks" and "irresponsible attacks." "The most vicious of these attacks" is the one that benefits may not be paid to future claimants. Payment is mandated by law, and Congress has done as much as it could to bind future Congresses to honor the program's commitments. The program "is, in effect, a compact between the people of the United States and their government." While acknowledging Congress' legal power to violate the "compact," Cohen fell back on the ultimate argument: for a Congress to do so would be political suicide.[31]

As to the nature of Congress' commitment to taxpayers, Cohen acknowledged that OASDI must be flexible to meet changing conditions. He talked only in terms of improvements, and acknowledged that no one could say that under no circumstances would any individual "suffer some loss" through "overall improvements in the system." What one could say is that "the congressional sense of fair play" (toward Nestor?) gives assurance that Congress will not abuse its power to amend the program.[32]

Assertions that OASDI is not insurance are "unfounded," Cohen maintained, arguing that Social Security embodies insurance's "central element" of financial protection against specific hazards through "a pooling of contributions and a pooling of risk," with benefits payable "as a matter of legal right" should hazards eventuate. We have seen how dubious the application of risk pooling is to OASDI, and as for "legal right," in private insurance, this right is contractual, whereas one's "legal right" under Social Security is contingent, tentative and statutory. Referring to both as a "legal right" and implying that the one carries the same force as the other, which was clearly Cohen's intent, is a conflation of two radically dissimilar things. "It is fallacious to argue, as some persons do," he added, "that the workers' payments are not insurance contributions because they are taxes." Apparently it was fallacious of the Justice Department to argue, in its brief for *Flemming v. Nestor,* presumably in consultation with the Social Security Administration, that Social Security's "contribution," being a true tax, "is not comparable to a premium under a policy of insurance promising the payment of an annuity commencing at a designated age." In another confirmation of "the power of the word," Cohen characterized Congress' designation of Social Security as "insurance" in the statute as an "indication of the character of the commitment it was undertaking," and noted that the Supreme Court "has stated that the term 'social insurance' accurately describes the program."[33] This of course is similar to Cohen's misreporting of *Flemming v. Nestor* in response to Stevenson.

Cohen dismissed the charge that the "trust fund" contained mere government IOUs and then refuted a charge Miller had not made, that the program is regressive—when all Miller had (rightly) argued was that the *tax* is regressive. As for the complaint that the poor were paying too much in Social Security taxes and that for many persons of modest means, the Social Security tax exceeded their income tax, Cohen asserted that "there is nothing inherently inequitable" in this and that to say that the poor are overtaxed for social security "is to say either that their protection should be reduced"—an assertion that one's taxes determine one's benefits ("protection"), which Cohen knew was untrue—or that they should be more subsidized by wealthier taxpayers.[34]

Cohen wound up by asserting over and over that benefits are "an earned right."[35] Nestor had appealed to that same assertion.

Just two days after Cohen et al. issued their white paper and held a press conference assuring the public that benefits were not in danger, the Hsiao panel informed the Senate Finance Committee that Social Security's finances were worse than previously believed, and that its benefit structure should be overhauled soon, and additional financing provided. Otherwise, the "trust fund" would be exhausted by the late 1980s.[36]

Similarly, in his 1972 debate with Milton Friedman, Cohen asserted that payment of benefits was

> a matter of right—a moral, political and statutory right similar (but not identical) to the contractual right of payment under private insurance policies. Again, while we may discover that there are no absolute rights, even with respect to private contracts, the effort is to make the right to social security as certain as it can be in an uncertain world.[37]

But the "right" to benefits is *not* "similar" to a private insurance policy's contractual right. It is quite different—as Altmeyer had testified, Wollenberg and the *Flemming v. Nestor* brief had argued, and Nestor's fate proved. Cohen of course knew about these things, and could hardly have not known that they refuted him. And saying that private contracts don't give absolute rights either is ungermane.

In response to criticism or concern about the program's future, then, Cohen and his confederates told less than they knew, and what they did tell was less than accurate.

Group Insurance: Another Untenable Analogy

Another recourse of Social Security's defenders in those years, either to parry criticism of the program or the insurance analogy or to keep the latter alive, was to analogize Social Security to private *group* insurance. In arguing that group insurance would not live up to Milton Friedman's definition of insurance, Cohen was implicitly making this analogy.[38] Former Chief Actuary Myers argued that Social Security resembles group insurance in many respects.[39] Responding to criticisms of Social Security by Robert Alberts in the *New York Times Magazine* in 1974, Social Security Deputy Commissioner Arthur Hess argued that critics of the alleged inequity of the retirement test "don't look at Social Security as the gigantic group insurance it actually is," whereby costs and benefits are supposed to "make sense from the group or social point of view, not just from the standpoint of individual equity."[40] Former Commissioner Ball went much further in describing OASDI as "a form of group insurance operated by the government" and "a very large-scale group insurance and retirement system." Social insurance and private group insurance have much in common, he wrote. Both social insurance and many private group plans charge all participants the same premium. Both are less concerned with individual equity—a close tie of the individual's risk to his premium—than with providing a certain amount of protection for all group members. An exact link of individual benefits to individual contributions "is no more relevant to the question of whether social security is insurance than . . . of whether group insurance is insurance."[41]

However, this is another adding of dissimilars, since taxpayers individually pay "contributions" to Social Security, which is not always true of group insurance. More fundamentally, while group insurance does transfer risk to the insurer, OASDI does not. And in any case its "premiums" have nothing to do with risk. Since Social Security is therefore not insurance, it cannot be group insurance.

Besides which, the earlier campaign to market Social Security had drawn explicit analogies to *individual policies:* "you pay a sort of premium on what might be called *an insurance policy*," "*your insurance policy* with the government," "*your* premiums," "*your* benefits," "*your* account." How did the same program which was analogized to *individual policies* suddenly become *group* insurance? Had its nature and operations changed? Since they had not, the new analogy was obviously a re-labeling for marketing purposes.

New Myths for Old: The "Compact Between Generations"

Even as the SSA and its sympathizers kept the insurance analogy alive, some mainstream professional economists were repudiating it. In a Brookings study of Social Security, Joseph Pechman, Henry Aaron, and Michael Taussig pointed out that despite a superficial resemblance to insurance and despite the reiteration of the insurance analogy by Cohen and others, "the insurance analogy is no longer applicable to the system as it has developed." For one thing, Social Security's taxes are levied on the current earnings of current workers and benefit payments are based on past earnings of insured workers, and the link between an individual's "contributions" and his benefits is "extremely tenuous," since benefits and taxes vary greatly for people within any age group, and as of 1968, when the study was published, current beneficiaries were getting benefits far above those they would have been entitled to based on their own tax payments.[42]

Pechman et al. recognized that private group retirement plans also have situations in which some beneficiaries get far more than they would based on their own contributions. As we saw, Social Security gave similar windfalls, for example, in 1950, hence at first glance the analogy between OASDI and group insurance looks strong. In fact, Pechman et al. argued, the program's analogy to private group insurance is "nearly as tenuous as the more general analogy between individual insurance and social security." For one thing, private group insurance lapses if a firm or industry fails to make premium payments for the plan, whereas OASDI's workers have portable quarters of coverage even if their employers go out of business.[43]

More to the point, Pechman et al. rightly argued that the distinction between private insurance and Social Security turns on whether the current
worker is paying with his payroll taxes for the benefits of current retirees and
survivors or for the benefits of himself and his family in the future. Under
private insurance, an individual's premiums are tied to his or his family's
future benefits. Under Social Security, though, one's taxes pay not for one's
own future benefits, but for those of current beneficiaries. One's own benefits
will be paid by future taxpayers. Also, under private insurance, one pays
higher premiums if one wants better future coverage or benefits. Social Security, by contrast, raises one's payroll taxes to pay higher benefits *for others;*
there's no link between one's taxes and the size of one's *own* benefits.[44]

John Brittain's study for Brookings of the payroll tax likewise noted the
weakness of the insurance analogy, pointing out that social insurance and
private insurance had several important differences, e.g., risks or expected
costs for social insurance can't be given the same sort of actuarial analysis as
is done in the private sector due to additional, imponderable, unforecastable
factors such as changes created by future legislation. Brittain concluded that
"the insurance analogy is a contrived one at best and is certainly not forced
upon us by the facts."[45]

It is worth noting that Brookings is ideologically liberal, not conservative, and that Pechman, Aaron, Taussig, and Brittain were *sympathetic* with
Social Security and its objectives. (Aaron has, as we saw, ridiculed the idea
that there's any crisis in Social Security, and denounced privatization.) Indeed, even while demolishing the insurance analogy, Pechman, Aaron, and
Taussig attempted to legitimize OASDI another way. Instead of thinking of it
as insurance, they argued, we should see it as

> an institutionalized compact between the working and nonworking generations, a
> compact that is continually renewed and strengthened by every amendment to the
> Social Security Act. When viewed in this light, a social security program has the
> eminently desirable function of forcing upon society a decision at each point of time
> on the appropriate division of income and consumption between workers (the young)
> and nonworkers (the old, survivors, and disabled). Workers and nonworkers alike
> participate in the democratic process that shapes this vital distributional decision. The
> social security system is the mechanism by which society settles the issue of
> intergenerational (worker-nonworker) income distribution through the political pro-
> cess rather than leaving its resolution to private decisions and the market.[46]

The "compact (or contract) between generations" view of Social Security
has gained, as we shall see, enormous credence. Hence subjecting it to critical
scrutiny is imperative.

Here again we see "the power of the word." "Contract" and "compact" are
powerful terms which, in a nonlegal context, evoke—and are intended to evoke—
an impression of a solemn and binding agreement which cannot be broken.

However, they *also* mean that the said agreement was entered into voluntarily, deliberately, and knowingly by all parties after informed discussion.

Social Security entails a coerced intergenerational income transfer, whereby each generation is supported by the taxes paid by the following generation, which in turn anticipates like support from the next generation. But no compact, express or implied, exists. The American people were never asked to make such a "compact," and never made one. A "contract" or "compact" which only one party (one generation—specifically, that generation's Congress) creates and forces on the other (young present and future taxpayers), while reserving to itself the sole power to rewrite it, and under which generations yet unborn are bound without being consulted, much less consenting, hardly lives up to the term. Payroll tax withholding removes the last vestiges of the "compact" fiction; the taxpayer's resources are extracted by *force majeure* in advance of any decision on his part to consent. Nor is he ever asked to consent to FICA withholding. As for the opinion polls expressing widespread support for Social Security in the thirties and forties, polls are not compacts. They have no power to bind one generation on another's behalf.

The reality is that a social-welfare measure was approved by Congress in 1935. Succeeding generations confronted not a "compact" but a *fait accompli.* They never explicitly gave their consent, and were never asked to. Rather, they went along with decisions taken by others, partly because of the huge "insurance" promotional campaign; partly because of the lopsided generosity of benefits relative to taxes in the early years and the enticing prospect that they, too, could get Social Security "insurance bargains"; partly because of the huge prestige enjoyed by Franklin Roosevelt and the New Deal after the Depression; and partly because it is most people's nature to accept their institutional and political milieu as almost metaphysically given, conform to it, and submit to its demands unless and until they become unbearable. But it is hardly accurate to label such passive acceptance as "consent," much less as entering into a "contract" or "compact," with these terms' implication of a specific agreement consciously made after informed discussion.

The depiction of "society" as actively making decisions to renew this compact "at each point of time" through the political process is also untenable. Discretionary spending flows from explicit, formal decisions and actions by Congress, in the form of appropriations bills "at each point of time," but entitlement spending, mandated by previously passed laws, does not. The absence of discussion and conscious decision is default, not consent. And the country and successive Congresses and presidents have preferred to *avoid* an intergenerational distribution decision rather than let Social Security "force" one "at each point of time"; there has been no major legislation embodying such a decision since 1983.

Far from renewing and strengthening the "compact," Social Security amendments such as the 1939 liquidation of the money-back guarantee and the original lump-sum death benefits, the 1977 tax increase, the 1983 increase in the retirement age and introduction of benefit taxation, make the claim of a "compact" or "contract" untenable. Through them, Congress has repeatedly torn up and rewritten the "contract" or "compact," and compelled the other "parties" to accept the result. Those injured by these contract violations—which is what these revisions are, if one accepts the word "contract"—have no recourse, which is untrue of real contracts.

As for the assertion that "Workers and nonworkers alike participate in the democratic process," the reality is seriously lopsided. Anticipating our next topic, retiree pressure groups such as the American Association of Retired Persons participate intensively indeed, and decisively shape the outcome. But the taxpayers, who had no organizations like Third Millennium as a countervailing force on their behalf until long after the 1977 and 1983 legislation which determined the tax-benefit hand they were dealt, barely participated in crafting those laws, and haplessly took what they were given.

The idea of Social Security as "a compact between generations" would have credence only if periodic nationwide plebiscites or referenda were held whereby each generation's workforce voted on whether or not they were willing to continue to support the Social Security program. Only if a majority of voters aged 18-64 voted to continue to support the program, could it be fairly said that that generation had in fact made a compact to support its elders through OASDI. But no such plebiscite or referendum has ever been held.

A variant on the "compact"/"contract" myth is that Social Security is an "implicit contract" between generations or between government and people. But Congress has already repeatedly broken and rewritten this "implicit contract."

The claim that Social Security represents a "compact between the generations," then, is utterly lacking in rigor and basis in reality. The point is not to attack motives, but to establish that this term is untenable, and fosters an inaccurate understanding of Social Security.

The Defenders: Unions and the Empire of the Elderly

Meanwhile, a very large and powerful interest group was rising in America: the elderly lobby. It played a decisive role in the history of Social Security, beginning with the sixties.

The rise of seniors' advocacy groups owed much to organized labor, which had always been a vigorous friend of Social Security. Unions had worked with the Social Security Board to combat the pay-envelope scare in 1936. The American Federation of Labor-Congress of Industrial Organizations (AFL-CIO) provided considerable support for the expansion of Social Security in the Eisenhower years to include disability insurance, and worked for further expansion to include health insurance, drafting bills and writing speeches for members of Congress who favored such expansion. Especially prominent among labor's supporters of Social Security was Nelson Cruikshank, who in 1944 became the American Federation of Labor's staff specialist in social insurance and in 1955, when the AFL and CIO merged, became the AFL-CIO's Social Security director, holding this post until his retirement in 1965.[47]

Unions also opened their publications to Social Security officials and advocates, thus providing transmission belts for disseminating Social Security's myths to members. In 1975, the *AFL-CIO American Federationist* printed Wilbur Cohen's white paper, and marked Social Security's fortieth anniversary with an article by Cohen lauding Social Security's achievements, its various kinds of "insurance protection," and the labor movement for defending "the 'earned right' and 'contributory social insurance' philosophy which assures workers and their families of the payment of benefits irrespective of the political ups-and-downs in Congress."[48] The January 9, 1975 issue of the *Machinist,* the monthly magazine of the International Association of Machinists, ran an article titled "Social Security Your 'Best' Insurance," consisting mostly of quotes by Cohen, Cruikshank, Social Security Commissioner James Cardwell, and others vouching for Social Security's soundness, superiority over private insurance, and so on.[49] Three years later, Cohen defended Social Security in the *American Federationist* again. It was a "myth," he wrote, that "social security is not insurance." On the contrary, "It is a social insurance program which . . . can give maximum insurance protection to individuals at relatively low premiums, since it does not have to build up relatively large reserves." OASDI is not welfare, but "a nationwide group insurance plan." And so on.[50]

Founded in 1958, the American Association of Retired Persons (AARP) was the first of the advocacy groups for seniors. Open to all Americans aged fifty-five or over, retired or not, it dealt comprehensively with the quality of life for the elderly. Besides providing services to members, such as drugs and hearing aids at reduced prices, it lobbied Congress on behalf of seniors, which meant in favor of Social Security and Medicare and their expansion. In 1961 came the National Council of Senior Citizens (NCSC), a federation of elderly groups which had developed from union locals, with labor providing the financial support for its creation. After retiring from the AFL-CIO, Cruikshank was elected president of the NCSC. It too supported Social Security and Medicare. At first these groups were small; as of 1968 the AARP had 800,000 members, the NCSC just 2,000.[51]

The Gray Panthers, in name and spirit reflecting the militancy of the times, followed in 1971. Founded by Margaret Kuhn, the Gray Panthers sought to combat "ageism" (discrimination due to age) and raise awareness about aging through seminars, organizing local groups to agitate about issues, and so on. Meanwhile the elderly population grew from 19.1 million Americans sixty-five and over in 1965 to 20.9 million in 1970 and 23.3 million in

1975.[52] By the mid-seventies the elderly lobby's numbers were formidable. In 1975 the AARP boasted 5,000,000 members; the NCSC had 3,000 autonomous clubs, councils and other groups with a total of 3,000,000 members.[53]

As a consequence of the rising controversy over Social Security in the 1970s, additional groups emerged dedicated to serving Social Security recipients and lobbying in favor of Social Security and Medicare. In 1979, prompted by Carter administration proposals to trim benefits, Save Our Security (SOS) was created, with Wilbur Cohen as chairman. A coalition of organizations containing Social Security beneficiaries and taxpayers, such as the AFL-CIO, Gray Panthers, and United Auto Workers, it sought through speeches and numerous publications to protect Social Security and Medicare from cuts and expand coverage. The National Committee to Save Social Security and Medicare followed in 1982, and had 847,000 members by 1986 and five million by 1990. Other Social Security advocacy groups included the Alliance for Social Security and Disability Recipients (founded in 1982) and the National Organization of Social Security Claimants' Representatives (founded in 1979). There were even two special groups, NOTCH and End Notch Discrimination, devoted exclusively to representing Social Security recipients born in 1917-1921, the "notch babies," whose benefits were trimmed by the 1977 Social Security rescue legislation, and to seek restoration of their benefits to pre-1977 levels.[54]

Concern over Social Security and Medicare also spurred the continued growth of other senior groups. Another factor was the accelerating growth in the senior population: to 26.1 million aged sixty-five and over in 1980, 29.1 million by 1985, and 32 million in 1990.[55] By 1986 the Gray Panthers had 100 local groups under its umbrella, the NCSC had 4,000,000 members, and the AARP had a staggering 16,000,000.[56] Just four years later, AARP membership topped 28,000,000; it stood at 32,000,000 in 1995.[57]

The picketing of the *Reader's Digest* had been done when the elderly lobby was small, the AARP having only 800,000 members the following year. By the time Social Security's finances faced a crisis in the seventies and eighties, the gray legions were a mighty force. As events would prove, a momentous and powerful symbiosis had developed: Social Security would protect its constituency, and its constituency would protect Social Security. Moreover, which was decisive, the gray legions' ranks were filled with people who had been steeped in Social Security's promotion as insurance and other myths since 1935—that is, in many cases, for most of their adult lives. And in the experience of most of them, Social Security *seemed* to live up to its advertising. Unsurprisingly, the false consciousness about Social Security was very widespread among the elderly. With the rise of the elderly lobby America now had a very large, well-organized, vigilant and militant pressure group steeped in the false consciousness, with sufficient political power to give that false consciousness a decisive influence on policymaking.

Notes

1. Gustave LeBon, *Gustave LeBon: The Man and his Works,* p. 211.
2. Michael Belloise, "Are You Missing Out on Social Security Payments?" *Reader's Digest,* June 1963, pp. 73-76.
3. "Back of the Questions About Social Security," *U.S. News & World Report,* December 7, 1964, pp. 54-55; "An Official Interview: How Safe is Your Social Security Pension?" *U.S. News & World Report,* December 7, 1964, p. 58.
4. Milton Friedman, "Truth in Advertising," *Newsweek,* June 14, 1971, p. 88.
5. Ibid.
6. Warren Shore, *Social Security: The Fraud in Your Future* (New York: Macmillan Publishing, 1975), p. 19.
7. "Personal business," *Business Week,* April 23, 1966, p. 137.
8. "Editorial: Dangerous Ground for Social Security," *Business Week,* August 26, 1967, p. 128.
9. Myers, *Social Insurance and Allied Government Programs,* pp. 8-10; Myers, *Social Security,* pp. 11-14; Myers, *Social Security,* 2nd ed., pp. 11-14; Myers, *Social Security,* 3rd ed., pp. 12-15; Myers, *Social Security,* 4th ed., pp. 12-16.
10. Robert M. Ball, *Social Security Today and Tomorrow* (New York: Columbia University Press, 1978), pp. 289, 300-302.
11. Ibid., p. 307.
12. Ibid., pp. 264-287, 121-123.
13. Shore, *Social Security: The Fraud in Your Future,* p. 6.
14. Letters to the Editor: What Social Security Is," *New York Times,* January 31, 1974, 32.
15. Henry Hazlitt, "Insurance—Or Handout?" *Newsweek,* June 13, 1960, p. 88; Raymond Moley, "Legislating in Dog Days," *Newsweek,* August 22, 1960, p. 92.
16. See chapter 3, pp. 1-3.
17. "Inequities Compounded," *Washington Post,* August 20, 1967, B6; "Letters to the Editor: Cohen on Social Security," *Washington Post,* September 1, 1967, A20.
18. Charles Stevenson, "How Secure Is Your Social Security?" *Reader's Digest,* October 1967, pp. 75-78.
19. Ibid., pp. 78-80.
20. Ibid., p. 80.
21. U. S., Congress, House, "Statement by Wilbur J. Cohen, Under Secretary of Health, Education, and Welfare," in Representative Wilbur D. Mills, "How Secure is Your Social Security," Extension of Remarks, 90th Cong., 1st sess., September 27, 1967, *Congressional Record,* 113: 27028.
22. Ibid., p. 27029.
23. Ibid. Stevenson later made a dignified and devastating reply to Cohen's rebuttal. Besides some of the falsehoods enumerated here, Stevenson exposed numerous others, for example, Cohen's misrepresentation of Rep. Byrnes's remarks. Stevenson's reply was entered in the *Congressional Record* by Representative Harold Collier (D-IL). (U. S., Congress, House, Representative Harold Collier, "How Secure is Your Social Security?" 90th Cong., 1st sess., November 20, 1967, *Congressional Record,* 113: 33271-33274.) Congressman Curtis of Missouri also entered a critical response to Cohen's rebuttal in the *Record.* While parting company with Stevenson on some points, Curtis maintained that Cohen's reply "seeks to build upon the half-truths and misleading conclusions the Social Security Administration has been promulgating" and "does not forthrightly state" basic differences of opinion about OASDI. (U. S., Congress, House, Representative Thomas

Curtis, "How Secure is Your Social Security?" 90th Cong., 1st sess., October 10, 1967, *Congressional Record*, 113: 28461-28466.)

24. U. S., Congress, Senate, Senator Abraham Ribicoff, "The Security of Social Security," Extension of Remarks, 90th Cong., 1st sess., September 29, 1967, *Congressional Record*, 113: 27358-27362.

25. U. S., Congress, House, Representative Charles H. Wilson, "How Scrupulous is the Reader's Digest?" 90th Cong., 1st sess., October 2, 1967, *Congressional Record*, 113: 27476.

26. U. S., Congress, House, Representative Charles Vanik, "The Reader's Digest and Social Security," 90th Cong., 1st sess., October 4, 1967, *Congressional Record*, 113:27788.

27. U. S., Congress, House, Representative James Scheuer, "Senior Citizens to Picket Reader's Digest," 90th Cong., 1st sess., December 6, 1967, *Congressional Record*, 113:35259.

28. Roger LeRoy Miller, "Social Security: The Cruelest Tax," *Harper's,* June 1974, pp. 22-27.

29. "The People's Own Corner," *The Oregonian,* June 7, 1974, quoted in William C. Mitchell, *The Popularity of Social Security: A Paradox in Public Choice* (Washington, DC: American Enterprise Institute, 1977), pp. 14-15.

30. "Social Security Is Defended; Attacks Called a Disservice," *Washington Post,* February 11, 1975, A1, A7; "Ex-Officials Back Pension System," *New York Times,* February 11, 1975, 23; "A Defense of Social Security—," *U.S. News & World Report,* February 24, 1975, pp. 74-75; U. S., Congress, House, Representative Stephen L. Neal, "Americans Raising Serious Questions About Social Security System," 94th Cong., 1st sess., February 19, 1975, *Congressional Record,* 121: 3654-3656; U. S., Congress, House, Representative James Burke, "White Paper on Social Security," 94th Cong., 1st sess., February 25, 1975, *Congressional Record,* 121: 4195-4197.

31. Wilbur Cohen et al., "Social Security: A Sound and Durable Institution of Great Value," in Burke, "White Paper on Social Security," *Congressional Record,* 121:4195-4196.

32. Ibid., p. 4196.

33. Ibid.

34. Ibid., pp. 4196-4197.

35. Ibid., p. 4198.

36. See chapter 3, pp. 3-4.

37. Cohen and Friedman, *Social Security: Universal or Selective?,* p. 3.

38. Ibid., p. 53.

39. See, e.g., Myers, *Social Security,* 2nd ed., pp. 13-14; Myers, *Social Security,* 3rd ed., pp. 14-15.

40. Arthur E. Hess, "What of the Price?" in "Letters," *New York Times Magazine,* September 8, 1974, p. 52.

41. Ball, *Social Security Today and Tomorrow,* pp. 4, 289, 303, 303-304.

42. Joseph A. Pechman, Henry J. Aaron, Michael K. Taussig, *Social Security: Perspectives for Reform* (Washington, DC: The Brookings Institution, 1968), pp. 68-69.

43. Ibid., pp. 69-70. Disputing Pechman et al. in their disavowal of the insurance analogy, former Chief Actuary Myers asserted, erroneously, that they "fail to consider the various group insurances," which in his view shared many features with social insurance (see, e.g., Myers, *Social Security,* 2nd ed., p. 13 n. 3).

44. Ibid., pp. 70-71.

45. John A. Brittain, *The Payroll Tax for Social Security*, pp. 7-12.
46. Pechman, Aaron and Taussig, *Social Security: Perspectives for Reform*, pp. 75-76.
47. Derthick, *Policymaking for Social Security*, pp. 110-128.
48. "Secure Retirement: Sorting Out the Myths," *AFL-CIO American Federationist*, April 1975, pp. 1-8; Wilbur J. Cohen, "Social Security 40 Years Later," *AFL-CIO American Federationist*, December 1975, pp. 9, 10.
49. U.S., Congress, Senate, Senator Frank Church, "The Truth About Social Security," 94th Cong., 1st sess., April 10, 1975, *Congressional Record*, 121:9914-9916.
50. Wilbur J. Cohen, "Social Security: Focusing on the Facts," *AFL-CIO American Federationist*, April 1978, pp. 7, 10. Other articles in the AFL-CIO's journal supportive of Social Security include Floyd E. Smith, "Social Security: Myths and Realities," *AFL-CIO American Federationist*, April 1974, pp. 11-12; Larry Smedley, "Maintaining the Balance in Social Security," *AFL-CIO American Federationist*, February, 1979, pp. 20-25.
51. *Encyclopedia of Associations*, 5th ed. (Detroit, MI: Gale Research Inc., 1968), vol. 1, pp. 532, 565; Derthick, *Policymaking for Social Security*, pp. 197-198.
52. *2000 OASDI Annual Report*, p. 147, Table II.H1.—Social Security Area Population as of July 1 and Dependency Ratios, by Alternative and Broad Age Group, Calendar Years 1950-2075.
53. *Encyclopedia of Associations*, 9th ed. (Detroit, MI: Gale Research Inc., 1975), vol. 1, pp. 613, 663.
54. *Encyclopedia of Associations*, 20th ed. (Detroit, MI: Gale Research Inc., 1986), vol. 1, pt. 2, p. 1364; Berkowitz, *Mr. Social Security: The Life of Wilbur J. Cohen*, pp. 300-302; *Encyclopedia of Associations*, 24th ed. (Detroit, MI: Gale Research Inc., 1990), vol. 1, pt. 2, p. 1752; *Encyclopedia of Associations*, 29th ed. (Detroit, MI: Gale Research Inc., 1995), vol. 1, pt. 2, p. 2160.
55. *2000 OASDI Annual Report*, p. 147, Table II.H1.
56. *Encyclopedia of Associations*, 20th ed., vol. 1, pt. 2, pp. 891, 893, 993.
57. *Encyclopedia of Associations*, 24th ed., vol. 1, pt. 2, p. 1234; *Encyclopedia of Associations*, 29th ed., vol. 1, pt. 2, pp. 1511-1512.

10

Fruits of the False Consciousness:
Drift, Evasion, Denial, Paralysis

*"None of the system's difficulties are likely to
be resolved as long as the idea that Social
Security is insurance persists."*

—Time, *1976*[1]

*"We retirees are 35 million strong.
Anyone who dares to tamper with this
program will be voted out of office."*

—*Letter to the editor,* U.S. News & World
Report, *1984*[2]

By 1975, a rapidly growing elderly population, reckless expansion of benefits, and an economy whose ability to pay for them had been impaired by inflationary stagnation, had gotten OASDI into serious trouble, requiring action by Congress to avert program bankruptcy.

Since Social Security is a program of taxes and transfer payments, a financial rescue necessarily requires increasing taxes, decreasing benefits, or some combination thereof. Because OASDI entails both present and future taxes and transfers, these options refine still further: (1) raise taxes on current taxpayers; (2) raise taxes on future taxpayers; (3) cut benefits for current beneficiaries; (4) cut benefits for future beneficiaries; or (5) a combination thereof.

The first and third are the riskiest politically, because of the possibility of political forfeits in the near future, and the third is by far the riskiest of all, given the enormous power and numbers of the elderly, their organization, their passionate interest in Social Security, and their numerous sympathizers in and out of government. Though more numerous, Social Security's taxpayers are nowhere near as well-organized and intensively engaged in Social Security issues. By far the least dangerous option politically is to push the pain of a Social Security rescue into the future, by raising future taxes and cutting future benefits. Of the groups participating in Social Security, the young have the least political power, hence are the least dangerous to inflict costs upon. Young adults have only recently organized, and to a very limited extent, hardly enough to offset the power of the huge, well-established elderly lobby; and in any event their interests and attention are divided. Children will bear the cost of present decisions about future taxes and benefits, but cannot vote and have no one to speak for them; many, indeed, are yet unborn.

These political considerations dictated the nature and consequences of the rescue attempts of the seventies and eighties. Efforts which relied on imposing costs on current beneficiaries were spurned, in one case vehemently, with decisive effects for the future. The 1977 rescue, which relied primarily on raising current and future taxes, was politically costly and cast long shadows. The most politically successful, the 1983 rescue, shifted most of the pain into the future. And all of these outcomes were decisively shaped by the false consciousness generated by Social Security's decades-old misleading promotion.

I do not, of course, mean to imply that that the false consciousness was the *only* cause of these outcomes. Beneficiaries will naturally oppose benefit cuts for the obvious reason of prospective loss. However, the singular ferocity of their response, and that of their allies, owed much to their beliefs about Social Security, which the program's advocates had made such an immense effort to shape.

The 1977 Rescue

The hapless Ford administration made brief but foredoomed efforts to deal with OASDI's worsening finances. In his 1975 State of the Union message, President Gerald Ford proposed putting a 5 percent ceiling on Social Security COLAs. Extremely unpopular, Ford's proposal found no takers; no bills were introduced for it, no hearings held. There was no further action in 1975.[3]

One factor driving Social Security toward ruin was "double indexing," an error in adjustment of benefits for inflation legislated in 1972. Until COLAs were adopted that year, Congress had made *ad hoc* increases in benefits to catch up with inflation at roughly two-year intervals, raising benefits by slightly more than prices. These adjustments were applied not only to current beneficiaries, but to new ones, even though the latter were earning higher average wages than current retirees had received. In those days, wage increases were running ahead of inflation, inflation itself was relatively modest, and the number of taxpaying workers supporting each beneficiary was quite high, so this "coupling" of current and future benefit adjustments did not strain the program's finances. But in the seventies, inflation exploded, and began driving up wages themselves as unions fought to protect real wages with hefty wage increases and COLAs. Hence current workers' (i.e., new and future beneficiaries') Average Monthly Earnings (AME), the basis for calculating one's basic Social Security benefit, the Primary Insurance Amount (PIA), were reflecting rising inflation. OASDI's COLAs then adjusted benefits for inflation. Benefits for new and future retirees were thus being indexed for inflation not once, but twice, hence growing far faster than employment income. What all this meant was that the replacement rate—Social Security benefits as a share of pre-retirement employment income—for new and future retirees would keep rising over time until eventually most retirees would get benefits replacing the lion's share of their work incomes, and some would get benefits actually exceeding those incomes.[4] Since Social Security was meant to be only a partial income replacement, and except for lower-income workers a fairly modest one at that, this double indexing would become unaffordable fairly quickly.

The 1975 Advisory Council on Social Security recommended revising the formula for calculating benefits to get rid of double indexing, and in 1976 President Ford proposed that Congress do so, and raise the tax rate for both employees and employers by 0.3 percent, effective in 1977. But the proposal did not get beyond hearings and bill markup sessions by the House Ways and Means Committee's Social Security subcommittee.[5] Meanwhile OASDI's long-term outlook was deteriorating rapidly; the projected seventy-five-year actuarial balance under intermediate assumptions, as a percentage of taxable payroll, was -5.32 in 1975, -7.96 in 1976, and -8.20 in 1977.[6] Something had to be done, and soon.

In a rare instance of perceptiveness and honesty about Social Security in the mainstream media, *Time* magazine reported in 1976 that although the program was not in danger of bankruptcy, it did need more money—but that "no lucid analysis of its requirements is possible as long as the idea that Social Security is insurance, rather than a federal tax, dominates debate." This was an admission that the insurance analogy was not only misleading, it had generated a false consciousness that governed how the program was being perceived and discussed. Once, Social Security had indeed resembled insurance, but, *Time* pointed out, the resemblance had disappeared long ago. Rather, Social Security "is largely a tax-financed welfare program." After reporting on the proposals afloat in the Ford Administration and Congress to shore up the program, *Time* concluded that "None of the system's difficulties are likely to be resolved as long as the idea that Social Security is insurance persists."[7] It was a prophecy abundantly fulfilled by events.

To his credit, President Jimmy Carter faced the problem promptly. On May 9, 1977, Carter announced his Social Security proposals, including decoupling the benefit formula so as to stabilize the replacement rate; gradually increasing the ceiling on earnings subject to the employer tax, and ultimately removing it, so that the employer would be taxed on his entire payroll; raising the maximum taxable income by $600 a year in 1979, 1981, 1983, and 1985; and using general revenues to make up for any shortfall in payroll tax revenue in 1975-1978 if unemployment exceeded 6 percent.[8]

But Carter's proposals collided with the false consciousness about Social Security. Wilbur Cohen endorsed Carter's proposal to use general revenues as "ingenious." However, he added, "under no circumstances" should general revenue finance more than a third of the total cost. Moreover, use of general revenues "should be justified by a very specific rationale . . . so that it does not invalidate the earned-right insurance concept of the program."[9] House Ways and Means Committee chairman Al Ullman (D-OR) rejected the general-revenue proposal outright. For one thing, he argued, it would destroy OASDI's fiscal discipline, whereby added benefits had to be paid for by increases in the payroll tax, thus imposing a check on benefit growth. For another, there was something unique about Social Security—something psychological—which general revenue financing would undermine:

> Social Security is something that should be available to every American—and available not as a gift, but available on a contributory, earned-right basis. This has been its real significance. People who get Social Security don't want to feel that they're taking funds from a welfare program. They like to feel they're taking funds from a system to which they have contributed and paid their fair share, and that they're accepting it as a matter of right—not just a right that society owes them, but a right they've earned.[10]

The proposal to use general revenues went nowhere.

And when Commerce Secretary Juanita Kreps suggested in an interview in July 1977 that delaying commencement of Social Security benefits until age sixty-eight would greatly help the program's finances, Social Security's defenders—the AFL-CIO and the elderly lobbies—pounced. The law provided for partial benefits if one retired at age sixty-two, and full benefits upon retirement at age sixty-five, and they weren't about to countenance a later retirement age. HEW Secretary Joseph Califano renounced the idea, but OASDI's defenders, unsatisfied, demanded—and got—a public statement by Kreps herself that the administration was proposing no such thing and that she hadn't been making a formal proposal.[11] The beneficiary lobbies had flexed their muscle, and the national government had backed off. The message was clear. Beneficiaries weren't about to give up anything. If restoring Social Security's soundness required sacrifices, they would have to be made by somebody else.

There was nothing for it but to raise taxes, and for the rest of the session Congress grappled with its unpalatable task. The final version of the 1977 rescue legislation passed the Senate on December 15, the very last day of the session, by 56-12; the House vote was much closer, 189-163, reflecting widespread unease in the House about the very heavy tax load the bill contained. Reluctant to call attention to a huge tax increase, President Carter signed the 1977 Amendments into law December 20, not in the White House, but in the Indian Treaty Room of the Executive Office Building in a (to Wilbur Cohen's disapproval) modest ceremony.[12]

Carter and the House had good reason to be apprehensive. The 1977 Amendments did "decouple" the benefit structure to get rid of the unintended overcompensation for inflation, and stabilize future replacement rates, but anyone becoming eligible for benefits before January 1979 was exempted. In any event, this simply undid a mistake; no beneficiary was actually hurt thereby. The central feature of the Amendments was an increase in payroll taxes by $227 billion over the 1978-1987 period, in dollar terms the largest payroll tax hike in history. The maximum taxable income was massively increased; whereas under the previous law it was $18,900 in 1879, $20,400 in 1980, and $21,900 in 1981, under the 1977 Amendments the corresponding figures were $22,900, $25,900, and $29,700, with automatic increases after 1981 to keep up with wage increases. At the same time, the payroll tax rate was significantly increased. Whereas the old law kept the employer-employee rate at 4.95 percent of taxable payroll through 2010, the new law raised it to 5.70 by 1985 and 6.20 by 1990.[13] The two taxing provisions interacted powerfully (see chapters 2 and 3) to enormously increase the tax burden on middle-class Americans—and with it, their discontent and anger about Social Security.

As soon as Congress reconvened, a movement arose to roll back the taxes. The House Ways and Means Committee voted for a payroll tax rollback, but reversed itself when Carter said he would veto it. The Social Security tax increase stayed.[14] Though unhappiness with it was widespread, nobody even thought of cutting current or future benefits enough to allow a tax rollback while keeping the program sound. When HEW Secretary Califano floated some modest benefit trims, they went nowhere (see below). Locked into benefit untouchability thanks in large measure to the false consciousness Social Security and its partisans had created, Congress and the president had no choice but to put the bulk of the burden on taxpayers, who got increasingly upset as their tax loads soared.

Califano's Defeat: Triumph of the True Believers

Although a friend of Social Security, HEW Secretary Califano had the intellectual honesty to observe in his Washington memoir that "It is a misconception to call Social Security benefits an 'earned right.'" Congress, he noted, has repeatedly revised benefits—downward as well as upward. "As a matter of law," the right to Social Security benefits "is no stronger than any other right under a federal statute that bestows benefits." What Congress does, it can undo. Moreover, Califano recognized that OASDI's levies are taxes, not contributions, and that OASDI "is very much an income transfer program." With those realities acknowledged, he wrote, "it becomes possible to look at Social Security with a view toward eliminating unnecessary benefits," such as those duplicated by other programs, and "changing the system to accommodate the needs of the 1980s and beyond." Accordingly, in 1978 Califano proposed to trim Social Security's rising costs with some benefit cuts. Under current law, one could retire early at age sixty-two and collect 80 percent of the benefits one could get by retiring at sixty-five; Califano proposed gradually phasing an increase in the earliest age of eligibility from sixty-two to sixty-five; gradually eliminating benefits for post-secondary school students, since other student-aid programs existed; and getting rid of the $255 lump-sum death benefit for burial costs, which by 1978 was worth only $90. Califano planned to grandfather persons receiving benefits before the law's enactment and apply his changes only to future beneficiaries. He estimated the proposals would trim costs by one percent.[15]

Califano's proposals alarmed and angered three of Social Security's key architects and defenders: Wilbur Cohen, former Social Security Commissioner Robert Ball, and Nelson Cruikshank, now Carter's White House Counselor and Chairman of the Federal Council on Aging. Cohen, Ball, and Cruikshank met President Carter on December 20, 1978 to argue against Califano's proposals. Carter flabbergasted Cohen with his closing remark, that "Social Security is not sacrosanct." Two days later, the three aging Social Security stalwarts met with Califano, Social Security Commissioner Stanford G. Ross, and HEW Undersecretary Hale Champion.[16]

What happened next was a vivid demonstration of the power of Social Security's myths over the minds of their true believers and their potential for exerting political pressure. Califano defended his proposals as not just money-savers but administrative reforms to improve OASDI. "But you are cutting benefits," Cruikshank retorted. "These benefits are earned rights that people have paid for and are entitled to."[17] Cruikshank and Cohen grew enraged as Califano held his ground; both repeatedly shouted at him. Even Ball, a calm and courtly man, flushed with anger. The confrontation, and the dialogue, dramatically epitomized the terrible core contradiction in Social Security Elmer Wollenberg had fingered so long ago: on the one hand, the need, for political and philosophical reasons, for both the rhetoric and the reality of inflexible, inviolate guarantees; on the other, the need to be flexible in the face of economic realities.

"There are reductions of over one billion dollars in benefits that people have earned," Cohen was almost shouting.

I responded firmly . . . "These are not 'earned' in any true sense. People get a lot more out of Social Security than they put in. Any program has to be changed as the times change. Benefits were added when the program had surplus funds. Today, it's under a severe financial strain that's going to get worse. . . . "

"The worst mistake," Cohen said, "was when Social Security became part of the federal budget. We should go back to separating it out. Then you wouldn't cut it to meet a budget target."

"The worst mistake would be to treat it separately." I was now getting annoyed. "The claims of senior citizens for tight dollars have to be weighed against other claims. The unified budget faces up to those kinds of considerations."

Cohen exploded. "What you just said proves you don't believe in the Social Security program. It is a separate program. People have rights. You don't believe that."

"Social Security needs to be reviewed periodically like any other program. We can ease the impact of cuts by not letting them apply to anyone now receiving those benefits. But changes have to be made."[18]

Repeatedly Cohen accused Califano of trying to destroy Social Security, of not having his heart in it. Moving, in Califano's words, "sideways and back and forth on the balls of his feet like a fighter ready to uncork a barrage of jabs," Cohen threatened Califano: "If you propose these changes, I'm going to organize all the senior citizens groups to picket you wherever you speak. Wherever you go, they'll be there picketing you."[19]

In February 1979, Cruikshank attacked Califano's proposals before the House Select Committee on Aging. Cutting benefits for budgetary reasons, he said, "represents a breach of faith between the government and the millions of Social Security contributors and could go a long way toward eroding the confidence people have in their government." Ball and Cohen concurred. Cohen organized Save Our Security (SOS) to picket Califano and put pressure on Congress. It worked. While Califano was picketed only once, Carter could not get anyone in Congress to introduce the proposed Social Security cuts, and they sank without a trace.[20] Once again the Social Security myths—and their true believers—had demonstrated their power.

Reagan's Rout: Victory for the False Consciousness

But the most spectacular demonstration came later. Enormous and onerous though it was, the 1977 tax increase failed to solve Social Security's problems. The long-term actuarial deficit had fallen from an appalling -8.20 percent of taxable payroll, but remained at a troublesome -1.46 percent. Moreover, Chief Actuary Haeworth Robertson warned, a very large actuarial deficit of -4.29 percent remained for the final third of the 75-year long-term period.[21] The short-run outlook was grim, too; in 1980, the Board of Trustees reported that OASDI had a deficit of nearly $2 billion in fiscal 1979; that by 1982 at the latest, OASI would be unable to pay benefits when due; and that OASDI's trust fund would be exhausted by calendar 1985. OASI's projected demise, the Trustees wrote, was "an immediate problem that requires early attention by the Congress."[22]

Like Carter, Ronald Reagan courageously grasped the Social Security nettle. On May 12, 1981, Health and Human Services Secretary Richard

Schweiker sent Congress the Reagan administration's proposals for Social Security reform. Rather than raise taxes further to strengthen OASDI's cash flow, the administration proposed to rely on benefit cuts. Among the most important were: (1) in 1982-1987, increase the Primary Insurance Amount benefit formula's "dollar bend points" (dollar amounts breaking up one's Average Indexed Monthly Wage into intervals to which percentages are applied for calculating the PIA) by 50 percent of the rise in the average annual wage, not 100 percent; (2) cut the benefit for persons retiring at sixty-two from 80 percent of the Primary Insurance Amount to 55 percent; (3) beginning in 1982, shift the date for applying the benefit COLA from June to September; (4) eliminate benefits for retired workers' children while the retirees were aged sixty-two to sixty-four. There were also numerous changes to tighten eligibility for Disability Insurance by relating DI more closely to the beneficiary's work history and medical condition, which was the original intent of Disability Insurance. The ceiling on income exempt from the retirement earnings test for persons sixty-five and older would be increased from its then-current $5,000 in $5,000 increments to $20,000 in 1985, and then removed altogether. There were also provisions to trim the scheduled OASDI FICA and self-employment tax rates, and introduce automatic tax rate adjustments to peg the Social Security tax rate to the ratio between the trust fund assets and annual expenditures, so that the tax rate would be trimmed when the ratio rose and increased when it fell. These measures, plus other Social Security provisions included in Reagan's March 1981 budget proposals, would save an estimated $81.9 billion by end-1986.[23]

It was an act of enormous political courage. For the first time, current and near-future beneficiaries were being asked to make significant sacrifices to shore up OASDI's finances. Unfortunately, the proposals had been hastily concocted and the administration had done nothing to prepare the climate of opinion for them or to assemble congressional support in advance. Moreover, while House Democrats, led by Congressman J. J. Pickle (D-TX), an authority on Social Security, were working on proposals to gradually reform the program, with the effect spread over many years, the administration wanted an immediate payoff. David Stockman, director of the Office of Management and Budget, remarked, "I'm just not going to spend a lot of political capital solving some other guy's problem in 2010." The clever but purblind Stockman didn't seem to realize that 64 percent of persons eligible for Social Security were opting for early retirement, which necessarily meant that huge numbers of beneficiaries would be hurt by the administration's proposal and certain to oppose it vigorously.[24] And neither Stockman nor Reagan showed any awareness of the decisive importance of beliefs and perceptions, or that they were attacking America's most heavily promoted program, guarded by a constituency steeped in myths.

The response—immediate, massive, and seethingly hostile—exploded in the Reagan administration's face like a bomb. It proved that by now Social

Security's false consciousness had an iron grip on powerful Social Security advocacy groups and constituencies—the unions and the elderly—as well as congressmen, senators, and millions of other Americans.

The very next day the attacks began thick and fast in Congress, and went on for weeks. After several defeats at Reagan's hands, the Democrats had been handed something they could work with, and they made the most of it. "I do not believe that Congress can break its promise to the American worker who has contributed to this program throughout a working lifetime," declared Congressman Jim Wright (D-TX), and several of his House colleagues were quick to echo him and denounce the "breach of faith" and "broken promise."[25] Congressman Bob Traxler (D-MI) denied that Social Security was going broke and asserted that Social Security is "an intergenerational social compact. People who pay taxes now must be able to know with certainty that the commitment will be kept when they retire. Tampering with the benefit scale now in place will destroy everyone's confidence in that social contract."[26] Similarly, Congressman Jonathan Bingham (D-NY) asserted that "social security represents a compact between a worker, his employer, and the Federal Government. The Reagan proposals, if enacted, would tear that compact asunder. Benefits are a right—an earned right—and any attempt to cut these benefits would be a statement that the U.S. Government is not as good as its word."[27] Other Democrats portrayed Social Security as a "contract with the American worker" and "a binding contract between the Government and the people."[28] "The scope of these cuts is unprecedented," said Claude Pepper (D-FL), then chairman of the House Committee on Aging and a stalwart defender of Social Security and the elderly. "These cuts constitute a major breach of contract for a worker who has paid for 30 or 40 years into the Social Security system."[29]

In the Senate, the story was the same. Senator Daniel Patrick Moynihan (D-NY) was especially vehement. If the cuts in early-retirement benefits went through, he said, "we have broken a contract with" early retirees. Moreover, "there are rights to which older Americans are entitled. . . . These are contracts we have made with our people, with ourselves—a social contract." Jim Sasser (D-TN) concurred that "this administration is indeed breaching a contract that was made with these beneficiaries as they paid into the social security system over the years. . . . social security is bought and paid for by the hard labor of the American worker." Senator John Stennis (D-MS), while refraining from polemics, cited "certain vested rights that so many people have in the fund" and argued that Social Security was a "trust fund" that should be considered separately from the rest of the budget and administered separately.[30]

Social Security's architects weighed in, too. Wilbur Cohen promptly denounced the proposed cuts as "unwise, unsound and unnecessary" and "a tragedy" for elderly Americans. Adopting them would make both beneficiaries and taxpayers "begin to lose faith in our government's promises." Cohen threw himself into the fray, spending six days a month in Washington to fight the proposed cuts, railing at the "breach of faith."[31] On May 21, the House Select Committee on Aging held a hearing on the proposals. In his prepared statement, Robert Ball, now chairman of the Save Our Security Advisory Committee, depicted Social Security protections as arising from "a compact between the contributing worker and his employer and the government." Being linked to past earnings and contributions, "benefits are paid as an earned right as well as a legal right." Social Security outlays, Ball argued, "*should* [italics in original] be 'uncontrollable,' because they are the product of an agreement to furnish certain protection in return for certain contributions." The government, he concluded, "must make it known beyond the shadow of a doubt" that it will honor "its compact with contributing workers under Social Security—that the government, as insurer, will meet its obligations . . . Social Security is a government promise that must be honored."[32]

Within hours of announcement of Reagan's proposals, the elderly lobbies began mobilizing against them. Hadn't they been told all their adult lives, from every quarter, that they had insurance policies with the government, that the taxes they had paid all those years were insurance premiums buying them retirement insurance, that they had bought their benefits, that the benefits were their money, that they were only getting back what they had paid in, that those benefits came as a matter of earned right? The AARP and the National Retired Teachers Association alerted 14,000 volunteer leaders, telling them to contact lawmakers and mobilize other group members to do likewise. Cohen's Save Our Security (SOS) swung into action with an emergency meeting. "The President's safety net is under water," charged Jack Ossofsky of the National Council on the Aging, "and old people are being thrown to the sharks." National Council of Senior Citizens president Jacob Clayman denounced the administration's proposal as "the biggest frontal attack on Social Security ever launched—an attack aimed at the ultimate destruction of the system." Besides their intensity, the elderly's strength lay in their numbers. As of 1980, over 47 million Americans were over fifty-five, and in the 1980 election seniors had made up 29 percent of the voting-age population and cast over a third of the ballots for president. No elected politician could afford to affront such a constituency, and everybody knew it. Said William Driver, executive vice president of SOS: "We make mention of our size and the fact that it's the group of people from which you get the largest percentage of the vote. We also impress upon congressmen that we're urging our members to oppose anyone who favors the cuts."[33]

Closely allied with the elderly, the unions jumped into the scrap. The United Auto Workers (UAW) ran a full-page newspaper advertisement in twenty-two newspapers, including the *New York Times*, the *Washington Post,* and the Detroit papers. It appeared in the May 22 *Detroit News*, depicting

Ronald Reagan's hand holding a pair of scissors, about to cut a Social Security card in two, and above, a boldfaced admonishment: **Don't Do It, Mr. President**. The text berated Reagan for proposing "breaking America's promise" and wanting to "change the rules in the middle of the game." It ended exhorting its readers to oppose Reagan's proposed cuts. "A letter, mailgram or call to your U.S. Senators and Representative will help mean Social Security will be there when you need it. Do it today."[34] A similar advertisement appeared on the back cover of the August 1981 issue of the UAW's magazine *Solidarity*, and in newspapers nationwide, warning that "Reagan still wants to cut Social Security," and adding that "Social Security is not a handout. It's a contract between the United States Government and the American people— a contract we've earned through lifetimes of hard work." After recommending general revenue financing and interfund borrowing to solve Social Security's problems, the ad urged its readers to tell their representatives in Congress that they want the government to keep its word: "Tell them you've paid into Social Security and want it to be there when you need it. . . . Don't let them take away what we've earned." It closed in boldface, telling the reader to remember that **Social Security is a Contract, Not a Handout!**[35] The June 1981 AFL-CIO *American Federationist* printed a lengthy extract from Ball's May 21 testimony.[36]

All of this was predictable. But much of the general public too was enraged by Reagan's proposals. Congressmen and senators were deluged with angry telephone calls and letters. In newspapers and magazines across the country, letters to the editor scourged both the Reagan administration and any editorials that dared suggest a version of reality other than the Social Security Administration's decades-old version. Clearly, millions of Americans were in the toils of the false consciousness which Social Security and its partisans had worked so hard to instill. From the *Detroit Free Press* of May 24:

Everyone who worked for the benefits deserves them. . . .

In your editorial, "Social Security: There are more humane remedies than these" (Free Press, May 14), you say, " . . . it faces an even more serious problem in the 1990's, when there will be far fewer workers to support the growing number of retirees."

Where do you get the nerve to insinuate that Social Security recipients are "supported" by workers?

Social Security is an insurance program, generously contributed to by workers and employers. It is only logical that such a program should come to fruition and maturation at a reasonable date. . . .

The establishment of the Social Security system embodies much that can be found in contract law, an agreement between two or more parties for the doing or not doing of something specified. . . .

I would suggest that any changes in the Social Security system that must now be made should recognized the original implied contract and the continuing viable support of that contract.[37]

From the *Los Angeles Times* of the same day:

> The Social Security system is in trouble. But there are other ways to solve the problems than to deprive beneficiaries who have earned their benefits . . .
>
>   . . . . The average Social Security check is $350 a month—not a giveaway at the expense of younger workers as we hear so often, but is a pension earned by a lifetime of work.[38]

A *U.S. News & World Report* editorial cited still more angry, ill-informed mail:

> I seriously doubt that the courts will permit the unethical and immoral tampering with the vested rights already acquired by implied contract under the Social Security system. If this type of abrogation were sanctioned, then the contractual obligations and rights under insurance policies or pension plans would be worthless and they could be altered or diminished at will . . .
>
>   In effect, the country has said to each of us, "Pay your Social Security taxes in good faith, select which retirement age you prefer, and make your retirement plans accordingly." I submit that this constitutes a moral obligation to all who have contributed to the program. The proposal itself is unjust, but to propose its immediate activation, without any graduated phasing-in period, is sickeningly cruel.[39]

On May 20 the House Democratic Caucus unanimously adopted a resolution branding Reagan's proposals "an unconscionable breach of faith." That same day, Moynihan introduced a Senate resolution saying pretty much the same, and the Senate, where the Republicans held a majority, fell only one vote short of approving it. Senator Robert Dole (R-KS) introduced a slightly softer one opposing cutting benefits "precipitously and unfairly"; it passed 96-0. It was Reagan's first defeat in Congress.[40]

The controversy dragged on through 1981. In the budget reconciliation bill approved in July, Congress actually voted to eliminate Social Security's $122 minimum monthly benefit for all new retirees beginning in December 1981 and for current retirees for benefits after February 1982. It also eliminated the $255 lump-sum death benefit for deaths after August 31, 1981 in which the worker was not survived by a spouse or dependent children, and made numerous other small trims. However, Reagan's proposals to postpone the July 1982 COLA increase and cut early-retiree benefits were defeated.[41] The elimination of the minimum benefit touched off another uproar, with senior-citizen demonstrations at the Capitol and a fresh torrent of angry mail:

> . . . . These seniors contributed many hours and dollars to Social Security during their working years. This is not a dole. Many of them need these funds. They deserve these funds.[42]
>
>   President Reagan . . . believes it is OK for the federal government to break its word to the 3 million persons whose minimum Social Security benefits are to be

canceled in February. . . their small pensions were earned by complying with regulations set up by the federal government. Evidently a contract is a contract only when Reagan says it is.[43]

Columnists should stop writing about Social Security as if it were social welfare for senior citizens. Where this notion got started we don't know, but it should be laid to rest once and for all.

Social Security is an insurance program establishing a trust fund separate from general revenue, even if several administrations have "robbed" the fund for their adventures.[44]

. . . . The Social Security system is an insurance system whereby our payroll deductions are the premiums we pay. It is a continually revolving fund. The pension received from it is incidentally *not taxed* [italics in original].[45]

The language of most of these attacks is further evidence of the dominion of the false consciousness. The false consciousness decisively determined the character of the opposition to Reagan's proposals in another sense. OASDI's self-promotion shaped belief not only by what it said but by what it had not said. The shock and fury at a perfidious Reagan proposing that Congress change the rules in the middle of the game proves that most Americans had never heard of Section 1104 of the Social Security Act, which empowers Congress to do just that. They had never heard of it, because their information sources—Social Security, its friends in Congress and advocates in academe and the media—had never told them; had chosen not to tell them.

Had Social Security's promoters made Section 1104 and its implications explicit from the beginning and given them due prominence, had it been impressed upon taxpayers and beneficiaries all along that OASDI benefits were contingent, subject to reduction by Congress later should events make retrenchment necessary, this firestorm would probably not have occurred. There would have been protests, to be sure, but the accusations of breach of faith, breach of contract, and changing the rules of the game could never have gained credence. People would have been unhappy, but they would have understood. But truthfulness and honesty about Social Security was the road not taken—not in the thirties, not later, and not now. That Reagan was proposing something literally unheard of goes far to explain the singularly hysterical and seething intensity of the opposition he encountered.

The House reversed itself in July and restored the minimum benefit. The administration's resolve collapsed. On September 24, Reagan too reversed himself, denied that he had intended to cut benefits to anyone in need, and asked Congress to restore the minimum benefit. He also withdrew his proposals and called for creation of a bipartisan commission to study Social Security and make recommendations. Its members were appointed in December and given a December 31, 1982 deadline for issuing their report. Finally, at the end of the session in December, both houses restored the minimum benefit and, to buy a little more time for Social Security until Reagan and Congress could agree on what was to be done, authorized the Old-Age and Survivors Insurance trust fund to borrow from the Disability Insurance and Hospital Insurance funds until the end of 1982.[46]

The administration had spent a lot of political capital, but not only had it solved nothing, it had made matters disastrously worse. As Nietzsche wrote, "There are terrible people who, instead of solving a problem, bungle it and make it more difficult for all who come after."[47] The administration's effort had aroused the wrath and vigilance of Social Security's myth-driven protectors, who had demonstrated their power and administered an unforgettable object lesson about what would happen to politicians who tried to tamper with Social Security—especially with current benefits. From now on, politicians' thoughts and actions about Social Security would progress in the shadow of Reagan's rout. For their part, the lobbies protecting Social Security, in order to frighten the elderly and rouse them to block any future attempt to modify the program, had only to point to what Reagan had attempted in 1981. It was this fiasco that spawned the saying, and belief, that Social Security is the third rail of American politics—touch it and you die. The program's misleading publicity had sown, and the administration had sprouted, many seeds of the paralysis, evasion and deadlock over Social Security that would characterize the next seventeen years.

The 1983 Rescue: Spare the Old and Scourge the Young

Chastened by its myth-driven rout in 1981, the administration did not make another attempt the following year. Congress was no more disposed to act. In the 1982 election campaign, Democrats made much of the administration's effort to cut benefits in the previous year. Congressman Claude Pepper, chairman of the House Select Committee on Aging, went to twenty-six states campaigning for seventy-three Democratic candidates for the House. Pepper, who was receiving Social Security himself, was an unabashed true believer in the program. "Social Security is an insurance program to which I have contributed," he said. "It isn't welfare." Fifty-four of the candidates Pepper stumped for won. All in all, the Democrats gained twenty-six House seats, and Social Security was a major factor in their victory.[48]

Meanwhile, argument continued about what to do about Social Security. The idea of raising the "retirement age"—that is, the earliest age at which one could retire and receive full Social Security retirement benefits—from sixty-five to sixty-seven or sixty-eight was advanced repeatedly, but encountered stubborn resistance. In 1979, former Chief Actuary Robert Myers endorsed raising the retirement age to sixty-eight. Increased life expectancy and better health in old age meant that "the country just couldn't afford a retirement age as low as sixty-five some thirty years from now, when people will be living lots longer than they do today." Moreover, Dr. Myers added, a higher retirement age would generate substantial savings and hold down the growth in payroll taxes, which would otherwise become unbearably high. Similarly, economist Rita Ricardo Campbell, a Senior Fellow at Stanford University's Hoover Institution, citing both the declining birth rate and improvements in life expectancy, argued that raising the retirement age would shore up the program's finances. But former Social Security Commissioner Robert Ball and Betty Duskin, Director of Research of the National Council of Senior Citizens, opposed changing the retirement age since it was a reduction in benefits.[49]

Instead, Wilbur Cohen favored raising the payroll tax, since "benefits are well worth the contributions [sic] that younger people pay." Besides, it was better than the other options. General revenue financing would increase the budget deficit, and cutting benefits was "not only politically infeasible, it would be morally wrong." Senator William Armstrong (R-CO) retorted that raising the payroll tax would be an extra burden on the economy. Yet even Armstrong went out of his way to reassure current beneficiaries that their benefits should not and would not be cut.[50]

An especially bitter wrangle ensued about Social Security COLAs. Some economists argued that the COLAs were a valid target for cutting, because they overadjusted for inflation, and observed that in 1978-1981, benefits rose 37 percent, versus a 25 percent increase in average wages. Opponents maintained that COLA cuts would push hundreds of thousands of retirees into poverty. Then, too, certain beliefs about Social Security exerted an additional force. In an apt demonstration of the collision between the need for Social Security to be flexible to meet changing circumstances and the rigidity imposed on the program by its own language of insurance, contracts, and earned rights, Senator Pete Domenici (R-NM) favored cutting COLAs back due to the need to "balance the budget of our Social Security system" and also to help keep the growth of federal spending and deficits in check—while Senator Howard Metzenbaum (D-OH) was vehemently opposed, arguing that "a contract was made with the people when they entered the Social Security system. This is their money. They had it deducted from their wages. You don't lead people down a primrose path, tell them they're going to get retirement benefits they paid for and then suddenly tell them they aren't going to get it." The elderly lobby lurked in the background to see to it that such views prevailed. The National Council of Senior Citizens exhorted its 350,000 members to threaten incumbent politicians with defeat in the coming 1982 election if they supported COLA cuts. And the combination American Association of Retired Persons-National Retired Teachers Association was lobbying Congress against tampering with COLAs.[51]

Unsurprisingly, then, Reagan and Congress decided to wait until the bipartisan National Commission on Social Security Reform, chaired by economist Alan Greenspan and including five members appointed by Reagan, five appointed by House Speaker Thomas O'Neill, and five appointed by Senate Majority Leader Howard Baker (R-TN), had made its report. The Commission would give them a political cover for doing unpopular things; should political heat flare up, they could say that they had only acted on the advice of a bipartisan expert commission. The Commission itself fought bitterly over what to do. Republican members wanted to gradually raise the age for retiring with full benefits; Democrats wanted an increase in the payroll tax. So deep were the divisions that the Commission missed its December 1982 deadline, and not until January 15, 1983 did the members agree on a compromise combining benefit cuts and tax increases.[52]

With the Commission's recommendations in hand, Reagan and Congress moved quickly. They were under intense pressure. Social Security's sands were running out; OASI's trust fund had borrowed almost $14 billion from the Disability Insurance and Hospital Insurance trust funds on December 31, 1982, and was projected to be exhausted in July 1983, meaning benefit checks would not go out on time.[53] In his State of the Union speech on January 25, Reagan urged Congress to adopt the Commission's plan by Easter; next day the proposals were introduced in Congress; the House Ways and Means Committee began hearings February 1; on March 25 both Houses passed the final version; and Reagan signed it April 20.[54]

Current retirees had the July 1983 COLA delayed six months, and paid in January 1984. Thereafter, COLAs would be on a calendar basis, payable in January rather than July (the beginning of the fiscal year before 1976, when the federal government adopted a fiscal year that begins October 1). Moreover, for some workers first eligible after 1985 for both Social Security retirement benefits and a pension from noncovered employments, windfall benefits would be gradually eliminated: the Social Security benefit would be cut by no more than one-half the amount of the pension. Another provision, that beginning with the December 1984 OASDI COLA, future automatic increases would be based on the lower of the increase in wages or prices if the ratio of the OASDI combined trust fund assets to estimated outlays fell below 15 percent through December 1988 and 20 percent thereafter, imposed a further trim in benefits, although merely a potential one, on current beneficiaries, as well as on future beneficiaries. Slightly offsetting the cuts on future beneficiaries, however, the legislation reduced the rate of benefit withholding under the earnings test beginning in 1990, from $1 of benefits for every $2 in earnings above the exempt amount, to $1 of benefits for every $3.[55]

For the first time, Social Security benefits would be taxed. Beginning in 1984, up to 50 percent of Social Security benefits would be included in taxable income for persons whose sum of adjusted gross income, taxable interest income, and one-half of Social Security benefits exceeded $25,000 for single beneficiaries and $32,000 for married beneficiaries.[56] While this did impose some cost on the more well-to-do current retirees, the cost of this

benefit taxation measure would in fact fall most heavily on future beneficiaries, because the income thresholds for triggering the taxation were not indexed for inflation. Thus as the years pass, inflation will push a greater and
greater share of beneficiaries over these thresholds, just as the "inflation tax"
pushed Americans into higher federal income tax brackets until the 1981 tax
law introduced tax indexing. Writing in 1987, Phillip Longman argued that
of all the features of the 1983 legislation, this benefit tax provision "most
reduces the benefits promised to baby boomers and their children." In the
mid-eighties, the benefit taxation affected only the richest 10 percent of
beneficiaries. However, Longman pointed out, even given the modest inflation rate assumed by the Social Security actuaries' intermediate analysis, in
2030 a $25,000 income would have less purchasing power than an income of
$4,000 in the mid-eighties. "So by the time the baby boomers qualify for
Social Security pensions, the program will be effectively means-tested, if it
survives at all. Under current law, only the poorest baby boomers are even
promised a fair return on their contributions to the system."[57]

The legislation also created numerous additional current and future OASDI
taxpayers and future beneficiaries. Federal employees newly hired on or after
January 1, 1984 were brought into the program, as were current employees of
the legislative branch not covered as of December 31, 1983 by the Civil
Service Retirement System. So were the president, vice president, members of Congress, federal judges, and most executive-level federal political appointees. Effective January 1, 1984, all present and future employees
of tax-exempt nonprofit organizations were also required to participate in
Social Security. Finally, the escape window for state and local government
employees, who had previously been allowed to opt out of Social Security,
was closed effective April 20, the day Reagan signed the bill into law.[58] The
effect was to increase current and future revenues, and future costs (since the
newly covered persons' benefits would be an additional cost to future taxpayers).

Current OASDI taxpayers were saddled with substantial tax increases. The
payroll tax rate increase scheduled for 1985 under the 1977 legislation was
advanced to 1984, and part of the increase scheduled for 1990 was advanced
to 1988. In addition, whereas the prior law would have increased the tax rate
on the self-employed to 75 percent of the sum of the employee and employer
tax rates for OASDI and 50 percent of the sum for HI (Medicare), the new law
raised the self-employment rate to 100 percent of the sum of the employee
and employer tax rates.[59]

Most of the package's benefit reduction was inflicted on future retirees.
The retirement age was gradually increased, to reach sixty-six in 2009 and
sixty-seven in 2027. Early retirement benefits would still be available at age
sixty-two, but would be gradually cut from 80 percent of full benefits in 1983
to 75 percent in 2009 and 70 percent in 2027.[60]

All of the foregoing benefit reductions, and the introduction of benefit taxation, are simply applications of Section 1104, the reservation of power clause. Moreover, these changes explode all the talk of "earned rights" to benefits, "the sure bet of social insurance," and "guarantees." They thereby confirm the arguments of the government's brief in *Flemming v. Nestor* that there are no accrued, vested rights to benefits.

The 1983 legislation did pull Social Security back from the brink. Moreover, *prima facie,* it would seem that it boldly broke the deadlock over Social Security and did politically risky, long-resisted things: raise the retirement age, trim COLAs, and raise payroll taxes. Mixing tax increases and benefit cuts, it distributed sacrifices among all four groups of Social Security participants: current beneficiaries, current taxpayers, future beneficiaries, and future taxpayers. However, the distribution was hugely lopsided, falling least heavily on the current beneficiaries, far more heavily on the three other groups, and most heavily of all on future generations.

Even in the short run of 1983-1989, it exacted the majority of its sacrifices from taxpayers rather than current beneficiaries. Using its 1983 Alternative II-B (intermediate) assumptions, the Office of the Actuary estimated that in that period, the new law would bring in an additional $39.4 billion from the higher FICA tax rates, another $18.5 billion from the higher taxes on the self-employed, and $21.8 billion from extending coverage to nonprofit employees and federal employees, elected officials, and appointees, for a total of $79.7 billion from current (including newly created) Social Security taxpayers. Introducing benefit taxation, which, as Longman pointed out, would affect only a minority of current beneficiaries, would raise an estimated $26.6 billion more. By contrast, the only major sacrifice by *all* current beneficiaries, the six-months' delay in COLAs, would reduce benefits an estimated $39.4 billion, for total current beneficiary sacrifices of $66.0 billion.[61]

Examination of the actuaries' 1983 estimates of the effect of the 1983 Social Security amendments on the long-range actuarial deficit, an estimated 2.09 percent of taxable payroll, gives another indicator of how much the new law relied on pushing the pain into the future and onto taxpayers (see table 10.1).[62] The measure making the largest single contribution to closing that deficit—the increase in the retirement age—disposed of over a third of it and fell wholly on future beneficiaries. The provision making the second largest, benefit taxation, fell mostly on them, too. These two provisions accounted for almost two-thirds of the long-term deficit. The tax and new coverage provisions dispatched most of the rest.

So, the one serious effort in the past twenty years to improve Social Security's finances relied almost wholly on exacting sacrifice from every group *except* the one most threatened by Reagan's 1981 proposals, and the one politically most dangerous to approach: current beneficiaries. The lesson

Table 10.1

Estimated Improvement in Long-Range Actuarial Deficit of Major Provisions
of 1983 Amendments by Group Affected, as Percent of Payroll

Provision	Group(s) making sacrifice	Effect
Bar state, local employee terminations	Current & future taxpayers	+ .06
Cover new Federal employees	Same	+ .28
Cover all nonprofit employees	Same	+ .10
Accelerate tax increase	Current taxpayers	+ .03
Adjust tax rate on self-employment	Current & future taxpayers	+ .19
Tax one-half of benefits	Current & (mostly) future beneficiaries	+ .61
Raise normal retirement age to 67	Future beneficiaries	+ .71
Delay benefit increases 6 months	Current & future beneficiaries	+ .30

Source: *Social Security Bulletin,* July 1983. Note: sum exceeds long-term actuarial deficit because individual figures do not reflect effect of interactions between provisions.

of the 1981 debacle had been learned. The contradiction between the political demand for certain, guaranteed benefits, and the fiscal need to keep Social Security flexible to meet changing circumstances, was resolved by maintaining as much benefit certainty as possible for politically powerful current beneficiaries, and pushing the cost of adjustment to changing conditions onto politically weak future ones.

To grasp just how much the 1977 and 1983 rescues relied on taxes and how much heavier tax burdens became as a result, compare the maximum taxable incomes that would have been in force in 1979-1998 and the FICA and self-employment (SE) tax rates scheduled for those years under pre-1977 Social Security law, with the actual maximum taxable incomes and tax rates that were in effect in those years due to these rescues (see table 10.2).[63]

The divergence of the actual maximum taxable income, FICA tax rate, and SE tax rate from those that would have obtained under pre-1977 law began promptly, and widened dramatically over time. By 1993, ten years after the 1983 rescue, the maximum taxable income was 34.3 percent above its pre-1977 level, the FICA rate 25.3 percent higher, and the SE rate a staggering 77 percent higher.

Social Security's only real "implicit contract" is that politicians will provoke current beneficiaries as little as possible and seek their sacrifices elsewhere, or face political annihilation. The politicians honored that contract in 1983. They would continue to do so.

Table 10.2

Pre-1977 Law and Actual Values for Maximum Taxable Income, FICA Tax Rate, and Self-Employment Tax Rate, 1979-1998

Year	Maximum Taxable Income			FICA tax rate		SE tax rate	
	Pre-1977	Actual	Increase	Pre-1977	Actual	Pre-1977	Actual
1979	$18,900	$22,900	$3,000	4.95	5.08	7.00	7.05
1980	20,400	25,900	5,500	4.95	5.08	7.00	7.05
1981	22,200	29,700	7,500	4.95	5.35	7.00	8.00
1982	24,300	32,400	8,100	4.95	5.40	7.00	8.05
1983	26,700	35,700	9,000	4.95	5.40	7.00	8.05
1984	28,200	37,800	9,600	4.95	5.70	7.00	11.40
1985	29,700	39,600	9,900	4.95	5.70	7.00	11.40
1986	31,500	42,000	10,500	4.95	5.70	7.00	11.40
1987	32,700	43,800	11,100	4.95	5.70	7.00	11.40
1988	33,600	45,000	11,400	4.95	6.06	7.00	12.12
1989	35,700	48,000	12,300	4.95	6.06	7.00	12.12
1990	38,100	51,300	13,200	4.95	6.20	7.00	12.40
1991	39,600	53,400	13,800	4.95	6.20	7.00	12.40
1992	41,400	55,500	14,100	4.95	6.20	7.00	12.40
1993	42,900	57,600	14,700	"	"	"	"
1994	45,000	60,600	15,600	"	"	"	"
1995	45,300	61,200	15,900	"	"	"	"
1996	46,500	62,700	16,200	"	"	"	"
1997	48,600	65,400	16,800				
1998	50,700	68,400	17,700				
1999	53,700	72,600	18,900	"	"	"	"
2000	56,700	76,200	19,500	"	"	"	"

Sources: *2000 OASDI Report; Social Security Bulletin,* March 1978

1980s-1990s: Chronicles of Wasted Time

Reagan's calamitous rout in 1981 had a decisive and disastrous effect, casting a long shadow down the years. Out of fear of political reprisals from well-organized and militant beneficiaries, nothing was done in the years that followed to obtain real, significant sacrifices from them, either to help with deficit reduction, or to reform OASDI so as to avoid a long-term financial crisis. Over and over, both political parties swerved away from a perilous confrontation with Social Security's defenders and very powerful constituency, who were quick to invoke the myths of Social Security to forestall any benefit trims. Over and over, the false consciousness's grip on Americans' minds defeated any effort to touch Social Security, with the mythical descriptions of Social Security—"insurance," "sacred compact," "contract between generations"—invoked repeatedly as grounds for refusing to make any substantial changes, especially any that would inflict pain on current retirees. Steeped in the false consciousness, the elderly wanted what they had been led to believe was coming to them—and they had the political power to get it, and hang the consequences and the cost. As a result, nearly two decades of opportunities to address Social Security were thrown away.

During the 1980s and 1990s, numerous measures were advanced, and some enacted, to cope with the rising tide of red ink. Several involved some sort of automatic mechanism or legal requirement to force Congress to do what it manifestly lacked the courage to do: cut spending enough to balance the budget, or at least impose some binding check on spending growth. Yet virtually all of them exempted Social Security from any current spending reduction whatsoever. And most exempted Social Security permanently.

The Gramm-Rudman-Hollings Act of 1985 set as its goal achievement of a balanced budget by 1991, by setting annual deficit targets for 1986-1991, and applying automatic spending cuts ("sequesters") if they were missed. This act, much trumpeted as a stern, brave act of self-control by Congress, was in fact an exercise in pusillanimity. It exempted Social Security—along with veterans' benefits, Medicaid, AFDC, WIC, food stamps, and other entitlements from sequester, and limited any cuts to Medicare.[64] In 1987, Gramm-Rudman-Hollings was revised. It limited Medicare cuts to 2 percent, and again exempted Social Security and poverty entitlements from sequesters altogether.[65]

The few attempts after 1983 to cut Social Security outlays were quickly defeated. In 1985 the Senate, which then had a Republican majority, actually did vote to eliminate the 1986 COLA for Social Security benefits as part of an effort to avert large future budget deficits. The elderly lobbies promptly swung into action. The National Council of Senior Citizens alone was responsible for elderly Americans inundating Congress with 800,000 postcards. Senators going home for Easter recess were confronted by angry elderly in scores of meetings. The following year was an election year, and the threat of political punishment was blatant. "We shall not forget if Congress behaves in an unfriendly fashion to the senior citizens of the United States," said NCSC president Jacob Clayman. "We shall remember—and 1986 is just around the corner." 1985 was the fiftieth anniversary of Social Security's creation, hence a singularly inauspicious year to be trimming benefits, and the elderly groups made the most of the connection, delivering Social Security anniversary cakes to lawmakers, many of whom chose not to appear at such embarrassing media events. Democrats in the House insisted that the COLA be restored, and the final budget resolution passed by Congress restored the full COLA for 1986.[66] In the next year's election, the Republicans lost nine seats and control of the

Senate, and the 1985 Senate vote to eliminate the Social Security COLA was a factor in the Republican rout. In Alabama, for example, Democratic Representative Richard Shelby, who defeated incumbent Senator Jeremiah Denton, ran advertisements accusing him of vowing to cut Social Security benefits.[67]

In the wake of the October 1987 "Black Monday" stock market crash, Congress and the Reagan administration held a "budget summit" to produce credible deficit reduction to calm the agitated financial markets. A proposal arose to delay COLAs for federal workers and retirees, including Social Security beneficiaries, for three months. Social Security's protectors promptly went into action. Former HEW Secretary Arthur Flemming, of *Flemming v. Nestor* fame, a signatory of the 1975 white paper, and active in the eighties in resisting Social Security cuts, threatened that "There will be political fallout if this is pursued." And House Rules Committee chairman Claude Pepper sent a short videotape from Florida in which he warned that if a deficit-reduction package included a cut in Social Security COLAs, he would insist on a separate vote on the cut on the House floor. The message was unstated but unmistakable: approval of any COLA cut would bring punishment in the 1988 election. The precedents of the 1982 and 1986 elections testified that this was no idle threat. With that, the "budget summit" retreated to politics-as-usual haggling over token cuts in discretionary spending.[68]

Reagan, whose fiscal leadership grew increasingly flaccid, made no more attempts to address Social Security, despite the warnings that were accumulating from well-informed and rightly worried observers such as Haeworth Robertson and Peter Peterson. He handed the poisoned chalice to his successor, who was no more willing to drink it.

In the fall of 1990, after posturing and partisan maneuvering by both the Democratic Congress and the Bush administration, there was yet another global budget agreement, the Omnibus Budget Reconciliation Act (OBRA). Bush broke his no-new-taxes pledge. In return, Congress supposedly embraced fiscal discipline with the 1990 Budget Enforcement Act (BEA), which was supposed to put caps on spending. But, like Gramm-Rudman, BEA was toothless. The caps applied only to discretionary spending; cutting Medicare by more than two percent to enforce a deficit target was forbidden; Social Security was exempted altogether.[69] The BEA's pay-as-you-go (PAYGO) entitlement limits applied only to creating new entitlements or expanding existing ones; they did nothing to contain the costs of existing benefits mandated by current law.[70]

Over and over, President Bush asserted that he would not touch Social Security to control deficits. In his 1992 State of the Union address, Bush said, "I will not tamper with Social Security." He reiterated his stand in his acceptance speech at the Republican convention that summer. Debating Bill Clinton and Ross Perot in St. Louis on October 11, Bush declared, "I'm the President that stood up and said don't mess with Social Security. And I'm not going to

and we haven't, and we are not going to go after the Social Security recipient
. . . I don't think we need to touch Social Security."[71] Similarly, candidate
Clinton promised, "We're not going to fool with Social Security. It's solid. It's
secure. It's sound."[72]

Proposals to impose a so-called "cap" on entitlement spending drew a
flurry of attention in 1992. Most proposed caps would have held entitlement
spending growth to the growth of the beneficiary population, adjusted for
inflation (usually as measured by the Consumer Price Index). Should spending growth exceed this ceiling, sequesters would be imposed.[73]

Examining cap proposals and how they could be implemented for eleven
programs, a 1994 U. S. General Accounting Office (GAO) study pointed out
that caps would have merely treated symptoms without touching the dis-
ease—the forces, such as demographics, driving entitlement outlays; "a cap
would have little, if any, effect on the longer-term growth trends in these
programs until issues of underlying eligibility and benefits which drive spending are addressed . . . most mandatory spending is driven by eligibility and
benefit formulas which a sequester may not change."[74]

Besides which, those who bandied about cap proposals could not muster
the courage to "cap" the biggest entitlement of all: Social Security. George
Bush repeatedly exempted Social Security from proposed entitlement caps.[75]
Similarly, in 1993 Jack Kemp proposed limiting entitlement spending growth
to beneficiary population growth plus inflation—except for Social Security.[76]

And even if Social Security *had* been included and a cap proposal had
been enacted, holding Social Security spending growth to inflation-adjusted
beneficiary population growth would simply have kept the program going
according to what is already mandated under current law, and achieved nothing. It is the growth in the beneficiary population itself from the Baby Boomers'
retirement, supported by a slower-growing worker population, which will
doom Social Security—and a cap would have done absolutely nothing about
it. After Bill Clinton entered the White House, cap proposals eventually vanished into oblivion. Given their problems, their bogus, gimmicky nature, and
the universal lack of will to include Social Security in them, their demise was
fortunate.

In January 1993, the newly arrived Clinton administration began advancing proposals to reduce the federal budget deficit. One was a freeze on Social
Security COLAs, which, it was estimated, could have saved $10 billion in
1994. The program's defenders in and out of Congress reacted quickly. Horace
Deets, executive director of the AARP, branded a COLA freeze or cut "the
wrong remedy to reduce the budget." Senator Moynihan, chairman of the
Senate Finance Committee, called the proposal "unacceptable," and revealed
that Social Security's insurance myth was bulking large in his mind. Tinkering with benefits, he said on "This Week With David Brinkley," would under-

mine the idea that Social Security is insurance. "I would like to see us acknowledge that this is a contributory insurance program," Moynihan added. "These monies are held in trust . . . That's not an entitlement program, where you get something for nothing. It's paid-up insurance." Proving that subscription to Social Security's false consciousness was bipartisan, Representative Newt Gingrich (R-GA) declared, "Social Security is unequivocally the one contract the country is overwhelmingly in favor of. I'm going to do everything I can to keep the Democrats from tampering with it." Wilting under the heat, President Clinton promptly reversed himself and decided against a COLA freeze, and in a White House meeting reassured leaders of the AARP that he believed that Social Security was a special contract with the elderly—an explicit embrace of one of Social Security's myths.[77] The deficit-reduction proposals he sent to Congress opted instead for higher taxes on Social Security benefits.

Ohio Congressman John Kasich's Republican alternative to Clinton's 1993 deficit-reduction plan exempted Social Security from spending cuts. Indicating the grip of the Social Security myths on even supposedly fiscally conservative Republican politicians' minds, Kasich reported this decision in language that would have warmed the cockles of Wilbur Cohen's heart: "Social Security was off limits. Republicans believe that Social Security represents a fundamental agreement between the Federal Government and the American people—an agreement that must be preserved. . . . Republicans would achieve their deficit reduction without cutting benefits that American senior citizens have come to consider a sacred trust."[78]

Two libertarian economists from the Cato Institute, William Niskanen and Stephen Moore, also dissented from Clinton's proposals. Their proposed alternative proved equally captive to the Social Security myths and equally unwilling to tackle Social Security—or rather, inflict any politically-dangerous pain in the present period. One principle of their plan was abandonment of the notion of "mandatory" or "uncontrollable" outlays—except for the following, which "should be regarded as fixed obligations of the federal government": interest on the federal debt, deposit insurance outlays, and "the real pension benefits" of retired federal employees and current Social Security beneficiaries.[79] They elaborated:

> Over time, Social Security has been interpreted as a political contract between the working-age population and retired persons. We accept that implicit contract and do not propose to reduce the real pension benefits of those who are now retired. This contract eliminates the possibility of any substantial saving in Social Security outlays in the near term, but it should not cause us to defer dealing with the immense long-term problems of the system.[80]

Rejecting President Clinton's increase in taxation of Social Security benefits as part of his 1993 deficit-reduction package as unfair and punitive to

currently-retired elderly, Niskanen and Moore went on to propose two reforms that would "put Social Security on a sustainable basis . . . without
breaking the contract with current retirees." Specifically, acceleration of the
already-scheduled increase in the retirement age, raising it two months per
year for the next thirty years (to sixty-six in 2000, sixty-eight in 2012,
and so on), and basing the formula for calculating future benefits on the
consumer price index rather than the retiree's wages while employed. These
two suggestions would supposedly save $400 billion by 2030.[81] They
amounted, of course, to an enormous cut in benefits for future retirees.
Future generations, apparently, had no such "implicit contract"—but then,
neither did they have any political clout in the here and now. The proposal was a transparently cynical exercise in shifting the pain of fixing
Social Security into the future. Current retirees' benefits would be kept
intact, not because there was an "implicit contract" or if there were, because Niskanen and Moore really believed in it—their proposal to massively penalize the future generations explodes both possibilities—but
because current beneficiaries could impose political penalties if their benefits were tampered with.

Political calculations continued to dictate treatment of Social Security as
the nineties wore on. When in October 1994 Alice Rivlin, director of the
Office of Management and Budget, sent President Clinton a memorandum on
possible budget options for the future, including freezing or cutting COLAs
for Social Security and other entitlement programs, and it was leaked to the
press, Republican politicians accused the administration of hypocrisy and
planning to break its promise not to touch Social Security. Rivlin tried to
limit the political damage by asserting that the administration was not "actively considering" any of the options, and Clinton declared, "I do not support cuts in Social Security."[82] After the 1994 Republican victory, Kasich
reiterated his pledge not to cut Social Security.[83] In March 1994, Representative Gerald B. H. Solomon (R-NY) proposed a plan to balance the budget in
five years, which entailed widespread painful specific spending cuts—but
exempted Social Security.[84]

A constitutional amendment to require that the budget be balanced annually (except in emergencies such as wars) was a favorite panacea of the eighties and nineties for restoring fiscal discipline. But balanced-budget
amendment proposals almost invariably exempted Social Security. House
Majority Leader Richard Gephardt (D-MO) endorsed the balanced-budget
amendment idea in 1992, but insisted on excluding Social Security from the
budget to be balanced. This, he said, was "a far better, more thoughtful and
effective" approach than the balanced-budget amendment proposal of Congressman Charles Stenholm (D-TX). "No member of Congress who believes
in the integrity of Social Security can posture as a friend of the elderly while
voting against the amendment."[85] Similarly, Senator Dianne Feinstein (D-

CA) stated in January 1995 that she would not vote for a balanced budget amendment unless Social Security was exempt.[86] The Republicans' 1995 proposals to balance the budget by 2002 exempted Social Security from cuts.[87]

And all the while, year after year, Social Security's long-term outlook was steadily worsening.

Short-Term Patchwork, Continued Paralysis

The 1983 annual report of the Board of Trustees had projected OASDI to be in long-term actuarial balance under intermediate assumptions. Just five years later, the actuarial balance was -.58 percent of taxable payroll. In 1993, ten years after the rescue that supposedly had saved Social Security, the long-term actuarial deficit was -1.46 percent; next year, it stood at -2.13 percent— *larger* than the -2.09 percent deficit which had prompted the 1983 rescue. Much of the deterioration was due to changes in actuarial assumptions, several of which were revised in a pessimistic direction.[88] Moreover, as we saw in chapter 1, the projected date of OASDI trust fund exhaustion was coming steadily closer. Successive Boards of Trustees warned Congress yearly that OASDI was not in long-term close actuarial balance, and that the Disability Insurance program was heading for bankruptcy in the very short run, and called for action—and got nothing for their pains but procrastination and short-term, *ad hoc* patching to fend off impending ruin of various provinces of the "social insurance" entitlement empire.

By the early nineties, Hospital Insurance (HI), widely known as Medicare, the hospital insurance branch of Social Security, separate from OASDI and outside the scope of this book, was under immense financial pressure from soaring health care costs. Its prospects were bleak and worsening rapidly. Whereas the 1991 report of HI's Board of Trustees projected trust fund exhaustion in 2005 under intermediate assumptions, the 1992 report projected it for 2002 and the 1993 report put it at 1999.[89] Repeatedly, the Trustees asked Congress to take steps to avert HI's financial ruin.[90] In 1993, Congress acted—not with fundamental reform of either health care costs or Medicare itself, but with a minor revenue increase. The Omnibus Budget Reconciliation Act of 1993 increased the maximum percentage of OASDI benefits subject to taxation, for taxable years after 1993, from 50 percent to 85 percent for single beneficiaries with "combined incomes" (adjusted gross income plus tax-exempt interest plus one-half of OASDI benefits) over $34,000 and for married coupled filing joint tax returns with "combined incomes" exceeding $44,000. Below these income levels, the old 50 percent tax rate still applied. The additional revenues from increasing the share of OASDI benefits subject to taxation were shunted to HI.[91] This blood transfusion improved Medicare's prospects, but very modestly; the 1994 HI Board of

Trustees' report put the trust fund's exhaustion date at 2001—a gain of just two years.[92]

Disability Insurance also received a belated rescue. Back in 1985, the Board of Trustees reported that DI faced possible "trust fund" depletion. Since 1982, a larger and larger share of the workforce was being awarded disability benefits, and since 1970 a smaller and smaller share of disability beneficiaries were having their benefits terminating due to death, recovery, or reaching age sixty-five. So more and more people were getting benefits from DI, and of these beneficiaries, more and more of them were collecting indefinitely. The number of new disability benefit awards soared from 415,000 in 1988 to over 640,000 in 1992. These trends badly strained DI's financing, and in 1992 and 1993 the Board of Trustees asked Congress to act to shore up the program, sending a separate letter to Congress calling for prompt action. In 1994, the Trustees repeated their warning: "It is imperative that legislative action be taken as soon as possible this year to strengthen the financial position of the DI program. . . . The DI Trust Fund will be exhausted in 1995 and benefit payments will cease unless Congressional action takes place." Specifically, the Trustees asked for reallocation of tax rates between the OASI and DI trust funds to strengthen the latter.[93] Finally, in 1994, after nine years of pleading by the Trustees, Congress acted. The Social Security Domestic Employment Reform Act allocated a greater portion of the OASDI payroll tax rate to DI as of December 31, 1993. DI's share went from 0.60 percent of payroll to 0.94 percent for employees and employers each for 1994-1995, from 0.60 percent to 0.85 percent in 1997-1999, and from 0.71 percent to 0.90 percent beginning in 2000. The 1995 report revised DI's projected "trust fund" exhaustion date under intermediate assumptions to 2016.[94]

While some ambitious efforts were made in the nineties to confront the problem of the future unaffordability of Social Security, Medicare and other entitlements, the people undertaking them proved unable to agree on a course of action, and in the end nothing happened. The Bipartisan Commission on Entitlement and Tax Reform, created by President Clinton in 1993 after the deficit reduction bill passed and chaired by Senators Robert Kerrey (D-NE) and John Danforth (R-MO), brought together thirty-two senators, representatives, university presidents, investment bankers and other notables to consider how to adjust federal entitlement programs and taxes to enable the federal government to meet its future entitlement commitments without undermining its finances. The Commission recognized the coming long-term financial problem in Social Security and other entitlement programs, and crafted numerous options for modifying the programs, but could not agree on a specific set of recommendations.[95] Senators Kerrey and Danforth proposed raising the age for eligibility for full Social Security retirement benefits from sixty-seven to seventy, phased in over thirty years, exempting everyone then over age fifty; indexing the "bend points" in the benefit formula for inflation, rather than average wage growth; cutting benefit growth for middle- and upper-wage workers by adding a third "bend point" to the formula; and cutting the payroll tax for workers under fifty-five by 1.5 percentage points in exchange for a required contribution to personal savings or Individual Retirement Accounts (IRAs).[96] The Kerrey-Danforth proposals received considerable dissent among Commissioners, and the myths of Social Security helped drive the Commission's failure to achieve consensus. One dissenter, Congressman John Dingell (D-MI), cited Social Security's nature as "social insurance," entailing an "explicit expectation" by contributors that they will be repaid in their old age, whereas options like means testing would turn Social Security into a welfare program. Thomas J. Downey, of Thomas J. Downey and Associates, Inc., described Social Security as the country's biggest insurance provider, and denied that it faced any crisis in either the short run or the long run. United Mine Workers president Richard Trumka, another opponent of the Kerrey-Danforth proposals, likewise asserted that Social Security's finances were sound, that "Social Security insurance" guarded families against disability, and that "life insurance protection provided by Social Security" exceeded that from all private providers, and rejected all of the proposed modifications in Social Security.[97] The Commission issued its final report in 1995; its proposals still await action, six years later.

The 1994-96 Advisory Council on Social Security, chaired by Professor Edward Gramlich, dean of the University of Michigan's School of Public Policy, and containing Robert Ball, Carolyn Weaver, Sylvester Schieber and other leading Social Security experts, was appointed in March 1994 to examine the program and advise the government on how to prepare it for the future. It too was unable to agree on a single plan to reform Social Security so as to restore long-term solvency. Its overdue report, finally released in January 1997, yielded divided counsel: its members broke out into three groups and offered three widely differing proposals for Social Security reform (which we shall examine in the next chapter). One group, deeply committed to preserving the program without fundamental change, even objected to how the Advisory Council's report began, and the report's summary of findings and recommendations was littered with footnotes getting various members' dissents from specific passages on the record.[98] Four years after the Council's proposals appeared, no action had been taken on any of them.

The 1997 budget bargain struck between President Clinton and the Republican-dominated Congress in July 1997 did absolutely nothing to address Social Security's long-term financial problems.[99] Even as of February 2001, nothing had been done.

There was, of course, intense controversy over Social Security in the past two decades. But significant aspects of that controversy were direct consequences of Social Security's long public relations campaign, and the misleading language itself still issued forth, continuing to inhibit action.

"Raiding the Trust Fund": A Public Relations Boomerang

As OASDI revenue surpluses from the 1983 rescue accumulated, the "trust fund" became an explosive issue. The "trust fund" was projected to rise to over $12 trillion by 2030. As we saw, since OASDI is off-budget, its surplus offsets any on-budget deficit, making the unified budget deficit smaller than it would be otherwise.

In sensationalist language, economics and political writers warned that Congress was stealing this huge "nest egg." It was almost a media campaign. "Can Washington keep its hands off Social Security's bulging coffers?" asked *Business Week* in March 1988. "Can Congress keep its mitts off the Social Security trust fund?" echoed *Time* a few months later.[100] *Business Week* writer Paul Magnusson announced that "The sad truth is that a quiet hoax is being perpetrated on the American public, and most people don't realize it. The U. S. government is spending the funds to make up for revenue shortfalls elsewhere." The surplus, he added, is not really being saved and is only "a glorious accounting fiction." The surplus and the interest it earns are spent immediately, yet prospective retirees, taken in by the surplus talk, think their retirement money is safe. "Meanwhile, Congress raids the nest, takes the eggs, and leaves a note."[101] Economist Alan Blinder warned that with "untold trillions sitting in the Social Security kitty, legislators surely will be tempted to spend some of it on worthy causes. This we must resist, for if we fail to squirrel the money away, we will not have the wherewithal to pay the retirement bills when they come due." Congress had to grasp, he added, that the surplus "is not spare money; it is spoken for."[102] It was all very much like the "old-age reserve fund" controversy of the thirties—with an important new twist caused by the presence of the term "trust fund."

While the authors of such pieces usually did mention that the surplus revenue was required by law to be used to buy Treasury debt, they conveyed two false and dangerous impressions: that there was a pile of money "spoken for" and sitting in the "trust fund"—and that a lightfingered and dastardly Congress had suddenly decided to rifle it and "leave a note," to paper over yawning budget deficits.

In a telling demonstration of the power of the Great Stereopticon and the credulity of the mass mind, angry letters about the alleged rifling of the "trust fund" began landing on editors' desks. One quite representative letter to *Business Week* in response to Magnusson's piece scourged the "ever-spending Congress" who could "steal it [Social Security] blind to cover up the deficit they've saddled us with over the years." Another reader wrote that he could "find little difference between the actions of labor unions that were indicted for fraud when they appropriated pension funds to use for purposes other than those prescribed by law, and the appropriation of Social Security surpluses to write down budget excesses."[103]

A like misunderstanding developed among politicians in Congress, including some knowledgeable ones. In 1989, the Senate Finance Committee's Subcommittee on Social Security and Family Policy held a hearing on bills intended to bolster public confidence in Social Security. Senator Moynihan, the subcommittee chairman, argued for such bills because of "a great problem that has emerged. . . the trust funds are in some important sense unguarded." The Committee learned in 1985, he added, that the Treasury "had in effect taken enormous sums of money out of the trust funds" to finance general government operations. Whereas the surpluses should be saved to provide for the baby boomers' retirement, the Treasury, Moynihan complained, "has used it as if it was general revenue. They issue a debt certificate to the trust funds, but spend the money for whatever purposes are at hand. . . . they spend it on things other than that for which the money was collected to be put in trust."[104] In another Social Security hearing in 1996, Moynihan was still complaining that "That whole surplus has been squandered" on current government expenditures.[105]

Sensationalist, misleading treatments of the "trust fund" persist even now. A recent book advocating privatization, for example, declares that "one of Washington's dirty little secrets is that there really are no trust funds. The government spent that money long ago to finance general government spending, hiding the true size of the budget deficit. The trust funds now consist only of government bonds, essentially IOUs . . ."[106] This, like the ill-informed magazine pieces of ten years earlier, conveys the totally untrue notion that once upon a time there *was* a stash of money to finance Social Security benefits, but Congress lifted it.

Such is "the power of the word" that even experts on Social Security sometimes gave an impression of being taken in by the term "trust fund." At a 1992 roundtable discussion held by the AARP's magazine *Modern Maturity,* Henry Aaron, Carolyn Weaver, and Laurence Kotlikoff wrangled over, among other things, whether or not it is possible for Congress to "raid" the "trust fund" and whether or not it was already being tapped to cover budget deficits.[107]

The public's misunderstanding, ignorance and anger over the "trust fund" endure to this day. Many Americans have come to believe that Congress is robbing the trust fund and that this is a major cause, if not *the* cause, of Social Security's weakening financial prospects. On July 15, 1998, Carolyn Lukensmeyer, director of the Americans Discuss Social Security project, testified before the Senate Special Committee on Aging about her findings. Funded by the Pew Charitable Trusts, the project polled 17,000 Americans and had substantial discussions with 3,700 Americans in fifteen states. Lukensmeyer found that confidence in Social Security's future is low; 55 percent of Americans in her survey think Social Security is going to face major financial problems, and only 10 percent evaluated it as secure and solid. Moreover, she reported, "the public's perception about the way the government has managed the Social Security trust fund dwarfs its concern about the demographic trends. The government's borrowing of excess payroll contributions to pay for other programs, unrelated to Social Security, is the real focus of the public's concern." Fully 79 percent of respondents identified government spending of Social Security's reserves on other, unrelated programs as one of the reasons why Social Security might have financial trouble in the future. Moreover, 45 percent of respondents said this is the *main* reason. (By contrast, only 26 percent answered, correctly, that the main reason is that growth of the elderly population is outstripping growth of the number of workers.)[108] In another hearing in 1997, the AARP itself observed that the widespread lack of confidence in Social Security's ability to pay benefits in the future is due in part to "the widely held belief that Congress has raided the trust funds."[109]

Elderly lobbies themselves have helped promote this belief. In September 1999 I received an unsolicited letter from an elderly lobby called The Seniors Coalition, warning that "something terrible is happening in Washington. . . . Something sinister and dangerous is happening as you read this note . . ." The Coalition had "exposed the truth about the looting of the Social Security Trust Fund." But when the Coalition's founder died, "our enemies saw an opportunity. . . . the Washington Insiders stole another $1.2 billion from the Social Security Trust Fund." After railing for four pages about these nefarious "Insiders," the author exhorted me to send money and to sign and return an enclosed petition demanding that Congress "Stop the raid on the Social Security Trust Funds. Immediately repay all monies that were illegally diverted from these Trust Funds."[110]

The Seniors Coalition claims to represent three million seniors.[111] Imagine three million elderly getting this scare mailing about how "they" are looting Social Security's "Trust Fund," and spreading the word to friends and relatives. Add the numerous misleading articles in the popular press, and small wonder letters to newspaper editors continue to reflect this virulent strain of the false consciousness:

> Congress has proved it is incapable of handling the "trust fund" without dipping its hands into the fund.[112]
>
> . . . . Let's go back in years and have the government replace all the millions of dollars it took—no, stole—from Social Security. Having the government replace the theft, there wouldn't be any need to gamble in the stock market or bond fund.[113]
>
> Our president and all members of Congress should be charged with criminal malfeasance if the surplus that is supposed to be available by the end of the year is not returned to the Social Security account. . . . [114]
>
> The way to save Social Security immediately is to transfer the administration of this fund to a private administrator. The government has been borrowing and stealing from this lucrative fund.[115]

About this destructive and dangerous misunderstanding, several things must be said. First, far being guilty of illegality or malfeasance, Congress was and is merely doing what the Social Security law has required all along. As we have seen, the requirement that unspent revenues be used to buy Treasuries was in the original Social Security Act.

Second, use of Social Security surplus revenue to defray general government outlays is likewise not new. The same thing had happened in every previous year when Social Security had run a surplus while the rest of the federal government ran a deficit.

Third, if there is an on-budget deficit, under current law there *is no* place for Social Security's surplus to go *except* to help finance current outlays. That is no fault of Congress (except insofar as its fiscal indiscipline produced a deficit). It is simply a financial, legal, and accounting reality.

Fourth, as we have already established (chapter 6), there *is no* Social Security "trust fund" in the proper sense of the term—merely Treasury accounts for the OASI and DI programs. That being so, it is completely erroneous to speak of payroll tax money being put or held "in trust." The whole uproar about robbing the trust fund is flawed at its core. There is no trust fund there to be robbed.

Fifth, there *is no* "nest egg" of money literally "sitting in the Social Security kitty" for Congress to "raid." OASI and DI tax receipts are swept into the Treasury general fund upon receipt and credited to their respective accounts in the form of Treasury securities, and when the Treasury sends out benefit checks, it debits the accounts by removing equivalent amounts of these securities. A given year's "surplus" consists of whatever securities remain at the year's end.[116] This is not a nefarious contrivance. It is a reality of modern finance.

Sixth, if the Social Security "trust fund" is not a true trust fund, neither is it a mere "accounting fiction" or gimmick, as journalists, true to the media's pattern of swinging from credulity to caustic skepticism, have charged.[117] It is a bona fide Treasury account. The "trust fund" is not *nothing,* it's *something*—although not the kind of something Social Security's use of language has led us to believe.

Seventh, the notion that benefits are or will be paid out of the "trust fund" is itself mistaken. Today's benefit payments are made out of current tax revenues, not an accumulated "trust fund." Only the residual of revenues above current benefit outlays actually accrues in the "trust fund." Nor will future benefits be paid out of a "nest egg," because the "trust fund" contains nothing to pay benefits *with.* The Treasuries in the "trust fund" are unmarketable special issues—internal IOUs of the government. They have no market value and cannot be sold to raise cash to pay benefits. Rather, future benefits will be paid with private resources extracted through taxing or borrowing from the public to pay off these bonds when presented by OASDI for payment.

Given all that, the popular anger about the purported robbing of the "trust fund" was, and is, unfair to Congress. But it is also understandable and blameless, for—which is our final, decisively important point about the "trust fund"—it is an unintended, unforeseen consequence of the decision in 1939 by Congress and the Roosevelt administration to re-label Social Security's Old Age Reserve Account at the Treasury as the "Old Age and Survivors Insurance Trust Fund" for public relations purposes. The use of "trust fund" language created, and was meant to create, an impression, powerfully reinforced by statements of various government officials, such as HEW Secretary Hobby, that there is a stock of assets which "belongs" to Social Security taxpayers and is being "held in trust" for them for their retirement. It was done, as we saw, to strengthen public faith in the program. However, if one believes that the Social Security "trust fund" really is a trust fund, one will quite understandably be incensed at the news of Congress using the money for current general operations—and the stronger one's (confected) belief in the reality of this "trust fund," the stronger will be one's anger and sense of betrayal. Whether the writers denouncing the "squandering" of the trust fund "nest egg" really believed Social Security's trust fund language, or were simply ill-informed as to the "trust fund's" true nature is uncertain; what mattered was that they waxed indignant at the rifling of a trust fund, and succeeded in communicating that information, and emotional slant, to their readers. In the wrathful letters to editors and in the Americans Discuss Social Security polls, "the power of the word" is again vividly manifest—but this time to Social Security's disadvantage.

Intended to bolster Social Security's prestige, the term "trust fund" is now having the opposite effect. Had the government opted in 1939 for an accurate and emotionally neutral term such as "Old-Age and Survivors Treasury Account," the vexing public relations problem that dogged Social Security over the Old Age Reserve Account would perhaps not have been solved. On the other hand, today's vexing public relations problem about "robbing the trust fund" would not exist.

"Money's Worth": Another Chicken's Homecoming

Another bad and worsening wound to Social Security's prestige is the issue of getting one's "money's worth" out of Social Security. The first few generations of beneficiaries got fantastic deals from Social Security, because they had paid in only for a few years, at modest tax rates on small taxable incomes, and the overwhelming bulk of the cost of their benefits was pushed onto future generations. However, Social Security offers an increasingly worse deal to each new generation, because as Social Security matured, succeeding generations spent their entire working lives paying ever-increasing Social Security taxes on an ever-increasing taxable income.

This natural diminution of returns attendant on program maturation was much exacerbated by the tax increases of 1977 and the 1983 increases in taxes and the retirement age and the introduction of benefit taxation, which will simultaneously increase the costs to the young and diminish the benefits they will get. Hence, as even the AARP's Public Policy Institute (PPI) acknowledged in 1992, with an honesty that does the AARP credit, it will take each succeeding generation of younger taxpayers longer and longer in retirement to recover what they paid into Social Security. The Public Policy Institute estimated that a median wage earner aged sixty-five in 1992 who had taken early retirement at age sixty-two would take less than ten years of retirement to recover his OAI taxes; if he had retired at sixty-five and was married, he'd recover his money in five. By contrast, a median wage earner aged ten years old in 1992 who retired early at age sixty-two would take over twenty-five years of retirement to recover his money, and if he had retired at sixty-five and was married, he'd take over ten years to get back what he'd paid. Thus, the PPI reported, "the money's worth of OAI is deteriorating over time."[118]

In response to the "money's worth" critique, Social Security officials such as Louis Enoff, Acting Commissioner of Social Security (in 1993), and Commissioner of Social Security Shirley Chater (in 1995 and since) and other advocates such as Henry Aaron, former Commissioner Ball, and the AARP have repeatedly argued that one really cannot assess the value of Social Security strictly in terms of rates of return on investments or a comparison of benefits and contributions. Focusing on such "money's worth" criteria loses sight of the financial security, stability and "social insurance" protections Social Security provides. Moreover, it passes over Social Security's social goals, such as redistribution toward lower-income workers, who get more of their labor income replaced by benefits than do higher-income workers, and prevention of poverty for millions of retirees.[119] Social Security's defenders such as Aaron also disparage "money's worth" concerns as "self interested" and "selfish."[120]

They also invoke the insurance myth. Chater closed her testimony at a 1996 Senate hearing by quoting from the March/April 1996 issue of the *Consumer's Digest Magazine*: "Making a money's worth calculation is basically irrelevant. Do you get your money's worth from insurance that protects your home, health and car if nothing catastrophic happens? Well, the same principle applies to Social Security, a social insurance fund that insures you, your family and everybody else who pays into the system."[121]

Despite these rejoinders, attacks on Social Security on "money's worth" grounds are multiplying. More and more observers are advocating privatization of Social Security; arguing that the program affords young taxpayers a worsening return on their taxes is an effective entering wedge for privatization arguments.

Here again, one of Social Security's public relations and marketing strategies is having unforeseen bad consequences. Precisely the essence of the "money's worth" criticism of Social Security in the nineties—comparison of taxes to benefits—had been one of the main selling points employed by the program's advocates for decades. Beginning in 1935, as we saw, they had reiterated what a splendid insurance buy Social Security is, far surpassing anything one could get for the same money (i.e., the worker's share of the payroll tax) in private insurance. And when Social Security was extended to the self-employed in the fifties, the change was heralded by media celebrations of pension "windfalls" and "bargains in insurance"—fantastic returns for newcomers to the program on only modest tax payments. In so doing, the program's advocates powerfully encouraged Americans to think about Social Security in, yes, self interested and selfish terms: what return they were getting on their money, "what's in it for me." The advocates did not seem to find "money's worth" considerations irrelevant then. They were willing to play up the self-interested angle when it made a strong selling point for the program. Now that it no longer does, Social Security advocates are anxious to downplay and even disparage it.

Moreover, in establishing "money's worth" as a criterion for evaluating the program, Social Security's proponents were giving a lead to later students of Social Security. The observers who, beginning with Colin and Rosemary Campbell in the mid-sixties, through Milton Friedman in the seventies, and on to the proliferating critics of the nineties, pointed out that Social Security was offering a worsening "deal" to the young, were only faithfully following in the footsteps of Social Security's boosters of two decades earlier. The difference was that with a maturing program, changing economic circumstances, and legislated increases in taxes and cuts in benefits for future generations, the calculations gave less attractive results.

The "money's worth" controversy is a child of Social Security's self-promotion in another, more important but indirect way. In a 1955 actuarial study of Social Security's self-financing nature, Chief Actuary Robert Myers wrote that the schedule of payroll tax rates is governed in part by the principle of individual equity, and that "According to this principle, the eventual contributions should not be so high that young entrants could purchase more protection with their own contributions from a private insurance company."[122] Social Security taxes, in other words, should not be driven so high that private insurance offers a better deal for the money. However, it stands to reason that for this outcome to be averted, there has to be some flexibility regarding Social Security benefits—specifically, they have to able to be cut if necessary to hold down the cost the taxes must cover, lest the taxes become unbearable. Recall that Dr. Myers himself said much the same thing in 1979 in recommending that the retirement age be raised. More specifically—which he did not mention—there must be freedom to cut benefits to *current* retirees. If the flexibility is found in cutting benefits to *future* retirees, this lowers the amount of protection the young "purchase" with their "contributions," making Social Security less attractive relative to private insurance. To maintain Social Security's attractiveness to the young, a considerable share of any necessary sacrifices would have to fall on current beneficiaries.

Unfortunately, the politics of Social Security made, and still make, that out of the question—and Social Security's politics flow in large measure from the false consciousness. The true believers' flat refusal to countenance benefit cuts left the Carter administration and Congress no choice except to massively increase payroll taxes, and to retain the tax increase despite its unpopularity. The ferocious resistance, likewise springing in large part from the contrived false consciousness, to Reagan's 1981 proposals to cut current benefits, led directly to the 1983 legislation's emphasis on higher taxes and benefit cuts for future generations. Boxed in by political constraints of which the false consciousness was a major architect, Congress was trapped into massively raising taxes and cutting future benefits, such that the program became a worsening "deal" for the young.

Since Social Security's partisans had made it their business to promote awareness of the program in "money's worth" terms, discovery of and complaint about this unpleasant fact was only a matter of time. Thus they had here again knotted a scourge for Social Security's own back.

There are only two ways to reverse the trend of worsening returns for the young and thereby retain their support for Social Security and their willingness to continue to pay its taxes. One is to capture the higher returns of equity markets. The other is to finally make substantial savings at the expense of *current* beneficiaries, which would permit cuts in current taxes—but which, absent demolition of the false consciousness, greatly increases the political risks attendant on Social Security reform.

Meanwhile the Social Security myths continued to issue from the program's publicity machine and its many partisans and sympathizers, and to find resting places in many minds in Congress and among the public.

Misleading Language Persists

All of the myths we have exposed and exploded—"insurance," "trust funds," "earned rights," and so on—are still being promoted as truths. Even now, Social Security employs the same misleading language—"contributions," "benefits," "insurance." And Part 1 of its booklet *Social Security: Understanding the Benefits* is titled, "Your Investment in Social Security,"[123] as if one were buying an annuity. Its *Basic Facts About Social Security* booklet claims that "Social Security protects more than 141 million workers."[124] What the SSA means is that more than 141 million people are paying Social Security taxes—but the wording it uses makes it sound as if these taxpayers have the "protection" of insurance policies. The booklet later asserts that the value of Social Security survivors' benefits for an average breadwinner leaving a spouse and two children "is equivalent to a $295,000 life insurance policy," and that "Social Security provides a valuable package of disability and survivors insurance to workers." There is, too, a misleading statement that OASDI "is designed so that there is a clear link between how much a worker pays into the system and how much he or she will get in benefits."[125]

As for the use of "trust fund" money for other purposes, the SSA's factsheet "Financing Social Security" has this to say:

> A persistent, but false, rumor is that the trust fund money has been used for purposes other than Social Security payments or operational expenses. For example, almost all presidents since Franklin D. Roosevelt have been characterized . . . as misusers of the trust funds for having allowed Social Security money to be used to finance wars, highway projects, foreign aid, and other government functions.
>
> There is confusion over this issue because of the trust fund investment procedures. . . . The government uses the money it has borrowed from Social Security for other purposes [flatly contradicting the denial in the opening sentence].[126]

Popular-level books by private-sector sympathizers and "experts," purporting to "explain" OASDI, are also keeping profound misunderstandings alive. *Social Security, The Inside Story* by Andy Landis, a former Social Security field representative and self-styled "expert," is a tissue of misstatements: "Social insurance means that the government acts as an insurance company"; "The [benefit] payments made are proportional to your contributions to the system (i.e., the Social Security FICA taxes you pay). Those payments, then, are due you and your family—your work paid for them. They are *earned* [italics in original]."; Social Security is "insurance, not public assistance"; "contributions" "buy" coverage, and so on.[127] A handbook titled *Your Social Security Benefits* takes a different but no less erroneous tack, telling its reader that if he or she is paying Social Security taxes, "As a result, you have built up substantial wealth [sic!] in the system" and that the book will explain "your rights to benefits" and how to "protect your investment [sic]."[128] These and other inaccuracies are waiting on the shelves of public libraries to mislead trusting, conscientious, information-seeking laymen who don't know any better and will innocently take them as facts.

Continuing apologetics for and advocacy of Social Security by private authors likewise perpetuate the analogy of Social Security taxes to insurance premiums; describe Social Security as "insurance for all Americans" and analogize it to private insurance, saying, for example, that Social Security provides a thirty-five-year-old worker with a non-working spouse and two small children "the equivalent of a life insurance policy and a disability insurance policy"; and claim that it offers benefits as an "earned right" and gives "guarantees" unavailable elsewhere; argue that Social Security is "an independent, self-financed insurance system" whose "central purpose" is to pay "a pension that has been earned as a matter of right" and whose "premiums" are the payroll taxes.[129]

The same sort of misleading talk persists among sympathetic Social Security scholars and policy advisers. The report of the 1994-1996 Advisory Council on Social Security conceals Social Security's true nature behind a veil of insurance terminology and euphemisms:

> Social Security is a defined-benefit plan, under which the government agrees to provide specific benefits based on past earnings. . . . About 141 million persons made *contributions* in 1996. They are *buying* more than retirement protection alone. . . .
>
> Social Security requires that all workers . . . *contribute* to their future security. A compulsory program ensures that these *contributions* take place. . . . Compulsion reduces the need for public assistance. In contrast, a voluntary program would allow the improvident to escape their share of paying for their own future retirement needs—leaving the community as a whole to pay for them . . . [130] (italics added)

As to compulsion reducing the need for public assistance, Social Security, redistributing income from current workers to current beneficiaries, *is* public assistance—in fact, the largest welfare program of all. Since one's own taxes paid the benefits of others and were *not* held in a "trust fund," one necessarily goes on welfare the minute one starts collecting benefits. The retirement earnings test increases the resemblance to welfare. This redistribution also means that Social Security taxpayers are *not* "paying for their own future retirement needs," they are financing the retirement of others. In short, "the community as a whole" supports retirees under Social Security—just what the Advisory Council says does *not* happen.

The description of Social Security as a "defined-benefit" pension plan is, unfortunately, inaccurate. The 1939 amendments, *Flemming v. Nestor,* the benefit cuts proposed by Califano and Reagan, and the benefit cuts enacted in 1983 demonstrate conclusively that benefits are *not* "defined," but tentative and malleable, subject to revision by Congress. This is a truth that the Advisory Council's members cannot fail to know.

One subgroup of the Council, including former Social Security Commissioner Ball; Thomas Jones, the vice chairman, president and chief operating officer of the Teachers Insurance and Annuity Association-College Retirement Equities Fund (TIAA-CREF); and various officials of the AFL-CIO, proposed to maintain benefits and pretty much preserve the present structure of Social Security. In advocating their proposal, they once again reiterated the old myths of Social Security, with a little updating: "In Social Security, the government is the administrator and fund manager of an enormous pension and group insurance plan. It collects dedicated taxes which are the equivalent of the premiums in a private insurance plan and the payments into the defined benefit plan of a private corporation or state retirement system. . . .

Social Security is an earned right growing out of past work and contributions. . . . Social Security provides more than $12 trillion in life insurance protection . . . Social Security is more [sic] than a statutory right; it is an *earned* right [italics in original], with eligibility for benefits and the benefit rate based on an individual's past earnings."[131]

Even knowledgeable, respected scholars continue to perpetuate Social Security's official, but erroneous, version of reality. Professor Gramlich refers to OASDI as "the nation's most extensive insurance program."[132] Henry Aaron, director of the Economic Studies Program at the Brookings Institution, testified before the Senate Finance Committee in 1993 that "The Social Security system is an ingenious and messy combination of insurance, income redistribution, all scrambled together. It is life insurance. It is disability insurance. It is survivor's insurance."[133] It is none of these things. Boston College professor Alicia Munnell, a staunch Social Security partisan, denounced privatization plans in a *Boston Globe* op-ed as especially injurious to women. By contrast, Social Security's benefits are, she wrote, "established rights, promised by law."[134] In light of Section 1104, the 1939 amendments, *Flemming v. Nestor,* and the 1983 benefit cuts, this is simply not true, as Munnell cannot fail to know.

The elderly advocacy groups are doing their bit too to preserve the Social Security illusions intact. "Social Security: Crucial Questions & Straight Answers," for example, a fact sheet produced jointly by the AARP and Save Our Security, retains the talk of "contributions" and "trust funds" and asserts that the working Americans contributing to the program through payroll taxes "are building the earned right to future retirement benefits," disability benefits, and survivor benefits. "Social Security benefits are an earned right . . . We all pay into Social Security, pooling our risks and earning the right to protection." Denying benefits to the better-off beneficiaries "would undermine the whole earned-right concept on which Social Security is based. After all, by contributing to the system we all earn the right to receive benefits."[135] This over thirty years after the *Flemming v. Nestor* decision that demolished the validity of depicting Social Security as an "earned right." Indeed the fact sheet made no mention of that decision.

The AARP's bimonthly magazine for its members, *Modern Maturity,* is another vehicle for disseminating Social Security's myths to its members, and in recent years has regularly run pieces doing so. In 1994, Senator Moynihan denied in *Modern Maturity* that Social Security is an "entitlement." Showing keen awareness of "the power of the word," he argued that this term emphasizes one's getting something and ignores what one has to do to qualify for it. Rather,

Social Security was envisioned from the beginning as a social insurance program. People would establish eligibility for Social Security through their work and contributions. Workers' contributions are even identified on their pay stubs as "FICA"—

Federal Insurance Contributions Act [Shades of Wilbur Cohen! Recall our observations in Chapter 8 about invoking the label to establish the reality] . . . the whole idea
of contributory insurance is neatly avoided by the word "entitlement."[136]

The next year, Eugene Lehrmann, AARP's president, denied that Social
Security was facing trouble, but recognized that changes might be necessary
"to honor the program's social contract for the long term." Any such changes,
however, "must preserve the concept of Social Security as an earned benefit."[137] In the same issue, Robert Ball described Social Security as "a complicated insurance program, biggest in the world. . . . family insurance . . .
[providing] more life insurance for American families than all private firms
combined."[138] Other articles in the same issue by Professor Alan Brinkley of
Columbia University and John Rother, Director of AARP's Legislation and
Public Policy Division, parts of an "AARP focus on Social Security," described Social Security as "insurance, not welfare," "a form of 'insurance',"
and "a compact between the generations" for "insurance protection."[139] Representative Bill Archer (R-TX) weighed in with a ringing declaration that
"Social Security has never been an entitlement program; it is an 'earned right'
program, and it's Congress' job to do whatever is necessary to deliver it—
today, tomorrow, and in the 21st century." Archer reaffirmed his strong opposition to means-testing and benefit taxation, because "it violates the
earned-right concept."[140] With AARP's millions of members reading such
things, it is small wonder that the elderly remain deeply committed to Social
Security and adamantly opposed to any reduction in benefits.

Whenever Social Security or Medicare benefit reductions were proposed,
the senior citizens' organizations mobilized their members with strident mailings full of urgent scare language, falsehoods, and insurance terminology.
After the Kerrey-Danforth Commission made its Interim Report, for example,
the National Committee to Preserve Social Security and Medicare sent out
mailings dated September 13, 1994 including a letter signed by NCPSSM
President Martha McSteen (acting Social Security commissioner, 1983-1986)
warning that "this powerful Commission" contained numerous members
"openly hostile to Social Security and Medicare," such as Peter Peterson,
"one of the biggest benefit cutters in Washington." (In fact, Peterson has
repeatedly insisted, in his book *Facing Up* and elsewhere, on protecting,
even increasing, poverty benefits.) The letter asserted that Social Security,
financed by a payroll tax yielding a surplus (true), is not responsible for
federal budget deficits (true for on-budget deficits, false for unified-budget
ones, since in the unified budget, with all revenues and all outlays combined,
a dollar spent on Social Security contributes as much to the deficit as a dollar
spent on anything else). "The big business Concord Coalition and other
entitlement cutters," the letter warned, wanted several budget cuts such as
means testing for Social Security and Medicare, which would cut benefits for

middle- and higher-income recipients, "thus transforming these social insurance programs into welfare programs"; increasing Social Security benefit taxation and taxing Medicare benefits' "insurance value"; and cutting or abolishing Social Security COLAs.[141] After bragging of how in 1985, 1987, 1989, 1990 and 1993 "we helped beat back serious attempts to cut or freeze your Social Security COLA," the letter warned that without the reader's help, it might lose, that the Commission's "scare tactics" could stampede Congress into cutting benefits, and concluded:

> RIGHT NOW IS THE TIME TO PULL TOGETHER AND TURN UP THE HEAT ON CONGRESS. YOUR CONTRIBUTION OF $10 OR $15 WILL HELP US DO IT.
> Your Social Security and Medicare benefits are called entitlements for a very good reason. You worked for them, you paid for them, you earned them, the government has promised them to you, and now you are **entitled** to them . . . and you must be willing to fight for them.
> THESE BENEFITS ARE WORTH THOUSANDS OF DOLLARS TO YOU. PLEASE SEND $10 OR $15 TO HELP US DEFEND THEM.
> **Time is of the essence. The Entitlements Commission needs your personal testimony immediately.**[142] (boldface and all capitals in original)

The mailing included a "personal testimony report" consisting of a one-page five-question questionnaire asking the reader whether the Commission's proposed cuts would affect the security of his retirement, whether he could afford a Social Security COLA cut, and finally, "Should Social Security and Medicare continue to operate as insurance programs, paying benefits to all who have paid into the programs, or should the programs be 'means tested' like welfare, paying benefits only to the poorest seniors?" There was also a "memorandum" from the NCPSSM's chief lobbyist, Max Richtman, to national committee members, warning of the Entitlement Commission's "alarmist message" and "scare tactics," claiming that "they are using scare tactics to try and silence you" (in fact, the Kerrey-Danforth Commission made no effort to silence anybody) and "They are coming after Social Security and Medicare [underlinings in original]," and exhorting the reader, "don't let the Commission silence you! Speak up! And speak up now!"[143]

Such powerful alarms and exhortations, as the reader can well imagine, easily goad beneficiaries into a state of hysteria and obdurate, seething militancy making reasoning with them about Social Security all but impossible.

And in both oral testimony and prepared statements at House and Senate hearings on Social Security throughout the nineties, the AARP continued to insist that Social Security is "insurance" or "social insurance," and that "benefits are an earned right."[144] The AARP was seconded by the National Council of Senior Citizens.[145]

As of this writing, the AARP's website contains a fifteen-question quiz about Social Security which perpetuates the myths. Question 14 asks why people get benefits regardless of their incomes. The answer begins, "Social Security benefits are not welfare. They are an earned right, based on a worker's earnings and time in the workforce. Since we all pay into Social Security and pool our risks, we all earn the right to protection regardless of income."[146] Given the retirement earnings test, this is simply not true.

Labor is likewise sustaining the false consciousness. An article in the August-September 1998 issue of the UAW's monthly *Solidarity* described Social Security as "a system of social insurance" and "the national old-age insurance system," adding that "Benefits are guaranteed by law." Invoking the close analogy to individual insurance policies, the piece described those benefits as "Like a $201,000 disability policy" and "$322,000 in life insurance."[147]

Social Security's false consciousness still has a powerful grip on politicians, too. In a vivid demonstration of this, in 1991 the Senate Special Committee on Aging prepared an "information paper" titled *Getting the Most from Federal Programs: Social Security (Retirement, Survivors, Disability), Supplemental Security Income, and Medicare* written for these programs' beneficiaries, telling its readers that "It is your right to receive the maximum benefits to which you are entitled" and exhorting them to "seek the full benefits to which you are entitled."[148] It also reiterated some of the same inaccuracies Social Security itself had been propagating for decades:

> It is important to remember that *the Social Security benefits you receive come from the money that you or your spouse have paid into the program during your working years.* . . .
> The Social Security program is based on a simple idea. You pay Social Security taxes into the system during your working years, and you and certain members of your family receive monthly benefits when you retire or become disabled. Or, your survivors collect benefits when you die. *Social Security benefits are paid from a government trust fund accumulated from taxes you and your employer have paid on your earnings.* These taxes are used to pay for all retirement, disability and survivors benefits.[149] (italics added)

In the years that followed, statements by politicians of both parties gave additional evidence that Social Security's false consciousness still prevails. At a 1993 hearing on "money's worth," Senator Donald Riegle (D-MI) said that the hearing's importance was "to underscore the broad insurance concept that is here." He described Social Security as "the most successful" insurance program because of its nationwide size, and as "this National insurance contract that we have with one another . . . . a cross-generational set of insurance protections so that younger workers have available to them at exactly the time they need it the most a form of social insurance that they would not have any other way."[150]

At a 1998 hearing on the goals of Social Security, Senator Harry Reid (D-NV) described it as "a social insurance package" and "a universal social insurance program." At the same hearing Senator Rick Santorum (R-PA) declared: "I believe Social Security needs to be maintained in some form. It is a social insurance program, but just that—an insurance program, not a transfer payment program that is a pay-as-you-go system. That is not a fair generational program."[151]

In 1998 the anti-deficit Concord Coalition and the AARP jointly sponsored a "great debate" on Social Security in Kansas City, Missouri. Opening the proceedings on April 7, President Clinton described Social Security as "a life-insurance policy" and "a rock-solid guarantee" and laid down as a principle of reform the assertion that "Social Security must provide a benefit that people can count on," a "solid and dependable foundation of retirement security."[152]

As a corollary, politicians of both parties adamantly insist that Social Security's "promises" to current beneficiaries must be kept.

The false consciousness still dominates the public mind, too. In 1997, Madelyn Hochstein, president and co-founder of DYG, Inc., a Danbury, Connecticut public opinion research firm, testified before the Senate Special Committee on Aging, about her firm's findings in its 1995-1996 Social Security and Medicare Anniversary Study for the AARP. Hochstein reported "extraordinary lack of confidence in Social Security's future financial viability"—but at the same time, fully 80 percent of respondents in her survey agreed with the statement that "the government made a commitment a long time ago [regarding Social Security] that cannot be broken."[153]

Hoist With Its Own Petard

It emerges, then, that the decades-old promotional campaign for Social Security succeeded only too well. It and the false consciousness it has created are in fact at the very heart of our gruesome predicament over Social Security: roots of crisis. The program, and with it the soundness of American public finance and the very legitimacy of American government, are caught between an irresistible force and an immovable object. On the one hand, changing economic and demographic conditions require Social Security to be flexible to meet them; on the other hand, the long mythmaking, intended to win public acceptance of and support for the program by fostering an atmosphere of security and certainty with talk of "earned rights," "insurance," and "trust funds," has created a climate of opinion making such adjustments impossible—or which made politicians believe for too long that such adjustments are too politically risky to be attempted, which for all practical purposes amounts to the same thing. And the time-honored way out of the trap—pushing the burden of adjustment onto younger Americans—is no longer feasible. It is finally dawning on the young that they have been forced to bear virtually all of the sacrifices necessary to keep Social Security going, and they are beginning to resist.

The adamant resistance during the Carter years to any trims in benefits, springing in large part from the false consciousness so carefully built up, left no choice but to pile the entire burden of rescuing Social Security onto the taxpayers. The ferocious opposition to Reagan's 1981 proposals, also the child of the false consciousness, led to a second rescue that again inflicted virtually all of the sacrifice on future generations. These rescues drove taxpayers over their threshold of pain for Social Security taxes, and spawned widespread resentment, making it unlikely that Americans will accept further Social Security tax increases. At a 1994 hearing, Congressman Pickle, although lauding the 1983 rescue, remarked, "I do not think, though, that we can raise taxes again. I just think you are going to reach a point where employers and employees are going to say, 'No more taxes.'"[154] Meanwhile, aroused and militant, the elderly lobby cowed every attempt since 1983 to adjust the program further even as its long-term outlook continued to deteriorate.

The time when a relatively easy adjustment could have been debated and made has been squandered. In 1997 former Chief Actuary Robertson observed grimly that

> if we do not take action by the year 2000, it will be too late. Frankly, it is already too late to make a smooth transition to a new system (we should have acted in the early 1980s). A very bumpy transition can be made in the late 1990s. But after the year 2000, we will be trapped: It will then be obvious to everyone that the present Social Security program won't work and that its continuation will result in massive social and economic turmoil, yet it will be too late to implement a revised program without causing a different form of social and economic turmoil that is equally disturbing.[155]

Because of our procrastination, substantial taxpayer and beneficiary suffering has become inevitable. "The power of the word" is operating with a vengeance. Social Security, in short, is hoist with its own petard of inaccurate, misleading language.

This language, and the false consciousness it has generated, still exert their baneful influence. Even now, many Americans, politicians and private citizens alike, cling to the notion of Social Security as "insurance." Even now, the powerful elderly lobby insists that benefits are an "earned right." Even now, Social Security's partisans deny that it faces any crisis. Even now, the public adamantly refuses to embrace painful measures to strengthen the program—increased taxes, benefit cuts, or raising the retirement age.

Instead, Americans are escaping into a search for deliverance, pinning their hopes on a perpetual bull market in stocks yielding fantastic returns. Unfortunately, these proposals to reform or "privatize" Social Security are yet another flight from reality, rather than a confrontation with it.

Notes

1. "No Bankruptcy—But a Need for Money," *Time*, February 16, 1976, p. 54.
2. "Social Security Debate—Readers Choose Up Sides," *U.S. News & World Report*, November 19, 1984, p. 107.
3. *Congressional Quarterly Almanac 1975* (Washington, DC: Congressional Quarterly, Inc., 1976), pp. 688-689.
4. Peterson and Howe, *On Borrowed Time*, pp. 244-245; John Snee and Mary Ross, "Social Security Amendments of 1977: Legislative History and Summary of Provisions," *Social Security Bulletin*, vol. 41, no. 3 (March 1978), pp. 12-13, especially Table 1—Replacement rates under old and new law; A. Haeworth Robertson, "Financial Status of Social Security Program After the Social Security Amendments of 1977," *Social Security Bulletin*, vol. 41, no. 3 (March 1978), p. 22.
5. Snee and Ross, "Social Security Amendments of 1977: Legislative History and Summary of Provisions," p. 5.
6. *1975 OASDI Annual Report*, p. 37; *1976 OASDI Annual Report*, p. 53; *1977 OASDI Annual Report*, p. 2.
7. "No Bankruptcy—But a Need for Money," *Time*, February 16, 1976, pp. 53-54.
8. Snee and Ross, "Social Security Amendments of 1977: Legislative History and Summary of Provisions," p. 6.
9. "How to Pay for Social Security?" *U.S. News & World Report*, July 4, 1977, p. 37.
10. Ibid.
11. Joseph A. Califano, Jr., *Governing America: An Insider's Report from the White House and the Cabinet* (New York: Simon & Schuster, 1981), pp. 376-377.
12. Snee and Ross, "Social Security Amendments of 1977: Legislative History and Summary of Provisions," p. 12; Califano, *Governing America*, p. 382.
13. Snee and Ross, "Social Security Amendments of 1977: Legislative History and Summary of Provisions," pp. 12-14, p. 18, Table 3.—Contribution and benefit base under old and new law, and p. 18, Table 4.—Tax rate schedule under old and new law; Califano, *Governing America*, p. 382.
14. Califano, *Governing America*, pp. 382-383.
15. Ibid., pp. 387-389.
16. Berkowitz, *Mr. Social Security: The Life of Wilbur J. Cohen*, pp. 301-302; Califano, *Governing America*, p. 389.
17. Califano, *Governing America*, p. 391.
18. Ibid., p. 392.
19. Ibid., p. 395.
20. Ibid., p. 397.
21. Robertson, "Financial Status of Social Security Program After the Social Security Amendments of 1977," p. 27.
22. *1980 Annual Report of the Board of Trustees of the Federal Old-Age and Survivors Insurance and Disability Insurance Trust Funds*, pp. 2-3, 57-58.
23. John A. Svahn, "Omnibus Reconciliation Act of 1981: Legislative History and Summary of OASDI and Medicare Provisions," *Social Security Bulletin*, vol. 44, no. 10 (October 1981), pp. 6-7; *Congressional Quarterly Almanac 1981* (Washington, DC: Congressional Quarterly, Inc., 1982), p. 118.
24. William Greider, "The Education of David Stockman," *Atlantic Monthly*, December 1981, pp. 43-44.
25. U.S., Congress, House, 97th Cong., 1st sess., May 13, 1981, *Congressional Record*, 127: 9638-9640, 9676-9677.

26. U.S., Congress, House, 97th Cong., 1st sess., May 20, 1981, *Congressional Record,* 127: 10327.
27. U.S., Congress, House, 97th Cong., 1st sess., June 4, 1981, *Congressional Record,* 127: 11622.
28. U.S., Congress, House, Representative Barbara A. Mikulski, "Remarks on Social Security Cuts," Extension of Remarks, 97th Cong., 1st sess., June 23, 1981, *Congressional Record,* 127:13513; U.S., Congress, House, Representative Stephen L. Neal, "We Must Honor Solemn Commitment to Older Americans," Extension of Remarks, 97th Cong., 1st sess., July 17, 1981, *Congressional Record,* 127:16406-16407.
29. "Pensions to fall 13%: Reagan plan analyzed," *Detroit News,* May 21, 1981, 2A.
30. U.S., Congress, Senate, 97th Cong., 1st sess., May 20, 1981, *Congressional Record,* 127: 10391-10394.
31. "Cohen questions Reagan cuts," *Detroit News,* May 13, 1981, A3; Richard A. Ryan, "Capital Connections," *Detroit News,* July 27, 1981, 12A.
32. U.S., Congress, House, Select Committee on Aging, *Impact of Administration's Social Security Proposals on the Elderly: Hearing before the House Select Committee on Aging,* 97th Cong., 1st sess., 1981, pp. 73, 100-101, 118-119.
33. "Senior Citizens Put On the War Paint," *U.S. News & World Report,* July 27, 1981, pp. 33-34; "Coalition Plans Drive Against Move to Trim Social Security Benefits," *New York Times,* May 14, 1981, B15.
34. "Save Our Security," *Solidarity,* June, 1981, p. 5; *Detroit News,* May 22, 1981, 12A.
35. *Solidarity,* August 1981, back cover.
36. Robert M. Ball, "Social Security Cuts: Violating a Trust," *AFL-CIO American Federationist,* June 1981, pp. 12-18.
37. "From our readers: Don't pull the rug out from under the elderly," *Detroit Free Press,* May 24, 1981, 2B.
38. "Letters to The Times," *Los Angeles Times,* May 24, 1981, IV:4.
39. Marvin Stone, "The Social Security Flare-Up," *U.S. News & World Report,* June 8, 1981, p. 92.
40. *Congressional Quarterly Almanac 1981,* p. 119; "The Gipper Loses One," *Newsweek,* June 1, 1981, p. 22.
41. *Congressional Quarterly Almanac 1981,* p. 120.
42. "Letters to The Times," *Los Angeles Times,* July 29, 1981, II:4.
43. "Letters to The Times," *Los Angeles Times,* August 21, 1981, II:10.
44. "Voice of the People," *Chicago Tribune,* August 24, 1981, I:20.
45. "Letters to The Times," *Los Angeles Times,* September 2, 1981, II:6.
46. *Congressional Quarterly Almanac 1981,* pp. 117-118.
47. Friedrich Nietzsche, *The Wanderer and His Shadow,* in Friedrich Nietzsche, *Basic Writings of Nietzsche,* tr. and ed. Walter Kaufmann (New York: Random House, Modern Library, 1968), pp. 165-166.
48. "Champion of the Elderly," *Time,* April 25, 1983, pp. 21, 22-23; Paul Light, *Artful Work: The Politics of Social Security Reform* (New York: Random House, 1985), pp. 152-161.
49. "Pro and Con: Delay Social Security Till Age 68?" *U.S. News & World Report,* February 19. 1979, pp. 49-50; "Pro and Con: Raise Social Security Retirement Age?" *U.S. News & World Report,* July 27, 1981, p. 35.
50. "Pro and Con: Raise Social Security Taxes Now?" *U.S. News & World Report,* November 1, 1982, p. 77.

51. "'The Great COLA War'—What's At Stake," *U.S. News & World Report,* April 26, 1982, p. 90; "Pro and Con: Limit Increases in Social Security?" *U.S. News & World Report,* May 10, 1982, p. 81.

52. *Congressional Quarterly Almanac 1983* (Washington, DC: Congressional Quarterly, Inc., 1986), pp. 221-222.

53. Light, *Artful Work,* pp. 137-138.

54. John A. Svahn and Mary Ross, "Social Security Amendments of 1983: Legislative History and Summary of Provisions," *Social Security Bulletin,* vol. 46, no. 7 (July 1983), pp. 8, 24.

55. Ibid., pp. 25-26.

56. Ibid., p. 26.

57. Phillip Longman, *Born to Pay: The New Politics of Aging in America* (Boston: Houghton Mifflin, 1987), pp. 73-74.

58. Svahn and Ross, "Social Security Amendments of 1983: Legislative History and Summary of Provisions," pp. 24-25.

59. Ibid., pp. 27-28.

60. Ibid., p. 30.

61. Ibid., p. 42, Table 10.1.—Estimated changes in OASDI tax income, general fund transfers, and benefit payments resulting from provisions in Public Law 98-21, under 1983 Alternative II-B assumptions, calendar years 1983-1989.

62. Table 10.1 source: Ibid., p. 44, Table 4.—Estimated long-range OASDI cost effect of the Social Security Amendments of 1983.

63. Table 10.2 sources: Snee and Ross, "Social Security Amendments of 1977: Legislative History and Summary of Provisions," p. 18, Table 4.—Tax rate schedule under old and new law; *2000 OASDI Annual Report,* p. 67, Table II.E2., and p. 70, Table II.E3.—Selected OASDI Program Amounts Determined Under the Automatic-Adjustment Provisions, Calendar Years 1978-2000, and Projected Future Amounts, Calendar Years 2001-09, on the Basis of the Intermediate Set of Assumptions.

64. "Budget Plan Highlights," *Congressional Quarterly Almanac 1985* (Washington, DC: Congressional Quarterly, Inc., 1986), p. 459.

65. "Debt Limit Bill/Gramm-Rudman 'Fix' Clears," *Congressional Quarterly Almanac 1987* (Washington, DC: Congressional Quarterly, Inc., 1988), p. 605.

66. "Congress Cuts Budget by More Than $55 Billion," *Congressional Quarterly Almanac 1985* (Washington, DC: Congressional Quarterly, Inc., 1986), pp. 441-457; "Graying Armies March to Defend Social Security," *U.S. News & World Report,* April 29, 1985, pp. 25-26.

67. "Voters Restore Democrats to Senate Control," *Congressional Quarterly Almanac 1986* (Washington, DC: Congressional Quarterly, Inc., 1986), pp. 5-B, 7-B.

68. "Hope Dims for Friday Budget Accord," *Washington Post,* November 17, 1987, A6; "The Narrow Road To Deficit Accord," *Washington Post,* November 22, 1987, A1, A4.

69. "Budget Reconciliation Act Provisions," *Congressional Quarterly Almanac 1990* (Washington, DC: Congressional Quarterly, Inc., 1991), pp. 161-162.

70. United States General Accounting Office [hereafter, GAO], *Budget Policy: Issues in Capping Mandatory Spending* (GAO/AIMD-94-155, July 1994), p. 4.

71. See, e.g., "The State of the Union: Bush Reviews Planned Cuts, Offers Economic Spurs," *Congressional Quarterly Weekly Report* [hereafter, *CQWR*], vol. 50, no. 5, February 1, 1992, p. 267; "Text of the President's Speech as He Accepted the Nomination," *New York Times,* August 22, 1992, 9; "Transcript of First TV Debate Among Bush, Clinton and Perot," *New York Times,* October 12, 1992, A15.

72. Carolyn Weaver, "Baby-Boom Retirees, Destined to Go Bust," *Wall Street Journal,* August 26, 1993, A10.
73. GAO, *Budget Policy: Issues in Capping Mandatory Spending,* pp. 43-45.
74. Ibid., p. 5.
75. "Proposal Indicates Bush Is Willing To Bend on the Issue of the Deficit," *Wall Street Journal,* January 30, 1992, A6; "Text of the President's Speech as He Accepted the Nomination," *New York Times,* August 22, 1992, 9.
76. Jack Kemp, "Taxes vs. Growth," *New York Times,* February 19, 1993, A15.
77. "Clinton Considers Curbs on Social Security Cost-of-Living Raises," *Washington Post,* January 29, 1993, A9; "Senators Differ on Deficit Cuts Involving Social Security," *Washington Post,* February 1, 1993, A4; "Clinton's Social Security Test: Selling Sacrifice to the Elderly," *New York Times,* February 7, 1993, 1; "Social Security Won't Be Subject To Freeze, White House Decides," *New York Times,* February 9, 1993, A1.
78. John R. Kasich, "On the Cutting Edge: The House GOP Alternative to Clinton's Budget," *Policy Review,* Summer 1993, p. 24.
79. William A. Niskanen and Stephen Moore, "May We Cut In, Mr. Clinton?" *Policy Review,* Spring 1993, p. 5.
80. Ibid., p. 6.
81. Ibid., pp. 6-7.
82. "Amid Republican Potshots, Clinton Tries to Limit Outcry Over Budget Memo," *New York Times,* October 24, 1994, A8; "Deficit-Cut Memos Reveal How Both Parties Gloss the Truth," *Washington Post,* October 25, 1994, A6.
83. "House GOP Budget Aide Vows to Devise Seven-Year Plan to Balance U.S. Books," *Wall Street Journal,* November 18, 1994, B4.
84. "A Balanced Budget: What One Looked Like," *New York Times,* November 28, 1994, A1, A10.
85. George Hager, "Opponents Launch Campaign to Stop Budget Amendment," *CQWR,* vol. 50., no. 22, May 30, 1992, p. 1520.
86. "GOP Is Pressed On How Budget Is to Be Balanced," *Wall Street Journal,* February 1, 1995, B3.
87. "The Zero Option: GOP's Plan to Erase Deficits Would Leave Few in U.S. Unscathed," *Wall Street Journal,* May 10, 1995, A1, A8.
88. *1994 OASDI Annual Report,* p. 191, Table III.D1.—Long-Range Actuarial Balances for the OASDI Program as Shown for the Intermediate Assumptions in the Trustees Reports Issued in Years 1984-1994.
89. *The 1992 Annual Report of the Board of Trustees of the Federal Hospital Insurance Trust Fund* [hereafter, *HI Annual Report*], p. 3, Table 1.—Status of the Hospital Insurance Trust Fund; *1994 HI Annual Report,* p. 3, Table 1.A.1.—Status of the HI Trust Fund.
90. *1992 HI Annual Report,* p. 4; *1993 HI Annual Report,* p. 4.
91. *1994 OASDI Annual Report,* p. 29.
92. *1994 HI Annual Report,* p. 3.
93. *1994 OASDI Annual Report,* pp. 14-15, 28.
94. *1995 OASDI Annual Report,* pp. 32, 26.
95. Bipartisan Commission on Entitlement and Tax Reform, *Final Report to the President* (Washington, DC: U.S. Government Printing Office, 1995), pp. ii-v.
96. Ibid., pp. 16, 22-26.
97. Ibid., pp. 108, 109, 148.
98. 1994-1996 Advisory Council on Social Security, *Report of the 1994-1996 Advisory Council on Social Security,* 2 vols., vol. I: *Findings and Recommendations* (Washington, DC: n. p., 1997), pp. 12, 14 n. 4, 18-21, n. 6, 7, 8, 11.

99. For a critical look at the 1997 budget deal, especially its failure to address future problems in Social Security and Medicare, see John Attarian, "Cancerous Budget," *National Review,* October 27, 1997, pp. 42-44.

100. "The $12 Trillion Temptation," *Time,* July 4, 1988, p. 58.

101. Paul Magnusson, "We Are Plundering the Social Security Till," *Business Week,* July 18, 1988, p. 92. Similar articles about the "trust fund" include "Social Security's 'Dirty Little Secret'," *Business Week,* January 29, 1990, pp. 66-67.

102. Alan S. Blinder, "Congress Should Keep Its Hands Off this Nest Egg," *Business Week,* July 4, 1988, p. 20.

103. "Readers Report: Congress is Spending Away a Crucial Safety Net," *Business Week,* August 8, 1988, p. 7. The foregoing title is itself erroneous and sensational.

104. U.S., Congress, Senate, Finance Committee, *Improving Public Confidence in Social Security: Hearing before the Subcommittee on Social Security and Family Policy, Senate Finance Committee,* 101st Cong., 1st sess., 1989, pp. 3-4.

105. U.S., Congress, Senate, Finance Committee, *Social Security and Future Retirees: Hearing before the Subcommittee on Social Security and Family Policy, Senate Finance Committee,* 104th Cong., 2nd sess., 1996, p. 5.

106. Peter J. Ferrara and Michael Tanner, *A New Deal for Social Security* (Washington, DC: The Cato Institute, Inc., 1998), p. 7.

107. "Social Security: Invaluable or outmoded?" *Modern Maturity,* April-May 1992, pp. 48, 84.

108. U.S., Congress, Senate, Special Committee on Aging, *Living Longer, Retiring Earlier: Rethinking the Social Security Retirement Age: Hearing before the Senate Special Committee on Aging,* 105th Cong., 2nd sess., 1998, pp. 84, 93, 121, 127.

109. U.S., Congress, House, Committee on Ways and Means, *The Future of Social Security for this Generation and the Next: Hearing before the Social Security Subcommittee, House Ways and Means Committee,* 105th Cong., 1st sess., 1997, p. 58.

110. The Seniors Coalition, unsolicited mailing, received September 10, 1999.

111. Ibid.

112. "Letters: Social Security: A scam or a safety net?" *Detroit News,* January 13, 1997, 6A.

113. Ibid.

114. "Letters: Insecurity on state of Social Security," *Detroit News,* May 7, 1998, 16A.

115. Ibid.

116. *1998 Green Book,* pp. 73, 75, 77.

117. See, e.g., Matthew Miller, "Public needs straight talk on saving Social Security," *Detroit News,* February 23, 1996, 9A.

118. U.S., Congress, Senate, Finance Committee, *"Money's Worth" of Social Security: Hearing before the Senate Finance Committee,* 103rd Cong., 1st sess., 1993, pp. 152-153.

119. Ibid., pp. 6-7, 30-31, 32; *Social Security and Future Retirees: Hearing,* pp. 6-7, 69-71; Shirley S. Chater, in "Letters to the Editor: Not a Ponzi Scheme," *Washington Post,* December 30, 1995, A18.

120. *"Money's Worth" of Social Security: Hearing,* pp. 30-31.

121. *Social Security and Future Retirees: Hearing,* pp. 8-9. It says something about the intellectual standards—or perhaps the desperation—of Social Security's defenders that Chater would resort to citing the *Consumer's Digest Magazine,* which she described as "a well-respected publication" (Ibid., p. 8).

122. Robert J. Myers, *The Financial Principle of Self-Support in the Old-Age and Survivors Insurance Program,* Social Security Administration, Division of the Actuary, Actuarial Study no. 40, April 1955, p. 3.

123. Social Security Administration, *Social Security: Understanding the Benefits,* SSA Publication No. 05-10024, January 1996, p. 4.
124. Social Security Administration, *Basic Facts About Social Security,* SSA Publication No. 05-10080, August 1995, p. 1.
125. Ibid., pp. 2, 16, 15.
126. Social Security Administration, "Financing Social Security," SSA Publication No. 05-10094, April 1995, p. 2; Social Security Administration, "Financing Social Security," SSA Publication No. 05-10094, May 1998, p. 2; Social Security Administration, "Financing Social Security," SSA Publication No. 05-10094, p. 2.
127. Andy Landis, *Social Security, The Inside Story: An Expert Explains Your Rights and Benefits* (Bellevue, WA: Mount Vernon Press, 1993), pp. 21, 22, 23, 26, 30-32, 35, 56, 238.
128. *Your Social Security Benefits* (New York: Retirement Living Publishing Co., Inc., 1995), p. 2.
129. Merton C. Bernstein and Joan Brodshaug Bernstein, *Social Security: The System That Works,* p. 13; Eric R. Kingson, *What You Must Know About Social Security and Medicare* (New York: Pharos Books, 1988), pp. 9, 12, 13, 14-15, 17; John L. Hess, "Social Security Is for Everybody," *Nation,* January 16, 1988, pp. 53, 54.
130. *Report of the 1994-1996 Advisory Council on Social Security,* vol 1: *Findings and Recommendations,* p. 15.
131. Ibid., pp. 83, 88, 89, 95.
132. Edward M. Gramlich, *Is It Time to Reform Social Security?* (Ann Arbor, MI: University of Michigan Press, 1998), p. 1.
133. *"Money's Worth" of Social Security: Hearing,* p. 30.
134. Alicia H. Munnell, "Privatization plans hit women hardest," *Boston Globe,* November 3, 1998, A17.
135. American Association of Retired Persons and Save Our Security, "Social Security: Crucial Questions & Straight Answers" (Washington, DC: n.d. [1995?]).
136. Senator Daniel Patrick Moynihan, "The case against entitlement cuts," *Modern Maturity,* November-December 1994, p. 13.
137. Eugene Lehrmann, "Heritage of the Depression," *Modern Maturity,* July-August 1995, pp. 94-95.
138. Robert M. Ball, "Social Security: the facts," *Modern Maturity,* July-August 1995, pp. 94-95.
139. Alan Brinkley, "Behind the numbers," *Modern Maturity,* July-August 1995, p. 97; John C. Rother, "Options for the future," *Modern Maturity,* July-August 1995, p. 100.
140. Representative Bill Archer, "Securing Social Security," *Modern Maturity,* July-August 1995, p. 98.
141. U.S., Congress, House, Committee on Ways and Means, *H.R. 4245, H.R. 4275, and Other Bills to Restore the Long-Term Solvency of Social Security: Hearing before the Social Security Subcommittee, House Ways and Means Committee,* 103rd Cong., 2nd sess., 1994, pp. 97-99.
142. Ibid., pp. 100-101.
143. Ibid., pp. 103, 104.
144. *H.R. 4245, H.R. 4275, and Other Bills to Restore the Long-Term Solvency of Social Security: Hearing,* pp. 45, 47, 50; *The Future of Social Security for this Generation and the Next: Hearing,* p. 66; U.S., Congress, Senate, Special Committee on Aging, *A Starting Point for Reform: Identifying the Goals of Social Security: Hearing before the Senate Special Committee on Aging,* 105th Cong., 2nd sess., 1998, pp. 40, 43; *Social Security and Future Retirees: Hearing,* pp. 69-77.

145. See, e.g., *H.R. 4245, H.R. 4275, and Other Bills to Restore the Long-Term Solvency of Social Security: Hearing,* pp. 63-64.
146. "The Facts," Question 14, at www.aarp.org/social security/facts.
147. "Will Social Security be fixed or weakened?" *Solidarity,* August/September 1998, pp. 13, 14, 16, 17. Predictably, the UAW is also adamantly opposed to privatization. See "At Risk," *Solidarity,* October 1998, pp. 9-12.
148. U.S., Congress, Senate, Special Committee on Aging, *Getting the Most from Federal Programs: Social Security (Retirement, Survivors, Disability), Supplemental Security Income, and Medicare: An Information Paper prepared for use by the Senate Special Committee on Aging,* 102nd Cong., 1st sess., 1991, pp. iii, 1.
149. Ibid., pp. 1-2.
150. *"Money's Worth" of Social Security: Hearing,* pp. 5-6.
151. *A Starting Point for Reform: Identifying the Goals of Social Security: Hearing,* pp. 6, 9.
152. The Concord Coalition, "Transcript of Proceedings, The Great Social Security Debate April 7, 1998, Kansas City, Missouri," p. 3 (www.concordcoalition.org).
153. U.S., Congress, Senate, Special Committee on Aging, *Retiring Baby Boomers: Meeting the Challenges: Hearing before the Senate Special Committee on Aging,* 105th Cong., 1st sess., 1997, pp. 86, 111.
154. *H.R. 4245, H.R. 4275, and Other Bills to Restore the Long-Term Solvency of Social Security: Hearing,* p. 13.
155. Robertson, *The Big Lie,* p. xiii.

Part 3

What Now?

11

A Critical Survey of Social Security Reform

*"In despair men turn to quacks who promise
them their dreams."*

—*Correlli Barnett[1]*

All reform or "privatization" proposals seek to capture higher returns on Social Security's taxes and to avert the coming crisis. Three commonly proposed approaches are: divert some of the existing tax into publicly or privately held individual retirement accounts; increase the tax and direct the additional portion into such accounts; or invest part of the "trust fund" in the stock market. Another possibility is to use general revenues from future budget surpluses, to fund either private accounts or government investment in stocks. A more radical idea is to replace Social Security with a system of private accounts resembling the system adopted by Chile in 1981. Scrutiny of the proliferating proposals individually would require a book in itself. Rather, let us examine the basic approaches, with some examples, to illuminate the problems of reform.

First, however, a recent development demands attention.

A Social Security "Lock Box"

In 1999, in response to the clamor that Congress is "raiding" the Social Security "trust fund," congressional Republicans proposed creating a "lock box" for the "fund," whereby Congress would be prohibited from using Social Security surpluses to finance non-Social Security spending or tax cuts. Pending reform of Social Security, the surpluses could only be used to pay down publicly held federal debt. In 1999 and 2000 the House passed bills creating a "lock box," but the Senate did not complete action on them.[2]

The "lock box" addresses a problem that does not exist. Congress is not "raiding the trust fund," and under current law Social Security's surplus has nowhere else to go but into Treasury debt. Moreover, in an interview with the

AARP Bulletin, former Congressional Budget Office director Robert Reischauer pointed out that there really is no way to create an effective "lock box," and that enactment of a "lock box" would not make the "trust fund" any safer, nor would failure to enact one make it any shakier. And the presence or absence of a "lock box" will make no difference whatever for Social Security's future finances, since its problems flow from an aging population and greater longevity, not "trust fund" raiding.[3] Reischauer is obviously correct. The "trust fund" would still be credited with unmarketable Treasuries, whether the surplus revenue financed on-budget spending or retired publicly held debt. "Lock box" or no "lock box," those Treasuries would still have to be redeemed to pay future benefits. That being so, creating a "lock box" is pointless.

Two-Tier Plans

Two-tier plans call for splitting the existing payroll tax into two parts, or "tiers," hence the name. One would pay benefits for current retirees under the existing Social Security program and a flat benefit for participants in its reformed version. The other would be diverted or "carved out" for deposit in mandatory individual retirement accounts, which would be invested in equities and other instruments, and capture higher returns.

One of the three subgroups of the 1994-1996 Social Security Advisory Council, for example, called for phasing in a two-tiered system, under which Tier I of the Social Security tax (7.4 percent of taxable payroll) would pay a flat benefits, and Tier II (5 percent of taxable payroll) would go into fully-funded, privately-held individual Personal Security Accounts (PSAs). All workers under fifty-five in 1998—that is, those born in 1943 or later, which includes the baby boomers—would participate, and would be able to start withdrawing funds from their accounts at age sixty-two. All workers under fifty-five, then, would have their payroll tax split in this way. Current retirees and workers over fifty-five would stay under the present Social Security system, which the two-tier system would gradually replace. Workers under twenty-five (those born in 1973 or later) would get benefits only from the new system: a flat benefit from the government paid for by Tier I taxes, and a Tier II benefit from the PSA's earnings. This plan, like the others offered by the Advisory Council, assumes that stocks will continue to earn the historical real return per year of about 7 percent. The gradual increase in the age of eligibility for full retirement benefits enacted in 1983 would be accelerated, reaching sixty-seven in 2011, and seventy by 2083. Fifty percent of Social Security benefits would be subject to federal income tax.[4]

Stanford University economist John Shoven has proposed a similar PSA plan which also keeps those age fifty-five and older under the existing program. Shoven too would put 5 percent of pay into individually held accounts, but do so through mandatory individual contributions of 2.5 percent of pay, matched dollar for dollar by Social Security taxes. The new plan would be phased in slowly, affecting only workers under age fifty-five. The retirement age would rise to sixty-seven in 2011. Upon retirement, half the account amount would be converted into an annuity.[5] Shoven and Sylvester Schieber, vice president of the retirement consulting firm Watson Wyatt Worldwide, proposed yet another two tier plan, PSA 2000, almost identical to Shoven's.[6] Although neither plan explains how transition costs will be met, presumably they will be financed by borrowing.

Obviously, much depends on how much of the current payroll tax is needed to finance current benefits. In 1985-1999, the surplus of payroll tax revenues over benefit payments averaged 13.5 percent of revenues, meaning paying benefits required an average of 86.5 percent of revenues.[7] With 86.5 percent of payroll tax revenues (about 10.7 percent of taxable payroll) spoken for, just 13.5 percent of revenues (1.7 percent of taxable payroll) are available for accounts. Moreover, under high cost assumptions, the payroll tax stops generating a cash flow surplus in 2010, and just a couple of years later under intermediate ones.[8] The cash stream available for personal accounts will dry up accordingly.

Funding the PSA plan's accounts with 5 percent of taxable payroll would divert 40.3 percent of payroll tax revenues to these accounts. The Shoven and PSA 2000 plans' earmarking of 2.5 percent of taxable payroll would divert 20.15 percent of revenues. Obviously, these plans would create huge revenue shortfalls.

Thus the problem of "transition costs." The current generation of taxpayers must simultaneously finance current beneficiaries' retirement and their own. These costs may be shifted, but not escaped. The only ways to close the revenue shortfall are to cut current benefits, cut future tax-funded benefits, impose additional Social Security or general-revenue taxes on current taxpayers, increase borrowing from the public, or some combination thereof.

Transition costs will be daunting large, in the trillions of dollars. The Advisory Council's two-tier plan anticipated a supplementary tax increase equal to 1.52 percent of taxable payroll, in effect until 2070, plus borrowing an estimated $1.9 trillion (1995 dollars) from the public by 2034.[9] Obviously, such huge costs will seriously burden the economy.

Some proposals to fund transition costs are dubious. In a pro-privatization Heritage Foundation backgrounder, economist Daniel Mitchell mentioned financing the transition through spending cuts on other government programs (all of which have constituencies, some of them powerful); sale of federal assets (which will depress asking prices in a wide variety of markets); and that patented standby of supply-siders and conservatives: faster economic growth (which, as I shall argue, may well turn out to be a weak reed on which to lean).[10]

These difficulties are sufficiently obvious as to need no further comment. Rather, let us raise another and worse problem: these plans consider Social Security in isolation and ignore the context of the larger entitlement crisis that will make transition costs insupportable. As OASDI grapples with baby boomer retirements, other programs will simultaneously come under like pressure.

Under its 2000 *Annual Report's* intermediate actuarial assumptions, Medicare's HI "trust fund" is projected to be exhausted in 2025, leaving Medicare, under present law, without authority to pay benefits; under high cost assumptions, the fund is exhausted in 2012.[11] Under intermediate assumptions, HI begins running cash deficits in 2010, rising to -$67 billion in 2020 and -$154 billion in 2025. Under high cost assumptions, HI starts running cash deficits in 2004, hitting -$50 billion in 2009—before the Baby Boomers retire. After that, things get catastrophically worse: -$150 billion in 2015, -$317 billion in 2020, and so on.[12]

Meanwhile, outlays for Supplementary Medical Insurance (SMI, or Medicare B), the part of Medicare which pays for physician, outpatient hospital, home health care, and other health services for the aged and disabled, will be exploding, too. Under intermediate assumptions, outlays will more than double from $82.3 billion in 1999 to $180.9 billion in 2009; under high cost assumptions they will nearly triple, to $228.1 billion.[13] This even *before* the Baby Boomers become SMI beneficiaries. When they do, SMI outlays will soar from 1.19 percent of GDP in 2009 to 2.13 percent in 2030 (intermediate assumptions), and still higher afterward.[14] While SMI does charge its beneficiaries premiums, it is over 70 percent financed with general revenue, so its demands on the budget will soar accordingly.

Even these grim figures are probably optimistic. In recent years' HI *Annual Reports,* Richard S. Foster, Chief Actuary of the Health Care Financing Administration, has included in his statement of actuarial opinion the warning that while the assumptions are "reasonable, much of the available evidence suggests that they may not be optimal." HI's finances should have a 50-50 chance of being better or worse than the intermediate projection. However, Foster believes, "a more adverse result (than the intermediate projection)" is more likely than a better one, and "an outcome more adverse than the high cost projection appears more probable than one that is better than the low cost projection."[15] In other words, Medicare's future will probably turn out worse than we expect.

This warning received substantial reinforcement in December 2000, when a Technical Review Panel of actuaries and experts in health care costs, established at the Board of Trustees's direction, reviewed the assumptions used in the HI and SMI annual reports. These reports' intermediate assumptions, the Panel noted, have long assumed that future per-beneficiary costs would grow at the same rate as the sources of funding for the programs. Thus HI assumes that per-capita costs will grow as fast as average hourly earnings (which pay HI's payroll taxes) and SMI has assumed that they will grow as fast as per-capita GDP (which pays SMI's general-revenue funding). However, program costs have consistently far outpaced per-capita GDP (as have health care costs in all OECD countries in the past three decades). Moreover, the major cause driving health-care costs has been improvements in medical science and technology, accounting for about half the real cost growth, and the Panel deemed this likely to continue. It therefore recommended that for both the short and long run, the age-adjusted, gender-adjusted per-beneficiary costs for both parts of Medicare be assumed to grow one percentage point faster than per-capita GDP. The anti-deficit Concord Coalition calculated that with this assumption, the intermediate actuarial analysis would substantially raise projected HI costs, for example, from 4.8 percent of GDP to 6.8 percent in 2040; the high cost analysis with this assumption would put 2040's cost at 8.2 percent of GDP.[16]

None of this, it is worth stressing, includes proposed Medicare expansions to include prescription drug benefits.

Writing in 1996, Phillip Longman observed that the civil service retirement system had unfunded liabilities of a present value of $1.1 trillion; the military retirement system had an unfunded liability with present value of over $713.4 billion; and the veterans' benefits program had an unfunded liability with present value of over $190 billion.[17]

Yet another crisis of unaffordability is coming for Medicaid, the means-tested program to pay for health care for the poor, created in 1965 along with Medicare. Medicaid, which finances about 31 percent of long-term care for the elderly and is the primary source of public funding for this care, paid $28.5 billion for it in 1995. The GAO has observed that while persons aged sixty-five and over today make up 13 percent of America's population, they will be about 20 percent of the population in 2030. Moreover, the population of the oldest old, those aged eighty-five and over, who are most likely to need long-term care, will more than double by 2030, going from 3.9 million in 1997 to about 8.5 million, and more than double again by 2050, going to roughly 18 million.[18] The budgetary implications are ominous. In 1999 the Congressional Budget Office estimated that Medicaid spending on long-term care, in constant 2000 dollars, would rise from $43.3 billion in calendar 2000 to $75.4 billion in 2020. If private health insurance does not assume some of the cost, Medicaid long-term care outlays would go to $87.8 billion.[19]

All this means that transition costs for Social Security reform will be competing with many other large and rapidly growing claims on federal tax revenues or borrowing from the public. Unless these programs absorb sweeping benefit reductions, meeting all of these other program costs will necessarily mean much higher taxes, much higher budget deficits, or both. This will make financing the transition costs problematic.

There would be three possible outcomes. The government could meet all other program benefit commitments plus those of a Social Security reform by making devastating resource extractions from the economy. Or it could make the resource extraction smaller by keeping the Social Security reform intact and forcing deep cuts on all other benefit programs and discretionary spending. Or it could make these other cuts smaller by reducing transition costs—that is, cutting current or future Social Security benefits by more than these reform plans contemplate.

Piggybacked Savings Accounts

Another subgroup of the 1994-1996 Advisory Council—chairman Edward Gramlich and Marc Twinney, the retired Director of Pensions for Ford Motor Company—called for raising the payroll tax 1.6 percentage points, and investing this additional money in publicly-held individual accounts (IAs). These accounts would be piggybacked onto the existing payroll tax, which would continue to pay OASDI benefits. When the individual retires, but no earlier than age sixty-two (the current age for earliest eligibility for Social Security), the accumulated funds would be converted to annuities containing a guarantee that some share of the annuity's purchase price would be payable in all cases. The IA plan also entailed measures such as raising the retirement age to sixty-seven by 2011 and seventy by year 2083; gradually making all benefits subject to federal income tax; slowing the growth of basic benefits for middle- and high-wage workers; and bringing all state and local government workers hired after 1997 under Social Security.[20]

The Committee for Economic Development, an organization of some 250 business leaders and educators which proposes policies to promote growth and prosperity, made a similar proposal in 1997. The CED plan would use similar measures to slow benefit growth, and add mandatory personal retirement accounts to the existing payroll tax, financed by mandatory levies of 1.5 percent of taxable payroll each on employers and employees, and 3.0 percent on the self-employed. Unlike the IAs, these accounts would be privately held.[21]

Many of the measures these plans advocate to trim benefit costs are steps in the right direction. And the CED and the IA plans' advocates are right about the need to increase savings, and do address that.[22] Unfortunately, investment of *small additional* payroll tax sums cannot possibly generate large individual retirement funds for any but the highest-income workers. Under the Advisory Council IA plan, a person earning $10,000 a year would have only $160 a year going into this account; someone making $50,000 a year would have $800 (see table 11.1). Even with compounding, investing these small annual injections of principal just simply will not accumulate much. The CED accounts, being built up from principal injections almost

Table 11.1

**Existing FICA Taxes and Amounts Generated for Individual Accounts
Additional 1.6 Percentage-Point Tax**

Taxable Income	Existing FICA tax for OASDI (6.2 percent rate)	Additional tax (1.6 percent rate)
$10,000	$620	$160
20,000	1,240	320
30,000	1,860	480
40,000	2,480	640
50,000	3,100	800

twice as large, will do almost twice as well—but still, in view of our poor savings rate, not enough.

Such piggybacked individual accounts, then, are more a public-relations gesture than a substantive change. The IA plan's advocates seemed to admit as much when they wrote that the plan "gives people an explicit stake in Social Security" and acknowledges the sentiment, especially among the young, that Social Security will not be there for them. "Small scale individual accounts will not totally change this view, but they should change it in a positive direction."[23] Similarly, the CED argued that its plan would, among other things, shore up the rate of return and "restore the faith of younger workers in the system."[24]

Piggybacked individual account plans offer essentially the Social Security status quo restored to solvency—the growth in future benefit costs gradually planed down to something more affordable, with additional revenue raised from various sources—with modest mandatory individual accounts tacked on in hopes of making young people feel better about the program. This approach does some useful things, and wisely refrains from any extravagant promises. A very great strength of this approach is its complete avoidance of transition costs. Moreover—and much to his credit—Gramlich is sufficiently aware of the larger picture to point out that "Social Security should not be looked at in isolation," that entitlement spending as a whole is rising rapidly, and that it must be curbed. He explicitly, and laudably, noted that the benefit cuts the IA plan offers will serve this important national priority by holding Social Security outlays' share of GDP constant into the twenty-first century.[25]

Both the IA and CED plans use Social Security's intermediate assumptions. But should the future turn out worse than that forecast, new tax increases and benefit cuts will be necessary, driving the rate of return down again. In those circumstances it is doubtful that younger generations will deem small added-on individual accounts an adequate compensation.

Government Investment in the Stock Market

The third approach is to leave the essential nature and structure of Social Security intact, but capture higher returns by direct government investment of part of the "trust fund" in stocks.

Under the "maintenance of benefits" (MB) plan concocted by the third subgroup of the Advisory Council, Social Security would (1) generate more revenue by increasing benefit taxation, bringing all state and local government employees hired after 1997 into the program, and redirecting payroll tax revenue now financing Medicare to Social Security; (2) either trim benefits by 3 percent or increase the payroll tax rate immediately by 0.15 percent each for both employers and employees; (3) if necessary, raise the payroll tax by another 1.6 percentage points fifty years out; and (4) consider investing up to 40 percent of the future "trust fund" accumulations in "stocks of private companies indexed to the broad market." Investment would commence in 2000 and reach up to 40 percent of the "trust fund" by 2014. With the majority of the "trust fund" still invested in Treasuries with a projected real return of 2.3 percent, and up to 40 percent of fund invested in equities enjoying the historical 7 percent return, the overall return on the "trust fund" would rise to 4.2 percent—a substantial improvement.[26]

There are, alas, several grave problems with direct government investment of part of the "trust fund" in stocks.

First, despite the seeming prospect of capturing a much higher return, such plans may in fact not do much to postpone "trust fund" exhaustion. An April 1998 GAO study of the effects of government investment of part of the "trust fund" in stocks used a historical long-term average real rate of return of 7 percent, the intermediate assumptions of OASDI's 1997 Board of Trustees Report, and two hypothetical investment strategies: (1) an "aggressive" scenario of investing OASDI's future annual cash surplus and interest earnings in stocks, while keeping sufficient investment in Treasuries to maintain a contingency reserve big enough to cover a year's outlays, and (2) a "conservative" scenario of investing only the cash surplus and selling stocks first to cover OASDI's cash deficits. The GAO found that the "aggressive" strategy would postpone the projected exhaustion of OASDI's "trust fund" from 2029 to 2040—but that this would require investing the lion's share of "trust fund" assets in stocks, peaking at over 70 percent in 2017. The "conservative" scenario, with a projected peak stock share of "trust fund" assets of 35 percent, would delay "trust fund" exhaustion just three years, from 2029 to 2032.[27] The GAO concluded that

> Investment in the stock market is one option to increase the trust fund's revenues, but by itself, is not the solution to Social Security's financial problem. Stock investing would have a relatively modest impact on long-term solvency as long as Social

Security remains largely a pay-as-you-go program. Restoring Social Security's long-term solvency will require some combination of benefit reductions and revenue increases.[28]

The MB plan does in fact use tax increases and future retirees' benefit cuts to eliminate the majority of the actuarial deficit of 2.17 percent of payroll—1.38 percent—with the investment in stocks disposing of the rest (0.80 percent).[29] However, the outcome is highly sensitive to the rate of return on stocks. If the actual future rate is one percentage point lower than the historical rate, the "aggressive" strategy would delay "trust fund" exhaustion just six years, to 2035; the "conservative" strategy delays exhaustion just two years, to 2031.[30] To offset these worse results, the plans would presumably have to make larger tax increases or benefit cuts than originally planned. But this necessarily means that the more the actual future stock returns fall short of the historical rate of return, the more such a direct-investment plan would collapse into another painful tax increase-benefit cut rescue, with all the political perils and intergenerational equity controversy such a rescue would entail.

Moreover, this investment would give the government enormous equity holdings, which would create vast difficulties. The MB plan's proponents estimated that the "trust fund" would contain $1 trillion in equities by 2015; the GAO's hypothetical "aggressive" strategy would have maximum holdings of roughly $4 trillion in 2025, and the "conservative" approach would have peak holdings of about $1.2 trillion in 2017.[31] Having such huge holdings, the federal government would have a compelling fiscal interest in maintaining a bull market in equities. This will likely lead to economic policy decisions being made so as to support share prices and protect the government's investment. Specifically, there would be pressure for easy credit and low interest rates, to facilitate investment in stocks and make stocks more attractive relative to bonds. This would necessarily impart an inflationary bias to economic policy. It would also threaten the independence of the Federal Reserve, which would come under intense pressure from future politicians to tailor monetary policy for this purpose.

Such a plan might also affect government regulation of stock and other financial markets. Would legislation and regulation be altered so as to give equities more favorable treatment compared to other investments? What of the stock market itself? Would there be pressure to ease regulations and oversight on, for example, purchases on margin, to facilitate purchases and support prices? Would short selling be more narrowly restricted or even forbidden? Should a bear market begin, would the federal government try to protect its holdings by introducing measures to avert substantial drops in equity values—say, a smaller decline in the Dow Jones Industrial Average sufficing to suspend trading on a given day?

With trillions of dollars at stake, it is unrealistic to think that Congress would not meddle like this. But this would be risky. The deregulation of banks and thrifts under the Monetary Control Act and Garn-St. Germain Act, resulting in rising federal deposit insurance exposure and weakened oversight, should give us pause.

Likewise, would tax laws be amended to give equity investments more favorable treatment compared to others, so as to encourage these investments and help support the stock market? Special favors are written into our tax laws routinely in response to pressure from industry lobbies. Given that, it is all but certain that Congress would grant tax favors to an investment market in which the federal government itself has a large position and a compelling fiscal interest in its performance.

Also, tinkering with regulations, tax treatment of investments and so on to favor equities over other investments would alter the composition of investments, creating distortions in resource allocation that may have major economic effects. Making equities artificially more attractive than corporate, state and municipal bonds will impair the ability of corporations and state and local governments to raise money for long-term improvements in physical productive capital and infrastructure. By a gruesome paradox, the tax and regulatory finaglings which would be artificially increasing paper wealth would be weakening that wealth's physical basis.

Finally, this would be, as Senator Vandenberg told Altmeyer, socialism. Government investment in stocks would necessarily mean partial government ownership of the means of production. Some degree of government control would be likely to follow.

To be fair, the MB advocates saw the need to "neutralize the effect of Social Security holdings on stockholder voting on company policy." One possibility they advanced is forbidding the voting of Social Security-held stocks. Another is to automatically allocate the votes of these stocks in the same proportions as other stockholder votes. Still another is to not count Social Security stocks in the base of stock to be voted in cases where a supermajority vote is needed for approval—for example, a vote to change corporate management.[32]

However, even if the Congress and president who enact a law intend its effects to be innocuous, future Congresses, administrations or courts may very well go beyond the original intent. Departures and reversals in policy, some very momentous, do occur. In 1939, just four years after passage of the Social Security Act, Congress reversed itself on the money-back guarantee, and in 1983, reversed itself on benefit taxation. Who can predict what another administration and Congress will do twenty years from now, as the baby boomers stream onto the beneficiary rolls and financial pressure on Social Security explodes?

General Revenue Infusion

Another idea is to supply Social Security with general revenues to furnish funds for either direct government investment in the stock market or principal for individual accounts.

Congressman Kasich and others have proposed allocating some share of budget surpluses—say, one-third—to create personal retirement accounts. The amount deposited in the accounts would vary with a worker's earnings. Some of these plans, such as Kasich's, would leave the existing program unchanged.[33]

On January 19, 1999, President Clinton proposed investing in the stock market $700 billion of the $4.4 trillion in federal budget surpluses expected over the next fifteen years. Clinton's plan assumed an annual rate of return of 6.75 percent, the historical average in 1959-1996. This, plus using another $2 trillion in expected surpluses to pay down the national debt, would, the administration claimed, postpone the exhaustion of the OASDI "trust fund" from 2032 to 2055.[34]

Clinton's proposal illustrates one problem with this approach: it is all contingent on surpluses actually appearing. The assumed $4.4 trillion in budget surpluses over fifteen years works out to an assumed average annual budget surplus of about $293 billion. This is optimistic, to put it mildly. The Reagan-Bush budgeteers' overly optimistic revenue, outlay and deficit projections ("rosy scenarios") did not eventuate. We should be leery of repeating the error.

Also, since direct government investment of general revenues is essentially the same approach as the MB plan, differing only in the source of money, the objections enumerated for the MB plan apply to Clinton's plan as well.

Furthermore, general revenue infusion would require a large ongoing stream of money into Social Security, over and above spending for the existing program. Clinton's fifteen-year plan would require an annual average revenue infusion of $46.7 billion. As for general revenue-funded accounts, in 1999 152 million persons paid OASDI taxes.[35] Assuming individual accounts are created for all of them, with an average annual injection of principal of $500 (which is not especially generous), this would have required $76 billion in general revenues in 1999. As our population grows and the number of covered workers and their accounts increases accordingly, the required annual revenue infusion would inexorably grow. Under intermediate assumptions, in 2040 there will be 181.6 million covered workers.[36] An average principal injection of $500 for 181.6 million accounts would cost $90.8 billion. More generous principal injections would, of course, cost more. Should the average annual principal be $750, the costs would be $114 billion in 2000 and $136.2 billion in 2040.

As for the aggregate costs for providing tax-surplus funded accounts for the entire workforce over the course of their careers, they would be enormous; giving just one million covered twenty-year-old workers an annual principal injection of $500 for forty-five years would cost $22.5 billion. Even allowing for the fact that many of today's covered workers are much older, if tomorrow we began such a system, it would cost trillions of dollars to give each of 151 million accounts $500 annually until each worker reached sixty-five. And each year the workforce, and thus the total cumulative cost, would grow.

Clearly, running on-budget surpluses for this purpose would require the most rigorous discipline over on-budget spending, not for a few years, but for decades on end. That Congresses and presidents will have the willpower for this is doubtful. Discipline over discretionary outlays is already collapsing. And the enormous pressure many other federal entitlements will experience as our population ages will further lengthen the odds against this approach.

A related problem is that general revenue infusion risks warping the rest of the federal government to fit the needs of Social Security. Other priorities such as infrastructure maintenance and defense might be starved of funds to produce the needed surpluses.

The only ways to mitigate the difficulties this approach poses for the rest of the budget would be to substantially raise taxes so as to provide sufficient general revenues for both OASDI *and* on-budget spending—or to reduce the required general revenue diversion. But the latter would necessarily mean reducing direct government investment, or reducing the number of individual accounts or principal injections to them or both. Which would necessarily diminish the additional returns these plans could capture.

Replacing Social Security with Private Accounts

A more drastic possibility would be to replace Social Security altogether with a system of private retirement accounts. The pioneering model for this is the new retirement system adopted by Chile in 1981. The Chileans replaced their pay-as-you-go social insurance program with mandatory individual retirement accounts. Beginning in 1983, persons entering the workforce were required to choose a private pension fund and put a share of their earnings into it. Workers under the old system could either stay in it (in which case they had to pay the full payroll tax, with no employer contribution) or enter the new one. Those who entered the new system received "recognition bonds" redeemable at retirement, for the accrued value of their payments under the old system. To finance the transition, Chile borrowed from the public, raised consumption taxes, and sold off government-owned enterprises. Chileans contribute a minimum of 10 percent of earnings for investment for old-age pensions under the new system, plus about 3.3 percent for survivor and disability benefits. The government guarantees a minimum benefit of 85 percent of minimum wage, and a minimum rate of return. Chile's new system has captured impressive returns; the private funds' average annual real rate of return has been 11.1 percent since the plan's beginning. Investment options are restricted and regulated by the government.[37]

This seems like a promising route to take. However, as Peter Peterson points out, Chile had several advantages which America lacks: substantial budget surpluses to help finance the transition, numerous government enterprises that could be liquidated to defray transition costs, and above all a much younger population (only 6 percent of Chileans were over sixty-five in the mid-nineties, vs. 12 percent of Americans), making the per-capita burden of financing retirement costs lower. Also, the recognition bonds for workers who switched to the new system will pose a substantial burden when redeemed.[38]

Laurence Kotlikoff and Jeffrey Sachs have proposed replacing Social Security with a Personal Security System (PSS). The Old-Age Insurance (OAI) payroll tax would be eliminated, replaced by equivalent contributions to PSS accounts, matched progressively by the government. Investment of the accounts would be regulated and supervised by the government, and the account balances converted to annuities when workers reach sixty-five. Current retirees would receive full benefits; current workers would receive benefits as of the time the reform began. To finance Social Security retirement benefits and government matches of PSS contributions during the transition, Kotlikoff and Sachs would levy a federal sales or value-added tax (VAT) which would start below 10 percent and decline to about 2 percent in 40 years.[39]

Peter Ferrara and Michael Tanner of the Cato Institute have offered another radical plan. They would give workers the option of investing 5 percentage points of their 6.2 percent FICA tax in a personal retirement account, matched dollar for dollar by their employers, for a total of 10 percent. Worker and employer would each continue to pay the FICA tax's remaining 1.2 percent of payroll for ten years after the worker left Social Security, to help defray current retiree benefits during the transition. Some of the account money would be used to purchase life and disability insurance to replace Social Security's survivor and disability benefits. The accounts would have restrictions similar to those for IRAs, with no withdrawals permitted until the account was large enough to purchase an annuity. Retirement benefits would equal the individual's deposits into his account plus whatever return they earned. They could be taken as an annuity, periodic withdrawals (limited to prevent account depletion), or a combination thereof. Workers who opted for this private system would also receive recognition bonds for past Social Security taxes. The government would guarantee all workers a generous minimum benefit, and there would be no reduction in benefits for current beneficiaries. Workers who chose to stay in Social Security, however, would have future benefits reduced by a continued raising of the retirement age to seventy and by a shift to basing Social Security benefits on prices rather than on wages.[40]

Here again, transition costs are the iceberg that could sink the ship. Since these approaches are more radical than the two-tier plans, entailing a much greater revenue diversion, the transition cost problem is much worse here. The Ferrara-Tanner plan does not give an actual figure for the transition cost, but by summing the annual revenue diversion from Social Security to the new system in 1998-2027, we arrive at $10.6 trillion in 1998 dollars.[41]

General Problem: Revenge of the False Consciousness

The transition cost problem is in large measure the revenge of the false consciousness. Many privatization advocates assert their commitment to keeping Social Security's promises to current beneficiaries—that is, paying all their benefits under current law.[42] Mitchell, for example, observes that "all privatization proposals explicitly guarantee" benefits for current retirees and those near retirement. This is partly for political reasons, but beyond that,

> There is also a moral argument that favors preserving the status quo for senior citizens. Simply stated, the government made a contract with them to provide a certain level in exchange for taxes paid, and it would be wrong to break that contract. . . . To renege on the deal now would disrupt the lives of millions of recipients who have assumed that the government would honor its word.[43]

This, of course, is a complete acquiescence in the false consciousness—benefits are an earned right, there is an unbreakable promise grounded in some sort of implicit contract.

Kotlikoff and Sachs deserve credit for facing the transition cost issue squarely and taking the pain in the immediate present rather than deferring it through borrowing. But their insistence on giving all current retirees full Social Security benefits and workers the OAI benefits accrued up to reform implementation means the tax burden would be staggering. Presumably the OAI share of the payroll tax would be replaced by a mandatory equivalent PSS levy—making the tax burden on the worker unchanged—with the sales tax or VAT piled on top of this. This tax, Henry Aaron observed, would have extracted $300 billion to $500 billion in 1997 alone, depending on what, if any, exemptions from it were allowed.[44]

The only way transition costs can be seriously mitigated is to substantially curtail benefits for current as well as future beneficiaries. That, however, is impossible as long as the false consciousness, the origin and driving force for much of the resistance to exacting sacrifices from current beneficiaries, reigns unchallenged. Because many privatizers and reformers are in the toils of the false consciousness, and do not seek to confront it and break its grip on the public mind, they are doomed to wrestle with the anaconda of transition costs, and driven to resort to complicated, costly, and politically awkward schemes to defray them.

General Problem: Too Late for the Boomers?

Another compelling problem with these proposals is that it is now too late for any plan to create personal accounts for Social Security beneficiaries to do anything effective for most baby boomers. All such systems depend on three factors: the amount of principal invested, the rate of return, and the period of accumulation. The power of compound interest depends decisively on *early money:* investments made early in one's life and left undisturbed to accumulate for a *long time.* Even if a plan creating personal accounts were enacted tomorrow, time is too short to generate substantial nest eggs for any but the youngest baby boomers. The oldest boomers will retire at age sixty-five with full benefits in 2010, just nine years away; the youngest will reach age sixty-five in 2030. The oldest will be able to take early retirement with reduced benefits at age sixty-two in 2007, just six years away.

David Koitz of the Congressional Research Service investigated the role which personal retirement accounts could play in Social Security reform. Koitz assumed that personal retirement accounts would go into effect no sooner than 2001, and that the nominal rate of return would be 10 percent annually, roughly the growth rate of the Standard and Poor 500 stock market index (including reinvested dividends) in 1926-2000, which, assuming a 3.3 percent annual rate of inflation, yields a real rate of return of 6.5 percent. He then calculated the value of personal retirement accounts for low-, average-, and maximum-wage earners, assuming annual investments of one, two, and three percent of pay.[45] Table 10.2 reproduces the results for a one-percent set-aside for an average-wage earner, multiplied by 1.6 and 5.0 to generate the

Table 11.2

Value of Personal Accounts as Percent of Current-Law Benefits for Average-Wage Workers Retiring 2010-2050

Yr. of retirement at age 65	Share of pay invested annually		
	1 %	1.6%	5%
2010	2.2%	3.5%	11.0%
2015	4.0	6.4	20.0
2020	6.3	10.1	31.5
2025	9.8	15.7	49.0
2030	13.8	22.1	69.0
2035	18.9	30.2	94.5
2040	25.5	40.8	127.5
2045	34.1	54.6	170.5
2050	33.7	53.9	168.5

Source: Congressional Research Service

results for the IA and PSA proposals of the Advisory Council, respectively. Clearly, personal accounts will be of little use to baby boomers unless they are very young, and the principal invested is very large.

Another implication is that workers with relatively lower incomes will, other things equal, build up far smaller accounts than affluent workers, since their principal injections will be much smaller in dollar terms.

Combining the two, we see that any scheme of personal accounts will work out worst for the oldest lowest-income baby boomers (modest principal injections over the shortest period of accumulation), better for the youngest affluent boomers (larger principal injections over a longer period of accumulation), better still for Generation X as a whole (a still longer period of accumulation) and best of all for the members of Generation X who are youngest and most affluent (largest principal injections over the maximum period of accumulation).

Thus, while these plans will certainly be a vast improvement over the existing Social Security program for the younger generations, their promise for all but the youngest, highest-income baby boomers is dubious, especially when benefit taxation and raised retirement ages are factored in.

General Problem: Politicized Investment Markets

The possible problems with direct government investment in stocks prompt another general concern: under a revised Social Security system—whether of two-tier individual accounts or direct "trust fund" investment—will investment markets be politicized? That is, will investment take place in a tax, regulatory and legislative climate rigged to try to influence investment so as to ensure an outcome favorable to this system or to the interests of powerful groups? Quite apart from the already-addressed huge government stake (which would also exist, albeit indirectly, in a two-tier plan) in a favorable outcome, there are additional compelling grounds for believing that it will.

The attractiveness of "reform" is due to political considerations at least as much as to economic ones. Current retirees do not want to lose benefits; nor do the baby boomers; Generation X does not want to be crushed by soaring payroll taxes to support their elders, and is rightly concerned about its own retirement. "Reform" seems to offer a way to avert this ugly collision of interests such that all parties are better off, or at least none is so grievously disadvantaged as to pose a political danger. What advocates of these plans do not seem to realize is that there are even more powerful psychological and political considerations which could easily work against them.

Most Americans have formed expectations about retirement and Social Security that are highly charged with emotion. In the last two decades the elderly have been lightning quick to exert intense pressure to enforce those expectations. That pressure sprang not only from the Social Security false consciousness itself, but from intense fear of indigence, expectation that comfortable retirement is a kind of right, and adamant insistence on "getting mine." The same sentiments certainly operate among younger Americans plumping for "privatization." And there is no reason, barring a revolution in American values, to think that they will not operate in the future.

While analytically formidable, reform schemes seem to have overlooked crucial political and psychological realities. First, powerful as the elderly lobby is today, it will become vastly more so after 2005, when the advance guard of the baby boom enters its sixties. Membership of senior citizens' organizations will begin soaring. So will the elderly as a share of the voting population—and they have higher voter turnouts than the young. It necessarily follows that the elderly will be far more politically formidable ten years out than they are now, and even more so twenty and thirty years out, as more and more of the baby boomers become old.

Second, the payroll tax exists primarily for psychological purposes. It was intended to not only make the insurance analogy believable by seeming to function in the office of an insurance premium, but to create a sense of entitlement to benefits, a sense whose power was compounded by its political enforceability. Any revision of Social Security which retains the payroll tax will thereby carry within itself the seed of a false consciousness and make itself vulnerable to psychological forces and political pressures similar to those that have afflicted policymaking for the existing program. Just as Social Security policymaking decisions in the past two decades were decisively shaped thereby, so may policy decisions for a "reformed" system during a future bear market be similarly warped. The fact that the investment money was extracted through a *tax on labor income,* will decisively affect participants' attitudes. Because of the disutility many jobs entail, people have different, and far stronger, attitudes about labor income than they do about, say, interest on a checking account, and very strong feelings as well about taxes on it and what is done with the tax money. Someone who freely invests his own money in stocks and loses it will be devastated, but has no one to blame but himself. His attitude will be vastly different—and very dangerous—if a system of forced savings financed by taxes on his emotionally charged labor income loses money. Initial public enthusiasm for stock-and-tax-based "privatization" or "reform" could quickly turn into fury under bear-market pressures. One can easily imagine the message a future Congress will get from taxpayers in those circumstances. *The idea was I'd get a great return for my old age. The market's going down the tube! You and your privatization [or trust fund investment]! You're shooting craps with my tax dollars! Will my money be there when I need it? After being forced to put my hard-earned money at risk I have a right to get something out of it, don't I? If you don't do something to protect my retirement money, I'll—*

This is political dynamite. Have tax-funded investment advocates thought of this? Do they know what they are doing?

Third, there is no such thing as permanent prosperity, and we are about due for hard times. Today's expansion is now about nine years old, and the bull market in equities has lasted since the fall of 1982. A recession and bear market will occur very probably within the next five years, certainly within the next ten. Americans are prone to anxiety, even panic, during downturns. They have too a strong tendency to demand that the government "do something" to protect them. This is not a favorable psychological climate for major revisions of a program long perceived as offering security. In an economic slump, the public mood may well shift from demanding a better return on Social Security taxes and toward clinging to a "guaranteed" floor of protection.

Fourth, when a downturn comes, it will be while the largest generation in American history is approaching retirement. A very great many people in that generation have taken pitifully inadequate measures to prepare themselves financially for old age. As Peter Peterson has pointed out, while many baby boomers expect to be at least as well-off in retirement as they are in their working years, median savings for adults in their late fifties were, as recently as 1993, below a paltry $10,000.[46] Such ill-prepared aging Americans are unlikely to be enthusiastic about converting Social Security to what amounts to a bet on the stock market, especially in the context of a recession and bear market. Even if they do endorse such a conversion, they may well insist on inclusion of a taxpayer-funded benefit equivalent to all or most of their current-law Social Security benefit as a backstop in case equity-investment outcomes fall short of projections. And they will have the political power to get their way. Provision of such a contingent backstop benefit will, of course, create a huge potential liability for the Treasury and the taxpayers, and vastly increase the pressure on Congress to tinker with regulations, tax treatment of investments, and monetary policy so as to try to ensure that equities perform well.

Fifth, reformers ignore the enormous lobbying pressures that Congress experiences whenever it modifies economic arrangements (consider what happens when it writes a tax law). The far-reaching changes most reform plans entail would give lobbyists from Wall Street to the AARP a huge opening for pressuring Congress into enacting innumerable specific tinkerings with investment markets.

Sixth, from now through 2010 there will be five federal elections, two of them presidential (2004, 2008)—and election years have powerful political imperatives of their own, which are greatly compounded in hard times.

Our likely prospect in the next ten years, then, is a simultaneous recession; bear market; and commencement of an unprecedentedly huge, hence unprecedentedly politically powerful, generation's passage into retirement, a condition from which many of them expect a great deal but for which many of them are woefully unready—at a time when the payroll tax will still be feeding a pernicious entitlement mentality and politicians will be grappling with elections. *It is in that unfavorable context that Social Security revision will be hammered out.*

The conclusion is virtually inescapable: any Social Security revision relying on equity investment, whether individual accounts or a portion of the "trust fund," will be rife with politically inspired but economically unsound and dangerous provisions to try to rig matters so as to ensure, or at least promote, a favorable outcome.

General Problem: Will the Brighter Tomorrow Really Come?

Another very grave problem is that the brighter tomorrow these plans assume may not come. Many considerations, from aspects of Social Security to economic fundamentals, add up to a powerful case for skepticism.

For one thing, except for Kotlikoff-Sachs, all the foregoing plans rely on Social Security's intermediate actuarial assumptions. However, as I have endeavored to show, the high cost assumptions are more prudent and probably more realistic. Should they indeed turn out to be more accurate, Social Security's costs will be far higher than these plans anticipate. We will then be forced into far more painful cuts in future benefits and increases in future taxes than these plans contemplate. That, of course, will again worsen Social Security's return for the young, and revive intergenerational tensions and "money's worth" issues. Also, the program will come under pressure sooner than under the intermediate assumptions.

Another problem is that the high long-term rates of return on equities invariably cited by reformers mask the reality of shorter-term bear markets, which may be deep and protracted. The Dow Jones Industrial Average did not return to 1929's pre-Crash high until November 1954—twenty-five years later.[47] Given the age of the current bull market, this short-term problem is very pertinent for the next twenty years—a dangerous period in which baby boomer retirement, and corresponding massive strain on Social Security and other federal programs, will commence. Even Wharton finance professor Jeremy Siegel, an influential advocate of stocks as a long-run investment, when asked in 1997 about putting Social Security money into stocks, sounded a cautionary note: "Suppose we come to a 10-year period when the return on stocks is not good. They happen."[48]

Moreover, advocates of equity investment for Social Security overlook the implications of globalization for the stock market. Integration of national capital markets into one global market and the perfection of communications technology necessarily mean that financial capital is more mobile than ever before in history, not only between national equity markets, but between all investments (stocks, corporate bonds, bonds of national governments, foreign currencies, commodity futures, etc.) in search of higher returns. It also means that disruptions in foreign markets have unprecedented potential for disrupting our own.[49] It stands to reason that short-term fluctuations in the stock market will become more violent and frequent, increasing the short-term market risk, and with it, the temptation for Congress to tamper with that market.

More fundamentally, much reform and "privatization" talk uncannily resembles the spirit of Social Security's advocates in its confident years: taking steady, brisk economic growth for granted, blithely assuming that the economy would be able to carry whatever load they placed on it. Recall Altmeyer's 1945 statement that Social Security would never be a finished thing, because "human aspirations are infinitely expansible," Wilbur Cohen's 1959 assertion of his belief that "during the next ten years the productivity of our nation will continue to grow," hence America would be able "to afford significant improvements in our Social Security system from these increased resources," and Paul Samuelson's 1967 crow that Social Security could give each generation more than it had paid in, because "the national product is growing at compound interest and can be expected to do so as far ahead as the eye cannot see." None of these men foresaw—how could they?—the economic convulsions of the seventies which left Social Security floundering. And none seems to have paid any attention to the demographics of an aging population, though Judd Benson had warned accurately in 1950 that our population would age and that Social Security's tax burden would rise accordingly.

Much "privatization" advocacy manifests the same hubris. Reading these plans, one often encounters a cocky sense of a sure thing. "There is no way to fix the current Social Security system," proclaims Daniel Mitchell of Heritage, "but there is a way to *guarantee* workers a *safe* and *secure* retirement. The answer lies in privatization, which has the added virtue of being relatively simple to implement" (italics added).[50] The invocation of the high historical real rates of return on stocks—6.5 percent or 7 percent, depending on whose proposal one reads—takes for granted that we will continue to enjoy these returns indefinitely, or that equity prices can rise without limit.

True, the average annual real compound return on stocks was an impressive 6.7 percent in the long 1802-1992 period, and 6.6 percent in 1871-1992. Returns were equally impressive in major subperiods: 7.0 percent in 1802-1870, 6.6 percent in 1871-1925, and 6.6 percent in 1926-1992, and 6.6 percent in the post-World War II period of 1946-1992.[51]

But is the past an infallible predictor of the future? Common sense and realism would argue that before projecting a historical rate of return into the future and placing all our Social Security bets on it, we should ask, what caused this rate of return, and how confident we can be that these causes will continue to operate, and make its continuation possible? Because all reform plans bet everything on this rate of return's persistence, giving these questions the most searching scrutiny is imperative.

This starts with the long-term performance of the real economy and what drives it. Financial markets have become so complicated, with such a bewildering proliferation of investment instruments—money market funds, equity index funds, puts, calls, futures, derivatives—that we risk forgetting fundamental realities. A reminder is in order. Stock prices are ultimately grounded in beliefs about a company's ability to earn a return on invested resources, which in turn rests on an ability to produce a good or service and sell it at a profit. This in fact is what makes the difference between a good stock and a bad one, especially in the long run. When the obscuring hyperbole and complexities are stripped away, the fact is that the financial sector is an epiphenomenon of the real economy; like money itself, it came into being to serve the needs of the real economy. It stands to reason that while mishaps in the financial sector can cause real-sector disruptions, and while in the short run the financial sector may be decoupled from the real economy by monetary and speculative phenomena, its long-term performance is grounded in, and disciplined by, what the real economy is capable of.

These assumed brisk long-term rates of return and growth of asset prices necessarily assume an underlying real economy steadily, robustly growing, in Samuelson's phrase, "as far as the eye cannot see." Yet whether sustained, long-term growth of national product at Samuelson's 3 percent, let alone a brisker pace, may obtain for most of the next century is highly questionable.

The ultimate, underlying cause of the high long-term rate of return on equities in 1802-1945 was the most gigantic real-economy growth and development in world history, which took place due to a unique combination of favorable phenomena: simultaneous revolutions in transportation (from horse carts and sailing ships to railroads, steel steamships, cars, trucks and airplanes, and from cart tracks to a continental rail and highway system), communication (from mail coaches to the telegraph, teletype, radio, and telephone), agriculture (cotton gins, reapers, combines, etc.) and manufacturing (interchangeable parts, machine tools, the sewing machine, the Bessemer process, the continuous moving assembly line, etc., etc.) *and* development of huge tracts of virgin land rich in resources, including almost limitless supplies of cheap energy, in a temperate climate by a uniquely vigorous and enterprising people; a government which was for most of this period minimal and low-cost and which not only imposed few impediments on invention, innovation and enterprise but promoted economic growth and development (protective patent laws and tariffs, generous land grants to transcontinental railroads, the Homestead Act); a long insulation from foreign competition due to protectionism; public schools that produced generations of solidly competent graduates.

Similarly, America began the post-World War II era with another set of unique highly favorable circumstances: a huge pent-up demand for consumer goods and housing; a huge pool of investible money to finance the meeting of that demand; a housing and durable goods boom; insulation from foreign

competition due to the slow recovery of our competitors from World War II; a
government which was, relative to today's, small and unobtrusive; plentiful,
cheap energy and raw materials; a stable currency; low inflation; and a high
savings rate and low real interest rates.

Of course long-term real returns were high in these periods. But how likely
are we to sustain those returns? Nothing remotely like the foregoing combinations of factors exists now or is likely to in the next several decades. Just
where will the economic expansion and prosperity which must underlie the
continuation of historical high real returns on equities come from?

Indeed, one need not look very hard to find some ominous signs that our
economy's long-term trend has been one of gradual slowdown (see table
11.3).[52] While the values of productivity growth and average real earnings
seem unremarkable over the forty-year period 1957-1996, when this long
period is disaggregated into ten-year periods, it reveals disturbing trends of
collapsing productivity and real wage growth. (These data are from the OASDI
1998 *Annual Report,* with which reformers are presumably familiar.) Meanwhile, the real interest rate, as measured by the interest rate on Moody's Aaa-
rated bonds minus the Consumer Price Index, which gives a rough measure of
the real cost of credit for corporate investment in plant and equipment, has
been steadily rising—indeed, its 1987-1996 average is almost double its
1957-1966 level. Which is not surprising, since meanwhile our net national
savings rate has been steadily falling. Taken together, these trends point not
to a coming boom but to stagnation, which of course will make continuation
of the historical return on equities unlikely. It will also make transition costs
more difficult to finance—a consideration which should give us pause, but
which no reform proponent seems to have considered.

It will be objected that the foregoing does not take account of the recent
productivity boom. But recall our argument in chapter 1 that the jury is still
out as to whether today's rapid productivity growth will in fact be sustained

Table 11.3

Warnings of Possible Coming Stagnation?

Period	Productivity growth	Real earnings growth	Real interest rate	Net national savings rate
1957-1996	1.7 %	0.8 %	3.3 %	6.1 %
1957-1966	3.1	2.3	2.5	8.6
1967-1976	2.0	0.5	1.7	7.6
1977-1986	1.1	-0.1	4.3	5.2
1987-1996	0.6	0.6	4.8	2.9

Sources: *1998 OASDI Annual Report; Economic Report of the President, 1991, 1998*

long term, which is what really matters, and that there are good reasons to think that it will not be.

Moreover, while productivity is usually measured in dollar terms, productivity growth must have a basis in physical reality. That is, productivity growth means, ultimately, that the physical process of producing goods and services is being completed more and more quickly in a unit of time. But is it really possible that physical output per man-hour can be increased indefinitely—put another way, that motions of human beings and machinery are capable of infinite acceleration? The absurdity of this becomes obvious when we realize that this implies that eventually people or machines would be producing almost instantaneously. Even with the best production technology, there are certain physical and physiological limits on how much can be done in a given time period to produce a good or service which simply cannot be overcome, just as a product's material content simply cannot be reduced below a certain point. Common sense and realism admit only one conclusion: unlimited productivity growth in a limited world is impossible.

Productivity growth of 1.5 percent a year (the 2000 *Annual Report's* intermediate assumption) implies that output per man-hour will be twice as high in 2049 as it is today. Is it seriously possible that forty-eight years from now, workers will assemble automobiles twice as quickly as they do now, or that barbers will be able to cut twice as many heads of hair per hour, or that computer keyboard operators will be able to perform twice as many keystrokes per minute? A far more likely possibility is that some time in this century a ceiling on productivity growth will be reached, productivity will stagnate, and economic growth will level off.

Enthusiasts of the Information Age of boundless growth and inconceivable prosperity which is supposedly coming will dismiss these sober speculations, and point out that after all, the dire predictions of the Club of Rome did not eventuate. But neither have *any* of the extravagant forecasts, many made as recently as the sixties, for today and early in this century: undersea cities, moon settlement, manned interplanetary voyages, huge manned space stations, planned cities equipped with monorails and moving sidewalks, and on and on. We still await even more-prosaic anticipated advances like practical electric or solar-powered cars.

And that shuffling information among computers—which is all the Information Economy amounts to when the hyperbole is stripped away—will come anywhere near repeating the fabulous performance that turned a huge undeveloped continent into the world's greatest economy is unlikely, to say the least.

The underlying causes of the historical high rates of return on equities which reform advocates are counting on, then, are extremely unlikely to recur. There are, too, ominous signs of gradual slowdown, perhaps prefiguring future stagnation. It follows, then, that those high rates of return will quite possibly not be achieved.

It bears emphasizing that this is not a prophecy of economic disaster. The point rather is that if actual future real long-term equities returns merely *fall short* of the historical ones, say to 3.0-5.0 percent—still respectable, hardly disastrous, the lower end equal to Samuelson's growth rate of the economy—it will render these plans untenable, and dash the high hopes pinned on them.

Moreover, privatizers likewise ignore the globalization of the American economy—its integration into a system of free trade, internationally mobile factors of production, and employers relocating overseas in search of lower labor costs and higher profits. In such a regime, factor-price equalization between the United States and other countries is well nigh inevitable. The factor price equalization theorem is well recognized in economic theory.[53] The essential idea is sensible and rests on supply and demand. Two countries have different endowments of factors of production—labor and capital, say. In the country with abundant labor and scarce capital (e.g., China), labor will be relatively cheap, capital relatively expensive; hence labor-intensive products will be cheap, and capital-intensive products costly. Where labor is scarce and capital abundant (as in America), labor will be relatively expensive, capital relatively cheap; hence capital-intensive products will be cheap, and labor-intensive products costly. Free trade combines these countries into one market. The expensive labor-intensive products of the costly-labor country now face competition from cheaper labor-intensive products of the cheap-labor country. This increases demand for the cheap product, driving up its price, hence raising the wages of its labor, and reduces demand for the expensive product, driving down its price, hence depressing the wages of its labor. Thus free trade between America and cheap-labor countries will tend to reduce American wages, and raise foreign wages. The downward pressure on U.S. wages will, of course, be exacerbated by continued mass immigration and exportation of high-wage manufacturing jobs.

This necessarily has dangerous implications for any benefit system, public or "privatized," financed by levies on labor incomes. Other things equal, real wage stagnation necessarily means stagnation of such a system's revenues. With beneficiary-population growth outstripping labor-force growth, this ineluctably spells eventual ruin. Reform plans based on equity market investments are counting on the higher rate of return on equities, *and* a sustained flow of principal from payroll tax revenues. Even if we do capture the historical equity returns, if the flow of principal into investment accounts stagnates or declines, the gain from the higher returns will be lessened or even nullified.

It must be emphasized that complete wage equalization between the United States and low-wage trade partners such as China need not occur to create this problem. Even if real wages fall only 10-20 percent, or stop growing, or merely *grow more slowly than expected,* it will seriously disrupt these plans, all of which use Social Security's intermediate actuarial assumptions. The 2000 *Annual Report's* intermediate actuarial analysis assumed an ultimate annual average wage growth of 4.3 percent and an ultimate annual Consumer Price Index increase of 3.3 percent. The "real wage differential," the difference between them, which is also the assumed growth in real wages, is thus 1.0 percent. To see the difference that a change in real wage growth can make to actuarial outcomes, Social Security's actuaries assumed real-wage differentials of 1.5 and 0.5, held all other variables constant at the intermediate values, and calculated new actuarial balances. This "sensitivity test" generated actuarial balances for the twenty-five-year 2000-2024 period of 1.35 and 0.73 percent of taxable payroll, respectively. The figure under intermediate assumptions was 1.04 percent. In other words, if annual real wage growth comes in at 0.5 percent instead of the intermediate assumption of 1.0 percent, the short-term actuarial balance drops almost 30 percent. The impact is also formidable over the long run (2000-2074); while intermediate assumptions generate a long-term actuarial deficit of -1.89 percent of taxable payroll, if annual real wage growth is 0.5 percent instead, the long-term deficit rises to -2.39 percent of payroll, a 26 percent increase.[54] If real wages stop growing or fall, of course, the outcomes are much worse.

Globalization, then, can substantially affect how these plans work out. Globalization's effect on American real wages will almost certainly be negative, exacerbating an already-worsening trend. And not one of the reform plans shows any awareness of this whatsoever.

In short, we are in uncharted economic waters, fraught with imponderables without precedent, any one of which could, and probably will, nullify the bright promises of privatization. All this is a profound cautionary tale about these proposals.

We should recall that Social Security's goal is, after all, security—providing a floor of protection so as to prevent poverty in old age. Security ends where speculation begins. Greater returns mean greater risks, meaning greater insecurity. There are fit objects for bold experimentation and risk taking, but retirement income is not one of them.

We should recall too Burke's sagacious argument that prudence is the first virtue in politics and statecraft. If history teaches anything about trying to devise a national system for old-age security, where so much depends on factors which are beyond one's control and impossible to predict, it is that we should be humble in our aspirations, mindful of constraints, prudent in our planning, keenly aware of the imponderable nature of the future, and deeply leery of wishful thinking and leaning on luck. These lessons do not seem to have registered with "reform" advocates any more than they did with Social Security's expansionists.

The expansionists certainly violated Burke's principle of prudence in their repeated expansions and liberalizations of Social Security. But reformers are equally imprudent in proposing to stake Social Security's future on the stock market even as our economy is entering an era of greater market volatility and uncertainty. We gain nothing by replacing one species of imprudence with another.

General Problem: A New False Consciousness

Nor do we gain anything by replacing one pernicious false consciousness with a new one. If the false consciousness of Social Security is one of nonexistent insurance, rights, and guarantees, the false consciousness of privatization is an equally dangerous one of costlessness—of getting something for nothing.

Some privatizers are going down the same road of inaccurate semantics. Shoven maintains that mandatory contributions to PSA accounts "are not taxes, however, because the individual retains title to the funds." Whereas taxes involve forced transfers with no say as to how the money is spent, Shoven argues, these mandatory contributions go into accounts in the individuals' names for their benefits, so they merely shift money from one pocket to another. This allows him to assert that his plan simultaneously secures OASDI's solvency, increases benefits, *and* cuts taxes. The Advisory Council's PSA plan, by contrast, he writes, "appears to be a marketing nightmare—it states that they have a tax increase, when actually it decreases the payroll tax." The Council's plan raises payroll taxes 1.52 percent of payroll and shunts 5 percent of payroll into an individual account. Actually, Shoven maintains, this is a "payroll tax cut" to 8.92 percent of payroll, plus a mandatory contribution of 5 percent of payroll to an account.[55]

In a fine piece of irony, Henry Aaron and Alicia Munnell, two of the staunchest defenders of Social Security as we know it, who have done their bit to propagate its false consciousness, take Shoven to task for this. Munnell insists that "a tax is a tax is a tax." Aaron defines a tax as "government action to require people to use their income for something that they did not want to use it for," and maintains that by this definition mandatory infusions to personal accounts are taxes.[56]

Munnell and Aaron are obviously right. The essence of a tax is a mandatory pecuniary levy by government on private income or wealth—an extraction of monies from private hands by state compulsion. The destination of the monies is irrelevant. Disbursement of these monies—whether to pave roads, pay government workers' salaries, pay existing OASDI benefits, or deposit sums to mandatory individual retirement accounts—is a separate transaction which does not affect the nature of the tax transaction. Both the Council's and Shoven's PSA plans increase the coerced extraction of monies from individuals by government: to 13.92 percent of payroll by the former and 14.90 percent by the latter. Therefore both raise taxes.

We see here Weaver's distinction between *vere loqui* (speaking truthfully) and *utiliter loqui* (speaking usefully) all over again. The Advisory Council's "marketing nightmare" is actually a laudable exercise in *vere loqui;* Shoven's

concern for "marketing" reveals an opting for *utiliter loqui* just as objectionable as that of Social Security's promoters. That privatizers such as Shoven
are perpetrating their own breach of the covenant of language is disturbing.
This is the entering wedge for propagating a new false consciousness, and
Munnell and Aaron deserve credit for resisting it.

Moreover, just as Social Security's partisans played up "earned rights" and
"guarantees," downplayed OASDI's retirement-earnings means test and suppressed Section 1104 altogether, privatizers play up the higher return of the
stock market, which is their strongest selling point, and give transition costs
nowhere near equal weight. Ferrara and Tanner never give an explicit cost
figure, though they do give data from which it can be calculated. The Shoven
PSA plan and the Schieber-Shoven PSA 2000 present neither a figure for the
transition cost nor an explanation of how it would be financed.

Another aspect of this problem is that money's worth calculations are
seriously misleading about the true costs of reform plans, and thus promote
an illusion of costlessness. Money's worth calculations for Social Security
are made by comparing expected lifetime benefits to expected lifetime taxes,
both expressed in present value. Money's worth calculations for the various
reformed versions of the program are made in the same way.[57] In other words,
these calculations deal only with benefits and costs which are *internal to the
program*. This is appropriate for Social Security since it is self-financing.
Using the same method for the reform plans—as one must to compare like
phenomena, that is, taxes and benefits within the existing program to those of
the reform plans—treats them as if they too are self-financing.

Unfortunately, they are not. Two-tier plans or plans replacing Social Security altogether with personal accounts rely heavily on additional non-Social
Security taxes (Kotlikoff-Sachs) or borrowing from the public (e.g., PSA plans)
to finance the transition. The added resource extraction from new taxes is
obvious. Additional borrowing of course means an enormous increase in publicly held debt and federal budget deficits. Federal interest costs will soar
accordingly. For example, in 1996 the Office of the Actuary calculated that
the annual interest cost to the budget from borrowing from the public for the
PSA plan would climb to $158 billion in 2010, $354 billion in 2020, and
$443 billion in 2030.[58] These interest charges must be paid from taxes. But
who will pay those taxes? The same persons who will be capturing higher
returns from the reformed Social Security program, of course.

But if one is paying new federal sales tax or VAT (Kotlikoff-Sachs) or
higher taxes for debt service (PSA et al.) as a result of privatization, one's total
return from privatization necessarily falls accordingly. When one focuses
narrowly on the Social Security program itself, reform plans do generate
higher returns for individuals (if their assumptions hold up). Since privatization
schemes push the cost—new taxes, higher debt service charges—outside this
frame of reference, they make them disappear for the purpose of comparing

reform plan returns to Social Security's. But in fact they have not disappeared. They have only been hidden. All economic costs must be paid by somebody, and since virtually the entire adult population participates in Social Security, the same people who receive a privatized Social Security program's benefits would also pay the higher general revenue taxes or debt service charge from its transition cost. Pushing the costs outside the program onto the budget simply extracts the resources from the same people in a different way. One's actual return from privatization would thus be significantly lower than money's worth calculations make it out to be. There is no such thing as a free lunch.

General Problem: Deeper into Statism and Paternalism

Finally, none of the reform plans frees us from the coercion and paternalism of Social Security. Indeed, they worsen them, and seriously disserve the major American values of individual liberty, responsibility and autonomy.

Any investment of tax monies, whether through individual accounts or the "trust fund" itself, will mean far greater involvement of the government in investment decisions. Not only will the government be making more investment decisions itself, it will have a compelling reason to manipulate the environment in which those decisions are made and transactions carried out.

Quite apart from this, the plans meet the difficulties of our largest government program with more government control over our lives, and address the consequences of Social Security's paternalism with more paternalism. Plans for "trust fund" investment in equities would almost certainly bring partial socialism. Tax-financed accounts merely impose socialism on individuals rather than companies. Under publicly held account plans, as the Advisory Council members said of their version, "Individuals would have constrained investment choices" for these monies. Under both the PSA and IA plans, individuals could start collecting their money only at age sixty-two, not before. The IA plan puts the fund into an annuity upon retirement because "It will be very hard for these workers, upon retirement, to determine how much money they will need to provide for their very old age, in the face of inflation and many other uncertainties. . . . Some restrictions on the potential overspending of the newly-retired seem to us sensible; some annuitization important." This "protects people against the financial risk of living a very long life."[59] The Ferrara-Tanner plan restricts withdrawals from accounts during employment; requires purchase of life and disability insurance; allows only annuitization or periodic withdrawals from the account at retirement; and restricts withdrawals during retirement, lest the retiree "use up all the funds early and then be left without retirement support."[60] The state, then, would tax Americans to force them to save their own money, tell them how they could save it, and decide when they could get back how much how often in what form.

This necessarily entails a vast increase of the "democratic despotism" and smothering paternalism Alexis de Tocqueville warned about so presciently in *Democracy in America.* His warning is worth quoting at length, since so many purported conservatives and libertarians seem to have forgotten it:

> Above this race of men stands an immense and tutelary power, which takes upon itself alone to secure their gratifications, and to watch over their fate. . . . It would be like the authority of a parent, if . . . its object was to prepare men for manhood; but it seeks on the contrary to keep them in perpetual childhood . . . For their happiness such a government willingly labours, but it chooses to be the sole agent and the only arbiter of that happiness: it provides for their security, foresees and supplies their necessities, facilitates their pleasures, manages their principal concerns, directs their industry, regulates the descent of property, and subdivides their inheritances—what remains, but to spare them all the care of thinking and all the trouble of living?
>
> Thus it every day renders the exercise of the free agency of man less useful and less frequent; it circumscribes the will within a narrower range, and gradually robs a man of all the uses of himself. . . .
>
> . . . . The will of man is not shattered, but softened, bent and guided: men are seldom forced by it to act, but they are constantly restrained from acting: such a power does not destroy, but it prevents existence; it does not tyrannize, but it compresses, enervates, extinguishes, and stupefies a people, till each nation is reduced to be nothing better than a flock of timid and industrious animals, of which the government is the shepherd.[61]

L'Envoi

This censorious treatment of Social Security reform does not flow from ideological hostility. The point, rather, is first, a counsel of prudence and realism: there are far more things in heaven and earth than are dreamt of in Social Security reform plans. Like watchmakers hunched intently over their workbenches in little cones of light, oblivious to their surroundings, the reformers are focusing narrowly on getting all the parts of their plans to mesh together into integrated, smoothly running wholes, while ignoring the larger economic, social and political universe outside those plans, which can and probably will make a hash of them.

Second, a counsel of honesty and the imperative need to avoid promoting a false consciousness. The economic costs of privatization are significant and real and cannot be escaped. Shifting them outside the program risks giving a misleading impression of costlessness. And there are serious losses of liberty and personal autonomy and responsibility that must also be considered.

Notes

1.   Correlli Barnett, *The Swordbearers: Supreme Command in the First World War* (New York: William Morrow & Co., 1964), p. 190.
2.   David Stuart Koitz, "Social Security, Medicare, and Public Debt Reduction 'Lock Boxes,'" Congressional Research Service Report RS20165.

3. "Interview with Robert D. Reischauer," *AARP Bulletin,* January 2000, pp. 3, 5 (www.aarp.org/bulletin/jan00).
4. *Report of the 1994-1996 Advisory Council on Social Security,* vol 1: *Findings and Recommendations,* pp. 30-31, 35. This approach was endorsed by Joan Bok, Anne Combs, Sylvester Schieber, Fidel Vargas, and Carolyn Weaver.
5. John B. Shoven, "Social Security Reform: Two Tiers Are Better Than One," in Aaron and Shoven, *Should the United States Privatize Social Security?,* pp. 30-47.
6. Sylvester J. Schieber and John B. Shoven, *The Real Deal: The History and Future of Social Security* (New Haven and London: Yale University Press, 1999), pp. 391-397.
7. Table II.F11 of the *2000 OASDI Annual Report* gives operations of the OASDI trust funds, combined, during selected fiscal years 1960-1999. Subtracting benefit payments from net contributions gives the payroll tax surplus. For 1985-1999 the average payroll tax surplus is 13.5 percent of revenues.
8. See chapter 1, tables 1.3 and 1.4.
9. *Report of the 1994-1996 Advisory Council on Social Security,* vol 1: *Findings and Recommendations,* pp. 32, 111-112.
10. Daniel J. Mitchell, "Creating a Better Social Security System for America," Backgrounder no. 1109, The Heritage Foundation, April 23, 1997, p. 26.
11. *2000 HI Annual Report,* p. 2.
12. *2000 OASDI Annual Report,* Table III.B4.—Estimated OASDI and HI Income Excluding Interest, Outgo, and Balance in Current Dollars by Alternative, Calendar Year 2000-75.
13. *2000 Annual Report of the Supplementary Medical Insurance Trust Fund,* Table II.D4.—Operations of the SMI Trust Fund (Cash Basis) under Alternative Sets of Assumptions, Calendar Years 1999-2009.
14. Ibid., Table II.D5.—SMI Disbursements (Incurred Basis) as a Percent of the Gross Domestic Product.
15. *2000 HI Annual Report,* p. 102.
16. Technical Review Panel on the Medicare Trustees Reports, *Review of Assumptions and Methods of the Medicare Trustees' Financial Projections,* December 2000, pp. 17, 27-42; The Concord Coalition, "A Wake Up Call on Medicare," January 29, 2001.
17. Longman, *The Return of Thrift,* pp. 8-9.
18. Ibid., p. 94; GAO, *Long-Term Care: Baby Boom Generation Presents Financing Challenges,* testimony before the Special Committee on Aging, U.S. Senate, March 9, 1998 (GAO/T-HEHS-98-107, March 1998), pp. 3-5.
19. Congressional Budget Office, Memorandum, "Projections of Expenditures for Long-Term Care Services for the Elderly," March 1999, pp. 3, 5 (http://www.cbo.gov/showdoc).
20. *Report of the 1994-1996 Advisory Council on Social Security,* vol 1: *Findings and Recommendations,* pp. 28-29.
21. Research and Policy Committee, Committee for Economic Development [hereafter, CED], *Fixing Social Security* (New York: Committee for Economic Development, 1997), pp. 15-18.
22. Ibid., p. 49; *Report of the 1994-1996 Advisory Council on Social Security,* vol 1: *Findings and Recommendations,* p. 155.
23. *Report of the 1994-1996 Advisory Council on Social Security,* vol 1: *Findings and Recommendations,* p. 155.
24. CED, *Fixing Social Security,* p. 54.
25. Gramlich, *Is It Time to Reform Social Security?,* pp. 39-41, 65.

26. *Report of the 1994-1996 Advisory Council on Social Security,* vol 1: *Findings and Recommendations,* pp. 25-26. The MB plan was advocated by Robert Ball, Gloria Johnson, Thomas Jones, George Kourpas, Gerald Shea, and (in most particulars) Edith Fierst.

27. GAO, *Social Security Financing: Implications of Government Stock Investing for the Trust Fund, the Federal Budget, and the Economy* (GAO/AIMD/HEHS-98-74, April 1998), pp. 6-7, 46-47.

28. Ibid., p. 51.

29. *Report of the 1994-1996 Advisory Council on Social Security,* vol 1: *Findings and Recommendations,* p. 80.

30. GAO, *Social Security Financing: Implications of Government Stock Investing for the Trust Fund, the Federal Budget, and the Economy,* pp. 47-48.

31. *Report of the 1994-1996 Advisory Council on Social Security,* vol 1: *Findings and Recommendations,* p. 100; GAO, *Social Security Financing: Implications of Government Stock Investing for the Trust Fund, the Federal Budget, and the Economy,* p. 47.

32. *Report of the 1994-1996 Advisory Council on Social Security,* vol 1: *Findings and Recommendations,* p. 26.

33. David Stuart Koitz, "Ideas for Privatizing Social Security," Congressional Research Service, Report 96-504 EPW, pp. 5-6 (www.concordcoaltion.org); David S. Koitz, "Social Security Reform," Congressional Research Service, p. 14.

34. "Unbowed, Clinton Presses Social Security Plan," *New York Times,* January 20, 1999, A21; "Clinton Plan to Strengthen Social Security Runs Into Opposition," *New York Times,* January 20, 1999, A19; "With Stock Plan, the President Hopes to Keep the Bulls Charging," *New York Times,* January 20, 1999, A19.

35. *2000 OASDI Annual Report,* p. 5.

36. Ibid., p. 122, Table II.F.19.—Comparison of OASDI Covered Workers and Beneficiaries by Alternative, Calendar Years 1945-2075.

37. Geoffrey Kollmann, "Social Security: The Chilean Example," Congressional Research Service Report 95-839 EPW, pp. 1-3, 4 n. 1.

38. Peterson, *Will America Grow Up Before It Grows Old?,* p. 135.

39. Kotlikoff and Sachs, "Privatizing Social Security: It's High Time to Privatize," pp. 20, 22.

40. Ferrara and Tanner, *A New Deal for Social Security,* pp. 168-173.

41. Ibid., pp. 196-197, table 9.3, Financing the Transition, col. 1.

42. See, e.g., Ibid., pp. 155-156, 173; Mitchell, "Creating a Better Social Security System for America," p. 22.

43. Mitchell, "Creating a Better Social Security System for America," p. 22.

44. Henry J. Aaron, "Privatizing Social Security: A Bad Idea Whose Time Will Never Come," p. 23. Other criticisms of the burden of transition costs may be found in, e.g., David R. Henderson, "Fix Social Security? Why Not Abolish It?" *Fortune,* September 8, 1997, p. 40; CED, *Fixing Social Security,* pp. 47-49; *Report of the 1994-1996 Advisory Council on Social Security,* vol 1: *Findings and Recommendations,* pp. 68, 156.

45. David Stuart Koitz, "Social Security Reform: How Much of a Role Could Personal Retirement Accounts Play?" Congressional Research Service, Report 98-195 EPW, pp. 6-8 and table 11. Projections of Personal Account Accumulations As Percent of Social Security Benefits—Retirement at Age 65.

46. Peterson, *Will America Grow Up Before It Grows Old?,* pp. 73-76.

47. Jeremy J. Siegel, *Stocks for the Long Run: A Guide to Selecting Markets for Long-Term Growth* (Chicago: Irwin Professional Publishing, 1994), p. 29.

48. "In the Market We Trust," *New York Times,* January 12, 1997, III:3.
49. For a discussion of the greater volatility of the modern financial capital market, see William Greider, *One World, Ready or Not: The Manic Logic of Global Capitalism* (New York: Simon & Schuster, 1997) Chapter 11, *passim.*
50. Mitchell, "Creating a Better Social Security System for America," p. 19.
51. Siegel, *Stocks for the Long Run,* p. 11, table 1-1, Annual Stock Market Returns.
52. Table 11.3 sources: (1) productivity and average real earnings: *1998 OASDI Annual Report,* p. 148; (2) real interest rate: *Economic Report of the President, February 1998,* p. 349, Table B-60.—Consumer price indexes for major expenditure classes, 1954-97; p. 353, Table B-63.—Changes in special consumer price indexes, 1960-97 (price index used in table 11.3 is all items, for all urban consumers); p. 366, Table B-73.—Bond yields and interest rates, 1929-1997; (3) net national savings: *Economic Report of the President, February 1991,* p. 296, Table B-8.—Gross national product by sector, 1929-90; p. 310, Table B-22.—Relation of gross national product, net national product, and national income, 1929-90; p. 318, Table B-28.—Gross saving and investment, 1929-90; *Economic Report of the President, February 1998,* p. 310, Table B-26.—Relation of gross domestic product, gross national product, net national product, and national income, 1959-97, and p. 318, Table B-32.—Gross saving and investment, 1959-97.
53. Among the major scholarly articles on factor-price equalization are Paul A. Samuelson, "International Factor-Price Equalisation Once Again," and Harry G. Johnson, "Factor Endowments, International Trade, and Factor Prices," both of which are in *Readings in International Economics* (Homewood, IL: Richard D. Irwin, Inc., 1968), pp. 58-71 and 78-89 respectively. The mathematics of both are quite formidable. A far more accessible treatment, relying purely on economic logic, is Ludwig von Mises, *Human Action: A Treatise on Economics,* 3rd rev. ed. (Chicago, IL: Henry Regnery Co., 1966), pp. 159-164.
54. *2000 OASDI Annual Report,* pp. 151-152, 137-138.
55. Shoven, "Social Security Reform: Two Tiers Are Better Than One," pp. 21-22, 46.
56. Alicia H. Munnell, "Comments," and Henry J. Aaron, "Responses," in Ibid., pp. 143-144, 160.
57. *Report of the 1994-1996 Advisory Council on Social Security,* vol. 1: *Findings and Recommendations,* p. 175.
58. Ibid., p. 193, Table UB, Comparison of Direct (First-Order) Effects on the U.S. Government Unified Budget Balance of Changes in the Nontax Income, Outgo, and Investment of the OASI, DI and HI Trust Funds as a Result of Advisory Council Proposals.
59. Ibid., pp. 28, 30, 157.
60. Ferrara and Tanner, *A New Deal for Social Security,* pp. 169-171.
61. Alexis de Tocqueville, *Democracy in America,* tr. Henry Reeve, 2 vols., intro. Erik von Kuehnelt-Leddihn (New Rochelle, NY: Arlington House, 1965), II:337-338.

12

A Modest Proposal

"Our survival depends on our
willingness to look reality in the face."
—Thomas Fleming[1]

"I learnt what one ought not to do,
and that is always something."
—The Duke of Wellington[2]

"I will not promise the moon."
—Alfred M. Landon[3]

Looking Reality in the Face

As we have seen, misleading rhetoric—"insurance," "earned right," "contract," etc.—still shapes thinking about Social Security and helps prevent action. Popular thinking is still dominated by the false consciousness, which is spawning new myths, for example, "robbing the trust fund." In order to revise or reform Social Security soundly, we must first see Social Security as it really is, with vision unclouded by rhetoric, so we can act on the basis of facts, not fictions. Therefore, dispelling the false consciousness about Social Security is imperative. To recapitulate the Social Security myths and their refutations:

Social Security is insurance. (1) In *Helvering v. Davis* and *Flemming v. Nestor,* the Justice Department, presumably after consultation with Social Security, argued explicitly that Social Security is *not* insurance. (2) There is no contract, so the analogy to an individual insurance policy is untenable. (3) More fundamentally, Social Security lacks the defining properties of insurance: risk pooling and risk transfer to the insurer. (4) Its mechanism is that of welfare, not insurance: coerced income transfer from one group to another for social-welfare purposes. (5) As Eveline Burns admitted, the insurance analogy has become inappropriate. (6) The career of the insurance analogy, as-

341

serted or denied depending on the need and audience of the moment, proves that the analogy was drawn not to accurately depict reality, but to influence opinion and belief.

Benefits are an earned right. (1) One's "rights" are contingent and tentative. Section 1104 empowers Congress to trammel, even wipe out, one's "earned rights." (2) Congress has done so repeatedly. (3) Nestor explicitly invoked this "earned right" concept in contesting his loss of benefits—and the Supreme Court ruled against him.

Taxpayers are building up vested rights to benefits. (1) Section 1104 nullifies "vested rights." (2) As Wollenberg rightly argued, Social Security's nature makes it impossible for vested rights to benefits to exist. (3) *Flemming v. Nestor* ruled that a system of "accrued property rights" deprives Social Security of flexibility needed to meet changing circumstances—that is, it ruled that such rights do not exist. (4) In cutting or eliminating benefits, Congress acted as if no vested rights exist.

OASDI taxes are "contributions" ("premiums"). (1) Since OASDI is not insurance, its taxes are not "contributions" ("premiums"). (2) The Justice Department argued explicitly in *Helvering v. Davis* and *Flemming v. Nestor* that Social Security taxes are true taxes; in the latter it denied the analogy to premiums. (3) When the Amish refused to pay these taxes on the grounds that they are insurance premiums, the IRS asserted that they are true taxes, not premiums. Amishmen who did not accept this were punished.

Benefits are bought and paid for by one's "contributions." (1) Benefit eligibility is determined by "quarters of coverage"—calendar quarters of "covered" employment—not payment of taxes. One's "contributions" thus buy nothing. (2) They pay for the benefits of current beneficiaries—not oneself. (3) One's tax is governed not by the cost of one's own benefits but by the cost of current benefits, which is driven largely by politics. As current (and future) benefits were increased, taxes were raised to pay for them. (4) One's benefits are paid for by other people's taxes. (5) As *Flemming v. Nestor* made clear, paying the tax does not "buy" anything.

Benefit payments are made out of a trust fund built up from contributions workers paid in while they were working. (1) The "trust fund" is bogus; it is not a true trust. (2) The term "trust fund" was adopted for public relations purposes and refers to a Treasury account holding unmarketable Treasuries. (3) Current benefits are paid from current revenues, not an accumulated fund.

Social Security is in trouble because Congress is robbing this trust fund. (1) Congress cannot be faulted for rifling a trust that does not exist. (2) Congress's actions were authorized by the Social Security Act from the beginning. (3) Social Security faces trouble because our population is aging and because its politics have precluded action—not because of purported "trust fund" looting.

Social Security is a compact/contract between generations, or between Americans and their government. (1) No such compact or contract, express or implied, was ever made. (2) The Social Security participant has no contract. (3) Section 1104 invalidates this myth. (4) Repeatedly, Congress has violated and rewritten the "contract."

Social Security is a commitment that we must honor. Congress has broken its "commitment" repeatedly, and rewritten the terms for honoring it, thus rendering the "commitment" notion vacuous.

Social Security is a defined-benefit pension plan. Benefits are *not* defined, but malleable—and have in fact already been revised repeatedly by Congress.

Besides making clear what Social Security *is not,* we must clarify what it *is:* income redistribution from the employed young to the unemployed elderly, survivors, and disabled. It is a welfare program in that it is means-tested and uses redistributive taxes and transfers to serve social-welfare goals. It is *not,* however, welfare in the generally understood sense of a poverty program, since it seeks to *prevent* poverty, not *relieve* it. The most accurate, judicious description is, a social-welfare, poverty prevention program.

It must be made clear too that taxes and benefits are subject to revision by Congress. Benefits may be cut or terminated; taxes may be increased. There are no guarantees. Taxes and benefits are *guaranteed contingently,* a contradiction in terms.

It is also imperative to face reality regarding Social Security's finances. This entails demolishing another set of myths:

There's no crisis coming. (1) Under the 2000 *Annual Report's* high cost assumptions, which are more prudent and realistic than the intermediate ones, OASDI's "trust fund" will be exhausted in 2026, leaving the program unable to pay full benefits on time. (2) Draining of the "trust fund" will begin sooner yet, and cause large and growing budget deficits and/or rising taxes, with corresponding economic and political pain, even before "trust fund" exhaustion.

Minor tax increases and/or benefit cuts will suffice. (1) The changes required for restoring actuarial balance will not be minor. (2) Restoring actuarial balance will not restore annual income and outlay balance. There will still be deficits in the later years of the long-run period, which will still create significant economic burdens.

Congress has ample time to take corrective measures, and will do so long before any crisis hits. If high cost assumptions are right, it has seventeen more years before the "trust fund" starts to drain, and twenty-five years before it is exhausted. And Congress's record does not inspire confidence; it has squandered the last eighteen years, and it procrastinated when Disability Insurance met difficulties.

Finally, there must be an admission that any reform will have heavy costs. Put another way, many of Social Security's promises must be broken—and the public must be told so, frankly.

Lessons and Larger Issues

The Social Security debate must also ponder the lessons taught by Social Security's history, and larger issues as well.

Social Security's experience confirms Wollenberg's contention that a large government benefit program simply cannot lock itself into a system of immutable guarantees or rights. To avoid fiscal crisis, Congress simply must leave itself free to make changes as necessary. Unforeseen, unforeseeable changes in circumstances will eventually break in and force modifications. This is a reality that must be faced and acknowledged by policymakers and public alike.

Indeed, *any* "social insurance" program is fatally flawed due to an inherent, inescapable conflict between a political demand for rigid benefit guarantees and an economic need for flexibility. A program which told the whole truth in its public-relations efforts, giving equal weight to its benefits *and* to their contingent nature, their being subject to reduction should circumstances require it, their lack of a true guarantee, would hardly have enjoyed the popularity that Social Security has. Social Security gave a strong appearance of security in an insecure world, at a time when the Depression-spawned desire for security was pandemic and frantic. Calling attention to Section 1104 and the inherent potential for benefit cuts would have been an admission—which critics would have seized upon—that the Social Security participant was merely substituting the insecurity of political and fiscal expediency for the insecurity of the market. In order to win support for Social Security, its architects and advocates stressed the security which it seemingly offered, and never mentioned Section 1104. Any such retirement program would likely adopt a similar strategy, and create a sense of entitlement that would generate a political need for rigidity regarding benefits—which would collide with the need for flexibility.

A mentality of entitlement is extremely pernicious for the same reason. It creates enormous political pressure to turn benefit outlays into fixed charges on the future and precludes retrenchment, and thereby sharply constrains the options open to policymakers.

Closely related is still another crucial lesson: manufacturing a false consciousness so as to create public support for such a program is extremely short-sighted and dangerous. The promoters of Social Security who sold the program to the country as insurance paying benefits as an earned right created an entitlement mentality with a dangerously rigid set of expectations, and thereby made Social Security's malleable benefit promises a fixed charge on the future—yet it never occurred to them that the government might some day not be able to make good on them. Once the program ran into financial trouble, and it seemed that the government not only could not keep its benefit promises but was actually trying to break them (Reagan's 1981 proposals), Social Security's politics turned explosively rancorous and risky. Thanks to globalization, economic life will likely become more turbulent, and our economy may very well be moving meanwhile into stagnation, all of which means that benefit promises above the most modest will be very difficult to keep. In such circumstances, the political perils from a false consciousness will be even worse than they are now.

Our Social Security experience also teaches that the nature of American politics—relentlessly short-run in orientation, terrified of public opinion, obsessed with popularity and the need to win the next election, and dominated by pressure groups—is extremely, perhaps fatally, harmful to the long-term financial soundness of any such program. It is almost foreordained that prescient warnings and early indications of oncoming trouble will be ignored; that measures which will injure powerful constituencies will be spurned; and that politicians will procrastinate until action can no longer be deferred, then respond with measures more painful and damaging than those which could have been enacted had politicians acted promptly.

This problem is well nigh insoluble. The great frequency of elections—every two years for the House, every four years for president, every six years for the Senate, with one-third of senators elected every two years—all but forces politicians to focus on the immediate short run, and to eschew fiscally sound but unpopular measures. Short of amending the Constitution to create longer intervals between elections (which has problems of its own), nothing can be done about this. Short of prohibiting it, nothing can be done about lobbying by interest groups. We seem incapable of producing a governing class capable of overcoming these flaws of our political system. Having the retirement program run by an unelected elite insulated from politics and empowered to modify benefits and taxes is inadmissible; the difficulties with constitutionality and reconciling such elitist control with representative democracy are clear.

This political problem and its intractability have grave implications about the wisdom of having any government retirement benefit program at all. Only by dint of the greatest statesmanship, maturity and self-denial by politicians and public alike could such a program possibly be kept modest and low-cost. Once it exists, any benefit program becomes subject to pernicious dynamics. Pressure to expand it arises both from within (administrators) and without (politicians, opinion leaders, constituencies). An inherent asymmetry exists whereby expansion is politically rewarded, but retrenchment is penalized, and an inherent tendency to a symbiosis whereby the program protects the constituency, and the constituency protects the program. An entitlement mentality disastrously compounds these tendencies. In the absence of unremitting vigilance, will, and courage in their defense, other important values such as sound public finance, sound money, small government, individual liberty and personal responsibility are all but predestined to lose out.

Social Security has also shown that entitlements, being zero-sum transfers, are extremely divisive. Far from encouraging solidarity, a sense that "we're all in this together," Social Security has pitted generation against generation: the old partaking in shrill demonstrations, angrily spurning even minor proposals to trim benefits; the young resenting their taxes and "raw deal" under Social Security, branding their elders "greedy geezers"—a sour epithet unknown before Social Security's taxes exploded.

Beyond these lessons specific to Social Security, there are larger issues that demand reflection. Beliefs, it should be clear by now, are decisive in determining actions. Social Security's advocates and promoters thought so, and they were right. It follows that the ultimate cure is a revolution in beliefs regarding many things.

One, clearly, is retirement, which is a new phenomenon historically and is probably no longer economically sustainable. As former Chief Actuary Robertson wisely observed, a leisurely, comfortable retirement has become an aspiration to which many Americans deem themselves entitled. "Indeed, this Great American Retirement Dream serves as a kind of opiate in making life more tolerable in the face of a sometimes onerous job, not to mention the everyday difficulties of living." However, he added, this dream has not only not materialized in the past, it probably will not do so in the future for most of us. "It is not affordable, at least at a price the nation will be willing to pay. It is not a healthful concept, particularly if there is so little chance it can be achieved. It is a sad commentary on our way of life that anyone would spend most of his or her adult years looking forward to retirement."[4]

We also need to jettison the entitlement mentality. Benefits are paid because people apply for them, out of a belief that they are "entitled." This not only has ethical problems, being a belief that one is entitled to live at others' expense, but is unaffordable in a society with a rapidly aging population.

Underlying both of these beliefs is a pernicious orientation toward existence. Many, perhaps most, of us have come to see life's purpose as maximizing material comfort, security and enjoyment, not as perfecting one's character or saving one's soul. The economic consequence is an aggregate demand on our economy far beyond what it can deliver. Not just a universal entitlement state and collapsing fiscal discipline, but our pervasive gluttony and obesity and record indebtedness, ratios of consumer debt to household incomes, and numbers of personal bankruptcies, are warnings that our prevailing philosophy of life is excessively demanding and materialistic; our way of life insupportable; our people losing their self-control, their appetites bursting all constraints of cost and perspective. Ultimately, we must rethink our nature, our purpose, and what life is all about.

We must also accept the reality that life is insecure. Adversity and suffering are man's lot. The instant we were conceived, we were doomed to die. The only guarantee in life is death.

Which takes us to our next point. For all its flaws, Social Security attempts to address a basic human predicament: finding security in an insecure world. This endeavor may ultimately be quixotic, but the nature of modern economic life makes such efforts inevitable. In the thirties and forties Social Security's advocates pointed out—rightly—that the security which obtains under a mostly agrarian society of widespread ownership of property and self-sufficient family farms does not exist in a highly interdependent and mobile urban and industrial society.[5] The drawback of a capitalist economy's dynamism and Schumpeterian "creative destruction" is a propensity for disruption and vertiginous, terrifying insecurity, making appeals for security understandable. Not every call for government help during the Depression was prompted by an unworthy desire to live at the expense of coerced others. Many came from people who earnestly wanted to be self-reliant and had worked hard and played by the rules, only to find themselves losing everything and sliding toward starvation. Insecurity has much worsened since, with leveraged buyouts, layoffs, and downsizings; employers' increasing reliance on part-time and temporary workers without pension or other benefits; the collapse in unionization; and rising foreign competition.

Many people find this insecurity psychologically insupportable. This problem is much exacerbated by the withering of the religious faith that gives people inner resources enabling them to withstand life's vicissitudes and traumas. Note that as fear has displaced faith in divine Providence as modern man's bedrock sentiment about existence, the incidence of suicide has soared.

Moreover, America's long affluence and preoccupation with comfort, convenience and entertainment have been mightily corrosive to character; our once-renowned stoicism is evaporating. And much of the demand for privatization is *not* motivated by a stoical desire to face life's uncertainty alone. Rather, as the obsession with capturing higher rates of return proves, it is driven by a desire to "get mine." (It is, in fact, no different from the resolve of the elderly, who fought all proposed Social Security trims for a quarter-century, to "get theirs.") The nature of the arguments for "privatization," full of appeals to avarice and devoid of calls for self-denying refusal to burden others, reveal their authors' own reading of the American character, the sort of appeals they think Americans will find persuasive. With insecurity waxing and stoicism waning, the demand for some government provision of security for old age will persist. Political realities being what they are, some response to that demand will be made. There are many frightened people in America, they have much to be frightened about, they are unlikely to embrace stoicism, and they vote.

What Goals Should Reform Pursue?

Common sense and realism suggest the following goals.

Restore truthfulness to public policy. Promotion of a false consciousness has been a disaster. It is a major reason why the rescues took the form they did, why policymakers have evaded Social Security ever since, why our likely outcome is either another painful rescue or unsound reform, why we risk a political crisis that may destroy faith in government. Misleading analogies to insurance, defined benefits, and trust funds must be abandoned. The ruptured covenant of language must be restored—which will do much to restore the covenant between the people and their government.

Reduce the burden on taxpayers. The payroll tax has become one of the federal government's most powerful resource extractors and is very burdensome to work and enterprise. Moreover, it falls most heavily on the middle class and working poor, and has done much to preclude them from saving for retirement.

Also, Americans have already been taxed as much for Social Security as they are likely to tolerate. Further increase in payroll taxes is almost certain to provoke taxpayer backlash and greatly worsen resentment of the old by the young. Social Security's apologists might retort that our tax burden is modest compared to those of Europeans. True, but Americans have a far lower threshold of pain for taxes than Europeans. From the 1770s, Shays's Rebellion, and the Whiskey Rebellion through Proposition 13 and beyond, taxes, especially taxes perceived as excessive, arbitrarily imposed, or not buying what they pay for, have never sat well with Americans. Any new retirement program must acknowledge that fact.

Avert fiscal crisis and serious damage to the economy. The true economic danger in Social Security is not that the program will founder, or that current or future beneficiaries won't "get theirs," but that OASDI's foundering will insupportably burden our public finance and economy. Avoiding this must be a high priority.

Avert intergenerational warfare. With division worsening over other matters, exacerbating strife between generations over entitlements will be disastrous, especially since OASDI involves almost everyone. Indeed it could very well destroy Americans' fraying sense of community and membership in one nation.

Acknowledge the necessity of sacrifice and suffering, and spread it widely and fairly. So far, the burden of sacrifice to shore up Social Security has fallen on the young. Continuing this approach while leaving current beneficiaries untouched is untenable. For the sake of fairness, feasibility, and political acceptability—to avoid wrecking our economy over Social Security, provoking a tax revolt or both—the elderly lobbies will have to be faced down, and current retirees will have to assume their rightful share of the burden.

Provide some benefits to current retirees and those soon to retire. Total benefit termination for these persons is politically impossible. They are too well organized and have too many partisans, and termination is too easily demagogued, for it to happen.

Moreover, a difficult moral problem exists, in that current and imminent retirees were long misled about Social Security, believed the "insurance" and "earned right" myths, and acted in good faith. Paradoxically, beneficiaries have a moral claim to get *something,* not because they *do* have contracts or earned rights, but because they *don't*—and were led to think that they do. Most elderly Americans are simple people, less well educated than the young; products of a less cynical era, raised to trust authority figures and believe in their government. Benefit termination for retirees who planned around Social Security in good faith and would be in penury without it, amounts to punishing them for believing in their government.

Encourage savings. This is too obvious to require elaboration.

Encourage personal responsibility, freedom, sturdiness of character and self-respect. Multitudes of Americans now depend on the government for sustenance, especially in old age and infirmity. Their control over their lives necessarily diminishes accordingly. So do their dignity and self-respect, which are ultimately replaced by a combination of a sense of entitlement to benefits and a fear of losing them. So does their incentive to take responsibility for their welfare. Both Social Security and today's "reform" schemes threaten to help turn us into the passive specimens Tocqueville warned about. We must give long and sober thought to the sort of human beings we are becoming and wish our descendants to become. We are already far down the road to becoming ciphers. We should neither retain nor adopt any program that takes that degradation still further.

Keep government involvement minimal. Social Security has made much of our public finance and our economy hostage to its politics and requirements, and burdened both federal finances and the economy, now and far into the future, with a colossal fixed charge. Most "reform" proposals not only fail to rectify this, they will almost inevitably vastly increase the government's interference in investment and financial markets.

Do not promise the moon. Whatever arrangement we make must shun extravagant talk of "guarantees," "earned rights," "entitlements," high rates of return, and such, that encourages rigid expectations that cannot be met. The benignant context of Social Security's golden years, 1945-1965—an affluent economy with little foreign competition; a highly unionized labor force securing rising real wages; a lower total tax burden; a much younger population; a higher savings rate; a much more respected (and respectable) government which furnished real leadership—is gone and will not return. The context in which any retirement program operates will become, and remain, more turbulent—meaning that any system which presumes to make fixed, long-term commitments will eventually endure traumatic revisions, just as Social Security has. Promising either guaranteed "earned rights" or lush retirement nest eggs would be the veriest folly.

A Modest Proposal

Given all this, what should be done is clear.

1. *Repeal the Social Security Act.* The Act is not sacrosanct. The *Helvering v. Davis* decision was almost certainly made under duress, to relieve political pressure, hence is of dubious validity. The opinion itself is a scissors-and-paste derivative of the government brief that skirts the main issues. Given all this, the Act's constitutionality is dubious. We are under no obligation to preserve OASDI in its present form, or keep the law itself on the books.

2. *Replace it with a program paying Social Security's benefits for current retirees and baby boomers based on presumed need, with benefits for better-off beneficiaries cut or eliminated.* Social Security was made universal for political reasons: giving almost everyone a stake in it would give almost everyone a reason to support it (an interest in its existence, so it could pay off)—whereas, so Wilbur Cohen argued, programs for the poor are poor programs, and not something most Americans would support.[6] But with our population aging, we can no longer afford to give the well-off Social Security as an inducement to accept preventing old-age poverty.

Pace the stereotype of poverty-stricken elderly, the fact is that many Social Security beneficiaries have substantial income from other sources. In 1995, 8.3 percent of all families and unrelated individuals with any member aged sixty-five and over had non-Social Security incomes of $50,000 or more; 11.8 percent, $40,000 or more; 17.7 percent, $30,000 or more; and 27.8 percent had non-Social Security incomes of $20,000 or more.[7]

Table 12.1

Breakdown of OASDI Beneficiaries and Aggregate Benefits by Individual and Couple Income, and Benefit Taxation, Calendar 2000
(thousands of beneficiaries, billions of dollars)

Individual or couple income	No. OASDI beneficiaries	Share of total	Aggregate OASDI benefits	Share of total	Aggregate benefit taxes	Taxes as share of benefits
< $10,000	7,410	18.8 %	$46.4	12.6 %	$0	0 %
$10-15,000	5,064	12.8	46.0	12.5	0	0
$15-20,000	4,244	10.8	39.7	10.8	0	0
$20-25,000	3,408	8.6	34.2	9.3	0	0
$25-30,000	2,964	7.5	28.9	7.9	.012	0
$30-40,000	4,747	12.0	47.0	12.8	.51	1.0
$40-50,000	3,702	9.4	36.5	9.9	1.8	5.0
$50-100,000	5,749	14.6	63.7	17.3	8.8	14.0
> $100,000	2,133	5.4	25.5	6.9	6.2	24.0
Total	39,421	100.0	$367.9	100.0	$17.3	5.0

Source: House Ways and Means Committee

Another perspective is provided by table 12.1, which, using Congressional Budget Office simulations based on data from the Current Population Survey, breaks down the projected OASDI beneficiary population and benefit outlays by individual or couple income (cash income plus realized capital gains).[8] We see that 24.2 percent of benefit spending goes to individuals or couples with incomes above $50,000; 34.1 percent goes to those with incomes above $40,000; 46.9 percent goes to those with incomes above $30,000; 54.8 percent goes to those with incomes above $25,000.

Moreover, the higher an individual's or couple's total income, the smaller Social Security benefits' contribution to income. In 1998, aged units (i.e., married aged couples or a nonmarried aged person) with incomes in the first income quintile (incomes below $8,792) received 82.1 percent of their total money income from Social Security. Those in the second quintile ($8,793-$14,224) received 80.5 percent from Social Security; those in the third ($14,225-$22,255), 63.8 percent; in the fourth ($22,256-$37,962), 45.2 percent; and those in the highest quintile (incomes above $37,962) received just 18.3 percent of their income from Social Security.[9]

Obviously, Social Security benefits for people with incomes below $25,000 are crucial, and should be left untouched. But such beneficiaries receive less than half the total benefits. At least half of benefit spending is going to persons who could get along decently without it. Those with incomes of $50,000 or more will suffer no real hardship if they lose all their benefits (reducing a $50,000 income by 18.3 percent leaves $40,850, which should suffice). And it would hardly inflict unbearable suffering if those with incomes between $30,000 and $50,000 gave up at least something. There is plenty of room for cutting benefits for current beneficiaries, while keeping Social Security's floor of protection intact.

Removing all benefits for incomes above $25,000—call it Option A—would have cut outlays in 2000 by 54.8 percent. A less draconian and more politically feasible Option B, removing all benefits for incomes above $30,000, would have cut outlays 47 percent. A more graduated Option C, removing 50 percent of benefits for incomes between $30,000 and $40,000, and all benefits for incomes above $40,000, would have shaved outlays 40.5 percent. Still milder, Option D—remove 50 percent for incomes between $30,000 and $40,000, 75 percent for incomes between $40,000 and $50,000, and all for incomes above $50,000—would still have yielded a sizeable outlay savings of 38 percent.

Using the outlay, cash income, and cash balance projections under the 2000 *Annual Report's* high cost assumptions, and assuming for simplicity's sake the foregoing breakdown of benefit outlays by income levels, we see that such income-based benefit reductions would generate very large outlay reductions (table 12.2).[10]

Table 12.2

**OASDI Current-Law Outlays, Income Less Interest, and Cash Balance, and
Outlays with Various Reduction Options, 2005-2040
(High-Cost Assumptions) (billions of current dollars)**

Calendar Year	Current Law			Outlays with Benefit Reduction			
	Outlays	Income less interest	Cash surplus/ deficit	Option A	Option B	Option C	Option D
2005	$586	$627	$41	$265	$311	$349	$362
2010	837	834	-3	378	444	498	519
2015	1,223	1,086	-136	553	648	728	758
2020	1,790	1,405	-385	809	949	1,065	1,110
2025	2,562	1,807	-755	1,158	1,358	1,524	1,588
2030	3,549	2,318	-1,231	1,604	1,881	2,112	2,200
2035	4,762	2,969	-1,793	2,152	2,524	2,833	2952
2040	6,220	3,785	-2,435	2,811	3,297	3,701	3,856

Source: *2000 OASDI Annual Report*

By inspection, *every* option replaces cash deficits with surpluses in *every* year, except Option D, which has a $71 billion deficit in 2040. The more rigorous the benefit reduction, the greater the reduction in projected outlays and the more affordable the program. My own preference would be for Option B.

The proposal, then, is that those who truly need their benefits to stay out of poverty will get them, and that those who can get along without their benefits will lose all or most of them.

Benefit reduction should be phased in, but since time is of the essence it would be advisable to have it fully in place by 2005, and certainly no later than 2010.

This does *not* affect the Social Security COLA. Social Security's inflation protection is valuable and should be retained. A COLA cut cuts benefits across the board, which falls most heavily on those least able to bear it. And given Longman's warning that inflation will push most persons over the current benefit tax threshold, it may be wise to adjust the benefit reduction threshold for inflation. But since this would reduce savings below the foregoing figures, to offset it, we should keep gradually raising the retirement age, to seventy.

How could this be done? (a) One way would be a means test—persons with income and/or assets below a certain amount would get all their benefits, while those with income and/or assets above it would lose some or all benefits. Both Peter Peterson and Longman have proposed a global, progressive means test for entitlements, including Social Security, to keep entitlements affordable.[11]

This does have problems. As Robertson sagely warned, means testing would encourage concealment of other income, which "would be extremely damaging to the character of our nation."[12] Means testing amounts, some argue, to punishing beneficiaries for doing good, socially desirable things: working and saving. Finally, it would entail higher administrative costs.[13]

(b) Another method, which skirts some of these problems, would be to assume a high correlation between lifetime earnings and retirement income, which is usually true. One's lifetime earnings record and OASDI tax payments are impossible to conceal, as Social Security already has the records. The benefit formula for the Primary Insurance Amount could be changed to preserve full current-law benefits for those with low Average Indexed Monthly Earnings but progressively cut benefits for higher AIMEs.[14]

(c) Table 12.1 suggests another way. Today's taxation of benefits inflicts progressive benefit reduction as income rises. This is for all practical purposes a means test; at any rate it has the same economic effect. Substantially raising the benefit tax, then, is another method.

However it is done, this is not too much to ask of current beneficiaries. Many would have to give up something; many would have to give up a good deal; but nobody would have to give up more than they could afford, and low income beneficiaries, who would be destitute without Social Security, would lose nothing.

Moreover, exacting some such sacrifice is politically feasible. Numerous polls have disclosed solid support for curtailing benefits to better-off beneficiaries by means testing Social Security or raising taxes on their benefits. For example, an August 1998 survey by the Princeton Survey Research Associates for the Americans Discuss Social Security project found that 54 percent of respondents supported reducing benefits for persons with retirement incomes above $60,000 a year. That same month a survey for the Democratic Leadership Council found 63 percent support for limiting benefits for the wealthy based on other income and assets.[15] Even the elderly are open to means testing. A 1994 poll for *Time* magazine and CNN found that 53 percent of Americans aged 65 and over agreed with the statement that better-off Social Security respondents should give up some of the benefits they receive beyond what they paid in taxes.[16] Thus, while lopsided majorities of poll respondents consistently reject raising taxes further, cutting benefits across the board, and raising the retirement age, reducing or eliminating benefits for more affluent beneficiaries is the one measure short of "reform" or "privatization" that does enjoy substantial support.

Of course, means testing or the equivalent will be ferociously resisted. The false consciousness will again draw blood: it will be protested that it is a breach of faith to force people to pay Social Security taxes, assure them that "benefits are an earned right"—and then apply means testing. Opponents will protest, as they did whenever means testing was broached, that it will "violate the earned-rights concept" of the program.[17] Geoffrey Kollmann of the Congressional Research Service ably summed up this argument:

> Opponents see means testing as a fundamental breach of Social Security principles. Benefits have always been paid regardless of a person's economic circumstances. Means testing benefits, opponents argue, would make Social Security similar to welfare. It would weaken a primary reason for the support of the program by the public — that people believe they have paid for their benefits and are not receiving a government "handout."
>
> Opponents say means testing is unfair . . . it would break an "implied compact" because workers paid a lifetime of taxes in the expectation of promised benefits.[18]

One sees here a vivid reminder of the decisive importance of the false consciousness in blocking modification of Social Security, and the need to dispel it to clear the way for reform. The truth—which the false consciousness has effectively concealed—is that means testing is not a new departure for Social Security. It is simply not true that "Benefits have always been paid regardless of a person's economic circumstances." In its retirement earnings test, as Dillard Stokes rightly observed so long ago,[19] *Social Security has always had a means test*—albeit an increasingly attenuated one as the earnings test was liberalized.[20] As both Arthur Larson and Robert Ball acknowledged (see chapters 7 and 9), the test was created for the selfsame reason our proposal is made: to keep the program affordable. It was repealed in 2000 for beneficiaries at or above the normal retirement age, currently sixty-five, but remains in force for those below retirement age.[21] Benefit taxation brought an additional element of means testing, which became more progressive in 1993. It bears repeating: Social Security is already means tested.

Moreover, some of the same Social Security supporters and marginal reformers who oppose means testing, such as Gramlich, Aaron, and Ball, also call for increasing taxation of benefits—specifically, including all benefits exceeding employee contributions in taxable income and phasing out the income thresholds on benefit taxation.[22] Yet this is the equivalent of a means test! Apparently means testing is acceptable, provided it is done *sub rosa*.

A means test or equivalent would not only reduce costs, but would be a powerful tool for demolishing the false consciousness. If today's means testing in Social Security was made prominent rather than suppressed, and a benefit reduction along the lines proposed enacted, this would drive home the reality that the "earned right" is a fiction and that Social Security benefits are redistributive transfers.

Finally, not only will Social Security itself become unaffordable soon, but Medicare, Medicaid, federal civilian and military pension systems, and veterans' benefits will also experience soaring costs. The only way to avoid economic stagnation or even implosion under this burden will be to sharply reduce those costs. The only way to do this while retaining a floor of protection will be with a rigorous means test or equivalent. However much program defenders and mainstream reformers disparage it, reality will make it inevitable.

3. *Abolish payroll and self-employment taxes, and finance the foregoing benefit with general revenues.* Defenders of the payroll tax make three points, which we will address in decreasing order of validity. First, the tax makes the program self-financing and puts no burden on the Treasury. This was President Roosevelt's own desire and subsequent defenders have reiterated this point. For most of the program's history it was adhered to. But a provision allowing for partial general-revenue financing was enacted in 1944 (and repealed in 1950), and when Social Security experienced crisis in the seventies, partial general-revenue financing was proposed—a sign that this self-financing rule will likely collapse under real stress.

Second, Social Security's more fiscally conservative proponents have argued that the payroll tax imposes a vital fiscal discipline on Social Security. The need to keep the program self-financing and in actuarial balance meant that any increase in benefits must be financed by an increase in payroll taxes. Payroll tax financing thus supposedly made the link between benefits and taxes prominent and thereby kept benefit growth more moderate than it would have been otherwise.[23] But in the event, the payroll tax proved a weak retaining wall against expansionism. It did not prevent the 1950 amendment whereby millions of elderly aged sixty-two or older qualified for full benefits with just six quarters of coverage, the expansions of 1954 and 1956, or the benefit binge of 1967-1972. It took the economic woes of the seventies and dawning awareness of demographic trends to finally chasten the expansionists. There have been no benefit increases since beyond the annual COLAs, and no further program expansions. The Social Security debate shifted from how to expand OASDI further to how to keep it solvent. External reality, not the payroll tax, administered the only real discipline.

Finally, the payroll tax gives benefits the character of an "earned right," something bought and paid for. This makes the taxpayer willing to pay the tax, since he thinks he is buying benefits for himself, and the beneficiary willing to receive them, since he thinks he paid for them. Over and over, we have seen politicians and Social Security administrators make this argument. Here we come to the heart of the matter. As Roosevelt admitted, the payroll tax is "politics all the way through." Its true purpose was and is to create a mentality of entitlement to benefits and give the insurance analogy an apparent basis in reality. Abolition of the Social Security tax is absolutely necessary to perform the crucial task of demolishing the false consciousness that it has done so much to foster.

In a crucial sense, the change to general revenue financing is no change at all. Thanks to the payroll tax-fed false consciousness, it is seldom grasped that *Social Security is already funded out of general revenue, and always has been.* The original Social Security Act, as the government's *Helvering v. Davis* brief stated, did not earmark its taxes, meaning they were general revenue. To pay benefits, it required Congress to make annual appropriations—obviously from general revenue. Today, OASDI tax receipts are, as we saw, swept into the Treasury's general revenue pool, commingled with all other tax monies, and Social Security's Treasury accounts ("trust funds") then credited for them with equivalent amounts of Treasuries. The Treasury, not Social Security, writes the benefit checks. Writes them on what? General revenue, of course.

In confirmation of this: when I pay my federal income taxes, I pay my income tax and Social Security self-employment tax with the same check, made out to the United States Treasury. Both taxes are thus necessarily general revenue, going to the same destination. There is no segregation of monies.

In short, this proposal *strips away the veil which the false consciousness has created and reveals Social Security for what it really is: a general-revenue financed, means-tested, poverty prevention welfare program—and scales it back to provide a floor of protection.*

4. *Write off the "trust fund."* With outlays cut enough to avert future cash deficits, there is no need for a "trust fund." Moreover, the "trust fund" does *nothing* to fund Social Security. The taxes and borrowing needed to redeem its Treasuries are merely the equivalent of the resource extraction through higher payroll taxes that would occur if the fund did not exist. Its existence or disappearance thus makes no economic difference. Since it is an internally held IOU written by the government to itself, its cancellation would entail no loss of economic welfare.

5. *Reduce general revenue taxes to match the benefit reduction.* With benefits to higher-income current and imminent retirees scaled back, the tax bill would be substantially less, so general revenues would not have to replace the payroll tax dollar for dollar. With the pretense of building up a "trust fund" abandoned, there would be no need to accumulate "surpluses." Taxes for this purpose would be no higher than outlays. Those now paying OASDI taxes would therefore get substantial tax relief. Option B cuts benefit outlays 47 percent, so revenues would have to equal 53 percent of current outlays. Since outlays have averaged 86.5 percent of revenues, and since we would no longer accumulate surpluses, the needed revenues would be 45.8 percent of current Social Security taxes (.53 x .865 = .458, or 45.8 percent). The tax for this purpose could therefore drop 54.2 percent. Since the payroll tax is regressive, this would give more than proportional relief for the lower middle class and working poor.

There would, however, be a price to pay. Younger generations would lose their benefits. They would have to recognize the OASDI taxes they have paid for what they are—redistributive transfers—and be disabused of the fiction of buying benefits with them. Many young persons wish to be rid of their Social Security tax and allowed to make their own arrangements for old age with that money. Cutting their tax by 54.2 percent gives them much of their wish.

6. *Acknowledging the demand for security in an insecure world, keep a safety net for those born after 1965.* The combination of globalization and eventual stagnation will inflict heavy social casualties: people who will be economically injured, as the Great Depression's sufferers were injured, by forces beyond their control, hence unable to make adequate provision for old age. For those born after 1965, there should be a means-tested old-age benefit along the lines of Supplemental Security Income, the successor to the original Social Security Act's Title I Old-Age Assistance benefit. With Social Security gone by the time these workers reach old age, we could afford to make this benefit more generous than the current SSI. It must always be described honestly: not an "entitlement" to which one has "rights," but a safety net to which one has recourse. In the interest of loosening the central government's hold on our lives, we should, ultimately, devolve provision of an old-age safety net onto states, localities and, better still, churches and families, which is where it properly belongs. For the next several decades, though, the only feasible option is to provide it at the federal level.

7. *Resist all temptation to expand this safety net.* For obvious reasons, the expansionism which characterized Social Security must not be allowed to recur. And to keep use of this safety net minimal, though, we should:

8. *Encourage saving for old age.* The $2,000 ceiling on IRA contributions is far too low given both the substantial inflation which has occurred since that ceiling was created and our urgent need to save more for old age. It should be raised immediately to $5,000, and increase automatically thereafter for inflation. Some members of Congress are already seeking this change.[24] Moreover, all taxes on IRAs should be abolished, except for a penalty for early withdrawal. This would maximize the incentive to save and to invest for old age, and to leave the money in the IRAs to accumulate.

This saving would entirely voluntary. By now young people are sufficiently aware of the need to invest for old age that most can safely be trusted to do so. The debate surrounding this reform would further publicize the retirement issue and provide a further spur to individual old-age provision. And with the foregoing tax relief, younger Americans would have the means at hand.

9. *Make purchase of disability insurance easier.* We have focused on old-age and survivors benefits, but Disability Insurance has its own financial woes; reducing dependence on it will be prudent. The self-employed are allowed a tax deduction on their health insurance cost. Both the self-em-

ployed and employees who lack employer-provided disability benefits should receive a similar deduction for purchase of long-term disability insurance.

10. *Reform employee pensions.* With employment insecurity likely to worsen, workers urgently need arrangements whereby they do not lose their pensions if they lose their jobs. Pensions should be made portable, vest promptly, and follow the TIAA-CREF approach. Employers who do not offer pensions should be encouraged to offer arrangements whereby workers voluntarily put some of their pay regularly into such pensions via direct deposits. Because pension plans are an instrument for ensuring security in old age, *not* a means to become a millionaire, they should be conservatively managed, and subject to federal oversight to avert fraud and irresponsibility.

Possible Objections

Criticisms are inevitable; let us anticipate and answer some.

It's not fair. Sacrifices would be inflicted according to ability to bear them, and would be in the nature of removing some or all of benefits, which is to say, windfalls furnished from other people's money. It is admittedly unfair in a sense to deny benefits altogether to the better-off elderly. But reducing benefits to which one's moral claim is debatable is fairer to the better-off than ever-greater extractions of their income, to which their claim is far stronger. And current workers would be able to use their tax relief to make investments to compensate for the loss of benefits.

In fact, this proposal is much fairer than Social Security's zero-sum transfer and the established pattern of rescuing Social Security by lopsidedly penalizing younger generations and leaving the elderly unscathed. There is an obvious problem of fairness in taxing struggling single mothers bagging groceries to send benefit checks to retired lawyers, doctors, bond traders, athletes and rock stars.

The unhappy truth is that there is no easy, cheap or painless way out—nor any perfectly fair one. We have been in the grip of a false consciousness for too long, and squandered too much time, for that. The best we can do is to find the least unfair, least painful, least dangerous—and most prudent, realistic and honest—solution.

It's politically impossible. Not if the false consciousness is exploded. And substantial support for means testing or its equivalent does exist. If benefit reduction were framed in terms of preserving benefits for those who would be destitute without them and asking better-off beneficiaries to make sacrifices they could afford, so as to make retention of a floor of protection affordable, and the proposed tax relief made clear, it should be a feasible sell.

In fact, most people should find this proposal appealing. Abolition of the regressive payroll tax, progressive benefit reduction and retention of Social Security's safety net would make old-age benefits and the tax code more progressive, which liberals should like. Gradual dismantlement of our biggest entitlement and prevention of fiscal and economic ruin will appeal to conservatives and libertarians. Current and imminent beneficiaries who need their benefits to live their twilight years decently would lose nothing. Taxpayers will have the payroll tax yoke lifted from them, and be enabled to save for old age. Those who are better off will not get their benefits, but can at least bear the loss without real suffering.

The tax cuts, larger IRA amounts, abolition of taxes on IRAs, and deductions for disability insurance will entail too much revenue loss. The increased saving will flow into investment, which will increase GDP and generate more revenue. Also, since this approach entails substantial outlay reduction for current retirees and eliminates OASDI's unfunded liability for persons born after 1965, it will require far less resource extraction than either the current program or "privatization" with its huge transition costs.

It's too harsh. The harshness is only relative; worse-off beneficiaries are spared. At some point we will be unable to evade hard choices about Social Security any longer. This plan is less harsh than what will happen if we do nothing, patch up a zero-sum game, or adopt "reform" with high, certain costs and uncertain returns.

While this proposal lacks glamor and makes no promises, it is realistic, honest, and prudent—unlike both the denials that trouble is coming, and the promotions of "reform" plans that have an uncanny and frightening resemblance to soap bubbles from a bubble toy: conjured up by clever manipulation, shining, smooth, seemingly complete and perfect in themselves, but hideously vulnerable to demolition by outside forces.

Parting Reflections

Our long prosperity has deluded us into disbelief in limits. The unaffordability of public and private gluttony will be driven home in the next few decades; the coming Social Security crisis is but one facet of a larger pattern of long indulgence in unrestraint finally colliding with the reality of limits and the limits of reality.

The coming entitlement crisis, Longman argues, will force a return to Victorian virtues: thrift, hard work and self-reliance.[25] True, but our only real cure—our only choice—is deeper than that.

We must radically rethink our beliefs about life, reality, and our purpose and destiny. We must accept limits on what life can feasibly give us, and demand less, consume less. A way of life grounded in self-restraint, perspective, and checks on appetite is not only moral and psychological wisdom, but in a limited world, political and economic wisdom as well. The only sound answer to insecurity, suffering, and mortality is to accept them as our lot, and learn the truth divined by William Blake:

Man was made for joy and woe;
And when this we rightly know,
Thro' the world we safely go.

Notes

1. Thomas Fleming, "A Not So Wonderful Life," *Chronicles,* July 1990, p. 13.
2. Elizabeth Longford, *Wellington: The Years of the Sword* (New York: Harper & Row, Publishers, 1969), p. 37.
3. Alfred M. Landon, "I Will Not Promise the Moon," *Vital Speeches of the Day,* October 15, 1936, p. 29.
4. Robertson, *The Coming Revolution in Social Security,* pp. 283-284.
5. See, e.g., Social Security Board, *Why Social Security?,* Publication no. 15, 1945.
6. Cohen and Friedman, *Social Security: Universal or Selective?,* pp. 54-56.
7. *1998 Green Book,* p. 1037, table A-8.—Amount of Income From Sources Other Than Social Security, Among Social Security Beneficiaries, Age 65 or Over, 1995.
8. Table 12.1 source: U.S., Congress, House, Committee on Ways and Means, *2000 Green Book: Background Material and Data on Programs Within the Jurisdiction of the Committee on Ways and Means,* p. 65, table 1-25.—Effect of Taxing Social Security Benefits by Income Class, Projected Calendar Year 2000. Beneficiary population share and aggregate benefit share calculations mine.
9. Social Security Administration, Office of Policy, *Income of the Population 55 or Older, 1998,* p. 123, table VII.5—Shares of aggregate income of aged units 65 or older by quintiles of total money income and marital status (www.ssa.gov).
10. Table 12.2 source: *2000 OASDI Annual Report,* p. 184, table III.B4.—Estimated OASDI and HI Income Excluding Interest, Outgo, and Balance in Current Dollars by Alternative, Calendar Years 2000-75. Outlays with benefit reduction calculations mine.
11. See Peter G. Peterson, *Facing Up: How to Rescue the Economy From Crushing Debt and Restore the American Dream* (New York: Simon & Schuster, 1993), pp. 272-276; Longman, *The Return of Thrift,* pp. 175-179.
12. A. Haeworth Robertson, "The National Commission's Failure to Achieve Real Reform," in Peter J. Ferrara, ed., *Social Security: Prospects for Real Reform* (Washington, DC: The Cato Institute, 1985), p. 43.
13. See, e.g., Gramlich, *Is it Time to Reform Social Security?,* p. 55; David R. Henderson, "The Sneak-Attack Tax on Seniors," *Fortune,* March 4, 1996, p. 60; American Academy of Actuaries, "Means Testing for Social Security," Issue Brief, September 1996, pp. 2-3.
14. See, e.g., American Academy of Actuaries, "Means Testing for Social Security," p. 3.
15. Bowman, "Social Security: A Report on Current Polls," p. 17, table 4: Means Testing.
16. "Speaking the Unspeakable to Retirees," *New York Times,* January 1, 1995, III:3.
17. See, e.g., Bill Archer, "Securing Social Security," p. 98.
18. Geoffrey Kollmann, "Means Testing Social Security Benefits: An Issue Summary," Congressional Research Service, Report 94-791 EPW, p. 2.
19. Stokes, "Does Our Social Security System Make Sense?" p. 570; Stokes, *Social Security—Fact and Fancy,* p. 86.
20. In 1975, the first $2,500 of retirement earnings were exempt from the test for all beneficiaries. Ten years later, the first $5,400 were exempt for those below the normal retirement age, and the first $7,320 for those at or above normal retirement

age. In 1999, the respective exempt amounts were $9,600 and $15,500 (*2000 OASDI Annual Report,* p. 67, table II.E2.—Cost-of-Living Benefit Increases, Average Wage Index Increases, OASDI Contribution and Benefit Bases, and Retirement Earnings Test Exempt Amounts).

21. Social Security Administration, *A Brief History of Social Security,* SSA Publication No. 21-059, 65th Anniversary ed., p. 23.
22. *Report of the Advisory Council on Social Security,* vol. 1, *Findings and Recommendations,* pp. 18, 20-21. Aaron, "Social Security: Tune It Up, Don't Trade It In," pp. 94-95, 108.
23. Derthick, *Policymaking for Social Security,* pp. 49-52, 152, 239.
24. "A Special Summary and Forecast Of Federal and State Tax Developments," *Wall Street Journal,* January 17, 2001, A1.
25. Longman, *The Return of Thrift,* chapter 14, *passim.*

Glossary

actuarial balance: the difference, over a given evaluation period, between (1) Social Security assets at the beginning of the period plus the ratio of the present value of the tax revenue projected over that period to present value of taxable payroll projected over the period and (2) the ratio of present value of expenditures projected over the period to present value of taxable payroll projected over the period. Essentially, OASDI's initial assets plus stream of income over the period, minus the stream of costs over the period, discounted to the present and expressed as a percentage of taxable payroll.

actuarial deficit: negative actuarial balance. The stream of costs exceeds the initial assets plus the stream of income.

AIME: Average Indexed Monthly Earnings. The amount of earnings used to calculated the Primary Insurance Amount (PIA) for most workers who reach age 62, become disabled, or die after 1978.

annual balance: difference between income and outlays in a given year.

bend point: dollar amount used to divide the AIME and PIA into intervals in the Social Security benefit formula. Bend points are adjusted automatically every year. See PIA.

fertility rate: average number of babies a woman would have in her lifetime if she experienced birth rates by age observed in, or assumed for, a specified year, and if she survived the entire childbearing period.

interfund borrowing: borrowing by one trust fund (OASI, DI, or HI) of assets from another when the first fund is in danger of exhaustion. Was authorized for 1982-1987, and done in 1982, when OASI borrowed from the DI and HI Trust Funds.

maximum taxable income: maximum annual income in covered employment on which OASDI taxes may be levied. Income above this amount is neither taxable nor used as a basis for calculating benefits. Aka "contribution and benefit base."

off budget: certain federal government transactions which are required by law to be excluded from the budget, even though they are part of total government transactions. Social Security and the Postal Service are off budget.

PIA: the monthly benefit for retired worker who starts receiving benefits at retirement age or is disabled. Based on AIME. The basic formula for calculating PIA for a worker who reaches age 62, dies or becomes disabled in 2000 is:

PIA = (90 percent of first $531 of AIME) + (32 percent of AIME > $531 but not exceeding $3,202) + (15 percent of AIME > $3,202)

$531 and $3,202 are bend points

retirement age: age at which one may first become eligible for full retirement benefits, currently 65. One may retire before 65, with a smaller monthly benefit. Under the 1983 Amendments, retirement age will increase gradually to 67 for persons reaching that age in 2027 or later, beginning with increase to 65 years and 2 months for persons reaching age 65 in 2003.

retirement earnings test: the provision of the Social Security Act requiring withholding of benefits if beneficiaries have earnings above exempt amounts. The test has been gradually liberalized, and as of 1999 applied for income over $9,600 for beneficiaries under 65 and for income over $15,500 for beneficiaries aged 65 to 70.

trust fund: Treasury account to which Social Security tax revenues are credited by depositing an equivalent amount of unmarketable Treasury debt, and which is debited to pay benefits by removing an equivalent value of debt. If revenue exceeds outlays in a year, the remaining stock of Treasuries is that year's "trust fund" surplus. Social Security has two "trust funds": the Old Age and Survivors Insurance Trust Fund and the Disability Insurance Trust Fund. They are often combined for analytical purposes.

trust fund exhaustion: the "trust fund" has no assets.

unified budget: a budget concept which includes all expenditures and outlays of the federal government, including Social Security. A given year's "budget deficit," as the term is commonly used, is the unified budget deficit, that is, the sum of the on-budget deficit plus any deficit (minus any surplus) in Social Security.

Index

Aaron, Henry, 167, 245, 246, 284
  denies crisis coming, 18, 19
  social insurance "sure bet," 18, 54
  disparages privatization, 18
  disparages "money's worth" concern, 288
  Social Security "insurance," 293
  on tax burden of Kotlikoff-Sachs plan, 322
  insists mandatory contributions taxes, 334, 335
  opposes means testing, 354
  favors more benefit taxation, 354
actuarial analysis, 5
actuarial assumptions, 5
  "low cost" ("optimistic"), 5
  "intermediate" ("most likely"), 5
  "high cost" ("pessimistic"), 5
    case for relying upon, 12-18
  importance of prudence and realism regarding, 12-13
  unforeseen disruptions and, 13
  Robertson on choice of, 13, 14
  need for debate on choice of, 19
  specific assumptions, see fertility, mortality, productivity
Advisory Council for Committee on Economic Security (1934), 65
Advisory Council for Social Security expansion (1938), 126, 127-128
Advisory Council on Social Security (1994-1996),
  unable to agree on recommendations, 282
  subgroup denies crisis coming, 18
  false consciousness of, 292-293
Agricultural Adjustment Act (AAA), 82, 98
Alberts, Robert, 244
Aldrich, Winthrop, attacks reserve fund, 122
Allen, Robert, 99

Alliance for Social Security and Disability Recipients, 250
Alsop, Joseph, 74, 100, 101
Altmeyer, Arthur, xiv, 65, 67, 80, 121, 179, 212, 230, 318
  Chairman of Social Security Board, xiv, 120
  Commissioner of Social Security, xiv, 145
  student of Commons, 63
  Assistant Secretary of Labor, 65
  picked to head Technical Board, 65
  inspired by Saint-Simon, 65
  recommends Witte as Executive Director, 66
  rejects proposed nameplate, 87
  in 1936 election campaign, 87
  opposes Vandenberg resolution, 123
  recommends Social Security expansion, 126
  testimony in 1939 Amendment hearings,
    public relations motive for "trust fund," 131
    no individual funds in "trust fund," 132-133
    "contributions" different from taxes, 136
    rationalizes injury to single beneficiaries, 137-139
  role in fostering false consciousness, "earned right"/"right," 81, 87
  OKs Cohen memo re calling program "insurance," 119
  "insurance," 81, 87, 120, 141
  "insurance bargain," 87
  expansionism of, 145-146, 328
  defends insurance analogy to Taft, 159-160
  leaves Social Security Administration, 160
  in Curtis hearings,

false consciousness of, 322
hubris of, 328
Mitchell, William, 242
Modern Maturity, 284
  disseminates Social Security myths, 293-294
Moley, Raymond, attacks insurance analogy, 238
money-back guarantee,
  in original Social Security Act, 48, 80
  1939 Amendments remove, 136-137, 247
  absence makes Social Security "longevity lottery," 48
money laundering, 77, 103, 127
"money's worth,"
  improving, wrong goal for reform, 37
  early promotion of program stressed, 87, 89, 120, 138, 140, 141, 238
  early windfalls, 47, 149
  declines due to program maturation, rising taxes, 287-288
  complaints about for young, 42, 222, 238, 239
  AARP admits declining, 288
  program defenders attack concern about, 288
  controversy as consequence of program publicity, 289-290
  Social Security politics and, 290
Monroney, A. S. Mike, *Collier's* article, 150
Moore, Stephen,
  false consciousness of, 278
  proposed Social Security cuts, 278-279
Morgenthau, Henry, 75
  Secretary of the Treasury, 65
  demands payroll tax raised to create reserve fund, 74-75
  recommends creating OASI Trust Fund, 129
  testifies to public relations motive for Trust Fund, 131
  recommends calling taxes "contributions," 136
mortality/mortality assumption,
  importance of for Social Security outlook, 14
  Robertson on realism of pessimistic assumption, 14

1999 Technical Panel recommends pessimistic revision in, 17
Moynihan, Daniel Patrick, 266, 277
  false consciousness of,
    "contract," 263
    Reagan cut proposal "breach of contract," 263
    "insurance," 277-278, 293-294
    "monies held in trust," 278
    "raiding trust fund," 284
    Social Security not entitlement, 293
    appeals to label to assert reality, 293-294
Municipal Bankruptcy Act, 98
Munnell, Alicia,
  on Social Security and saving, 33
  false consciousness of, 293
  insists mandatory contributions taxes, 334, 335
Murphy, Frank, 89
Murphy, Ray, attacks insurance analogy, 188
Myers, Robert J., 182, 239
  former Chief Actuary of Social Security, 18
  denies crisis coming, 18-19
  argues payroll tax disciplines spending, 69
  opposes general revenue financing, 69
  resigns as Chief Actuary (1970), 236
  admits rights flexible, 218
  appeals to insurance label to assert reality, 230
  admits insurance analogy overdone, 230
  insists Social Security insurance, 236
  endorses raising retirement age, 268-269, 289
  on individual equity principle in taxes, 289

National Association of Insurance Agents resolution, similar to NALU resolution, ignored, 189
National Association of Life Underwriters (NALU) resolution,
  attacks insurance analogy, recommends disavowal, 189
  widespread distribution, 189
  ignored, 189